Sherlock Holmes S

T0283157

"The Adventure of the Three Students"

"The Adventure of the
Golden Pince-Nez"

"The Adventure of the
Missing Three-Quarter"

"The Adventure of the Abbey Grange"

"The Adventure of the Second Stain"

1908

"The Adventure of Wisteria Lodge"

"The Adventure of the Bruce-
Partington Plans"

1910

"The Adventure of the Devil's Foot"

1911

"The Adventure of the Red Circle"

"The Disappearance of
Lady Frances Carfax"

1913

"The Adventure of the
Dying Detective"

1914

The Valley of Fear

1917

"His Last Bow"

"The Adven...
Mazarin Stone"

1922

"The Problem of Thor Bridge"

1923

"The Adventure of the Creeping Man"

1924

"The Adventure of the
Sussex Vampire"

"The Adventure of the
Three Garridebs"

"The Adventure of the
Illustrious Client"

1926

"The Adventure of the Three Gables"

"The Adventure of the
Blanched Soldier"

"The Adventure of the Lion's Mane"

"The Adventure of the
Retired Colourman"

1927

"The Adventure of the Veiled Lodger"

"The Adventure of Shoscombe
Old Place"

*Story titles in quotation marks signify "short stories" –
titles in *italics* signify "novels"

Praise for
The Strange Case of Dr. Doyle

"Offers us an opportunity to see how Conan Doyle might have approached the Ripper investigation, had he been involved with it, and, in a larger sense, how Conan Doyle's keen analytic mind mirrored, in many ways, that of his most famous creation [Sherlock Holmes]."

—*Booklist*

"[A]ccurate and well researched. . . . [A]n engaging examination . . . will raise eyebrows. . . . [B]ound to be read by fans of Victorian murder real and invented."

—*Library Journal*

"A gripping and fascinating read. Give the authors a chance and, well, you may start to look at Sherlock Holmes in an altogether different light."

—*Paul Begg, Ripperologist Magazine (UK)*

"[A] spectacular undertaking by Drs. Daniel and Eugene Friedman, who must be very good physicians if they can be judged by their passion, exhaustive research, and absolutely flawless writing."

—*The Durango Herald, "Murder Ink" columnist Jeff Mannix*

"The authors, long-time fans of the writings of Sir Arthur Conan Doyle, have turned the tables on this great author, using techniques that the great Sherlock Holmes and his creator would have applauded."

—*The Oakland Journal*

"[A] fascinating tale . . . extremely insightful, and well researched . . . illuminating. Highly recommended."

—Tom Johnson, columnist for *Detective Mystery Stories*

DOYLE'S WORLD LOST & FOUND

DOYLE'S WORLD LOST & FOUND

THE UNKNOWN HISTORIES OF SHERLOCK HOLMES AND SIR ARTHUR CONAN DOYLE

DANIEL FRIEDMAN, MD
EUGENE FRIEDMAN, MD

SQUAREONE
PUBLISHERS

EDITOR: Anthony Pomes
COVER DESIGN & TYPESETTING: Gary A. Rosenberg

Square One Publishers
115 Herricks Road
Garden City Park, NY 11040
(516) 535-2010 • squareonepublishers.com

[CIP DATA TO COME]

Artwork on page 9 (Stonyhurst College), public domain.
Artwork on page 14 by Diana Leto. Used by permission.
Photograph on page 16 (Bryan Charles Waller), public domain.
Map on page 130 from *Treasure Island* by Robert Louis Stevenson, Charles
    Scribner's Sons, 1897, public domain.
Artwork on page 194 by Scott Hanna. Used by permission.
Artwork on page 217 by Ramona Fradon. Used by permission.
Artwork on page 232 ("Is Conan Doyle Mad?") from *Sunday Express*, 1918,
    public domain.
Artwork on pages 264, 266–267, 272, 279, 282, 284, 289, 291, and 293 by
    Ben Moody. Used by permission.

Library of Congress Cataloging and Control in Publication Number:
2023024262

ISBN 978-0-7570-0448-3 (hardback)
ISBN 978-0-7570-5448-8 (ebook)

Printed in India

10   9   8   7   6   5   4   3   2   1

Contents

We dedicate this book to our wives,
Elena Friedman and Sheryl Friedman,
who sacrificed their time and unconditionally
devoted themselves to ensuring that
this new work of ours found its way to print.

We also dedicate this book to those who read
the Sherlock Holmes canon with sheer pleasure and
wonder, who appreciate the life and adventures of "Sir Arthur,"
and who adhere to the Holmes credo—

"'Eliminate all other factors, and the one which remains
must be the truth.'"

Note to Readers

As you read through this book, there will be various instances where the authors have applied their own *italics* on key points, themes, concepts, or even fragments of language found within cited portions of previously published text. When the authors have done this, you will see either *[emphasis added]* or—in cases when more than one spot in a citation has been italicized—as *[emphases added throughout]*.

Acknowledgments

We would like to begin by thanking Matthew Friedman, whose contributions to this book are present in each and every chapter. Matthew has spent hours tirelessly working with us to ensure that Sir Arthur Conan Doyle's story could be told in a manner that would be easily understood and appreciated by all of his fans. Without his assistance, we could never have completed this Herculean task.

We would also like to thank Dominick J. Grillo, librarian extraordinaire, for helping us track down rare manuscripts and newspaper clippings, and for adding his own thoughts to the book. If Sherlock Holmes had been a librarian, he surely would have been the embodiment of Dominick.

Many thanks to the gifted and talented *New York Times* best-selling author Ben Mezrich, who encouraged me to transfer my thoughts onto paper.

We would also like to thank Jennifer Johnstone, for providing us with Charles Doyle's admission and chart notes at the time he was incarcerated at Morningside Lunatic Asylum.

Thank you, David Knight, former archivist at Stonyhurst College, for sharing with us your personal notes on Doyle's years as a student there, and also for furnishing us with Doyle's academic records.

Thanks to Sally Pagan and Claire Button of the University of Edinburgh for supplying us with Doyle's medical school transcript, his thesis paper, and a few other documents contained in his folder.

As a single picture is said to be worth a thousand words, we would like to thank Benjamin Houston Moody for illustrating the "lost" Doyle stories "What the Moon Revealed" and "His Word of Honour" in this book. We would also like to thank artist Diana Leto for bringing the insane prefect "Mr. Chrea" to vivid pictorial life. And we are also honored that two award-winning comic book illustrators have shared their talents with us—Eisner Award recipient Scott Hanna, whose pencil and ink depiction of Richard Sherburne lying dead in Stonyhurst's "Dark Walk" enhances the reader's comprehension of the scene, and legendary Eisner and Woman's Cartoonist Hall of Famer Ramona Fradon, whose pencil illustration of Doyle attending a séance captures the excitement and fear associated with these strange and mystical events.

We very much appreciate the efforts of Michael Kean, president of the Baker Street Irregulars, for making sure that the fans of Doyle's characters have forums around the world where they can express their views on all things related to Sherlock Holmes. And we also extend our gratitude to Steven Rothman, Adrian Braddy, Dan Andriacco, Mark Alberstat, JoAnn Alberstat, Bill Barnes, Shai Porter, Susan Parry, Crystal Noll, Jayantika Ganguly, and Evelyn Herzog, each of whom have honored us by publishing several of our original articles in their prestigious magazines and journals.

And, of course, we would like to express our sincere thanks to our wonderful editor—Anthony Pomes, who worked day and night to make certain that the material contained in *Doyle's World* was accurate, intellectually stimulating, systematically organized, and written to the best of our ability. You are a taskmaster, Anthony, but now that we are done, we owe you a debt of gratitude for all that *you* have done.

And thank you to our publisher, Rudy Shur, whose belief in this project—and in us—allowed us the opportunity to put together a biography on Doyle, told in a nontraditional style.

Preface

The inspiration for *Doyle's World* can be traced back to our first book—*The Strange Case of Dr. Doyle*—where we wrote a series of biographical chapters primarily emphasizing Sir Arthur Conan Doyle's development and evolution before he reached the age of thirty. It should be noted that our fact-laden yet wholly conjectural "Tour" section of the book, presented as chapters that alternated with our biography-oriented work, was set in 1910.

This was twenty-two years beyond our targeted age parameters, by which time Doyle had turned fifty-one. Our self-imposed chronological barrier then compelled us to meticulously research Doyle's life and experiences through 1910, so that we could maintain an appropriate and consistent level of realism and academic fidelity throughout our fictive tour day.

Once the completed manuscript for *The Strange Case of Dr. Doyle* was submitted for publication, we found ourselves swimming in stacks of riveting—and frequently heretofore unrevealed information—uncovered during our research efforts. Upon subsequent examination of this copious Doyle-related material, we decided to write another book where we could share all our discoveries about Doyle's life and works.

At first, we were a bit stymied about how we would properly arrange this work. Just days into the first chapter, something fortuitous occurred. While researching Edinburgh's architecture, we stumbled upon a statue that appeared at first glance to be a depiction of Doyle himself. Surprisingly, it turned out that it was not Doyle at all—rather, it was the sculpted image of his fictional creation, Sherlock Holmes, topped with deerstalker hat and smoking his trademark calabash pipe. It dawned on us that, even in a city replete with historic markers identifying the schools he had attended and the residences in which he had lived, it was Doyle's *fictional creation*—and *not the actual man*—that his hometown chose to commemorate. Since much of the research for our first book by necessity required detailed examination of Doyle's two greatest characters—Sherlock Holmes and Dr. John H. Watson—we decided to modify our book to include a close study of that imaginary realm as well.

The world continues to associate Doyle with his "Sherlock Holmes" tales, but has basically consigned his many other literary contributions and accolades to oblivion. It is easy to forget—or never to learn—that Doyle was a multifaceted person who accrued a vast list of accomplishments that amounted to far more than the sum of the individual parts. In truth, that bronze figure of Holmes could have just as easily been replaced by a statue representing Doyle as: a physician, caring for an ill patient; a weathered seafarer, wielding a harpoon; an avid pioneer of photography, giving chase to and trying to capture the images of fairies and elves; a skilled pugilist, lacing up his boxing gloves prior to a spirited bout; a politician, delivering a fiery oration from his lectern; or even a psychic medium, gazing into the depths of a crystal ball. All of these were essential elements of Doyle's world.

And so, we opted to scrap everything we had previously done and redesign our manuscript from scratch. We returned to the same methodology we had employed when we wrote "The Tour" chapters in *The Strange Case of Dr. Doyle*—that is, we divided a variety of general subjects and topics into their component parts. Files labeled as "Hobbies," "Personal Interests," "Occupations," "Political Pursuits," and even "Religious Beliefs" were then further subdivided as we accumulated even more data about Doyle's life. Only when we were satisfied with the contents in each respective folder did we then begin to craft the individual chapters contained in the book that you are now holding in your hands.

Just as in *The Strange Case of Dr. Doyle*, we have made a deliberate choice not to turn to any contemporary biographies of Doyle written after 1943. Instead, we have made use of primary sources (letters, diary entries, newspapers and magazine articles) alongside first-hand accounts we were able to track down in Doyle's autobiographical books and further writings. As a result, much of what is contained in *Doyle's World* differs markedly from the information contained in the many other Doyle biographies you can readily find on shelves in stores and libraries alike.

In our shared opinion, Doyle said it best in his 1907 book of articles, *Through the Magic Door*, when he wrote the following:

"One would like the frail, human side of a man as well as the other. I cannot believe that any one in the world was ever quite so good as the subject of most of our biographies. Surely these worthy people swore a little sometimes, or had a keen eye for a pretty face, or opened the second bottle when they would have done better to have stopped at the first, or did something to make us feel that they were men and brothers."

It is our firm belief that the life of Sir Arthur Conan Doyle—whether it is examined through his admirable achievements or through his occasionally less-than-praiseworthy qualities therein—warrants being subjected to even greater scrutiny. Our hope is that our unique findings will provide readers with enjoyment, and a more thorough understanding of Doyle's literary works together with his life's copious experiences, efforts—and yes, **adventures**.

Welcome to *Doyle's World*.

Introduction

"All the world's a stage,
And all the men and women merely players;
They have their exits and their entrances;
And one man in his time plays many parts."
—WILLIAM SHAKESPEARE, *AS YOU LIKE IT* (ACT 2, SCENE 7)

For those who live and die by the written word, Sir Arthur Conan Doyle remains a permanent frame of reference against which all others are measured—a true titan of storytelling. Once readers are granted access to Doyle's overflowing cornucopia of language, they find themselves caught up in a whirlwind of creative expression—something we experienced as we continued on our quest to explore, discover, and admire this remarkable individual's output.

This book is not based *solely* on Doyle's life. It also considers the fictitious life of the "consulting detective" with whom this legendary British writer will forever be associated—Sherlock Holmes. The now-ubiquitous Holmes was first introduced to readers when Doyle was a struggling young physician, trying his best to supplement his meager income by submitting self-penned tales to London's publishing houses. Once his *A Study in Scarlet* had been accepted for publication in 1887, the only path that Doyle could take became clearly set in front of him. It would be his destiny to present a hungry reading public with a deeply satisfying detective novel, a genre that he updated and actually reinvented.

During the course of sixty thrilling adventures, Sherlock Holmes emerged as the prototypical *scientific* detective. By 1891—only four years from the publication of that first story—Holmes' name was universally known and globally beloved. These tales served as the inspiration for a new generation of writers to adopt, adapt, and occasionally improve upon Doyle's compelling literary style—one that brought scores of entertaining characters to life. Doyle had paved the way toward a new kind of realistic and captivating detective mystery story, where the events of the tale took place in *real time*.

Had this accomplishment represented the totality of Doyle's contribution to literature, it would have allowed him to rest casually on his laurels. But Doyle was not a man ready to bask in early glory. In addition to giving us the intellectually gifted Holmes, Doyle went on to expand his horizons with plays, poems, editorials, science fiction stories, and historical novels spread out over more than four decades.

Doyle waded fearlessly into the fields of medicine, politics, photography, athletics, exploration, and Spiritualism. His continuous high-quality work in these categories makes Doyle worthy of stand-alone status—indeed, many books have been written about his involvement in each of these areas. To help the reader gain a better understanding of the level and range of his versatility, our book places focuses on many of Doyle's talents—and eccentricities—by breaking them down into separate strands of research and analysis. It is our intention to provide the reader with a chronicle of Doyle's life that begins at his birth and ends on the date of his death on July 7, 1930. By adhering firmly to the tenets espoused by Doyle in *Through the Magic Door*, we have remained as "perfectly impartial" as possible—and better yet, we have done this to look at Doyle "with a sympathetic mind" and a "stern determination to tell the absolute truth." While it wasn't our mission to glorify the man, we were also cautious about minimizing his numerous accomplishments. We have reported only documented facts, whether they are favorable or not. Although Doyle's life was a complex one, we have worked throughout this book to deconstruct his written works—as well as Doyle himself—into a series of interconnected parts that should make the author, and his world of characters, more understandable.

The book is divided into three parts. In the five chapters that comprise Part I ("Building a World"), we dove into those life-based incidents that led Doyle to create the Sherlock Holmes universe—among them, some unpleasant events that guided him along on his path toward becoming a master storyteller; the bevy of distinguished medical men who were to become key elements in the genesis of the Holmes character; the chance meeting with an African-American dignitary, the result of which informed Doyle on issues of race; and how his struggles as a practicing physician finally gave way to a far more successful career as a man of letters.

In Part II ("Becoming a World"), we provide an in-depth examination of the myriad themes, strategies, and influences that Doyle was able to incorporate effortlessly into his work. We also made sure to discuss the political and spiritual beliefs that lay near and dear to Doyle's heart. Certainly, the man who brought Sherlock Holmes to life in 1887 was a far different one than the deeply conflicted knight of the British Empire in 1902. We are confident that what we are offering the reader is a resonant portrait of the true Sir Arthur Conan Doyle, one that transcends mere biography and literary criticism. In the spirit of all well-tested hybrid systems—and for the first time—the facts of Doyle's life stand in place as an unbent reflection of his *fiction* . . . and vice versa.

And in Part III ("Uncovering a Hidden World"), we are proud to share with our readers two *lost stories* that we are certain were written by Doyle, yet purposely attributed to another physician who Doyle greatly admired, and worked with, during his medical school years.

It is our hope that the approach employed by us throughout *Doyle's World* will furnish our readers with a fresh and unexpected perspective on this man—and the characters he introduced to us.

PART I

Building a World

CHAPTER 1

Doyle and *Holmes*
A Study in Origins

Sir Arthur Conan Doyle created some of the most unforgettable characters in Western literature. People around the world recognize Consulting Detective Sherlock Holmes just by his silhouette, which was first drawn by Doyle's father, Charles Doyle, and then revised and popularized by Sidney Paget when the Holmes stories appeared in *The Strand* magazine in the early 1890s. The master sleuth has also transitioned well over time into a multitude of media formats—books, theater, radio programs, comic books, television shows, graphic novels, blockbuster movies, and streaming series have all projected different variations on Doyle's most famous literary creation. Indeed, Sherlock Holmes has become the very symbol of the detective story. Even though the most recent of the Holmes adventures are nearly a century old, they continue to entice and entrap readers of all ages. For those who have been captivated by the stories themselves, there are hundreds of global organizations whose members are devotees of the fictional world of the partnership between Holmes and his trusty sidekick, Dr. John H. Watson. Although the modern detective story originated in the work of American writer Edgar Allan Poe nearly a half-century before Holmes made his formal debut, it was the imaginative talents of Britain-based Doyle who promoted the evolution of the genre into its current format.

Yet, Doyle made a curious choice when he decided not to delve too deeply into the early origins or family dynamics of his main characters. When Doyle touches upon these subjects at all, he typically gives them short shrift. In the 1893 short story "The Adventure of the Greek Interpreter," Sherlock Holmes casually divulges that his ancestors had been "country squires," and then mentions—almost in passing—that he has an older and more brilliant sibling, "Mycroft." These scant biographical details, provided nearly six years after the publication of the first Holmes story *A Study in Scarlet* in 1887, are all the family background made available to us by Doyle about his chief character. Where Sherlock had attended school, the names and occupations of his parents, the date and year of his birth, and the details of his college education are never revealed. In the case of a prose stylist who was as exacting and fastidious in technique as Doyle, the dramatic absence of these basic elements in his characters' lives must be considered as mysterious as it is notable.

Fortunately, certain clues relevant to the origins of Holmes and Watson are present in the life events of Doyle himself. And so, by exploring some of the pivotal moments in Sir Arthur Conan Doyle's early childhood and adolescence, we can collect enough keys to unlock the doors that can grant us access to a treasure trove of crucial information about the crime-fighting duo's formative years.

Arthur Ignatius Conan Doyle was born on May 22, 1859, in Edinburgh, Scotland's capital city. His father, Charles, who was employed as a draftsman at Her Majesty's Office of Public Works, was one of the four surviving sons of John Doyle, the most celebrated print caricaturist of his time. Charles succumbed to the demons of alcohol, and this expensive and lifelong habit was to lead his family on a financial rollercoaster ride that continually teetered between periods of prosperity and poverty. Doyle's mother, Mary, was an educated woman who instilled in her precocious son her love of literature. It was her daily ritual to read aloud to her son the Arthurian tales and Shakespeare's masterful works. Young Arthur soon emerged as an overflowing fountain of information and by the age of four had already written and illustrated an adventure story of his own. When his great-uncle, renowned art critic Michael Conan, received a copy of his great-nephew's story featuring a hunter who had unwisely chosen to enter the cave of a Bengal tiger, Doyle's destiny to become a professional writer was all but carved in stone.

So taken was Michael Conan by the scope of his great-nephew's vivid imagination, his hand-drawn comical illustrations, and his innate grasp of mature concepts that he began following Doyle's "development with great interest." In time, he saw the potential genius of his great-nephew, and recommended that Mary enroll him in a Jesuit school to receive his formal education. As Edinburgh lacked a school that measured up to Michael Conan's exacting standards, Doyle soon found himself sent off to Hodder House in England's north country town of Preston Hollow. Two years later, he moved up to its upper affiliate, Stonyhurst College. This decision meant that for the next seven years, Doyle would be apart from his parents and siblings.

School days—Stonyhurst Hall at Stonyhurst College circa 1870s.

The education one received at Stonyhurst was first-rate, especially when it came to astronomy. As there was a huge telescope and planetarium right on campus, students were afforded the opportunity to see firsthand the rings of Saturn, the moons of Jupiter, and other objects of the solar system. Doyle learned the Copernican theory and Newton's laws of gravity from Father Walter Sidgreaves and Father Stephen Perry, two of the most influential astronomers of their time. With a touch of irony, in *A Study in Scarlet*, Doyle has Dr. Watson describe Sherlock Holmes as completely "ignorant of the Copernican Theory and of the composition of the Solar System." Dr. Watson also finds it difficult to believe "that any civilized human being . . . should not be aware that the earth travelled round the sun . . . ." If this had been the case, then Sherlock Holmes certainly had never set foot in Stonyhurst.

At Stonyhurst, Doyle was subjected to the harsh disciplinary rules and corporal punishment of its prefects and faculty. A *tolley*—an eight-inch slab of India-rubber—was the instrument of choice to "correct" those students who strayed from the path of righteousness. Doyle was the student who had his hands lashed with it the most. Of these incidents, Doyle later wrote the following:

> "I think, however, that it was good for us in the end, for it was a point of honour with many of us not to show that we were hurt, and that is one of the best trainings for a hard life. If I was more beaten than others it was not that I was in any way vicious, but it was that I had a nature which responded eagerly to affectionate kindness (which I never received), but which rebelled against threats and took a perverted pride in showing that it would not be cowed by violence. I went out of my way to do really mischievous and outrageous things simply to show that my spirit was unbroken. An appeal to my better nature and not to my fears would have found an answer at once. I deserved all I got for what I did, but I did it because I was mishandled."

Hodder House and Stonyhurst were also firm proponents of outdoor activities, requiring all students, no matter how young or old, to participate in long walks, football games, cricket matches, and cold swims in the river. Doyle excelled in all of them. Cricket, football, rugby, and boxing ranked highest on his list. And so, when Doyle created his crime-fighting duo, he made sure to imbue Holmes with his own considerable boxer prowess while imparting his rugby talents to Dr. Watson.

When Arthur Conan Doyle was a fourteen-year-old student at Stonyhurst, a sensational trial that would indirectly, yet dramatically, involve the "playgrounds" of Stonyhurst College dominated the front pages of newspapers throughout the country. The case, known as the "Tichborne Trial," centered on the apparent return of Roger Charles Tichborne to the United Kingdom. In 1854, this heir to an immense fortune had been declared lost at sea and presumed dead off the South American coast. Twelve years after his disappearance, Roger's mother, Lady Dowager Tichborne, received a letter that bore an Australian postmark, and whose author claimed to be her "missing" son. She was completely convinced of the letter's authenticity and invited her "son" (regarded by most as an impostor) to re-enter her life and to gain access to her purse.

Any doubts that Lady Tichborne had about the identity of this long-lost wanderer were put to rest after she had personally inspected the young man's back. She was absolutely convinced that its overall shape and muscularity bore a striking resemblance to that of her departed husband's. She also was further taken by the structure of his ears, which were "exactly his uncle's." As Roger Tichborne had spent three full years as a student at Stonyhurst, Doyle saw his current professors being summoned to court one by one to offer testimony. Any member of the staff and faculty who had been on campus in 1845 was now considered to be a potentially valuable witness. On March 2, 1874, the following run-on sentence describing the bizarre events of the trial appeared in the *London Times*:

> "In this extraordinary drama are wonderfully combined, and played, one against the other, all the characters, all the ranks and classes, all the places, all the circumstances, all the styles and modes, all the spreading nations and universal languages, the chief religions, the prevailing tendencies, the traditions and anticipations, the old world and the new, the most fixed and forced conditions of life and the most unsettled and chaotic, the weaknesses and the strengths of a world always dying to be born again."

Ironically, the man purporting to be Roger Tichborne was brought down by a game that was played on the school's playground. At the trial, when the Solicitor-General asked, "What does 'bandy' mean?" the self-proclaimed *Roger* replied, "To the best of my recollection, it strikes me part of Stonyhurst was called 'Bandy'." The solicitor then countered with, 'Would it surprise you that bandy was a game played with balls by the philosophers at Stonyhurst, and in which Roger Tichborne was a great proficient?" *Roger's* response was a meek, "My memory isn't correct enough to enable me to speak of it." The Solicitor-General then closed the session with a sarcastic, 'Well, there is a difference between a game and a part of a building you know."

It is highly improbable that anyone other than a bona fide Stonyhurst student would have known about bandy, a game where a stick was used to get a ball past a goalpost, as it was exclusively played there. The actual Roger Tichborne had achieved legendary status among the students there, owing to his mastery of the game. With his reply that "bandy" was a section of the school, *Roger's* charade came to a sudden and abrupt halt. It was not long before it was confirmed that the imposter was Thomas Castro, a butcher from Wagga Wagga, Australia, and soon after this, a second discovery was made—Castro was really Arthur Orton from London, England. Although Mr. Orton failed to get hold of the Tichborne family fortune, he did receive the consolation prize of ten years in prison.

Doyle was later to put his own literary spin on the Tichborne case in "The Disappearance of Lady Frances Carfax" (1911). In this tale we find the title character nursing "Rev. Dr. Shlessinger" (a missionary "recovering from a disease contracted in the exercise of his apostolic duties" in South America) back to health. Holmes uncovers the disturbing fact that this Dr. Shlessinger is "none other than Holy Peters, one of the most unscrupulous rascals that Australia has ever evolved." The "particular specialty" of this conman "is the beguiling of lonely ladies," which is highly suggestive that Shlessinger's affliction has been a sexually transmitted disease, most likely syphilis. This parallels the Tichborne case in which Thomas Castro/Arthur Orton beguiled a lonely woman who was still in the process of mourning the loss of her son.

The "Lady Frances Carfax" adventure was not the only time that Doyle incorporated elements drawn from his Stonyhurst days into his Holmes tales. When Doyle first arrived at Stonyhurst College, the administration assigned him the number 31, a number that remained unchanged throughout his entire time there. Doyle paid homage to his number several times. In "The Adventure of the Retired Colourman" (1926), the seat number on Mr. Josiah Amberley's Haymarket theater ticket is number 31-B, while in "The Adventure of the Illustrious Client" (1924), the private phone number that Colonel James Damery uses at the Carlton Club is XX.31. In "A Case of Identity" (1891), Doyle goes even further by having Miss Mary Sutherland reside at "31, Lyon Place Camberwell." Not only did Doyle recycle his long-held college number, but the choice of the street name, "*Lyon* Place," hearkens back to the "Red *Lion* Inn," the customary meeting place for Hodder and Stonyhurst students when they stepped off the train upon its arrival at Preston Hollow.

Doyle's student years at Hodder House and Stonyhurst helped transform him into a master storyteller and consummate writer. One of his favorite

Stonyhurst teachers, Father Cyprian Splaine, got a kick out of frightening his students with his spine-tingling tales. One of these "jolly" stories, as young Doyle referred to it in a letter home to his mother, was an English version of August Lewald's 1829 German thriller, *Der Rächer* (The *Avenger*). Doyle described the plot of this "bedtime" thriller as "a lot of horrible murders," and pleaded with her to pick up a copy for herself. In 1873, Doyle's mother Mary abruptly stopped writing to him, a situation that filled the fourteen-year-old Doyle with trepidation. He wrote the following note to her: "I was a little frightened at not receiving any letter from you for so long." He then sent off a second letter to her that centered on a horrible event that had taken place on campus:

> "We have had a great commotion here lately, from the fact that our third prefect has gone stark staring mad. I expected it all along, he always seemed to have the most singular antipathy to me, and I am called among the boys 'Mr. *Chrea's friend.*' Ironically, of course. The first signs of madness were at Vespers the other day. I was near him & I saw him, just as the Laudate Dominum began, *pull out his handkerchief and begin waving it over his head.* Two of the community took him and at once led him out. *They say that in his delirium he mentioned my name several times.* A story is going about that before entering the society he fell in love with a maiden, but *the maiden absconded with an individual named Doyle,* and Mr Chrea in his despair entered the society, and the name of Doyle has ever since had an irritating effect on him. I can't however answer for the truth of this. We are having the most detestable weather possible over here. Rain, rain, rain and nothing but rain. I shall soon at this rate die of ennui, my great comfort however is the thought of seeing you all again at Xmas." *[emphases added throughout]*

Doyle's vivid description of a chaotic event that occurred during the Vesper service showcases his natural storytelling ability. His eerie letter begins by informing his mother that a Mr. Chrea, the school's "third prefect," had apparently suffered an acute nervous breakdown in front of the students in attendance. He immediately changes the subject by informing his mother that this same Mr. Chrea has been holding a long-term grudge against him and that his sudden outburst had been no surprise to him at all. He then complains to his mother that this "madman" has "the most antipathy to me" and that, ironically, his classmates always refer to him as "Mr. Chrea's friend." And yet, in none of his prior letters home had he mentioned any such person, even though he had told his mother the names of the other teachers who had been abusive toward him. Doyle goes on to write that "the first signs of madness" became evident at Vespers, declaring that his fellow teachers had to subdue Mr. Chrea before he could inflict harm on anyone else. Although the letter's wording seems to indicate that this was the sole occasion on which this particular prefect harassed him, the phrase, "I expected it all along" and "Mr Chrea's friend" contradicts Doyle's surprised tone regarding what took place earlier that evening.

Doyle's imagined "Mr. Chrea" story, written in a letter home to his mother.

How much of this letter from Doyle to his mother is fact—and how much is fiction? First, we need to determine whether or not there was a third prefect named "Mr. Chrea" at all. A review of the Stonyhurst teaching and administrative rosters of 1873 lists a Mr. Thomas Knowles as "Third Prefect." The name Chrea does not appear on that roster. An intensive search of Stonyhurst College documents revealed that there has never been a student nor faculty member with the name Chrea, which makes it highly unlikely that Doyle's tormenter ever existed. But it does suggest that Doyle's letter was a figment of his imagination. Lonely children crave attention and tend to exaggerate certain aspects of their experiences.

In that same letter, Mr. Chrea is described as having removed a handkerchief from his pocket and then waving it frantically above his head. This descriptive detail may have been Doyle's symbol for something rather significant—something Doyle's well-read mother would have easily deciphered. When he wrote this letter, Doyle had already read, seen, or been a performer in several Shakespearean plays, among them *The Tempest*, *King John*, and *Macbeth*. It is quite likely he had read (or heard his mother read to him) *Othello*, a tragedy marked by Desdemona's (Othello's wife) handkerchief being converted into a symbol of domestic infidelity by the evil Iago. Mr. Chrea's waving handkerchief may have been Doyle's way of admonishing his mother that he was aware that she had been unfaithful to his father. That same letter contains the following weird sentence: "A story is going about that before entering the society he fell in love with a maiden, but the maiden absconded with an individual named Doyle." Was Doyle's mother the *maiden* at the center of his letter home?

In order to unlock the letter's secret meaning, we have to take a look at Doyle's extended family. First, Doyle's grandfather, John Doyle, had been an expert in concealing his true identity from the general public. For more than fifteen years, he signed his artwork using the pseudonym H. B., initials derived from the letter J of John and D of Doyle and then doubling them. This was his way of poking gentle fun at Britain's Members of Parliament without having to fear any repercussions. Doyle's father, the brilliant but deeply troubled Charles, shared his affinity for word games and logic puzzles with his son. In *A Study in Scarlet*, the first of the Holmes stories, Inspector Lestrade of Scotland Yard observes the five-letter word "*Rache*" written on a wall—*in blood*. Lestrade immediately assumes that the killer's name is a "woman named Rachel," but Holmes is quick to correct him, pointing out that RACHE is the German equivalent for the word "revenge." As mentioned earlier, one of Doyle's teachers had read the story *Der Rächer* (The *Avenger*) to his class, the same book Doyle had begged his mother to purchase for herself. As the letters in "CHREA" are an anagram of "RACHE," it is our theory that the deranged Mr. Chrea was Doyle's vehicle for exacting a form of revenge against his mother and the person he believed to be her lover.

While Doyle, always the master of complex but subtle plot, doesn't go as far as telling us the name of his mother's lover, he indirectly names the philanderer in the form of a riddle that appears on the cover of that book. *Der Rächer* was written in 1829 by a German author, August Lewald. While this fact might be regarded as a mere piece of trivia, Lewald's English nom de plume, Kurt *Waller*, puts the pieces of this complex puzzle together. In 1873, Bryan Charles Waller, a brilliant third-year University of Edinburgh medical student, began boarding at the Doyle home to supplement the family's diminishing income. In the "Chrea" letter, Doyle seems to be offering a hint to his mother that he knew all about her inappropriate relationship with this wealthy, well-bred, future physician and future poet laureate of the Freemasons. The source of this damning information most likely was Doyle's sister Annette, who once had a relationship of her own with Waller. Once Waller began focusing his

Bryan Charles Waller (1853–1932). Doyle blamed him for having seduced his mother.

affections on Mrs. Doyle—who was fifteen years his senior—the spurned Annette had no compunction about letting her younger brother in on the family secret. Four years later, Doyle's forty-year-old mother gave birth to a daughter who she christened with the telling name "Bryan Julia Doyle." Worsening domestic matters, Charles Doyle was adamant in his refusal to go down to the local courthouse to register *his* purported child's birth. It is likely that Charles doubted that the child was his, and that it had been Bryan Waller who had fathered "Bryan Julia."

Doyle would allude to this family scandal in "A Case of Identity" (1891), where its opening gambit has Miss *Mary* Sutherland providing

Holmes with personal information regarding the members of her current household. Her stepfather (Mr. Windibank) is five years her senior (the same age difference between Waller and Doyle) and her mother is fifteen years senior to her new husband (the same age difference between Mary Doyle and Bryan Waller). "A Case of Identity" and the Mr. Chrea letter both revolve around love triangles gone terribly wrong, and free us to "fly out of that window hand in hand, hover over this great city, gently remove the roofs, and peep in at the queer things which are going on, the strange coincidences, the plannings, the cross-purposes, the wonderful chains of events, working through generations, and leading to the most outré results."

Doyle's *Study in Scarlet* holds the key for unlocking the true identity of "Mr. Chrea," who had to have been the aforementioned Dr. Bryan Charles Waller. That he and Mary Doyle shared a deep affection is undeniable, and so, when Mary Doyle's husband Charles became a permanent inmate of several of Scotland's mental sanitariums, Mary seized the opportunity to make her escape from Edinburgh and join her young lover at his Yorkshire Masongill estate. Well after her son had achieved fame and fortune in the world of literature, Mary Doyle remained a "tenant" there, rejecting her now famous and wealthy son's invitation to move in with him. It would take thirty-five years before she left Waller's estate. Even in her old age, she refused to move into her son's lavish home. Rather, she moved in with her daughter Connie and her noted husband, writer E. W. Hornung, for the remainder of her long life.

That Mary Doyle stopped writing to her son prior to his "Chrea" letter has been firmly established by the historical record. We have concluded that Doyle knew all about his mother's affair and found a way to condemn her for it by way of the "Chrea" letter. This would certainly explain Mary's ongoing relationship with Waller and her long-term estrangement from her son.

A Study in Scarlet and Stonyhurst College also hold important clues to Dr. John H. Watson's backstory. In the first paragraph to that very first Holmes tale, Watson informs us that he received his Doctor of Medicine degree from the University of London, and then went off to "Netley to go through the course prescribed for surgeons in the army." From there, he was dispatched to India where he was assigned to "the Fifth Northumberland Fusiliers as Assistant Surgeon." He was soon reassigned to the Berkshire Regiment in Afghanistan, where the combination of a bullet wound and a bout of dysentery brought his military career to a quick halt.

In the Holmes short story "The Adventure of the Naval Treaty" (first serialized in *The Strand* from October to November 1893), Watson tells the reader that he had attended private school with a young man named "Percy Phelps." When "The Adventure of the Sussex Vampire" was published more than 20 years later in 1924, readers learned that Watson played rugby for Blackheath in his younger years. Scant information at best, when it comes to personal details. Doyle is far more interested in Watson's present circumstances as a friend and collaborator of Holmes than what his life had been like before moving into 221 B, Baker Street. This glaring *lack* of family background has served as a seed for many Sherlockians to perform their own investigations into Watson's origins. There are many astute literary detectives who insist they have been able to find clues scattered throughout the Holmes canon that suggest Watson hails from Australia. Are their deductions correct? Or do they fail the test?

In his 1967 book *The Annotated Sherlock Holmes*, renowned Holmes expert William S. Baring-Gould refers to Watson's "Down Under" roots on several occasions. In his "Naval Treaty" annotations, Baring-Gould declares that Watson is "guilty of two 'colonialisms,' pointing to his boyhood in Australia: 'playground,' to a youngster reared in England would be 'playing field,' and 'wicket' would be 'stump.'" Although this interpretation of Watson's beginnings might initially appear plausible, Baring-Gould fails to recall that Doyle had spent a total of seven years between Hodder House and Stonyhurst College, where "playing fields" *were* referred to as "playgrounds." Irrefutable proof can be found in the 1870 historical volume *Stonyhurst College: Its Past and Present*, published during a period that overlapped with Doyle's days on campus. One of its chapter headings reads "*School-room, Playground, and Gymnasium.*" Like all Stonyhurst students, Doyle would also have referred to a ball field as a "playground" and not as a "playing field."

Another contemporaneous book that is related to Doyle's alma mater is *Stonyhurst College: Its Life Beyond the Seas* (1894). On its pages is the following wistful phrase: "It was not till long afterwards that what is now known as the Old Playground was brought into the form which many still remember." And so it follows that the author of the Holmes tales would have used the term "playground," and *not* "playing field," when he crafted his stories. And at Stonyhurst, students played "wicket-cricket," which most other English schools referred to as "cricket," and the three vertical posts that suspended the ball were referred to as a "wicket," and not "stump." Quite fittingly, the team that represented Stonyhurst was nicknamed The Wickets. In all likelihood, when Watson tells us that Percy Phelps was beaten "over the shins with a wicket," Doyle was recalling his own experience back at Stonyhurst. In fact, Doyle was probably beaten over the shins with a wicket, too, while a student there, as his autobiography states that "corporal punishment was severe" at Stonyhurst, and that "few, if any, boys of my time endured more of it." That punishment not only came from the teachers, but from the older students, too.

As for his being a native of Australia, Watson's statements "In an experience of women which extends over many nations and three separate continents" and his recollection that "I have seen something of the sort on the side of a hill near Ballarat, where the prospectors had been at work" run contrary to such a notion. While it is a possibility Watson sojourned there as a young medical student, it is unlikely he would have been romantically involved with women prior to entering the third form in England. And the hill described by Watson as being situated near Ballarat had already seen its golden treasure extracted by the time he would have arrived there, as Ballarat's gold rush began in 1851 and had settled down by the late 1860s. Watson would most likely have been in the state of Victoria in the early 1870s, a period that corresponds to his medical school days. And in "The Boscombe Valley Mystery" (1891), Watson knows nothing about either the "distinctively Australian cry" of "cooee" or the legend of Black Jack of Ballarat and the infamous Ballarat Gang. And when Holmes places a map of Victoria on a table and then covers the letters "B-A-L-L-" of "Ballarat" with his hand, Watson finds it necessary for Holmes to remove his hand from the map in order to appreciate that he isn't looking at a city named "ARAT." Certainly, if Watson had been raised in Victoria, he would have had no trouble deducing that Holmes' fingers had been partially covering the letters of the town of Ballarat.

Although the second Holmes tale, *The Sign of the Four* (1890), suggests that Watson had spent at least some time in Victoria, there might have been an ulterior motive behind Doyle's crafting of another story that had a relationship to Australia and New Zealand. We must keep in mind that "The Boscombe Valley Mystery" was not Doyle's first attempt at writing an authentic-sounding tale that used Oceania as its backdrop. That honor belongs to his non-Sherlockian adventure, "The Gully of Bluemansdyke" (published in 1894), a murder mystery he wrote while he was serving as ship's surgeon immediately upon graduating from medical school. This is an important literary work for several reasons. First, we find the American prospector-turned-hero, Chicago Bill, standing "with his gun still smoking in his hand." A modified form of this phrase was also used in the Sherlock Holmes tale from 1893, "The Adventure of the *Gloria Scott*" (an adventure that also has a connection with Australia), where "the chaplain stood with a smoking pistol in his hand." Although many Sherlockians attribute the origin of the phrase "smoking gun" to the "*Gloria Scott*," they are correct about its writer, but not the story. And "The Gully of Bluemansdyke" also foreshadows Holmes' particular choice of pipe, as the character Jim Burton's "meerschaums were always a weakness," and he would repeatedly say, "'[A] gentleman is known by his pipe. When he comes down in the world his pipe has most vitality.'"

We owe a debt of gratitude to E. W. Hornung, for he was the man most likely responsible for Doyle having directed some of his energies into the Australian-themed "Boscombe Valley Mystery." Before he had even laid eyes on his future wife, Hornung had already made a name for himself as an up-and-coming writer. Although he is best remembered for his "amateur cracksman" Raffles, he is regarded as "The Bret Harte of Australia." Hornung, who had lived a large part of his life in the land Down Under, had a natural ability to scatter proper colonialisms like "cooee" into his works, and gave us detailed and accurate descriptions of Australia's rivers, streams, and towns. When Arthur Conan Doyle wrote "The Gully of Bluemansdyke," he had not yet met Hornung, and conveniently created the non-existent Wawirra River and Gully of Bluemansdyke. Additionally, he placed the Australian town of Trafalgar in close proximity to New Zealand's Tapu Mountains (which are hundreds of miles away across the Tasman Sea). By the time Doyle was writing "The Boscombe Valley Mystery," he was engaged in a friendly competition against Hornung for supremacy in bookstores and on the cricket field. Doyle certainly sought to make "The Boscombe Valley Mystery" read at least as well as the works of his future brother-in-law. And by most accounts, Doyle succeeded in this quest.

In Doyle's "The Adventure of the Yellow Face" (1893), there is a scene where Holmes' new client accidentally leaves his amber pipe behind. Holmes studies it and tells Watson that it's a "'nice old brier with a good long stem of what the tobacconists call amber. I wonder how many real amber mouthpieces there are in London?'" That description also has its origins in Stonyhurst, as it matches the first pipe a fourteen-year-old Doyle purchased for himself ("a nice little pipe with an amber mouthpiece"). Holmes continues on, telling Watson, "'Pipes are occasionally of extraordinary interest . . . Nothing has more individuality, save perhaps watches and bootlaces,'" words of praise that parallel the sentiments expressed by "The Gully of Bluemansdyke"'s Jim Burton.

The more we look at Watson's life pre-Baker Street under the lens of a microscope, the clearer it becomes that he is descended from the same genetic material of his creator. Not only does Watson conform to the prototypical Stonyhurst student, but the history of his family bears remarkable resemblance to that of the Doyles. Watson's older brother—a man "with good prospects" who "threw away his chances"—was constantly alternating between "poverty with occasional short intervals of prosperity," which is akin to that of the Doyles. Holmes deduces that Watson's brother was only able to pay off his debts by pawning and re-pawning the gold watch his father had left him. All this did was enable him to drink himself to an early death. This vignette had to have been extremely difficult for Doyle to write about, as it describes the similar plight of his own beloved father—Charles Altamont Doyle. Even though Charles Doyle was a gifted draftsman, he was never able to climb up to the top of the governmental ladder at the Office of Public Works. And his addiction to alcohol (initially, burgundy wine, but then furniture polish) eased his depressed mental state. But it did nothing to mitigate his chronic absenteeism from his work desk, and eventually his supervisor, Robert Matheson, was forced to halve his salary before finally having to let go of a man he otherwise admired. During this period, Charles accrued enormous drinking tabs at many of Edinburgh's bars and taverns. In order to pay off his creditors, Charles would pawn, and sometimes sell, the valuable art collection he had amassed from his father, the famous caricaturist John Doyle. By the time he had reached forty-two, Charles had hit rock bottom, and he was forced to become a permanent resident of mental asylums throughout Scotland. It was in one of these facilities that he died from medical complications, one of them chronic alcoholism, at age sixty-one.

With so many of the puzzle pieces fitted together, it becomes clear that Arthur Conan Doyle based Dr. Watson's origins on a series of sensational events that occurred during his student years in the mountains of Northern England. Both creator and character had family members who were alcoholics; were sportsmen who played *rugby* and *wicket-cricket*, not on playing fields, but on *playgrounds*; and had spent some time on three continents. Dr. Watson's passport would have been stamped with India, Afghanistan (Asia), Europe, and Australia while Doyle's would have bore the marks of Greenland (North America), the European continent, and Africa.

So just as Doyle inserts portions of his personality and life events during his formative years into his Sherlock Holmes character, here he does the same for Dr. Watson. But a move to the European continent was to have a profound effect on Doyle's ability to add substance to his literary characters. He even found himself involved in a mystery of his own.

CHAPTER 2

Doyle's War
Friends, Enemies,
and the Words Between

In June 1875, a sixteen-year-old Arthur Conan Doyle—along with fourteen other Stonyhurst upperclassmen—traveled to England's capital city to wage war with the challenging matriculation exams held at the University of London, "the first university in England offering degrees on terms acceptable to Catholics." Stonyhurst students at that time were not permitted to take the Oxford and Cambridge higher certificate examination, as anti-Catholic sanctions were strictly enforced at these two ancient educational bastions. Twenty-one years were to go by before this ban would be officially lifted.

The London matriculation exam was designed to assess whether a candidate for admission was academically prepared and qualified for acceptance to one of the city's several prestigious colleges and universities. The higher the score, the more likely it was that an applicant would be permitted the honor of pursuing their studies at one of the world's premier city's law or medical schools. Conversely, a low score could potentially signify the abrupt end to a young student's educational journey.

Higher pressure than usual was placed on test candidates during 1875. That particular year marked the introduction of "a new system in the Examens." This unexpected and unpredictable factor only served to increase anxiety levels, especially as it was now impossible to know precisely how the test would be formatted. Further complicating matters, the Stonyhurst administration placed before their own students an additional obstacle by restricting exam participation only to those candidates who had passed the school's own rigorous trial examination.

Earlier that month on June 5, Doyle sat for the Stonyhurst exam and wound up "passing first class." Ironically, his "weakest paper was chemistry"—the discipline in which his Sherlock Holmes character would be an absolute master. Fourteen other Stonyhurst students were able to make it through the trial exam along with Doyle, and on June 28, they—with five hundred one other students from around the nation—sat for the admission test in London. Fortunately for Doyle, he possessed nerves of steel—one of his letters home about this experience read, "I did not feel a bit sleepy during the examens." One week later, the Stonyhurst administration proudly announced to the student body "that of the fourteen who had gone up thirteen had passed, the most that has ever passed since Stonyhurst was Stonyhurst."

Doyle and his dozen other successful classmates were cheered by their peers and faculty members for their astonishing accomplishment that day, although none of them knew where they had actually ranked—Honours, First Class, or Second Class. That "classified list" would not be revealed until a few days later. Doyle's "ambition" was "to get in the First Class." But when Stonyhurst received the list, Doyle learned that he had exceeded that lofty goal. He now ranked among the fifty-nine other British students who had made Honours, "the very highest class which can be attained." Doyle wrote to his mother that not only had he been taken aback by this news, but that "everybody else was equally astonished." He (together with the select few other students who had been designated Honours recipients) was paraded around the playground on the collective shoulders of his cheering fellow form members. According to Doyle's account of this moment, it represented "the greatest triumph ever recorded in the whole annals of Stonyhurst."

His golden moment—the one that garnered him the respect he had been seeking so desperately from the faculty members and his peers—was to be short-lived. Even though he had been singled out as one of the top students in the country, he failed to receive the coveted invitation he longed for that would have made him a member of the school's elite Gentleman Philosophers group. Furthermore, the Stonyhurst faculty proceeded to add insult to injury when it next deemed Doyle unprepared for university-level studies. Instead, the school where he had spent so many years "dispatched" him to a postgraduate "year of exile" for him at Stella Matutina, a relatively mediocre Jesuit preparatory school in the Vorarlberg province of Austria.

After a month of catching up with his family and friends back in Edinburgh, Doyle received a letter from Stonyhurst that included his upcoming travel arrangements. The administration took the liberty of assigning him a traveling companion who was a scion of the wealthy Rockliff publishing family. Doyle was instructed to make a stopover in Birkdale, a suburb of Liverpool, so he could meet up with the fellow classmate who would be joining him at Stella Matutina. A few days later, Doyle bid his family farewell and boarded a train bound for Liverpool. The first part of the journey was identical to the one he was used to taking to Stonyhurst. But for the first time in seven years, he could remain in his seat when the train pulled into Preston Station. Minutes later, Doyle entered unfamiliar territory, and got his first opportunity to admire the picturesque landscape of the Pennine Mountains as the train chugged toward the port city of Liverpool.

Doyle was scheduled to change trains at Liverpool's Exchange Station, but when he missed his stop, he was forced to hire a carriage that took him to the Lime Street Station. Several hours went by before he caught the next train to Birkdale Station. Although he was concerned about arriving late for his scheduled appointment, when he stepped off the platform he was greeted by "a hoary headed old chap who proved to be Mr Rockliff." Francis Rockliff was the family patriarch and was gracious enough to refrain from commenting on his guest's less-than-punctual arrival. His carriage transported the two of them to the family's estate on Oxford Road. Once their gig had pulled up to the house, Arthur received a cordial introduction to his host's "two daughters and three sons" who were present in the home at that time—"Ellen, Alice, Henry, Francis, and his traveling companion." Somewhat oddly, Doyle failed to designate his fellow classmate and traveling companion with a name in any of his letters or memoirs.

As a point of interest, in 1926 the Reverend James A. Rockliff, S.J., wrote an article published by the Cleveland, Ohio-based Jesuit *John Carroll Magazine* in which he states that he had been Doyle's "fellow-student" at both Stonyhurst College and Stella Matutina in the Austrian city of Feldkirch. Indeed, it would seem logical that James *must* have been the unnamed third son who was introduced to Doyle that day in Birkdale—and that it had been the two of them who had traveled across the English Channel together into France, and finally on to the Tyrol region of Austria. However, the account given by the Reverend could not have been true—there are, in fact, multiple holes in the story.

James Rockliff was born on October 4, 1852, and commenced "his religious life as a Novitiate of the Jesuit Society on September 30, 1872 in Gorheim, Germany." He entered Stonyhurst College in January 1863— when Doyle was two years old—and he left Stonyhurst for Feldkirch in January 1868, a few months before Doyle was about to enter Hodder House for the very first time. No possibility exists that the two were ever in the same school at the same time, let alone in the same class. And during the 1875 academic year—the only year in which Doyle matriculated at Stella Matutina—James Rockliff resided in Holland. Years later, Rockliff was invited back to Feldkirch, but this was not until 1879—a year when Doyle was studying medicine both at Edinburgh, Scotland and Birmingham, England. If James Rockliff and Doyle were never in school together at the same time, then why did the reverend choose to lie about it? And who was it that Doyle met that day in Birkdale? Just why James Rockliff would have made such a wild and false claim may never be known, but it is likely that he desired some of the residual prestige that comes from associating oneself with an international literary celebrity. As to who Doyle traveled along with to school, this is a mystery that can only be solved if there had been another Rockliff sibling—one who would have been similar in age to Doyle.

Actually, there are *two* other Rockliffs who might fit the bill—Richard or Charles. According to the ledgers of Stonyhurst College, Richard and Charles—but *not* James—had been enrolled at Stonyhurst when Doyle was there. Additionally, both brothers had attended Stella Matutina after they had graduated from Stonyhurst. The college's records reveal that Richard was awarded his diploma on August 8, 1876, and Charles had received his diploma two years earlier on August 5, 1874. And so, as Richard could not possibly have been at Stella Matutina until at least September 1876, we can deduce that the only Rockliff who could have been Doyle's traveling companion to Feldkirch was *Charles*.

As far as his desire to be associated with the now-famous Doyle, too much criticism of Father James Rockliff's false claims is not warranted. After all, he was just stretching the truth a bit in an attempt to convince the world that he had been friends with one of the greatest writers—and celebrated figures—of the turn-of-the-twentieth century. Unfortunately, Doyle—who had not been able to forge many close friendships during his Stonyhurst school days—did not fare any better in establishing relationships with his fellow students at Stella Matutina. Although Doyle described his time at Feldkirch as being "much more humane" and stated that he had been "met with far more human kindness than at Stonyhurst," he was *quite* embarrassed about being forced to complete his primary education at what was considered to be a second-rate institution. Close scrutiny of his medical school transcript gives us proof that Doyle didn't cease "to be a resentful young rebel" who became "a pillar of law and order" after traveling back to Edinburgh. The shame associated with that prep year abroad compelled him to take action, and to *remove* what he perceived to be a blemish on his record. Sometime during his Edinburgh years, he somehow managed to edit and arrange his transcript to read "Stonyhurst London Matriculation Exam 1876." By doing so, there would be no need to explain a gap year in his studies—instead, it would appear that he had gone directly from Stonyhurst to medical school. And it would be that previously described rebellious and "resentful" nature that would attract Doyle to those other students whom he perceived to be like him.

We have all known someone who is a little different—a bit eccentric. Most of us do our best to avoid such individuals—but sometimes there is that certain *someone* whose charisma draws us in like a magnet. Doyle encountered such a person a few days after he had entered medical school in his home city of Edinburgh. This student was the unconventional and irrepressible George Turnavine Budd. It wouldn't be long before Budd became one of Doyle's closest friends—and though their relationship eventually devolved into a muted yet mutual skirmish, eventually this same Budd *would* serve as the inspiration and model for many of Doyle's most memorable characters. Who was this enigmatic associate of Doyle's anyway, and in which of his stories are men of Budd's ilk to be found?

George T. Budd was a member of one of England's most respected medical families. His grandfather, Samuel, a "surgeon of considerable repute" in North Tawton, England, sired and homeschooled nine sons, seven of whom became medical professionals. Five of his offspring attended the University of Cambridge, where each of them distinguished themselves by being named a "wrangler"—a student who gains first-place Honours in their final year of study.

Budd's father, William, who had received his MD from the University of Edinburgh, had been awarded a gold medal upon graduation for his revolutionary medical thesis on rheumatic fever. During his celebrated career as a physician, he wrote dozens of groundbreaking articles on an assortment of medical conditions with titles like "Rheumatism and Gout," "Malignant Cholera," "Variola Ovina, Sheep's Small-pox," "Pathology of the Spinal Cord," and "Laws of Contagious Epidemics" among them. It was this William Budd who championed the rights of medical students in the late 1840s by putting forth his "resolution protesting against the regulation of the College of Surgeons," a policy that mandated all surgical candidates to spend a minimum of "three years of their student life passed in London." By 1855, he had been able to singlehandedly transform the then-struggling Provincial Medical and Surgical Association into the powerful British Medical Association.

A visionary who foresaw the place of photography in the practice of medicine, he also was in the vanguard of those who sought to construct water treatment facilities capable of preventing deadly cholera and typhoid epidemics. Nevertheless, William Budd is best remembered for his magnum opus, *Typhoid Fever: its Nature, Mode of Spreading, and Prevention*. And it was his Holmes-like powers of observation that allowed him to correctly determine that typhoid was "communicated from person to person, and that the specific poison which is the cause of the fever breeds and multiplies in the living body of the intestines." The public health measures he proposed were soon adopted by multiple municipalities and proved successful in preventing the spread of the disease.

George T. Budd's uncle, *also* named George, was every bit as brilliant and ambitious as his brother William. Educated at Cambridge, "Uncle George" went on to study medicine in Paris and Middlesex Hospital. Revered by his peers, he soon was named Professor of Medicine at King's College, London, and was promptly promoted to Chairman, a position he held for twenty-three years. During the entire course of his distinguished career, he was held in the highest esteem as a true "scientific physician," authoring the landmark treatise *Diseases of the Stomach* and the influential textbook *Diseases of the Liver*. He was asked to deliver the Goulstonian Lecture to the Royal College of Medicine in 1843, and the Croonian Lecture in 1847. George Budd was "the first to call attention to the fallacy of imagining that abscesses of the liver differ from each other according to climate," and it is he who is the *Budd* of the Budd-Chiari Syndrome, a liver condition that is all-too-familiar to the medical students and physicians of the past century.

Some of George T. Budd's other uncles were also remarkable achievers. Among them was his uncle Samuel—named after Budd's aforementioned grandfather—who for forty years was honorary physician to the Devon and Exeter Hospital. Samuel also served as president of the British Medical Association and as a magistrate of the city of Exeter. He married socialite Cordelia Turquand Budd, the great-granddaughter of James Christie, the founder of the famed London-based auction house.

Budd's "Uncle Richard" had credentials that matched those of his "Uncle Samuel"—he too served as a magistrate, and also a consulting physician for the North Devonshire Infirmary. Suffice it to say, George T. Budd would have a lot to live up to when it came to comparing him to the legacy left behind by his predecessors.

But the defiant nature of young George T. Budd made him the proverbial black sheep of the family—the one Budd who was *quite* different from the rest . . . except for *one other* uncle, John Wreford Budd. "Uncle John" was a prominent physician in the channel port city of Plymouth. He had acquired an unfavorable reputation due to his unsportsmanlike and reckless behavior, "rough manners," and a compulsive willingness to involve himself in street fights. Unlike his other siblings, John "did not take the MD degree," and settled for the less prestigious "M.B., C.M." (*Bachelor of Medicine, Bachelor of Chirurgery*) degrees that are conferred on those medical students who graduate without submitting an MD thesis or without sitting for the finishing examination. Despite not having the title of "MD" appear after his name, John Wreford Budd was still "regarded by the country folk as something more than human in his power of wrestling with disease and death."

Crazy stories and wild rumors about Budd's most peculiar uncle circulated throughout the entire Empire. Among the many anecdotes attributed to him was one that involved a mother whose daughter refused to remove herself from a wooden crate during an anxiety attack. Dr. Budd casually took out his gun and, removing some toxic chemicals from a vial, proceeded to ask, "Which shall it be, pistol or poison?" With that, a quick end to the young lady's malady ensued. Dr. John Wreford Budd was also purportedly so ugly in appearance that he had been able to cure a woman of her involuntary arm movements by issuing the following threat: "Every time you make one of those jerks, I'll force you to kiss me." Another vignette involved a young child with a nervous cough. Dr. Budd "planted her on the mantel shelf" above a raging fire and told her, "Balance yourself here for half an hour. If you cough, you will infallibly tumble over among the fire-irons and cut your head." Despite these unorthodox and, at times, unethical methods that often bordered on quackery, John Budd remained a sought-after physician—one who had gained the respect of his colleagues for his "aptitude to diagnose his patients at a glance."

By the time Arthur Conan Doyle entered the University of Edinburgh in 1877, George Turnavine Budd was already a virtual clone of John Wreford Budd. Although George Budd was intellectually gifted, he was prone to reckless and violent behavior. Somehow, these less-than-noble character traits, combined with his strange nature, enchanted the impressionable eighteen-year-old Doyle.

When Doyle first met him, Budd (who by then had completed his first year) had already established quite a reputation for himself with the student body. Not only was he an academic scholar and accomplished clinical researcher, but he had proven himself to be equally impressive on the football and rugby fields. His one considerable flaw, according to Doyle, was that he was "rather handicapped by the berserk fury with which he would play." Somehow, that didn't prevent Budd from being named captain of the Edinburgh Wanderers in their 1879–80 season—a position once held by his older brother Arthur two years earlier. Doyle had also tried out for the Wanderers, but unlike Budd, he hadn't made the team.

Doyle, who had to work hard for his grades, was more than a bit envious of his new friend's ability to habitually receive the highest marks on examinations seemingly without having to open a textbook. The medical faculty named Budd the recipient of the coveted Anatomy prize, which meant that he had beaten out the ultra-competitive "ten hour a dayers." Budd's "infernal" temper had quickly become a nightmarish recurring topic of discussion among the university's faculty and students. Doyle was to later recall that Budd had gained a reputation for going on "wild escapes, which ended usually in fisticuffs or in a transitory appearance in a police court." And his aggressive nature was occasionally manifested in the classroom. One of Doyle's favorite medical school anecdotes involved the time Budd had gotten annoyed at a fellow student for having asked a "banal" question during a crowded Anatomy lecture. When his demand that his fellow student's "mundane inquiries" cease went unheeded, Budd calmly took matters into his own hands. He walked atop a series of desks until he reached the offender, and then hopped back down to the floor. He then commanded his classmate to end his distracting nonsense. His fellow student's response was a quick punch to Budd's nose, a jab that drew blood. Once Budd recovered from his initial shock, he grabbed his opponent nonchalantly by the neck and dragged him outside the lecture hall. Before anyone could get up from their seats to see what was going on, a noise akin to "the delivery of a ton of coal" was heard outside the door. A few minutes later, a now-saintly George Budd returned to the auditorium and took his seat. The other student failed to reappear in class that day.

Budd's uncivilized behavior made such an impact on Doyle that his later fictional works would include several characters whose personalities were a reflection of his mercurial friend's eccentric and often capricious traits.

Once he had graduated from medical school, the new "Doctor" Doyle tried desperately to build up a practice of his own—but he failed at it. To fill in the often long bouts of time between patient visits, he would sit at his desk and write fictional stories in the hope that his hobby (at the time) might provide him with the money he needed to support himself. In the mid-1880s, Doyle sent off several of his manuscripts to carefully targeted London publishing houses—and to his astonishment, a few of them were accepted. None of those early literary works earned him enough money to permit him to quit his day job, though. That would not happen until the early 1890s.

In 1884, Doyle ventured off in a different literary direction and made the decision to try his hand at a different genre. Instead of his customary fictional tales, he tried his hand at writing a semi-autobiographical account of the trials and tribulations he had encountered upon his entry into the medical profession. His "Crabbe's Practice"—as this short story was titled when it appeared in December of that year—not only drew its source material from his first year of building up a medical practice of his own, but also alluded to some of his experiences working with his former colleague and former friend, George T. Budd.

Eleven years later in 1895, Doyle—by then an international celebrity writer—expounded further upon his dealings with George Budd and wrote a semi-autobiographical novel titled *The Stark Munro Letters*. This time, Doyle's protagonist was the fictitious "Dr. J. Stark Munro," who sent off "a series of sixteen letters" to his "friend and former fellow-student, Harold Swanborough, of Lowell, Massachusetts, during the years 1881–1884."

These correspondences became the vehicle Doyle needed to discuss his religious views without being considered *too* confrontational. But so as not to lose his devoted followers, he thought it wise to incorporate his madcap adventures with George Budd as a form of comic relief. In order to disguise his former medical partner's identity, he changed Budd's name to "James Cullingworth," and appended the book's preface with a note stating that Munro's letters had been "Edited and Arranged by A. Conan Doyle."

Some clarifications regarding the *Stark Munro*'s subtitle, preface, and its strange introduction should be presented here. First, we must define the word "arranged," which appears in the subtitle. "Arranged" could have been defined as "to draw up in rank or in lines of battle"—a somewhat obsolete definition, but quite relevant to what Doyle had actually done when he wrote this story. It can also be defined as "to put into proper, or requisite, order," which is something Doyle accomplished when he wrote and arranged these "letters." In his effort to rewrite the history of this bizarre period of his life, Doyle did his best to convince the world that it had been George Budd, and *only* George Budd, who had acted inappropriately. Doyle presented himself as an innocent victim who had had the misfortune to be at the wrong place at the wrong time. Nothing could have been further from the truth, but Doyle, taking full and powerful advantage of his mighty pen, shaped and crafted what would soon become *The Stark Munro Letters.*

Next, Doyle employed the word "edit," which is defined as "to bring into order for publication prepared by rearrangement, cutting, or collation of reported material to form a unified sequence." That complex definition was utilized by Doyle as he took the liberty of editing out the name "Herbert" (Bertie) from the 1895 version of *The Stark Munro Letters* and then rechristening him "Harold." And although Munro purportedly added four more letters to the story (a change from twelve to sixteen), sixteen chapters are present in both editions. In the second printing of *The Stark Munro Letters*, Doyle erased his prior statement that the book had been "edited and arranged" by A. Conan Doyle, and, further, he omits Swanborough's preface, "The letters of my friend Mr. Stark Munro *appear to me* to form so connected a whole, and to give so plain an account of some of the troubles which a young man may be called upon to face right away at the outset of his career, that I have *handed them over* to the gentleman who is about to edit them." That person, of course, was A. Conan Doyle. [*emphases added throughout*]

The words contained in this sentence must have so bothered Doyle that he jumped at the first opportunity he was given to hide it from future readers. What *was* it that pressed on Doyle's psyche? After subjecting this sentence to close scrutiny, things become clear. The phrase, "handed them over" implies total innocence and lack of ulterior motive, while the words, "appear to me" represent its polar opposite—that is, an attempt to deceive the reader by sleight of hand.

In his autobiography, *Memories and Adventures* (1924), written thirty years after *The Stark Munro Letters*, Doyle confessed that "the whole history of my association with the man I called Cullingworth, his extraordinary character, our parting and the way in which I was left to what seemed certain ruin, were all as depicted." When he chose those words, Doyle was acknowledging that *The Stark Munro Letters* represented a true account of his two failed attempts to establish medical practices with George Budd—one in Bristol, the other in Plymouth.

Doyle's association with Budd was one you might expect to see on a television soap opera—plenty of love triangles, plot twists, moral conflicts, and dramatic events. Not only was Cullingworth modeled after George Budd, but there are also some remarkable similarities between Thomas Crabbe and James Cullingworth. It follows that the dialogue and outlandish circumstances of "Crabbe's Practice" often mirror Doyle's adventures with Budd.

In "Crabbe's Practice," we are introduced to Dr. Tom Waterhouse Crabbe, a "powerfully built, square-shouldered fellow" with "a voice like a bull." Doyle's 1895 description of Dr. James Cullingworth resembles that of Crabbe, being "well-grown, five foot nine perhaps, with square shoulders, an arching chest, and a quick jerky way of walking." Doyle adds that Cullingworth had "short wiry black hair." In his autobiography, Doyle refers to George Budd by his alias, Cullingworth, and describes him as "5 ft 9 in. in height, perfectly built, with a bulldog jaw, bloodshot deep-set eyes, overhanging brows, and yellowish hair as stiff as wire, which spurted up above his brows." In *The Stark Munro Letters*, however, Cullingworth's hair is described as black. Doyle made this seemingly contradictory statement because, at one point in Budd's life, he "stained his yellow hair black," and for years his "hair presented curious iridescent tints which were the remains of his disguise." The physical traits described suggest that Doyle modeled both Crabbe and Cullingworth after George Budd. The only actual difference is that Doyle chose to mention Budd's odd manner of walking. Doyle had more freedom to include Budd's negative attributes in *The Stark Munro Letters*, as George Budd had been dead and buried for more than a half-dozen years before its publication. Conversely, Budd was still hale and hearty when "Crabbe's Practice" was first published. Had Doyle placed emphasis on Budd's awkward "jerky walk" in the surrogate character he created for "Crabbe's Practice," it would not have been surprising if he might have found it necessary to defend himself against a man with a notorious propensity for violent fits and outbursts. With George Budd's premature death in 1889, Doyle had no need to concern himself with any potentially negative repercussions.

Dr. Crabbe is depicted as "a man who it was not easy to forget if you had once come across him," while Cullingworth is also depicted as unforgettable due to an "ugliness of character, which is as attractive as beauty." This is further stressed when Munro asks his classmate Herbert Swanborough, "Can you remember Cullingworth at the University? . . . I'm sure that you would know his photograph, however, for the reason that he was the ugliest and queerest-looking man of our year." Yet, a single look at an actual photograph of George Budd reveals him to be the antithesis of "ugliest and queerest-looking." His eyes were far from bloodshot, his eyebrows were not bushy nor were they overhanging, and he did not have a slack jaw. The descriptions, written by Doyle about George Budd, were anything but accurate and imply that Doyle was doing his best to avenge the misdeeds of the man he believed to have ruined his life.

In *The Stark Munro Letters*, Cullingworth is described by Munro as being "a fine athlete—one of the fastest and most determined Rugby forwards that I have ever known . . . ," and Crabbe is portrayed as being "one of the best Rugby forwards in Edinburgh." In *Memories and Adventures*, Doyle wrote that the actual Cullingworth came from "athletic stock, and was a great Rugby forward . . ." Once again, it becomes apparent that Crabbe and Cullingworth are, in actuality, George Budd. Doyle's memory is not accurate when he states that George's "younger brother was reckoned by good judges to be about the best forward who ever donned the rose-embroidered jersey of England." George was Arthur's Budd's *youngest* brother, something that someone with Doyle's incredible memory surely would have recalled. Nevertheless, Crabbe and Cullingworth's physical gifts and athletic talents are a strong hint that these two characters come from the same mold—George Budd.

In both *The Stark Munro Letters* and "Crabbe's Practice," Doyle frequently alludes to George Budd's profound intellect. In *The Stark Munro Letters*, Munro goes as far as defining genius, as it relates to Cullingworth, as something that "allows the possessor of it to attain results by a sort of instinct which other men could only reach by hard work." In "Crabbe's Practice," Doyle's alter ego, Jack Barton, states that "geniuses are more commonly read about than seen, but one couldn't speak five minutes with Crabbe without recognising that he had inherited some touch of that subtle, indefinable essence. There was a bold originality in his thought, and a convincing earnestness in his mode of expressing it, which pointed to something higher than mere cleverness. He studied spasmodically and irregularly, yet he was one of the first men—certainly the most independent thinker—of his year."

These thoughts are mirrored to a degree in *The Stark Munro Letters*, when Munro confesses to Swanborough that "Cullingworth was the greatest genius that I have ever known." He "never seemed to work, and yet he took the anatomy prize over the heads of all the ten-hour-a-day men." The similarities that exist among Cullingworth, Crabbe, and Budd suggest that the three are all variations on the same man. These statements also suggest that Doyle resents not being fortunate enough to possess these incredible natural gifts. Of course, these deficiencies could have been some of the triggers that eventually put an end to their friendship.

The not-so-subtle punches thrown at Cullingworth, but not at Crabbe, can be safely attributed to the fact that when "Crabbe's Practice" was published, George Budd was still alive and well, but when *The Stark Munro Letters* appeared in print, Budd had already been dead for six years. Doyle must have feared that if he had the temerity to insult George Budd in "Crabbe's Practice," there would be dire consequences to his actions. But by the time *The Stark Munro Letters* was released, there was no need to hold back. Doyle even has Munro ominously predict that, "I believe that in ten years he [Cullingworth] would either be in his grave, or would have the Continent." In its strictest sense, the first of these prophecies proved to be the correct one. *The Stark Munro Letters* should be considered Doyle's apologia to George Budd's widow, Kate, who was an onlooker at most of the brawls that involved her husband and Doyle.

As "Crabbe's Practice" moves forward, its narrator, Jack Barton, forges a friendship with his partner, one based on his infatuation with Crabbe's sheer cunning and overpowering individuality. This story is a mirror of events that took place during the Doyle-Budd partnership. And just as Budd was a class ahead of Doyle in medical school, Crabbe is a class ahead of Barton. Doyle states that Crabbe "went down" after graduating "with his young degree, and a still younger wife, to settle in this town, which we will call Brisport." In *The Stark Munro Letters*, Doyle tells his readers that Cullingworth had to lock his wife's "governess into her room" and dye his hair to make his escape with her. This claim was to be verified years later in Doyle's autobiography, where he offers a more detailed version of this episode, writing "he had run off with a charming young lady and married her, she being a ward in Chancery and under age." Apparently, Doyle had written about actual events in the lives of George and Kate Budd. Although she may have been under the supervision of a guardian, according to her birth records, Kate Budd—née Russell—was born in 1861. This places her at the very legal age of nineteen in 1880, the year of her purported elopement with George. A nineteen-year-old would not be regarded as being underage, even though Doyle tries to convince us of that. Some of the wording contained in *The Stark Munro Letters* suggests that Doyle had a crush on his friend's wife, as when Heddy (*Kate*) demands to know why her husband's nose is gushing blood, Munro (*Doyle*) confesses to his friend Swanborough that at that very moment, he "felt an insane impulse to pick her up and kiss her."

Munro goes on to inform Swanborough that after medical school, Cullingworth had broken all lines of communication with him. Then he justifies his friend's actions by stating that Cullingworth "prided himself upon never writing a letter." This is completely untrue, as Doyle wrote in his autobiography, "Just before I started for Africa I got a long telegram from Cullingworth imploring me to go to Bristol," and when Doyle arrived in Southsea, Budd sent him "a curt letter—not a telegram for a wonder." Here we have another attempt by Doyle to rewrite history and place all the blame on his friend-turned-enemy.

There was a period when Budd actually enjoyed sending letters to Doyle. Early in their relationship, he kept constant tabs on Doyle's whereabouts, as evidenced by this correspondence from Budd to Doyle:

> "Started here in Bradfield last June. Colossal success. My example must revolutionize medical practice. Rapidly making fortune. Have invention which is worth millions. Unless our Admiralty take it up shall make Brazil the leading naval power. Come down on next train on receiving this. Have plenty for you to do."

Revisiting *The Stark Munro Letters*, when Dr. Munro fails to respond to Cullingworth's telegram after ten days have passed, an irate Cullingworth dashes off the following telegram:

"Your letter to hand. Why not call me a liar at once? I tell you that I have seen thirty thousand patients in the last year. My actual takings have been over four thousand pounds. All patients come to me. Would not cross the street to see Queen Victoria. You can have all visiting, all surgery, all midwifery. Make what you like of it. Will guarantee three hundred pounds the first year."

The words of the *Stark Munro* telegrams were based on actual ones Doyle had received from George Budd, and run counter to sentiments that Doyle was later to express about Budd. And that Doyle fell under Budd's hypnotic, irresponsible, and hypomanic spell is evidenced by Doyle taking a train down to visit Budd as well as the following statement Munro addresses to Swanborough: "And you would be swept along by his words and would be carried every foot of the way with him . . . You suddenly fell back to earth again."

When Munro arrives at Cullingworth's mansion in Bradfield, he is taken to a large magnet powered by electricity that, when fully charged, is capable of attracting bullets and warheads. Cullingworth boasts to his houseguest that whichever country buys the rights to his defense system will have "naval supremacy." In the 1908 Holmes short story "The Adventure of the Bruce-Partington Plans," we learn that the blueprints for a revolutionary submarine—with the capacity to change the tactical balance of naval power—have been stolen. Certainly, Doyle may have based some of this adventure's plot on one of Budd's hare-brained schemes.

Events similar to these are described in "Crabbe's Practice," although it is Crabbe's wife who sends Jack Barton the telegram that begs him to assist her husband in his Brisport (a portmanteau of Bristol and Portsmouth) practice. Doyle created this fictitious town to commemorate both his and Budd's first home offices. Once again, Doyle rewrites history by making it seem that it was Budd, and not Munro, who was the crazy one of the two. Evidence of this is provided in Munro's letter in which he discusses establishing a printing press. He claimed that Cullingworth had an idea about starting a "weekly paper" of his own called the Scorpion, so that he could make anyone who crosses him "wish they had never been born." Doyle actually had brought this idea to fruition twenty-years prior as a student at Stonyhurst. In *The Wasp*, a publication of his own creation, Doyle, as had Munro, "would do the fiction and poetry" while his friend Roskell would write "the snappy paragraphs." And when the Stonyhurst administration shut down Doyle's printing press, he simply started a new one he named *The Figaro* (after the French newspaper of the same name). This second magazine's mission was to lampoon certain members of his class, the prefects, the faculty, and the administration. Unsurprisingly, Doyle's second venture into satirical publications was soon shut down. In reality, it was Doyle, and not Budd, who masterminded the concept of a gossip newspaper. Doyle simply transferred the blame for this venture onto Budd, who was no longer around to defend himself. Doyle's meticulous scheme to reinvent himself ensured that the public's perception would be that he had been the innocent victim of Budd's malevolent capers.

And in the last chapter of *The Stark Munro Letters*, Doyle has Cullingworth leaving England for South America, where he will be starting a new career as an ophthalmologist. In truth, it had been Munro—that is to say, *Doyle*—who dreamed of leaving England for South America. And it was Doyle who trained for several years in several countries to become a licensed ophthalmologist. Doyle misguides the reader into believing that Budd had abandoned his lucrative medical practice in Plymouth to perform corrective eye surgery from "the Equator to the icebergs."

Another real-life event that is similar to one described in "Crabbe's Practice" and *The Stark Munro Letters* took place in 1882 between Doyle and Budd. A few weeks after their partnership began, Doyle was unceremoniously booted out by Budd, who claimed the decision was purely business-based. Doyle tells this story in *The Stark Munro Letters* when he has Cullingworth inform Munro:

> "You see, many of my patients are simple country folk, half imbecile for the most part, but then the half-crown of an imbecile is as good as any other half-crown. They come to my door, and they see two names, and their silly jaws begin to drop, and they say to each other, 'There's two of 'em here. It's Cullingworth we want to see, but if we go in we'll be shown as likely not to Dr. Munro.' So it ends in some cases in their not coming in at all."

After he fired Doyle, Budd (Cullingworth) offered his former partner financial support to help him in starting his own practice elsewhere. In *The*

Stark Munro Letters, Cullingworth offers Munro "one pound a week until you [Munro] got your legs under you" while Doyle wrote his mother that, "Budd volunteers to pay my passage there, and to find me a pound a week until I earn more than that." But once Doyle had arrived in Southsea to set up his own practice, he wrote this to his mother: "Serves me right for not being more careful in tearing up my letters." The reason for Doyle's dismissal had nothing to do with patient complaints, but rather, Doyle writing (or his mother sending) inflammatory letters about Budd. Doyle also displays a bit of paranoia here when he informs his mother that Budd has been "scheming my ruin."

Ironically, when Doyle was on the verge of leaving Plymouth to start his own practice in Southsea, George Budd fell ill. Kate had no other option but to plead with Doyle to stay on so that the practice could avoid financial ruin. *The Stark Munro Letters* alludes to this incident when a weeping Heddy tells Munro that her husband "has been very strange all night, and I am afraid that he is ill."

Doyle might actually have been right in his assessment that George Budd was plotting to ruin him. But he might have failed to appreciate the much bigger picture—that George was on a mission to destroy the entire Doyle family, not just Doyle. As Doyle was packing his belongings and moving to Southsea, Christie's auction house was scheduled to showcase and sell artwork that had once belonged to John Doyle. As we have already established, John Doyle, under the alias "H.B.," was one of the most respected caricaturists and painters of the nineteenth century. His lithographs were immensely popular as "they were far superior to everything that had preceded them, inasmuch as they were painted with a strong political allusion, and the persons represented were not monstrously caricatured." In an effort to avoid any dire repercussions from the Members of Parliament (a group he chose as his subject matter on many occasions), he cloaked his identity employing the initials HB.

When John Doyle died in 1868, he left behind his extensive art collection of paintings and lithographs. In early 1882, the famous London-based auction house Christie's was fully engaged in preparations to sell John Doyle's collection, which was expected to fetch thousands of pounds. But days before the event was scheduled to take place, Christie's abruptly canceled it—ostensibly due to a lack of potential buyers. This given excuse does not seem credible though, as HB is *still* considered to be the founder of British lampooning and one of the most renowned and celebrated artists of his era. So what was the real reason that led to this auction being called off? It should be pointed out that George Budd's uncle Samuel was married to Cordelia Turquand, the great-granddaughter of the Christie family's auction house. Armed with this information, one can infer that George Budd sabotaged the auction by explaining the fractious situation he was involved in with a member of the Doyle family—it is likely that this would have helped him convince his aunt and uncle to cancel the sale of HB's work. If this were the case, then George Budd wasn't just trying to ruin the life of his former partner—he was also attempting to malign and destroy the reputation of the entire Doyle family, starting with Arthur's well-respected grandfather.

Regarded by some as a visionary, history has exposed George Budd as the consummate "con man" whose ultimate goal was to make as much money as he could. That he was not the least bit averse to resorting to quackery is discussed at length in Doyle's *The Stark Munro Letters*. But Budd had other unethical tactics he would employ to build up his practice. In "Crabbe's Practice," Crabbe hatches a scheme that would have Barton pretending to stagger outside a church "and fall senseless upon the pavement." He would then be "taken up and carried writhing in terrible convulsions into the surgery of . . . Doctor Crabbe," where he would make a miraculous recovery under the medical supervision of Dr. Crabbe. This same plot is resurrected in *The Stark Munro Letters*, where Cullingworth instructs Munro "to lie senseless in the roadway, and to be carried into him [Cullingworth] by a sympathising crowd, while the footman ran with a paragraph to the newspapers." Once he is in Cullingworth's hands, Munro would "feign fits at his door . . . then I was to die—absolutely to expire—and all Scotland was to resound with how Dr. Cullingworth, of Avonmouth, had resuscitated me."

In "Crabbe's Practice," we also learn of Dr. Crabbe's habit of polishing an ice-slick outside of a church in an effort to have a parishioner slip and fall on their way out and then limp over to his office—which happened to be right across the street—for treatment. He would then make certain to get his "name into the *Brisport Chronicle*." Coincidentally, an event almost identical to this one occurred within weeks of Doyle setting up his medical practice in Southsea. A spooked horse tossed its rider off, and by mere chance, Doyle happened to witness the accident. He ran over to attend to the victim and, after he had patched him up, Doyle sent his brother "Innes off to get it in the evening papers." Amazingly, another fortuitous event like this was to take place a few days later, and then according to a letter sent to his mother, he had yet "another lucky hit—A man broke his jaw & fractured his skull just outside the house today." Doyle returned to his role as a first responder, attended to the man's injuries, and sent Innes off to get his name into *The Hampshire Telegraph*. These three equestrian-related events that so magically occurred within sight of Doyle's office may appear to be too coincidental to be "coincidental," especially when compared to the invisible ice-slick trick tactics employed in "Crabbe's Practice."

Another "Crabbe's"-devised scheme involved Barton feigning drowning and then getting rescued by a group of Good Samaritans who proceed to carry him over to Dr. Crabbe's office. Crabbe immediately constructs a defibrillator, and, after attaching its electrodes to Barton's chest, revives him in a quite unpleasant (but humorous) way. The idea that lay behind Doyle's makeshift defibrillator can be traced back to his pre-teen days when he received electrotherapy for his headaches from William Hart-hill, a respected Glasgow-trained physician. Harthill, a pioneer in the then-emerging field of galvanism, took out advertisements in newspapers and medical journals that claimed he had developed a painless apparatus "whereby the shock is counteracted," enabling him to apply electrical current safely to "delicate ladies and weakly children." The defibrillator in "Crabbe's Practice" predates the medical debut of the actual defibrillator by fourteen years. Although Doyle credits the famed Viennese pathologist-anatomist, Carl von Rokitansky, as its inventor, he was not at all the man behind it. There is a real possibility that its true inventors, Jean-Louis Prevost and Frederic Batelli, had read "Crabbe's Practice" and drawn inspiration from Doyle's fictional device.

Doyle goes as far as to summarize the evolution of artificial resuscitation in "Crabbe's Practice," and although we might assume that there were several methods available to revive near-drowning victims, it wasn't until 1893—a full decade after Doyle's short story appeared in print—that the first clinically effective method of cardiopulmonary resuscitation was developed. In 1866 the physicians at St. Bartholomew's Hospital successfully used methods that had been devised independently by a Dr. Henry Robert Silvester and a Dr. Marshall Hall to revive a near-drowning patient victim. In the Silvester technique, the victim is placed on their back, and air is expelled from the lungs by pressing the arms over the chest while fresh air is drawn in by pulling them above the head. In the Hall technique, the rescuer places the victim in a prone position, followed immediately by pressing on his back, a process that activates spontaneous expiration. The victim is then turned over on his side with the shoulder raised to initiate active inspiration. Both of these life-saving techniques are mentioned and illustrated in "Crabbe's Practice" prior to Dr. Crabbe shocking his friend, and both of these procedures were taught to England's Sanitary Inspectors, Water Police, and Police Surgeons. Doyle, true in his fashion, was a bit careless and spelled Silvester incorrectly as "Sylvestre."

"Crabbe's Practice" and *The Stark Munro Letters* serve as prime examples of Doyle's tendency to turn to his actual life experience for the foundations of his stories. Although 1879 was the first year in which anything written by Doyle appeared in print, those early works were fictional short stories, ghost tales, or articles submitted to medical and photography journals. "Crabbe's Practice" (1884) is significant in that it marks the appearance of Doyle's first semi-autobiographical effort, and alludes to the convoluted relationship he shared with George and Kate Budd. *The Stark Munro Letters* that followed eleven years later would be built upon the framework of that short story. Here, Doyle made no attempt to suppress his animosity toward the Budds, and instead subjected them to ridicule. And the most likely reason Doyle chose to include more personal vignettes relating to George and Kate Budd in *The Stark Munro Letters* is that George had been deceased for over six years at the time of its publication. At that point, Doyle had not only won a battle against the Budds—he had won the *war*, through his brilliant and brash use of the English language.

Fortunately for Doyle, he was a student of several brilliant physicians, among them Joe Bell, William Rutherford, and Henry Duncan Little-john—doctors he could turn to when he began his literary career. And when it came time to introduce Sherlock Holmes to the world, Doyle had already developed a secret formula for splicing together the genetic sequences of the people he knew in Edinburgh to create a most memorable and immortal character.

CHAPTER 3

Doyle's Medical Professors and *His* Detective

The Sherlock Holmes adventures owe a large portion of their continuing appeal to Arthur Conan Doyle's foresight in combining scientific method and logical reasoning with comprehensive, nose-to-the-grindstone detective work. It was this perfect blend of theory and realism that launched the character of Sherlock Holmes to heretofore unreached literary heights, making him an international phenomenon and the dominant fictional detective of his time. However, those prodigious talents conferred by Doyle onto his creation did not materialize miraculously out of thin air. Rather, Holmes' singular skill set was a conglomerate of traits possessed by the remarkably gifted coterie of physicians responsible for Doyle's medical education while at the University of Edinburgh. Much like the legendary alchemist who could transform lead into gold, Doyle collected the real-life attributes of his extraordinary teachers, and transmuted them into a fictional sleuth and criminologist who was imbued with a unique amalgam of gifts.

Robert Louis Stevenson—another of Edinburgh's favorite sons, famous in his own right as the author of classic tales like *Treasure Island* (1883) and *The Strange Case of Dr. Jekyll & Mr. Hyde* (1886)—was the first writer to formally recognize how Doyle deftly weaved many of his own professors' favorable personality traits into the Holmes persona. In a letter dated April 5, 1893, Stevenson, who knew that Dr. Doyle was a graduate of the University of Edinburgh's School of Medicine, wrote him the following Holmes-like letter from his home in faraway Samoa:

"Dear Sir, You have taken many occasions to make yourself agreeable to me, for which I might in decency have thanked you earlier. It is now my turn; and I hope you will allow me to offer you my compliments on your very ingenious and very interesting adventures of Sherlock Holmes. That is the class of literature that I like when I have the toothache. As a matter of fact, it was a pleurisy I was enjoying when I took the volume up; and it will interest you as a medical man to know that the cure was for the moment effectual. Only the one thing troubles me: can this be my old friend Joe Bell?"

Stevenson—ten thousand miles away from London at the time—was unaware that Doyle had already confessed to the London press that it had been his anatomy professor, Dr. Joseph Bell, who served as the primary model for his Holmes character. Stevenson had no need for Doyle's revelatory statement to spot some of the similarities that the real-life Bell and the fictional Holmes share—it is more than likely that they were as clear as day to him. The phraseology employed by Holmes in the stories surely would have reminded Stevenson of Dr. Bell's unique speech patterns and use of vernacular. Although he never had the opportunity to observe Dr. Bell in the classroom, Stevenson's good friend—the noted English poet William Ernest Henley—had in early February 1875 personally introduced the two on the hospital ward where Henley was then a patient. The fact that Stevenson was not a physician prevented him from ever detecting the far subtler influences exerted on Doyle by his other professors when he conjured up his legendary Consulting Detective. Who, then, were among these other luminaries in Edinburgh's pantheon of physicians, whose DNA strands had been spliced directly into Sherlock's chromosomes?

Dr. Henry Duncan Littlejohn

One of these influential professors was Dr. Henry Duncan Littlejohn, a pioneer in forensic medicine. A homegrown talent who had come to prominence as Edinburgh's first Medical Officer of Health, Littlejohn was in his early fifties when Doyle first sat in his classroom. A renowned clinical researcher, Littlejohn was also a skilled actor who seemed able to portray anyone he wanted. He often incorporated this unique talent into his well-attended lectures. Although he habitually arrived late to his classroom, "his boys" (as he called his students) would never even think to leave their seats. On the contrary, they were always willing to wait patiently in anticipation of his masterful one-man performances. During one of these lectures, Littlejohn spoke not a single word—and wrote not a single thing upon the blackboard. Instead, he pantomimed an entire murder case from 1857 that had involved a beautiful twenty-one-year-old Glaswegian socialite named Madeleine Hamilton Smith. Littlejohn's students looked on in wonderment as their professor literally *became* the accused, "denying indignantly the accusation" that she had poisoned her lover with arsenic. Moments later, Littlejohn transformed himself into Pierre Emile L'Angelier, Madeleine's ill-fated "lover creeping through the window." His "ever-changing" face then took on the appearance of Scotland's leading defense attorney, Lord Inglis, who Littlejohn had respectfully dubbed "that great man." Despite restricting himself to the nuances of body language, facial expressions, and gestures, Littlejohn was able to win over his students-turned-jurors, just as Lord Inglis had done in Glasgow when he had "got her off in a trial which ended in a 'Not Proven' verdict."

Littlejohn was an absolute original, and a great many of his former students claimed that "no teacher ever took a greater interest" in them, both within and beyond the university's walls. Littlejohn regaled in taking his students on field trips, refusing to waste his time taking his "boys" to "routine museums" or hospital wards. What he wanted to do was to expose these future physicians to the realities of city life—to give them a firsthand look at the grime and filth of Edinburgh's slaughterhouses, reservoirs, prisons, and outdated sewer systems.

Dr. Littlejohn constantly petitioned city officials not only to enact stricter rules and regulations but to stringently enforce a series of urban mandates that, during his time as Police Surgeon, had been often overlooked by the authorities. As the city's Medical Officer of Health and Chief Inspector of Abattoirs, he was eventually able to bring about significant hygienic improvements in Edinburgh. He issued a health mandate, requiring that all infectious diseases be reported to his office—an edict that led to a marked reduction in both morbidity and mortality rates. Littlejohn's policy proved such a success that it was soon implemented throughout all of Great Britain. When a smallpox epidemic broke out in Edinburgh in the late 1860s, Littlejohn—along with fellow Scot and business entrepreneur James Marwick—was able to extend the Vaccination Act across all of Scotland. Later on, he would be instrumental in gaining the support of Parliament in making the vaccination of infants compulsory (a cause that Doyle would also strongly advocate years later). After an outbreak of cholera in Edinburgh in 1866, Littlejohn prepared an exposé on the unsanitary conditions of the city—overcrowding of houses, poor drainage and improper sewer systems, and unacceptable roadways. His work led to the passing of the Edinburgh City Improvement Act of 1867, a measure that called for the demolition of many dilapidated dwellings (especially in the Old Town district), construction of new buildings, widening of streets, and the removal and replacement of defective gas and water pipes.

The passion with which Dr. Littlejohn fought for social welfare was equally matched by the fervor of his medical lectures—a commitment that left an indelible mark on his students, among them Arthur Conan Doyle. In 1914, when Doyle was given a private tour of New York's Sing Sing Correctional Facility, he drew upon his previous experiences with Littlejohn, angrily suggesting to the Warden that they "Burn it down! The buildings are absolutely antiquated and it is nothing less than a disgrace for a State so great and wealthy as New York to have a prison which is a hundred years behind the times."

By the time Doyle had begun his medical studies at Edinburgh, Littlejohn had already established a ritual of taking his students to crime scenes—where he would review the salient features that made each case unique. His reputation as the top expert witness in the region was so well established that whenever the Crown called on him to testify on their behalf, the courthouse was always overrun by small mobs of his students and hosts of admirers. The best anyone could hope for was to be granted "standing room only" status, either in a jammed hallway or outside on a nearby street. Littlejohn's courtroom persona was so intimidating, and his presentations so cogent, that it was said he "never got the worst of the argument. He was never entrapped by the smartest of lawyers, and never disconcerted by the severest of cross-examinations."

Serendipitously, Doyle happened to be in the student audience during one of Littlejohn's more entrancing school lectures. At first, Littlejohn took on the role of Dr. William Palmer, a London-trained physician and compulsive gambler, who was soon to become known as the "Prince of Poisoners." Racing to his desk, Littlejohn picked up a glass of water and feigned slipping something into it. Then, switching parts to become Palmer's friend and associate, John Parson Cook, he pretended to drink the contents of the glass. Within seconds, "Cook" was screaming, "Good God! There's something in it; it burns my throat!" Then, Dr. Littlejohn "returned," and after explaining to his "audience" that Dr. Palmer had poured strychnine into Cook's brandy, he proceeded to recreate Cook's grisly death. His knees trembled as his hands frantically patted down his neck and chest. Littlejohn (now in the role of "Cook"), gasped in agony, "I can't lie down; I shall be suffocated if I lie down. Oh, fetch Mr. Palmer!" With that bitterly ironic phrase, Littlejohn fell to the floor where he lay motionless on the planks—for a full minute. When he finally stood up, Littlejohn gave an elegant discussion of how the Crown managed to convict the unrepentant perpetrator. His closing tour de force was a reenactment of Palmer's death on the gallows where he placed an imaginary noose around his neck, looked down at the "trapdoor beneath him," and pretended that his neck had been snapped. His students rolled on the floor with delight, but after things had quieted down, Dr. Littlejohn's authoritative countenance and demeanor were restored. He addressed the class and reiterated that this was not at all a unique event—that physicians had been evildoers on other occasions. One of the cases he alluded to was that of Dr. Edward William Pritchard of Glasgow, who had murdered his wife and his mother-in-law and may have been involved in the premature "departures" of several others.

It turned out that Dr. Littlejohn had played an active role in helping to secure Pritchard's conviction. At this juncture, though Littlejohn had already seen just about everything under the sun, even *he* was surprised by Dr. Pritchard's ability to maintain his calm demeanor in the face of such serious charges. At the time of this 1856 trial, Littlejohn was forced to admit that Pritchard's stately appearance made him second-guess his presumption that Pritchard was guilty. After all, neither Drs. Pritchard nor Palmer confessed to the murders, implying that they had been falsely accused or they were among the most imaginative liars who had ever lived. Dr. Littlejohn told his students that he had already determined that both men were indeed liars, and that their training and privileged status as physicians furnished them with the ability to perform criminal acts almost without being detected.

In the especially inventive Holmes short story "The Adventure of the Speckled Band" (1892), Doyle drew upon the knowledge he gained from observing Professor Littlejohn's memorable lectures when he has Sherlock Holmes tell Watson, "'Subtle enough, and horrible enough. When a doctor does go wrong, he is the first of criminals. He has nerve and he has knowledge. Palmer and Pritchard were among the heads of their profession.'" Years afterward, Doyle endowed his master detective with his old professor's theatrical skills. In "The Adventure of the Six Napoleons" (1904), after smashing open the bust of Napoleon, Holmes discovers that "'the famous black pearl of Borgias'" is lodged within one of its broken shards. This startling revelation gains him the literal applause of both Watson and Inspector Lestrade. Holmes then proceeds to take a bow, "like the master dramatist who receives the homage of his audience."

Once again Holmes' theatrical skills are on display in the 1904 short story "The Adventure of the Priory School," when he feigns an ankle injury in order to acquire crucial information without arousing suspicion. A further example of his showmanship is found in the 1893 short story "The Adventure of the Reigate Squire," where Holmes succeeds in preventing salient facts from being divulged. He does so by becoming the sudden victim of a "'nervous attack.'" At this point, Watson gives the following vivid description of Holmes: "His face had suddenly assumed the most dreadful expression. His eyes rolled upwards, his features writhed in agony, and with a suppressed groan he dropped on his face upon the ground. Horrified at the suddenness and severity of the attack, we carried him into the kitchen, where he lay back in a large chair, and breathed heavily for some minutes." It turns out that Watson, along with the others who were witnesses of Holmes' apparent convulsion in this scene, is completely fooled by his partner's virtuoso performance.

Doyle frequently presented Holmes as a master of disguise, and makes available to him "at least five small refuges in different parts of London in which he was able to change his personality." In "The Adventure of Charles Augustus Milverton" (1904), Holmes artfully transforms himself into an up-and-coming plumber named Escott who, in order to get his hands on a damning series of blackmail letters, asks the villain's maid to marry him—and she accepts his proposal. In the 1904 short story "The Adventure of Black Peter," an especially dark tale of greed and gore, Holmes transforms himself into "Captain Basil," someone who "rough-looking men" turn to when they are desperate for work. In "A Scandal in Bohemia" (1891), the first of the Holmes short stories, Watson offers this description of his partner: "His broad black hat, his baggy trousers, his white tie, his sympathetic smile, and general look of peering and benevolent curiosity were such as Mr. John Hare alone could have equaled. It was not merely that Holmes changed his costume. His expression, his manner, his very soul seemed to vary with every fresh part that he assumed. The stage lost a fine actor, even as science lost an acute reasoner, when he became a specialist in crime." These same sentiments are reiterated in "The Adventure of the Mazarin Stone" (1921)—not by Holmes' client or assistant, but by a potential assassin. This passage is found in the latter half of the story when Count Sylvius confronts Holmes in his Baker Street apartment and reprimands him for having put his "'creatures'" upon his tracks. When Holmes attempts to assure the Count that he has done no such thing, the nobleman retorts that "'Other people can observe as well as you. Yesterday there was an old sporting man. To-day it was an elderly woman. They held me in view all day.'" With that, Holmes, who had played both those roles, replies, "'Really, sir, you compliment me. Old Baron Dowson said the night before he was hanged that in my case what the law had gained the stage had lost. And now you give my little impersonations your kindly praise?'" The incorporation of acting into Holmes' proverbial "bag of tricks" echoes the sheer joy that Doyle and his classmates experienced when they watched the performances of Dr. Littlejohn in the University of Edinburgh's medical theater.

Dr. Robert Christison

> *"Burke an' Hare*
> *Fell doun the stair,*
> *Wi' a body in a box,*
> *Gaun to Doctor Knox"*
> —*ANONYMOUS STREET CHANT, CIRCA 1830*

For the first half of the nineteenth century, the University of Edinburgh Medical School faculty followed the guiding principle that the sole way to advance medical knowledge and the art of healing was to study dead subjects. They were fiercely opposed by many members of the public, who remained convinced that their loved ones could not "rise if the bodies were cut up in dissection." The result of this was a limited supply of cadavers for gross anatomy classes. Certain industrious individuals would enter graveyards clandestinely to dig up fresh bodies—that they then sold at exorbitant prices to medical schools. This illegal trafficking gave rise to what became known as the "resurrectionist trade." Cemeteries responded to this body snatching by installing high fences, while many families hired guards to keep watch over the gravesites of their relatives.

And yet, there were two Scottish "entrepreneurs," William Burke and William Hare, who had no problem at all in obtaining dead bodies. They found an eager buyer in an Edinburgh professor named Dr. Robert Knox, who never asked questions as to the origins of the cadavers he purchased. It was not until a woman who was boarding with Burke discovered a corpse hidden beneath a pile of straw that Burke's and his accomplice's joint sixteen-month reign of terror in the "West Port" region ended abruptly. Dr. Robert Christison (Professor Emeritus at Edinburgh when Doyle entered medical school) was called upon to ascertain whether Burke and Hare had been murderers, and not merely grave robbers. He was also asked to determine how the nefarious duo managed to get away with their misdeeds for as long as they had. Christison, unfazed by the assignment, embarked on a series of meticulously and elegantly performed experiments on cadavers, both canine and human. He was able to demonstrate that Burke and Hare had asphyxiated many unsuspecting wanderers by tightly fastening pinches of plaster over their noses and faces. In the case involving "Mrs. Campbell" (whose body was found under the pile of straw), the medical evidence rested on proving if "certain bruised marks and subcutaneous extravasation of blood, found on different parts of the body, were indications of injuries received before death." Christison put his hypothesis to the test by smashing the extremities of human cadavers with heavy sticks and then compared them to the bruising patterns left on the dead woman's body. Christison concluded that she had been the victim of a cold-blooded murderer—and having convinced the jury the veracity of his findings, Burke and Hare were found guilty.

Burke met his end on January 27, 1829, when he was hanged in the public square before a crowd of cheering onlookers. His corpse was then transported over to the medical school where anatomy students dissected it in front of a large crowd of enthusiastic future physicians. The man who oversaw Burke's dissection was anatomy professor Alexander Munro III. After completing the "demonstration," he dipped his quill pen into a portion of the blood he had drained from Burke's head to inscribe the death certificate as follows: "This is written with the blood of Wm Burke, who was hanged at Edinburgh. This blood was taken from his head." Although Hare managed to escape the penalty he should have paid for his crimes by turning over King's evidence, it was not long before he too was punished for his evil deeds. Once his trial was over, he departed from Edinburgh and headed straight for London, where he changed his name and gained employment at a lime works facility. Somehow, his co-workers discovered his true identity, and decided to take matters into their own hands. They "flung him into a lime pit, whence he escaped with the loss of his sight." With that, Hare had no recourse other than turning to begging on the streets of London. Although the Anatomy Act that was passed three years later would allow medical schools to receive unclaimed bodies legally from hospitals, prisons, and workhouses, its enactment had a negative effect on the impoverished—many of whom continued to die inside hospitals and serve as the ongoing source of cadavers for anatomy lessons. These disenfranchised members of society had no choice but to engage in criminal activities if they did not want to subsist in deplorable workhouses. Those of the lower class were not consulted about the proper disposal of their bodies, and, of course, the upper classes gave little or no thought to their plight. The trials and tribulations of a poor person's life were never lost on Doyle, who himself had been brought up in less-than-advantageous circumstances.

Even if Doyle had received his medical education at an institution other than the University of Edinburgh, he would have known about legendary professors Christison and Knox—and the murderous duo of Burke and Hare. As an author who used his own life as a source for his fiction, Doyle was clearly intrigued enough by this cast of characters to mold them together—as if they were clay—and to shape them into a singular entity. *A Study in Scarlet* pays nuanced homage to Professor Christison's diligent detective work at the moment in the story when Watson and his former medical assistant, Stamford, discuss Holmes' "'passion for definite and exact knowledge.'" Stamford goes on to inform Watson that he "'saw with his own eyes'" Holmes "'beating'" cadavers "'in the dissecting-rooms with a stick,'" although Holmes "'is not a medical student'"—and further, he has never been one.

Another important facet of Professor Christison's personality entered the Holmes canon—and it was one that the strait-laced Dr. Watson would not at all condone. While at work as a clinical researcher, Christison made it a point to set aside time to experiment with opium to confirm for himself "its influence upon longevity when it was habitually used as an indulgence." Although we as readers never witness Holmes turn to opium whenever he is mired in the ennui that tends to overwhelm him between cases, in the 1891 short story "The Man with the Twisted Lip" he *does* go to an East End opium den to perform some undercover work.

Doyle's description of this seamy place captures perfectly the essence of the London netherworld:

> "Through the gloom one could dimly catch a glimpse of bodies lying in strange fantastic poses, bowed shoulders, bent knees, heads thrown back, and chins pointing upward, with here and there a dark, lack-lustre eye turned upon the newcomer. Out of the black shadows there glimmered little red circles of light, now bright, now faint, as the burning poison waxed or waned in the bowls of the metal pipes. Most lay silent, but some muttered to themselves, and others talked together in a strange, low, monotonous voice, their conversation coming in gushes, and then suddenly tailing off into silence, each mumbling out his own thoughts and paying little heed to the words of his neighbour. At the farther end was a small brazier of burning charcoal, beside which on a three-legged wooden stool there sat a tall, thin old man, with his jaw resting upon his two fists, and his elbows upon his knees, staring into the fire. As I entered, a sallow Malay attendant had hurried up with a pipe for me and a supply of the drug, beckoning me to an empty berth."

How much of Doyle's description of that opium den was based on his imagination, rather than on direct experience, remains an unsolved mystery. Nonetheless, the details of the story clearly indicate that Doyle knew a lot about the properties of this drug. In the short story "The Adventure of Silver Blaze" (1892), Holmes' prior experiences have taught him that "'powdered opium is by no means tasteless'" and that its "'flavour is not disagreeable.'" Holmes' knowledge of opium allows him to deduce by story's end that a serving of curry-seasoned mutton had been the agent responsible for concealing the taste of the deadly poison contained within. Drawing further upon Christison's proven expertise in the field of chemistry, the later Holmes story "The Adventure of the Illustrious Client" (1924) includes an intriguing plot point reminiscent of William Hare's deserved fate after Dr. Christison revealed the pair to be murderous criminals a century before. The scorned Miss Kitty Winter is given an opportunity to avenge herself against her former lover, the blackmailing Baron Gruner. She permanently blinds him by tossing sulfuric acid into his face—just as the lime works group had done to Hare in real life. These are only a few of the indispensable contributions made by Professor Christison to the Holmes character, all of which imparted a substantive layer toward the evolution of Doyle's great detective.

Dr. William Rutherford

Another Edinburgh faculty member, Dr. William Rutherford, so excited Doyle's imagination that he became the prototype for George Edward Challenger, the volatile fictional professor who Doyle featured in two of his later science fiction short stories—"When the World Screamed" (1928) and "The Disintegration Machine" (1928)—and in three of his novels *The Lost World* (1912), *The Poison Belt* (1913), and *The Land of Mist* (1926). In his prime, Rutherford's instantly recognizable "fine, sonorous voice of rich timbre and great power" imparted upon him an air of supreme confidence that gained him the instant respect of the student body. Rutherford was a staunch advocate for the surgical use of curare—a South American plant-based paralytic agent—during vivisections. Although he regarded curare as an anesthetic, he totally *disregarded* the fact that the animals used in these experiments—in his case, dogs—remain fully awake during such operations, and feel every single cut of the cold surgical knife. Even though Doyle first used curare when he served as Professor Rutherford's medical assistant, he already knew it was a potent medicinal dating back to his Stonyhurst years. After all, the school's most celebrated alumnus during Doyle's time there was Charles Waterton, the first European to successfully demonstrate the paralytic effects of curare. And so it follows that when Doyle created his Sherlock Holmes character, the consulting detective would be knowledgeable about curare, including its place of origin and its experimental misuse on dogs. Much of this is detailed vividly by Doyle in the following passage from "The Adventure of the Sussex Vampire" (1924):

> "'A South American household. My instinct felt the presence of those weapons upon the wall before my eyes ever saw them. It might have been other poison, but was what occurred to me. When I saw that little empty quiver beside the small bird-bow, it was just what I expected to see. If the child were pricked with one of those arrows dipped in curare or some other devilish drug, it would mean death if the venom were not sucked out. And the dog! If one were to use such a poison, would one not try it first in order to see it had not lost its power? I did not foresee the dog, but at least I understand him and he fitted into my reconstruction.'"

Doyle may have been purposeful in giving Sherlock Holmes the singular facial expression of Dr. Rutherford, that of keeping his eyelids "half-closed . . . as if oblivious to everything going on about him." And like Holmes, Rutherford "was a lover of music," a genius "capable of composing complex melodies of his own songs." Yet there were moments when Holmes exhibited several of Professor Rutherford's less-than-admirable traits, among them being described as "haughty, affected, supercilious," and a person "to be avoided at social functions."

Dr. Joseph Bell

Most readers of the Sherlock Holmes adventures know the name Joseph Bell. This distinguished Edinburgh professor of anatomy and pioneering forensic scientist earned his MD degree in 1859 (the same year Conan Doyle was born) from the University of Edinburgh. Like Henry Duncan Littlejohn, Bell's expertise in criminal toxicology led to his being summoned to court to represent the Crown in many of the sensational trials that took place in Edinburgh or Glasgow. Dr. Bell always tried his best to keep his name out of the papers, a trait that mirrors that of the fictional Holmes. Nevertheless, Bell was not able to keep his name out of the newspapers when he was called on by the Crown to appear in court at a sensational 1878 murder case. It was his testimony that convinced a jury that Eugéne-Marie Chantrelle—a French-born educator, and the man thought to be the inspiration for Robert Louis Stevenson's *Dr. Jekyll* character—was a cold-blooded murderer who had poisoned his wife Elizabeth with a lethal quantity of opium. Seconds before he was hanged at the gallows of Calton Prison, Chantrelle is said to have uttered these rather strange last words: "Bye-bye Littlejohn. Don't forget to give my compliments to Joe Bell. You both did a good job of bringing me to the scaffold." News of this bizarre farewell address escalated Dr. Bell to unsought celebrity status all throughout Scotland.

Not only was Doyle a student of the great Dr. Bell, he also had the good fortune to work for him as his clerk at the Edinburgh Royal Infirmary. This gave Doyle plenty of time to carefully study his mannerisms, listen to his stories, and learn his observational techniques. Doyle would go on to dedicate his short story collection *The Adventures of Sherlock Holmes* (1892) to Dr. Bell, and wrote him these words of praise, which stated, "Though in the stories I have the advantage of being able to place him [Sherlock] in all sorts of dramatic positions, I do not think that his analytical work is in the least an exaggeration of some effects which I have seen you produce in the outpatient ward."

Bell had a reputation for having perfected the art of visual medical diagnosis—rumor had it that he broke the ice with his patients by telling them "something about themselves and their doings gleaned solely from observation of their persons or clothing." With the publication of the Holmes tales, Bell's superior observational and deductive powers became known well beyond the walls of the medical school and turned him into a high-profile target of magazines and newspapers seeking to get the "inside scoop" on both Doyle and Holmes. During an interview with *The Book Buyer* in 1894, Bell related the following vignette about his special abilities:

> "'A man walked into the room where I was instructing the students, and his case seemed to be a very simple one. I was talking about what was wrong with him. "Of course, gentlemen," I happened to say, "he has been a soldier in a Highland regiment, and probably a bandsman." I pointed out the swagger in his walk, suggestive of the piper; while his shortness told me that if he had been a soldier it was probably as a bandsman. In fact, he had the whole appearance of a man in one of the Highland regiments. The man turned out to be nothing but a shoemaker, and said he had never been in the army in his life. This was rather a floorer; but being absolutely certain I was right, and seeing that something was up, I did a pretty cool thing. I told two of the strongest clerks, or dressers, to remove the man to a side room, and to detain him till I came. I went and had him stripped—and I daresay your own acuteness has told you the sequel."—"You have given me credit for that which I don't possess, I assure you."—"Why, under the left breast I instantly detected a little blue 'D' branded on his skin. He was a deserter. That was how they used to mark them in the Crimean days, and later, although it is not permitted now. Of course, the reason of his evasion was at once clear.'"

In his final Sherlock Holmes novel *The Valley of Fear* (1915), Doyle would put his own spin on Bell's ability to decipher the meaning of tattoos and branding marks when he has Holmes identify the character John Douglas as a member of a specific Freemason lodge only by observing a "'triangle within a circle'" that was branded on the dead man's arm. We then learn that, like Bell's "'deserter'" patient who tried to escape from his band of brothers as told in the passage above, Douglas has also attempted to sever his ties with his secret society.

Doyle's fascination with Bell's perceptive wizardry runs through so many of the Sherlock Holmes adventures. Doyle—who had borne witness to Dr. Bell's incredible gift of being able to determine a person's trade, hobbies, or social status just by glancing at their hands, clothing, and jewelry—conferred this same power on Sherlock Holmes. In "The Adventure of the Copper Beeches" (1892), Holmes is critical of "'the great unobservant public, who could hardly tell a weaver by his tooth or a compositor by his left thumb,'" and all those who lack "'the finer shades of analysis and deduction!'" What Holmes fails to realize is that it is his unique and seemingly psychic powers of observation that have let him climb to the pinnacle of his profession in the first place.

Dr. Bell considered Doyle to be one of his better students, and later remarked that Doyle was "exceedingly interested always upon anything connected with diagnosis, and was never tired of trying to discover all those little details which one looks for." Bell was able to recall the precise instant that he became Doyle's idol—it was when he determined that a patient had walked through an area known as "The Link" by observing a small splash of reddish clay on the man's shoes. Bell stated unequivocally that this material was only found in one spot in the entire city of Edinburgh. Doyle paid literary homage to that moment of epiphany in *The Sign of the Four* (1890), when Holmes draws startling inferences and conclusions about his partner's morning stroll around the streets of London. Holmes tells a shocked Watson, "'It is simplicity itself . . . so absurdly simple that an explanation is superfluous; and yet it may serve to define the limits of observation and of deduction. Observation tells me that you have a little reddish mould adhering to your instep. Just opposite the Seymour Street Office they have taken up the pavement and thrown up some earth which lies in such a way that it is difficult to avoid treading in it in entering. The earth is of this particular reddish tint which is found, as far as I know, nowhere else in from the neighborhood.'"

Bell's influence upon Doyle is *also* displayed in stories outside the Sherlock Holmes canon. In Doyle's "The Recollections of Captain Wilkie" (1895), the story's narrator passes the time trying to guess the occupation of his second-class traveling companion. First, he asks himself, "Who can he be?" Then he pridefully boasts "on being able to spot a man's trade or profession by a good look at his exterior. I had the advantage of *studying under a master of the art*, who used to electrify both his patients and his clinical classes by long shots, sometimes at the most unlikely of pursuits; and never very far from the mark." *[emphasis added]*

The narrator continues his algorithmic approach by listing the steps that the masterful doctor taught him:

"General appearance, vulgar; fairly opulent and extremely self-possessed; looks like a man who could out-chaff a bargee, and yet be at his ease in middle-class society. Eyes well set together and nose rather prominent; would be a good long-range marksman. Cheeks flabby, but the softness of expression redeemed by a square-cut jaw and a well-set lower lip. On the whole, a powerful type. Now for the hands—rather disappointed there. Though he was a self-made man by the look of him, but there is no callous in the palm and no thickness at the joints. Has never been engaged in any real physical work, I should think. No tanning on the backs of the hands; on the contrary, they are very white, with blue projecting veins and long, delicate fingers. Couldn't be an artist with that face, and yet he has the hands of a man engaged in delicate manipulations. No red acid spots upon his clothes, no ink stains, no nitrate of silver marks upon the hands (this helps to negative my half-formed opinion that he was a photographer). Clothes not worn in any particular part. Coat made of tweed, and fairly old; but the left elbow, as far as I can see it, has as much of the fluff left on as the right, which is seldom the case with men who do much writing. Might be a commercial traveller, but the little pocketbook in the waistcoat is wanting, nor has he any of those handy valises suggestive of samples."

The narrator's cautionary "look but don't touch" postulate matches up perfectly with a remembrance of Dr. Bell by Dr. Harold Emery Jones, one of Doyle's classmates at Edinburgh. Jones recalled how Dr. Bell admonished his students that when first examining a new patient, they should only "look at" but "mustn't touch" them. Rather, he instructed his class to "Use your eyes sir! Use your ears, use your brain, your bump of perception, and use your powers of deduction." Bell's systematic method of differentiating *seeing* from *observing* things, in the hope of *perceiving* and *deducing* their importance, was adopted—and then modified—by Holmes.

Dr. Bell made it a point to teach his students how to speedily ascertain the "small points in which the diseased differ from the healthy state." Although Sherlock Holmes is not a physician, Doyle endows him with this same Bell-like ability. In the first Holmes novel *A Study in Scarlet* (1887), Holmes—to the astonishment of the Scotland Yard detectives who are there with him—instructs them to look for a man with a "'florid face'" after he has viewed blood on the floor of a crime scene. He then draws the correct conclusion that when the murderer was committing his crime, his nose began to bleed—a consequence of a heart condition that has ruddied his complexion.

Dr. Bell was "much interested in the reading of character through hand-writing and composition," and Doyle made sure to bestow this hobby on Holmes as well. In "A Scandal in Bohemia" (1891), Holmes correctly determines that a letter he has recently received had to have been written by a German. He asks Watson the following question: "'Do you note the peculiar construction of the sentence—"This account of you we have from all quarters received." A Frenchman or Russian could not have written that. It is the German who is so uncourteous to his verbs.'" In *The Sign of the Four* (published a year earlier in 1890), a didactic Holmes instructs Watson that "'Men of character always differentiate their long letters, however illegibly they may write. There is vacillation in his k's and self-esteem in his capitals.'" It is unquestionable that Doyle made sure his Sherlock Holmes would be a virtual clone of his beloved college professor.

Dr. Joseph Bell was a social-minded philanthropist who donated ten percent of his income to the Free Church of Scotland and worked gratis at the Hill Street Refuge for Girls—known colloquially as "The Cripples' Home." During his earlier years when he was serving as ward assistant to the renowned Scottish surgeon Dr. James Syme, Bell saved a young child's life by heroically sucking out several thick diphtheritic membranes from the back of the young lad's throat that would have otherwise suffocated him. Bell's selflessness came with a price: The partial paralysis of his own vocal cords, which left him with a high-pitched and noticeably breathy speech pattern. Nevertheless, he held true to his credo that "We must not give the poor soul away."

And Sherlock Holmes stayed true to this same motto—in Doyle's short story "The Adventure of the Devil's Foot" (1910), a murderer is allowed to escape the hand of justice because Holmes judges the fugitive to be in the right. In "The Adventure of Charles Augustus Milverton" (1904), Holmes opts to do nothing when a woman fires bullet after bullet into the chest of the blackmailer who has ruined her life. When Watson attempts to stop her, Holmes uses all the force he can muster to pull him back, an action that permits his particular brand of justice to be served and affords the lady in distress the opportunity to escape scot-free. In "The Adventure of the Abbey Grange" (also published in 1904), Holmes is willing to allow a murderous sea captain to escape from the British authorities so long as he promises to keep his criminal secret to himself and remains off English soil for precisely one year. Holmes' decisions in these two cases are a reflection of Bell's own paraphrased mantra of *not turning in the poor soul* to the authorities. In homage to Dr. Bell, Doyle's character Sherlock Holmes is quite willing to do *pro bono* detective work if he deems a potential client to be worthy of being afforded free services. In "The Adventure of the Speckled Band" (1892), despite the words of a potential client who tells him, "'At present it is out of my power to reward you for your services,'" Holmes takes on her case, while in the later 1903 tale "The Adventure of the Norwood Builder," he is willing to take on the case of a man who is on the run from police.

Additionally, in the first Holmes novel *A Study in Scarlet* (1887)—and in "The Adventure of the Six Napoleons" (1904), "The Adventure of the Retired Colourman" (1926), and many other Sherlock Holmes adventures—Holmes works with the Scotland Yard's inspectors for no fee and allows them to put themselves in the limelight he deserves, despite their false claims that they are the ones who have cracked the cases. And in the second Holmes novel *The Sign of the Four* (1890), Doyle pays a nuanced tribute to Bell's heroically acquired affliction by weaponizing blow darts with lethal diphtheria toxin.

Bell was a man of honor—the epitome of high morality. He earned the respect of others by his refusal to divulge the slightest morsel of private and privileged information. Bell wrote, "I have been engaged in the practice of medical jurisprudence on behalf of the Crown, but there is little I can tell you about it. It would not be fair to mention that which is the private knowledge of the Crown and those associated there with, and the cases which have been made public would not bear repetition." And Holmes adhered to this same creed by his unwillingness to disclose any information that might compromise another person. In the short story "The Adventure of the Noble Bachelor" (1892), the condescending Lord St. Simon consults Holmes on "'a most painful matter . . .'" and tells him, "'I understand that you have already managed several delicate cases of this sort, sir, though I presume that they were hardly from the same class of society.'" When Holmes replies that "'his last client of the sort was a king,'" then the St. Simon character, prying into the nature of that case, is stymied by Holmes' Bell-like response: "'I extend to the affairs of my other clients the same secrecy which I promise to you in yours.'" In "His Last Bow" (1917), Sherlock Holmes comes out of retirement after the Premier of England recruits him to break a German spy ring. Holmes' decision is reminiscent of the one made by Cincinnatus, the first dictator of Rome, who became the symbol of manliness and civic virtue with his willingness to leave his plow (or in Holmes' case, his bee farm) in order to handle a clear and present danger. Dr. Watson is also a proponent of that same code of honor that Holmes and Bell share. In the 1927 short story "The Problem of Thor Bridge," Watson tells us "there are some [sic. cases] which involve the secrets of private families to an extent which would mean consternation in many exalted quarters if it were thought possible that they might find their way into print. I need not say that such a breach of confidence is unthinkable, and that these records will be separated and destroyed now that my friend has time to turn his energies to the matter."

Bell, a dyed-in-the-wool critic of the methods employed in the training of the London police force, went on the record with this somewhat demeaning statement:

> "It would be a great thing if the police generally could be trained to observe more closely. The lines upon which it might be done would be to make the prizes bigger for the educated man . . . The fatal mistake which the ordinary policeman makes is this, that he gets his theory first, and then makes the facts fit it, instead of getting his facts and first of all and making all his little observations and deductions until he is driven irresistibly by them into an elucidation in a direction he may never have originally contemplated."

In Doyle's 1891 short story "A Scandal in Bohemia," the following words spoken by Holmes echo previous sentiments expressed by Bell: "'I have no data yet. It is a capital mistake to theorize before one has data. Insensibly one begins to twist facts to suit theories, instead of theories to suit facts.'" In "The Five Orange Pips" published in the same year, the following statement made by Holmes also mirrors Joe Bell's attitude:

> "'The ideal reasoner would, when he had once been shown a single fact in all its bearings, deduce from it not only all the chain of events

which led up to it but also all the results which would follow from it. As Cuvier could correctly describe a whole animal by the contemplation of a single bone, so the observer who has thoroughly understood one link in a series of incidents should be able to accurately state all the other ones, both before and after. We have not yet grasped the results which the reason alone can attain to. Problems may be solved in the study which have baffled all those who have sought a solution by the aid of their senses. To carry the art, however, to its highest pitch, it is necessary that the reasoner should be able to utilise all the facts which have come to his knowledge; and this in itself implies, as you will readily see, a possession of all knowledge, which, even in these days of free education and encyclopaedias, is a somewhat rare accomplishment. It is not so impossible, however, that a man should possess all knowledge which is likely to be useful to him in his work, and this I have endeavoured in my case to do.'"

Dr. Thomas Laycock

While we know that Dr. Joseph Bell exerted a profound influence on the personality traits of Sherlock Holmes, few know who the man was who helped shape and refine Bell's style of critical thinking. That person was Dr. Thomas Laycock. The two first met on the wards of the Royal Infirmary of Edinburgh, when Bell was a student and Laycock was "Chair of Practice of Physic" at the University of Edinburgh. Many medical students during his tenure did their best to avoid enrolling in any of Laycock's classes, primarily due to his reputation for habitually going off on irrelevant tangents and off-topic digressions during his lectures. As to his diagnostic abilities, Laycock was strictly "hit or miss." He remained convinced that a person's intelligence could be determined simply by studying his or her facial characteristics or head size, and became the precursor of actual men like Dr. Joseph Bell and Doyle, and fictional characters like Sherlock Holmes and Dr. Watson—all of whom thought the same way.

In the 1892 short story "The Adventure of the Blue Carbuncle," Holmes applies Laycock's methodology to predict that an unknown man is highly intelligent simply by observing the cubic capacity of his lost hat. In "The Adventure of Charles Augustus Milverton" (1904), a blackmailer is described by Watson as being "a man of fifty, with a large, intellectual head . . .", while in a short story from that same year, "The Adventure of the Missing Three-Quarter," he "could not fail to be impressed by a mere glance at the man, the square, massive face, the brooding eyes under the thatched brows, and the granite moulding of the inflexible jaw. A man of deep character, a man with an alert mind, grim, ascetic, self-contained, formidable—so I read Dr. Leslie Armstrong." Although it is now considered to be a pseudoscience, Holmes and Watson were proponents of anthropological criminology—a system that was employed to classify an individual's personality traits by *looking* at that individual. Although this field was considered to have been founded by Cesare Lombroso, Dr. Laycock was certainly an advocate of this system and was a contemporary—and perhaps forerunner—of Lombroso.

In 1904, Doyle included this type of specious reasoning in "The Adventure of the Golden Pince-Nez," where he has Holmes claim that his "'deductions are simplicity itself'" after he has merely examined a pair of spectacles:

> "'It would be difficult to name any articles which afford a finer field for inference than a pair of glasses, especially so remarkable a pair as these. That they belong to a woman I infer from their delicacy, and also, of course, from the last words of the dying man. As to her being a person of refinement and well dressed, they are, as you perceive, handsomely mounted in solid gold, and it is inconceivable that anyone who wore such glasses could be slatternly in other respects. You will find that the clips are too wide for your nose, showing that the lady's nose was very broad at the base. This sort of nose is usually a short and coarse one, but there are a sufficient number of exceptions to prevent me from being dogmatic or from insisting upon this point in my description. My own face is a narrow one, and yet I find that I cannot get my eyes into the centre, or near the centre, of these glasses. Therefore the lady's eyes are set very near to the sides of the nose. You will perceive, Watson, that the glasses are concave and of unusual strength. A lady whose vision has been so extremely contracted all her life is sure to have the physical characteristics of such vision, which are seen in the forehead, the eyelids, and the shoulders.'"

Professor Laycock was notorious for his "brilliant diagnoses, and . . . great mistakes." He often strode "through a ward to look at a man" so he could label them with a diagnosis. But there were many times when he was way off the mark. One incident in particular encapsulates his erratic deductions. Laycock was called to a man's bedside and proceeded to diagnose him by "the condition of the patient's teeth." To Laycock's embarrassment, the patient casually removed his false teeth from his mouth and sarcastically asked him, "Please, Sir, shall I hand them round?" But a student should always strive to surpass his teacher by being able to filter out the good from the bad, and that was precisely what Dr. Joseph Bell was able to accomplish.

Dr. Thomas Richard Fraser

Dr. Thomas Richard Fraser was born in Calcutta in 1841 and moved to Edinburgh in his early youth, where he received his primary education before later attending medical school at the University of Edinburgh. When he was twenty-one years old, Fraser's thesis "Characters, Actions, and Therapeutics of the Ordeal Bean of Calabar (Physostigma Venenosumon)" earned him the Medical School's coveted gold medal—and with it, an international reputation. In 1877, he was appointed lecturer in Materia Medica. Doyle was among the fortunate students who attended Fraser's inaugural class. The two of them shared similar interests, among them "fishing, shooting, golf, and photography." And both Fraser and Doyle had ties to the Arctic—Fraser having been a member of the "Admiralty Committee on Sir George Nares" 1877 expedition, and Doyle having served as ship's physician aboard a Greenland whaling vessel. The possibility exists that it was Fraser who inspired Doyle to try his luck with such "dangerous work."

Fraser's groundbreaking research on the chemical properties of physostigmine was to provide the field of medicine with cutting-edge therapeutic approaches to ophthalmology, rheumatology, anesthesiology, immunology, and toxicology. Intent on determining physostigmine's mechanism of action, Fraser had no qualms about sacrificing himself in the name of science. On each occasion when he ingested the potentially deadly calabar bean, Fraser was willingly putting his life on the line. Doyle passed this risk-taking behavior onto Sherlock Holmes, who bears an eerie resemblance to Dr. Fraser in his willingness to act as his own guinea pig. In *A Study in Scarlet*, Holmes tells Watson that he has been known to "'dabble with poisons a good deal'"—and in "The Adventure of the Devil's Foot" (1910), Holmes participates in an "'unjustifiable experiment'" when he inhales a toxic gas to verify whether or not his proposed rationale for the methods used to kill others is, indeed, provable.

It was Dr. Fraser who made the major discovery that the atropine derivative of the belladonna plant can reverse the paralytic effects of physostigmine. Doyle pays warranted tribute to Dr. Fraser's work in *A Study in Scarlet*, which opens with Stamford telling Watson, "'Holmes is a little too scientific for my tastes—it approaches to cold-bloodedness. I could imagine his giving a friend a little pinch of the latest vegetable alkaloid, not out of malevolence, you understand, but simply out of a spirit of inquiry in order to have an accurate idea of the effects. To do him justice, I think that he would take it himself with the same readiness.'" And when Dr. Watson presents the reader with a written list of Holmes' strengths and weaknesses, item five is: "Botany—Variable," but all the time he makes sure to mention that Sherlock is "well up in belladonna." It was Fraser's lecture series on Materia Medica that familiarized Doyle (and, by extension, the fictive Holmes) with the amazing properties of these pharmacologic agents.

Fraser's sterling reputation as a physician, professor, and investigator earned him a prized spot in the medical school's elite "Big Five"—its other members being Andrew Douglas Maclagan, Thomas Grainger Stewart, Alexander Simpson, and William Smith Greenfield. Fraser was to be the last survivor of this exclusive group.

Fraser also "took on an unexpected interest and even fascination" with "tobacco, alcohol, and the arrow poisons and ordeal beans." Sherlock Holmes, who shares Fraser's intricate knowledge of tobacco and its derivatives, "can distinguish at a glance the ash of any known brand, either of cigar or of tobacco." And in "The Boscombe Valley Tragedy" (1891), Holmes tells us that not only has he "'devoted some attention to this'" topic, but he has also "'written a little monograph on the ashes of 140 different varieties of pipe, cigar, and cigarette tobacco.'" And poison-tipped arrows appear in not one, not two, but *three* Sherlock Holmes adventures. In *A Study in Scarlet*, Mr. Hope's story of his janitorial days at York College seems to have been extracted directly from Doyle's daily journal:

> "One day the professor was lecturing on poisons, and he showed his students some alkaloid, as he called it, which he had extracted from some South American arrow poison, and which was so powerful that the least grain meant instant death. I spotted the bottle in which this preparation was kept, and when they were all gone, I helped myself to a little of it. I was a fairly good dispenser, so I worked this alkaloid into small, soluble pills, and each pill I put in a box with a similar pill made without the poison. I determined at the time that when I

had my chance, my gentlemen should each have a draw out of one of these boxes, while I ate the pill that remained."

In *A Sign of the Four*, we learn that one of the antagonists, the cannibal Tonga, can paralyze his chosen prey by blowing poisonous darts at them. And in Doyle's 1924 Holmes short story "The Adventure of the Sussex Vampire," curare-tipped arrows are used first to paralyze a dog and then for the failed murder of an infant. In addition to what we have already established about Doyle's experiences with curare when he worked alongside Dr. Rutherford, we also know he would have gained even more detailed knowledge of other South American toxins and venoms at Dr. Fraser's symposiums.

And it was Dr. Fraser who early on served as Dr. Robert Christison's assistant in Materia Medica and then was selected to replace him. Although his name may not be familiar to many of Doyle's readers, this same Dr. Christison performed forensic experiments on cadavers by first beating them with sticks and then studying how the process of bruising progressed. This same weird procedure was replicated by Holmes in *A Study in Scarlet*.

But most significantly is that Fraser's name will be most closely associated with "snake poisoning . . . his work on serpent's venom, on the limitations to the antidotal power of antitoxins, on immunization against serpent's venom, and on the antivenomous properties of the bile of serpents was of high interest and great practical value." Doyle's favorite Holmes tale was "The Adventure of the Speckled Band" (1892), where Fraser's knowledge of snake venoms is transferred to Dr. Roylott (who was born in India, as was Fraser). Here, the evil doctor uses his pet swamp adder to do away with one of his stepdaughters. Unfortunately, Doyle did not employ Dr. Fraser's revolutionary work on finding antidotes to snake venom, a success that has saved thousands throughout the world—and, possibly, would have saved the doomed character Miss Julia Stoner.

Somewhat strangely, Doyle and Fraser were conferred with knighthoods on the same day and year—October 24, 1902. When Fraser died on January 4, 1920, the obituary that appeared in *Nature* magazine could have easily served as Holmes':

"Gifted with *acute senses* and a *fearlessly logical mind*, and trained in the habits of *accurate observation* and *experiment in the laboratory* . . . Endowed with a remarkably lucid and quick mind himself, Fraser was *intolerant of mental slowness in others, sparing of praise, and at times not slow to censure* . . . He carried himself—a keen, spare, scholarly figure—with a faint, indefinable hauteur, which may have been to many a *barrier to close intimacy*. But when this barrier was surmounted, and when he could lay aside the cares of too unremitting labour and of indifferent health, he would weave a *grace and charm which few could resist or forget.*" [emphases added throughout]

Sherlock Holmes has these very same attributes. Not only does he have an observant eye, he also has the "gift" of the keenest sense of hearing. In "The Man with the Twisted Lip" (1891), when an astonished Watson stumbles upon Holmes inside a dangerous East End opium house, he whispers cautiously to his partner, "'[W]hat on earth are you doing in this den?'" Holmes immediately retorts, "'As low as you can . . . I have excellent ears.'" Holmes, like Fraser, has a "disinclination to form new friendships"—but as we learn in "The Adventure of the Dying Detective" (1913), he also displays a "remarkable gentleness and courtesy in his dealings with women." Throughout the entirety of the canon, Holmes is the picture of masculine grace and charm. In "The Adventure of Charles Augustus Milverton" (1904), Holmes is able to sweep a housekeeper off her feet in less than a day, and then persuades her to accept his very hasty marriage proposal. And in 1891's "A Scandal in Bohemia," Holmes—having gained the confidence of the stable hands—is able to obtain critical information about the habits of the central character, Irene Adler.

Yet Holmes is not quick to heap praise on others—indeed, on several occasions, he has chastised Watson for his tendency to "'embellish . . . the many causes celebres and sensational trials'" with which these two partners have been involved. In "The Adventure of the Empty House" (1903), Holmes disparages Watson by alluding to his "'mental slowness.'" As the two partners lie in wait in a dark abandoned apartment (one of Holmes' covert lairs), Watson becomes aghast when he peers out a window and watches a bust of Holmes change position in the sitting room of his former London apartment at 221 B, Baker Street. Holmes cuts Watson to the quick with the following reply: "'Of course it has moved.'" Later in his narrative, Watson recalls that he knew what Holmes' words of derision had signified: "Three years had certainly not smoothed the asperities of his temper or his impatience with a less active intelligence than his own." And in "The Adventure of the Abbey Grange," he tells Watson that he "'deplores'" such behavior in the narratives of his chronicler and then scolds him for having "'ruined what might have been an instructive and even classical series of demonstrations.'"

One of Holmes' pet peeves is the outdated methodologies and faulty deductions made by the inspectors of the prestigious Scotland Yard. A sterling example of this occurs in the 1891 short story "The Five Orange Pips" when, having learned that the inspectors believe that the letters received by his client are nothing more than practical jokes, Holmes blurts out, "'incredible imbecility!'" His genetic material has endowed him with a fearlessly logical mind, which is accompanied by remarkable skills in the chemistry lab. He goes as far as attaching his name to a blood test he has devised in *A Study in Scarlet*. Each of these traits is present in the chromosomes of Dr. Thomas Richard Fraser.

This vast collection of memorable medical school experiences was of aid to Doyle in his quest to provide us with some of literature's most unforgettable and, sometimes, immortal figures. They also furnished him with the capacity to orchestrate and arrange some of the greatest and gripping detective stories ever written.

Arthur Conan Doyle—The *Creator*

As one might expect, Doyle's DNA is also an integral part of the Holmes character. Doyle was a trailblazer who, as a teenager, immersed himself in the embryonic field of photography. While he was still in medical school, he began contributing articles to the *British Journal of Photography*. Within a few years, he gained so much respect from its board that he was given an editorial column of his own. Like his creator, Holmes also constantly familiarizes himself with the newest advances in his chosen profession and often puts down his thoughts on paper. Who of us can forget his "'little monograph on the ashes of 140 different varieties of pipe, cigar, and cigarette tobacco,'" or his "'trifling monograph upon the subject'" of secret writing. Holmes, indeed, was the *true* father of the Consulting Detective—while Doyle was the *true* father of the modern detective story. And Doyle was the ultimate risk taker, a man totally unafraid of throwing himself into new and dangerous activities. When it came to swimming with sharks, or skiing down mountains, or participating in high-speed motor car races, Doyle was always ready, willing, and able. And his Holmes character shared this same adventurous spirit—a willingness to put his life at risk by trekking up the Himalayan mountains into mystical Tibet to have an audience with the Dalai Lama, or placing his life in peril for the sake of His Majesty by going undercover as a goatee-sporting Irish

American to prevent Germany from winning the Great War, or spying on the Khalifa in war-torn Khartoum . . . or, of course, fighting the nefarious Moriarty in hand-to-hand combat atop Reichenbach Falls.

It was this insatiable thirst to always be *the first* to do something that Doyle passed down to his literary son, Sherlock Holmes. State-of-the-art police techniques and equipment are features of Doyle's adventure stories, as is the mention of the most avant-garde technologies like phonographs, telephones, and motor cars. Doyle was among the first authors to make use of the typewriter for his manuscripts—he dictated his stories to his attractive sister Lottie, who was adept enough on the keyboard to type them out with blazing speed. It was during one of these sessions that Doyle came up with a plot that revolves around the unique features of the typewriter. Doyle, always the keen observer, studied the science involved in this revolutionary machine's strike keys and levers, as well as the inherent problem of paper alignment. Once he had completed this self-assignment, he wrote "A Case of Identity" (1891), a tale that used the lovely Lottie as the inspiration for its female protagonist and Doyle's intricate knowledge of the typewriter as the plot's fodder.

Little did Doyle know that in fewer than three years after its publication, Sherlock Holmes would be making a surprise appearance in a far-off court-house. As Doyle was writing this story in England, the American county of Milwaukee, Wisconsin was in the midst of an exponential population increase, with an accompanying increase in the number of its homeless citi-zens. To properly address this problem, the county's municipal government issued a blanket invitation to any architectural firm willing to participate in drawing up and submitting blueprints for a brand-new almshouse in the town of Wanwantoss. Their one stipulation was that the structure had to be able to provide shelter for "500 inmates and necessary officers." In return, the winner would be awarded a lucrative contract to construct that facility. Only three firms were brave enough to enter the competition, and it wasn't long before two of them opted out. This left the firm of H. J. Van Ryn and Charles Lesser the winner by default. Both Mr. Van Ryn and Mr. Lesser were already well-known in the community, as their firm had previously constructed three local public schools for Milwaukee County. Once the architectural plans for the three-story homeless shelter had been drafted, the bid for general contractor was awarded to Joseph A. Meyers.

A special committee was then set up to oversee how the construc-tion was coming along, and to determine whether the funds provided were being properly allocated. But when that committee completed their assessment, they realized that much was amiss. According to their report, unacceptable shortcuts had been taken and the approved architectural blueprints were not being adhered to. In many of the building's rooms and hallways, plaster was being applied "directly to the walls," the roofing material being used was not the specified "No. 1 Black Pennsylvania Slate," inferior quality flooring had been laid down, and that cheap "Blue Ohio sand stone" had been used as a substitute for high-quality "No. 1 Buff Bedford lime stone."

Once the committee had discovered these irregularities, they felt it their duty to apprise A. C. Brazee, Milwaukee County's district attorney, of its findings, and on September 4, 1894, Brazee officially charged Van Ryn and Lesser with attempting to alter plans and specifications for the almshouse. Soon after, Meyers and subcontractor Sullivan were contacted by Brazee, with all four of them being brought up on charges of conspiring to defraud the city of Milwaukee by tampering with public documents, charging for work that had never been carried out, and substituting inferior product and embezzling the profit.

How does this incident relate to the Sherlock Holmes character? Well, Miss Leonora Northrop, the typist and stenographer for the county clerk, was called to the witness stand, where she asserted that on October 28, 1893, a "strange man came into her office" and instructed her to make six copies of page twenty-eight of the blueprint that pertained to the almshouse. That page, among others, had words written on it that would have originated from *her* typewriter. When she was asked by the defense attorney to look over that page, and the blueprints that accompanied it, Miss Northrop stated that she could "positively identify all the sheets she copied for insertion in the specifications," and learned how to do so after she had read Arthur Conan Doyle's "A Case of Identity." When the defense attorney retorted, "You say you can now identify these pages, while at the preliminary examination you said you could not do so. How is that?," Miss Northrop replied with, "Since the examination I have discovered some distinctive marks in my work." The defense attorney, who had been working under the impression that all type was standardized, countered with, "In what way? Is your type different from that in any other machine?" Miss Northrop's cool unfazed reply was, "Yes. I can distinguish my work by two distinct peculiarities in the type of my machine. The capital 'U' has a slight break on one end, and the upper right-hand corner of the capital 'I' is worn away." With this, the defense attorney was rendered speechless. But Miss Northrop wasn't quite done yet. She waited for just the right moment to break the stark silence she had created by adding "the ink on the page was slightly darker than that used in making the other pages." She went on to tell the judge and jury that the document purportedly written by her "showed signs of being written at a later date."

Without Miss Northrop's casual yet cogent testimony—and its allusion to this particular Holmes tale—the verdict would have gone differently. Soon, it was brought to light that Charles Lesser had authorized the alterations to the blueprints, although the other three defendants claimed to have no knowledge of that adulteration. As the state of Wisconsin defined the word "conspiracy" as requiring two or more individuals acting in concert to perform some harmful or unlawful act, Judge Burnell had no other option available to him to keep the case moving forward, and so he had to dismiss the case. Had the state "charged a conspiracy to defraud instead of a conspiracy to alter plans and specifications," the trial would have continued, with a guilty verdict more than likely. Ironically, once the trial had ended, Lesser and Van Ryn (whose shared reputation was on the line) sued Milwaukee County for services rendered on their magnificent work—and, of course, won.

So, not only was Arthur Conan Doyle the first to write about the typewriter's potential for aiding in identifying criminal activity, but his short story "A Case of Identity" was *the* source referenced in the first trial to use the uniqueness of all typewriters as evidence in a court of law. With this, the fictional methodology Doyle provided to his Sherlock Holmes character in the solving of crimes became transferable to the real world of forensic science.

Although Dr. Joseph Bell will be forever associated with Sherlock Holmes, we should not overlook the significant contributions that we now see were all made by many other of Doyle's professors—Drs. William Rutherford, Thomas Laycock, Robert Christison, Henry Duncan Littlejohn, and Thomas Richard Fraser—each of them having supplied Doyle with the critical elements he needed to grind up within his mind's own crucible of creativity. The upshot of their vast influence was that Doyle was able as a result to give life to the world's perennially favorite detective.

CHAPTER 4

Doyle and Race
An Epiphany Aboard the *Mayumba*

The 1960s gave us two powerful slogans—"Freedom Now" and "Black Power"—each of them a response to the ongoing mistreatment and resultant lack of influence of a significant portion of the American populace. More than a half-century later, the United States still falls short of adequately confronting and addressing so many of the injustices that Dr. Martin Luther King, Jr. and Stokely Carmichael fought to correct—albeit in quite different styles. A new rallying cry, "Black Lives Matter," is now a sonorous echo reverberating from coast to coast and around the world.

Back in 1882, a relatively unknown Arthur Conan Doyle engaged in several "long chats" while he served as ship's physician aboard the steamship *Mayumba* with one of the first Black men to attain an American governmental post once the Civil War had ended. The dignitary with whom Doyle conversed was an American diplomat—a man who not only served two non-consecutive terms as ambassador to Liberia, but who would exert a profound influence on the fledgling British author's perception of race relations and, later, on some of Doyle's future works. By sharing experiences drawn from his own life, this outstanding individual also helped to pave the way toward racial equality in America. In fact, several of the Sherlock Holmes adventures allude directly to the unfair practices and dangerous secret societies that the former slaves had to continuously confront and deal with—and so it follows that this fateful meeting aboard the *Mayumba* affected Doyle's work, and his life.

Although Doyle was able to acknowledge some of America's most noted abolitionists in his Holmes stories—among them Henry Ward Beecher and Samuel Clemens (a.k.a., Mark Twain)—it is this long overlooked and virtually unknown Black leader Doyle met aboard the *Mayumba* who lurks behind his civil rights-inspired talés. The seeds this man scattered were reaped by the multitude of Doyle's loyal readers throughout the world. Now, more than ever, it behooves us to remember and appreciate this dauntless pioneer's contribution to our society.

When Republican candidate Abraham Lincoln was elected President of the United States in 1860, most Southerners and many Northerners were equally infuriated. Fearful that Lincoln and the men around him would cripple an economy based almost solely on the harvesting of highly profitable cotton—a slogan that Southerners would refer to as "King Cotton"—and entirely dependent upon the continuation of slavery, eleven states broke their ties with the Union and seceded from the United States of America. These dissenters banded together to form a rival nation within a nation, calling themselves the Confederate States of America. On April 12, 1861, when Confederate troops launched an attack against federal soldiers stationed at Fort Sumter in South Carolina's Charleston Harbor, they were unofficially declaring war on the Union. For four difficult years, this war fought between "brothers" resulted in 650,000 deaths—which, even by contemporary standards, represents an immense and sickening casualty toll. It wasn't until Robert E. Lee—the most revered of the Confederate generals—formally surrendered to the Union's General Ulysses S. Grant at Appomattox Court House on April 9, 1865 that there was even a glimmer of hope for the reconciliation of a torn nation.

As so much damage and destruction had been wrought by both opposing forces, it became necessary to rebuild the nation's infrastructure from the ground up. The period between 1865 and 1877 became known as the Reconstruction Era. Its first order of business was to reword and reinterpret the antiquated laws that had allowed the "peculiar institution" of slavery to exist for more than two centuries. In less than a period of five years, three amendments related to these issues had been added to the Constitution. The first of them, the Thirteenth Amendment, declared an official end to the legal practice of slavery. Next came the Fourteenth, which permitted the recently freed slaves to become citizens of the United States. It was the Fifteenth Amendment that cleared the way for people of color to pursue and obtain governmental positions of prominence and power, paving the way for better representation of the Black community on the local, state, and federal level. In 1869, Ebenezer Bassett broke the color barrier by becoming the first African American to hold an official diplomatic position when he was appointed Consul-General to Haiti. A year later, Hiram Rhodes Revels replaced Jefferson Davis (the former president of the Confederacy) as the senator from Mississippi, which made him the first Black man to hold the legislative branch's highest position. Nevertheless, these changes did not take place in a vacuum. Even before the war had ended, other Black men and women of courage and distinction had already made names for themselves—people like Frederick Douglass, Sojourner Truth, Benjamin Turner, Harriet Tubman, Robert Elliott, and Henry Highland Garnet among others.

A few months after his 1881 medical school graduation, a twenty-two-year-old Arthur Conan Doyle responded to an advertisement placed in *The Young Doctor's Future* by the African Navigation Steam Ship Company. It read as follows:

> "The African Steam Navigation Company. Offices:- 21, Great St. Helen's, London. Ships sail from Liverpool and Hamburg for St. Paul de Loanda, calling at Madeira, Tenerife, and all ports on the West Coast of Africa. Voyage out and home in 84 days. Salary 8 (pounds) per month. Surgeon ranks with chief officer and purser. Company finds instruments and drugs. Uniform optional; cap usually worn."

Doyle heard back from the company almost immediately. He had been assigned to the *Mayumba*—one of the fleet's twelve steamers—on its upcoming round-trip voyage from Liverpool, making stops along the West African coast. This would be Doyle's second stint as a ship's surgeon. In the year prior to this, while still a medical student, he had held that same position while aboard the whaling vessel *Hope*, which sailed out of Peterhead (a remote fishing port in northern Scotland). During that Arctic expedition, he had seen double duty for six months as both a physician and a hunter of whales and seals. Although officially he was considered a novice, Doyle was a natural seaman with skills that sometimes exceeded those of his more seasoned shipmates. He was quickly able to earn the respect of his fellow crew members, as well as the admiration of an officer staff that included the renowned Scottish mariner Captain John Gray. At voyage's end, Doyle received an open invitation to return to the *Hope* on its next sailing—although this time, he was to serve only as a sealer-whaler, and not as a doctor.

For some unknown reason, Doyle accepted an offer to serve as ship physician on the Africa-bound steamship *Mayumba* rather than returning to the *Hope*. In mid-October 1881, he traveled from Birmingham to Liverpool—once there, he busied himself shopping and purchasing "cartridges for a splendid little revolving rifle" that his mentor at the time, Birmingham physician Reginald Ratcliff Hoare, had given him as a parting gift. On Friday, October 22, 1881, the *Mayumba* steamed out of Liverpool en route to the Portuguese island of Madeira, its first scheduled port of call. Other stops along the way would include Tenerife off the Spanish coast, followed by stops at the West African ports of Cape Palmas, Liberia, Sierra Leone, and Cape Coast Castle—and then the steamer was to retrace its sea journey back to Liverpool. Once he was aboard ship, Doyle had ample opportunity to socialize with its passengers, go canoeing, hunt snakes, and read books written by his two favorite authors, Thomas Carlyle and Oliver Wendell Holmes.

On November 22, 1881, Doyle wrote to his family friend Charlotte Drummond that he was "steaming from one dirty little port to another dirty little port, all as like as two peas, and only to be distinguished by comparing the smell of the inhabitants, though they all smell as if they had become prematurely putrid and should be buried without unnecessary delay." A month later, as his ship sailed out from Liberia's principal port and capital city of Monrovia, Doyle's diary reflected a sudden and dramatic change of attitude. His diary entry on December 24 read as follows:

> "American Consul came as a passenger with us. Rather a well read intelligent fellow, had a long chat with him about American and English literature, Emerson, Prescott, Irving, Bancroft & Motley. He was as black as your hat however. He told me what I myself think, that the way to explore Africa is to go without arms and without servants. We wouldn't like it in England if a body of men came armed to the teeth and marched through our country, and the Africans are quite as touchy. Thats why they begin getting their stewpans and sauces out when they see a Stanley coming."

It has been assumed—that is, until now—that the unnamed ambassador who helped Doyle understand that *all* Black lives matter was the

Reverend Henry Highland Garnet, the then-incoming United States Ambassador to Liberia. And yet, until three days before Christmas that same year, Henry Highland Garnet had never even set foot on African soil. Furthermore, the man Doyle described in his log entry possessed stunningly detailed knowledge about the attitudes and sentiments of the people who lived there—more specifically, a nation that now welcomed newly emancipated slaves who were looking to start new lives in a land far away from the country that had mistreated them. As it is documented that Garnet had never been to Africa before this, it would have been impossible for him to have had the depth of knowledge required to engage Doyle in detailed discussions about the inappropriate and unsuccessful methodologies exploited by the European colonialists and missionaries who had come to western Africa. The only explanation for this is that all of Doyle's previous biographers have *misidentified* this American statesman.

Reverend Henry Highland Garnet was born in New Market, Maryland on December 23, 1815. When he was only nine years old, Garnet and his family joined the ranks of those runaway slaves who had followed the "drinking gourd" to freedom. His family had taken the Underground Railroad to New Hope, Pennsylvania, where they became respected members of the community. At the age of eleven, Garnet was accepted to the New York African Free School on Mulberry Street—four years later, he became a merchant seaman and traveled first to Cuba and then to Washington, DC. Upon his return, he entered New York's High School for Colored Youths where he was taken under the wing of Theodore Sedgwick Wright. Through Wright's encouragement and tutelage, Garnet soon developed into a brilliant orator and dynamic minister, and at the age of twenty-four delivered his maiden speech at the annual meeting of the American Anti-Slavery Society. His "fire and brimstone"-laced sermon gained him national prominence with the abolitionists.

Although nature had afflicted him with "white spreading"—tuberculosis—of the knee, which necessitated the amputation of his right leg, he continued to spread the word that slaves were obligated to rise up against those who enslaved them. His "pure English, deep thought and manly dignity," combined with his charisma, held audiences spellbound. During the Civil War, he volunteered his services as Chaplain of the Black troops on New York City's Rikers Island, and then served as Chaplain of the 20th, 26th and 31st regiments of Black soldiers until their deployment to the battlefield. In 1864, Garnet moved to Washington, DC where he served as Pastor of the Fifteenth Street Presbyterian Church. As his reputation grew, so did his esteem. On February 12, 1865, he received an invitation to speak before Congress on President Lincoln's fifth-sixth—and, unfortunately, final—birthday. Garnet delivered a no-holds-barred "Let the Monster Perish" speech, making him the "first colored man who has on any occasion spoken in our National Capitol." Four years later, he was named President of Avery College in Pittsburgh, Pennsylvania—a year later, he returned to the uptown Harlem section of New York City where he was installed as the Pastor of Shiloh Baptist Church.

On June 30, 1881, Garnet was named "Minister-resident and consul-general" to Liberia. This marked the fifth time in United States history that an African-American individual had been given such a high-ranking diplomatic position—his predecessors were E. D. Bassett and John M. Langston, both Ministers to Haiti, along with J. Milton Turner and John Henry Smyth, who were both Ministers to Liberia. What is especially significant about Garnet's ascension to this post is that it marked "the last appointment made by President Garfield" prior to his assassination less than two months later in New Jersey.

A farewell party at Chickering Hall was held in Garnet's honor on October 5 of that year. Among the notables in attendance that evening was Frederick Douglass and T. McCants Stewart, both of whom sang his praises in front of an audience that included J. N. Gloucester, C. F. Dorsey, Rufys L. Perry, J. Beulah Murray, A. N. Freeman, and J. B. Smith.

A month later, on November 6, Garnet delivered a farewell sermon at Shiloh Baptist Church—six days later, he sailed aboard the S.S. *Egypt* from New York to Liverpool. Although Garnet "desired to get off quietly," a squadron of fully uniformed guards led a procession to the wharf and accompanied him down to the ship. What most people did not know at this juncture was that Garnet was determined to live out the remaining years of his life in Liberia, in the company of his family. In essence, Garnet was a precursor to Marcus Garvey's "Back to Africa" mantra of the early 1900s, which sought to transport well-to-do Black Americans aboard the Black Star Line to a designated colony on Liberian soil. On the date the ship departed, a certain Dr. Arthur Conan Doyle was on the S.S. *Mayumba*, sprawled out in his cabin off the West African coast suffering from the ravaging effects of "coastal fever"—in all likelihood known today as dengue fever, a tropical disease spread by mosquitoes that can cause a flu-like reaction.

Although Garnet had sailed previously across the Atlantic without issue, the sea air on this occasion purportedly brought on a near-fatal episode of "asthmatic complaint"—a recurring condition that left him incapacitated for weeks to come. Considering his prior history of "the white swelling" of his knee, it can be inferred that this episode of asthma represented an exacerbation of his preexisting (but undiagnosed) *tuberculous bronchitis*. From then on, the "nearly prostrated" Garnet was confined to his cabin—and when the *Egypt* docked at Liverpool on November 22, some old friends took him to their home and nursed him back to reasonably good health within two weeks' time. This unforeseen illness necessitated the rescheduling of his Liverpool departure date from Saturday, November 26 to the following week. And so, on December 3, 1881, while Garnet was boarding the S.S. *Nubia*, Doyle was swimming with sharks somewhere near Nigeria's Bonny River. Suffice it to say, these two men were destined never to cross paths. After all, when Garnet stepped off the gangplank at the Port of Monrovia on Thursday, December 22, the *Mayumba* (with Doyle aboard) was a two days' journey south, which precluded any possibility of Doyle having ever met or conversed with Garnet. Although the *Mayumba* and the *Nubia* did pass each other on the night of December 23, by then Garnet was already on African soil—celebrating his sixty-sixth (and *final*) birthday and settling in at the American embassy. When Doyle's steamer arrived in Monrovia on Christmas Eve, Garnet was already ensconced inside his new home surrounded by his family.

So, had Doyle fabricated his shipboard talks with the American Consul-General to Liberia? He certainly did *not*. Doyle's diary explicitly states that December 24 was the date on which the "American consul came as a passenger with us" aboard the *Mayumba* when it departed northward from Liberia. If it wasn't Henry Highland Garnet whom he had met, then who was the person he *had* met? The answer to this question is, in fact, quite elementary. When Henry Highland Garnet presented his credentials to the United States embassy, the departing Consul-General, **John Henry Smyth** (who had already completed a four-year term of office in Liberia) was now free to return to the United States. Unlike Garnet, whose intention was to become a permanent resident in Liberia, John Henry Smyth was eager to return home to North Carolina. After all the legal proceedings were over and done, Smyth boarded the first vessel he could get out of Monrovia—and so, on December 24, he was happily aboard the *Mayumba*. Courtesy called for him to be introduced to each of the high-ranking officers aboard, including the ship's physician, **Arthur Conan Doyle**. This became the moment when the two initiated their discussion of prominent American and British writers—Emerson, Prescott, Irving, Bancroft, and Motley among them—along with exchanges related to the problematic nature of attempting to convert the native populations of Africa to Christianity.

If Doyle *had* met with Garnet, the words uttered by the "American Ambassador" would never have included remarks that ran counter to the importance of zealous missionary work. Garnet (and his family) placed emphasis on ensuring that Christianity would be incorporated into Liberian culture through the establishment of Christian schools. Smyth, on the other hand, vehemently opposed such tactics. The words spoken by the American ambassador to Doyle on the topics of "stewpans" and "Stanley" reflect sentiments more consistent with views held by Smyth. In a letter dated April 28, 1881 to Secretary of State James Blaine, Smyth wrote:

> "A great deal of money has been spent and many valuable lives lost in the effort to evangelize the natives of this country on the purely spiritual line, but the experience of nearly one hundred years has shown that any effort for the benefit of these tribes, apart from secular agencies, will never be successful . . . there is nowhere on this coast any missionary station which has become self-supporting."

Once the *Mayumba* was berthed in Liverpool, Doyle returned to Birmingham to resume his assistantship with Dr. Hoare while Smyth spent some leisurely time in England before he headed home aboard the S.S. *Peruvian*.

Who *was* this John Henry Smyth who Doyle had judged so favorably during the *Mayumba*'s three-week return voyage from Monrovia to Liverpool? The Honorable John Henry Smyth was born July 14, 1844 in Richmond, Virginia, and had learned how to read—in secret—by the age of five. When he was seven, he was sent to Philadelphia to be educated and became "the first colored newsboy in Philadelphia." He attended public school for four years and then was enrolled in two private schools, both under the direct control of a Christian organization called the Society of Friends—more popularly known as the Quakers. Upon his father's death in 1857, Smyth was forced to take a leave of absence from school so he could begin to earn money for his family. Two years later, he returned to school and finished his formal education at the Institute for Colored Youth. This school was headed by Ebenezer Don Carlos Bassett, who eventually became the first African-American diplomat of the United States, serving as the Consul-General to Haiti. Smyth displayed a decided taste and strong aptitude for the fine arts and when he was sixteen, he became the first Black student at Philadelphia's Life School of the Academy of Fine Arts. There he developed into an accomplished landscape artist, while he worked as a laborer in the city's Tyndale and Mitchell China House.

Smyth was also an aspiring actor and in 1865, through the encouragement of John Weiss Forney—then Secretary to the United States Senate—and Shelton Mackenzie (theater critic of the *Philadelphia Press*), Smyth left for London to find his place in the limelight. He had with him a letter of introduction from Mackenzie to present to world-famous Shakespearean tragedian Samuel Phelps, and to the equally legendary African-American actor Ira Frederick Aldridge. Smyth's trip could not have come at a worse time for him. Immediately upon his arrival, he learned that Aldridge was in St. Petersburg, Russia performing with a theater company—and Phelps' training fees were far too steep. This left Smyth with no option other than to sail back home.

By 1869, he abandoned his dream of becoming an actor and, instead, entered Howard University's School of Law. While still a student, he was appointed clerk in the War Department's Bureau of Refugees, Freedmen and Abandoned Lands. After his 1870 graduation, he married Fannie Ellen Shippen, daughter of Reverend John Shippen, of Washington, DC. He then moved from his clerkship over to the Department of the Interior's Census Office. Within two years, he was appointed an Internal Revenue agent for the Treasury Department—three months later, thanks to the intervention of Secretary of the Treasury George Boutwell, he was named the Internal Revenue storekeeper.

On April 23, 1878, North Carolina's Democrat Senator Matt Whitaker Ransom sent a letter to Secretary of State William M. Evarts, in which he recommended that Smyth fill the vacancy of Ambassador to Liberia. A month later, President Rutherford B. Hayes, at the further behest of Mississippi's Republican Senator Blanche Kelso Bruce along with Ransom and noted abolitionist Frederick Douglass, approved John Henry Smyth for the position of Consul-General to Liberia.

Smyth would have his work cut out for him as Liberia was then mired in political, social, and economic turmoil. James S. Payne, Jr., son of the former President of Liberia, was arraigned on charges of "having conspired with a number of persons to assassinate three members of" the Liberian House of Representatives. During this time, two well-known members of the Liberian government were being impeached. One trial involved Benjamin Joseph Knight (B. J. K.) Anderson, the Secretary of the Liberian Treasury who had been accused of "malfeasance in office and using the public funds without the authorization of law." The other involved the senior James S. Payne, who had been unceremoniously suspended only six days before the end of his term in office for having failed to suspend Anderson from duty. To make matters worse, Liberia's Attorney General— along with its Secretary of State—had *both* handed in their resignations. Liberia, this purported haven of liberty and democracy, found itself in utter chaos—and Smyth was sailing straight into the middle of it. However, by the time Smyth arrived in Monrovia on July 31, 1878, a fortuitous political shift had already taken place with the election and inauguration of President Anthony W. Gardner and Vice President Daniel B. Warner.

During his tenure as Consul-General, Smyth "imbibed the teachings" of Dr. Edward Blyden, an early proponent of the Pan-Africanism political movement who was a zealous advocate for "the supremacy of the black race unadulterated with Caucasian blood over all others." Smyth had also sent out a general letter, in which he petitioned the companies whose ships crossed the Atlantic to establish a run between West Africa's coast and the large port cities of New York and Baltimore.

One of Smyth's first orders of business was to petition the President of Liberia for "the amount due for arms and ammunition furnished to this government {Liberia} in 1868." He then addressed the Senate and House of Representatives to "enable the secretary of the treasury to meet the demand." Smyth was off to a good start as a negotiator but was then informed by Liberia's new Secretary of State of a plot designed to have France declare Liberia one of its Dependencies. The Secretary had learned that the French government's reason for wanting to acquire Liberia was for "a commercial character and a postal one, due to the nearness of Liberia to Senegal, and desires immediate action to be taken by Liberia in the matter." Smyth was swift to warn Acting-Secretary Frederick W. Seward that the United States must secure "some direct influence in Africa" to prevent other European nations from establishing so-called outposts of progress. His words to the Acting-Secretary read as follows: "It would be idle to indulge the thought that the English and French Governments are influenced by humanitarian, civilizing motives, solely, in the acquisition of territory on this continent." Smyth further reminded Seward that the United States would "need more markets for our manufactured articles, and the need increases with every new invention made, every article for which we have not an immediate customer which we produce." It is not known whether it was the warning Smyth issued to Seward, or the French government's assertion that it had never proposed such a plan, that kept French forces out of Liberia from that day forward.

Deep into his four-year term as Consul-General, President Garfield recalled Smyth and replaced him with the Reverend Henry Highland Garnet. Prior to Garnet's nomination for the post, Smyth had been dealing with an incident that wound up having international repercussions. In October 1880, "piratical depredations" were committed by the Krumen tribe upon the *Carlos*, a large shipwrecked German merchant steamer. After the natives had plundered "every removable article which the ship contained," they had instructed all passengers—male and female—to remove their clothing and march "to the nearest civilized settlement some twenty-five miles distant." The German government's immediate response to this unfortunate event was to demand monetary reparations that, according to Smyth's account, the Liberian government had promised to indemnify. According to Smyth's October 29 letter to Secretary of State (and later Presidential candidate) James Blaine, the Liberian government had "disregarded" their promise. The German foreign office was infuriated by this perceived slight, and dispatched Commander Victor von Valois and his cruiser warship *Victoria*—originally built for the Confederacy and purchased by Germany after the Civil War—to exact reparations from the Liberian government. That is when, with diplomatic guidance and mediation provided by Smyth and "after two interviews had by Commander Valois and the acting German consul with the {Liberian} secretary of state, a settlement of the indemnity due" was made in "the entire sum of $5,375." The Liberian government was able to pay it only "by the co-operation of the European merchants settled at Monrovia." Commander Valois, realizing that the Liberian government had no effective power over the villagers, ordered the *Victoria* to deliver a literal "parting shot" that laid waste to the towns surrounding the *Carlos* shipwreck.

While Henry Highland Garnet sailed across the Atlantic to assume his post as the new Consul-General, John Smyth was delivering a speech in Monrovia at Liberian College. In attendance that day were "the president of the republic, the cabinet, the chief justice, distinguished citizens, and the consul of the Netherlands." Smyth told a rapt audience the following:

> "The work of the negro race and Africa is your work, the negroes' work, and will not be done until the negro is fitted for its accomplishment by proper culture of heart and head, and full, untrammelled development of his racial instincts. Delay is not failure. The future for us is in the keeping of God. His work never fails. And, gentlemen, you no doubt, in the secrecy of your own reflection as future citizens of Liberia, ask yourselves to what end is this preparation, is this work. It has a special political bearing: The making of Liberia, in the language of my government, through the late Secretary of State, Hon. Wm. M. Evarts, 'what her rulers should value before all else, a thoroughly independent and strong power.'"

Two days before Garnet's ship departed from Liverpool, Smyth, along with "the cabinet and diplomatic and consular officers residents" present in Liberia, celebrated the day on which Black pioneers had been victorious in their battle to settle in "Cape Messurado, the site now occupied by and known as Monrovia." Smyth expressed his pleasure with the change in attitude of the Liberian people that had taken place from the time of his arrival up until that day. His address ran counter to the custom of speech that kept "alive a feeling of alienation from the native races, which has so long existed and which has been so harmful to Liberia's progress." And the speeches delivered in the Methodist Church that day were similar in tone to Smyth's, a reflection of a radical change in the sentiments of those who were charged in leading the country.

On his final day in Liberia, Smyth and Garnet spent the day together performing a detailed inventory of the books housed "in the Library of the U.S. Legation at Monrovia and Archives." Once completed, Garnet officially transferred power over to his successor. Garnet died unexpectedly seven weeks after his arrival in Monrovia, which left America's new president Chester A. Arthur responsible for filling this now-vacant position. President Arthur simplified things for himself by reappointing Smyth to another four-year term. Smyth returned in 1882 and, one year later, his wife crossed the Atlantic to join him in Monrovia. Once his tenure in

Liberia was completed, the Smyths returned to New York City where John did his best to focus the public's attention on New York's newly opened American Museum of Natural History.

Smyth did not remain in New York City for long, deciding then to pursue a teaching job in the Pennsylvania public school system. Seven years later, he reopened his law practice in both North Carolina and South Carolina along with an office in Washington, DC. Upon his retirement from the diplomatic corps, an honorary LLD (Doctor of Laws) degree was conferred on him by Liberia College along with the designation "Knight Commander of Liberia's Humane Order of African Redemption" (which had been founded by Liberian president Anthony William Gardner in 1879). In 1891, American press reports indicated that President Benjamin Harrison was likely to reappoint Smyth to a third term as Consul-General to Liberia. This prediction was based on a speech in which Smyth took a stand "in favor of a division in the social relations of the black and mulatto people." However, Smyth's stance aroused enough opposition among other prominent and influential African Americans that President Harrison's efforts to return Smyth to Monrovia were quashed.

Three years after the death of Frederick Douglass, Smyth was called upon to eulogize "The Lion of Anacostia" at a monument built in his honor in Rochester, New York. In the audience that day were, among other notables, suffragette Susan B. Anthony and noted Black leader John C. Dancy. Smyth told his listeners, "Through the warp and woof of his private and public life, one purpose ran: Honesty, incorruptibility and loyalty to the interests of his race. His uncompromising hatred of oppression and American prejudice distinguished him from 1838 to the end of an eventful, useful, effective and beautiful life. His name will ever be 'great in tongues of wisest censure.'"

In 1897, Smyth was named head of the Negro Reformatory Association of Virginia and was granted the authority to establish "reform schools for delinquent Negro minors of both sexes." A decade later, on September 5, 1908, John H. Smyth passed away at the age of sixty-four.

And so, although we have shown that Doyle never exchanged a word with Henry Highland Garnet, he *did* have several "long chats" with John Henry Smyth aboard the *Mayumba*. And while Doyle did not diarize the details of what had transpired between them, we do know that Smyth told an audience at the Cotton States and International Exposition world's fair held in Atlanta, Georgia in 1895 the following:

"I should perhaps leave an impression which would be misleading as to Liberia and Africa unless I be more explicit. If you have observed, in any utterance of mine, anything about Africa which seems to possess in itself or as to the races of that continent, a roseate hue, be pleased to remember that I have faintly, and with unartistic hand, shown you a part of this garden of the Lord and limned its inhabitants with the pencil and brush of an amateur; and I appeal to Mungo Park, the sainted Livingstone, Barth, Schweinfurth, Nachtigal, and I may risk Stanley in the rear of this galaxy of friends of Africa, for more accurate data and for larger and fuller experiences. But I may astound you when I say that Africa fears not the invasion of her shores by Europe and the rightful acquisition of her territory, and that no Negro who knows Africa regards the European's advent there as a menace to the progress and advancement of her races, except when they bring with them rum and fire-arms."

These words bear a close resemblance to the sentiments Doyle entered in his journal and explain his about-face when it came to selling arms and ammunition to the native population. In his journal entry, Doyle confesses that he had smuggled some guns aboard the *Mayumba* "which he hoped to sell for gold." Fortunately, this attempted underground operation was unsuccessful, and the best he could do was barter "one gun for a toothbrush." Years later, Doyle would make amends for his inappropriate behavior—very likely in response to hearing what Smyth said in the speech above—when he put pen to paper to help make the world aware of the atrocities that had been committed by Belgium King Leopold II against the indigenous population in his 1909 book *The Crime of the Congo*.

In Doyle's autobiography, *Memories and Adventures* (1924), he included the following statement:

"My starved literary side was eager for good talk, and it was wonderful to sit on deck discussing Bancroft and Motley, and then suddenly realize that you were talking to one who had possibly been a slave himself, and was certainly the son of slaves. This negro gentleman did me good, for a man's brain is an organ for the formation of his own thoughts and also for the digestion of other people's, and it needs fresh fodder."

As we will now show, Doyle used this "fresh fodder" to inform his mind and to shape the plots of some of his Sherlock Holmes tales. For instance, the plot of "The Five Orange Pips" (1891) is centered around a white supremacy group rooted in the early Reconstruction era—a largely secret society that grew from an unfavorable response to the extension of the vote to Blacks, their ability to own property, and their right to intermarry. In this tale, Elias Openshaw—an Englishman who somehow manages to rise to the rank of colonel in the Confederate Army—becomes a charter member of the Ku Klux Klan. Openshaw is "'mostly concerned with politics for he had evidently taken a strong part in opposing the carpet-bag politicians who had been sent down from the North.'"

Holmes tells Watson the following about the origins of the name "Ku Klux Klan":

> "'[It was] derived from the fanciful resemblance to the sound produced by cocking a rifle. This terrible secret society was formed by some ex-Confederate soldiers in the Southern states after the Civil War, and it rapidly formed local branches in different parts of the country, notably in Tennessee, Louisiana, the Carolinas, Georgia, and Florida. Its power was used for political purposes, principally for the terrorising of the negro voters and the murdering and driving from the country of those who were opposed to its views. Its outrages were usually preceded by a warning sent to the marked man in some fantastic but generally recognised shape—a sprig of oak-leaves in some parts, melon seeds or orange pips in others. On receiving this the victim might either openly abjure his former ways, or might fly from the country. If he braved the matter out, death would unfailingly come upon him, and usually in some strange and unforeseen manner. So perfect was the organisation of the society, and so systematic its methods, that there is hardly a case upon record where any man succeeded in braving it with impunity, or in which any of its outrages were traced home to the perpetrators. For some years the organisation flourished in spite of the efforts of the United States government and of the better classes of the community in the South. Eventually, in the year 1869, the movement rather suddenly collapsed, although there have been sporadic outbreaks of the same sort since that date.'"

While Holmes correctly deduces that the Klan disbanded precisely upon Openshaw's return to English soil, he continues to remain in the dark about the sad fact that the Ku Klux Klan was able to resurrect and reorganize itself. Even now in the twenty-first century, organizations that denounce certain racial groups, genders, religions, and foreigners still pose a threat to our nation's principles. The words spoken by Holmes and Watson clearly demonstrate that Doyle was way ahead of his time in alerting his readers—then and now—to the perennial threat posed by organizations of this type.

In "The Adventure of the Yellow Face" (1893), Doyle is courageous enough to discuss the topic of racial interbreeding and the dangers that accompanied mixed marriages in the days following what Southern sympathizers called the "War of Northern Aggression." Here, Holmes and Watson are consulted by Jack Grant Munro, who seeks to know the reason for his wife's recent secretiveness. Holmes proceeds to investigate the matter and determines that Munro's wife, Effie, had previously been wed to an African-American lawyer from Atlanta, Georgia. Effie soon confesses to Holmes, Watson, and her current spouse that her first husband, John Hebron, died from yellow fever several years before her second marriage.

Lucy, the offspring of that first union, has skin that is "'darker far than ever her father was.'" It is Effie's good fortune in the story that Munro is open-minded enough to welcome Lucy into their home. Doyle inserts some thematic undertones throughout the tale regarding the perils inherent in being a Black man in the South. Holmes finds out that Effie had to "'cut [herself] off from [her own] race in order to wed him,'" and that her Georgia home—along with the entirety of her personal possessions—had been burned to the ground. Doyle made sure to tell the reader that Effie's first husband was a well-to-do "strikingly handsome and intelligent-looking" lawyer, and that "'a nobler man never walked the earth.'" It is likely that his description of John Hebron is based on that of John Smyth—both are educated lawyers, impressive in appearance and manner, and each hailed from the deep South.

In "The Adventure of the Cardboard Box" (1893), Holmes seems able to read Watson's mind after he observes him studying a photograph of the noted abolitionist Reverend Henry Ward Beecher. The great detective uses his magic to tell his partner that he had been "'recalling the incidents of Beecher's career. I was well aware that you could not do this without thinking of the mission which he undertook on behalf of the North at the time of the Civil War, for I remember your expressing your passionate indignation at the way in which he was received by the more turbulent of our people. You felt so strongly about it that I knew you could not think of Beecher without thinking of that also. When a moment later I saw your eyes wander away from the picture, I suspected that your mind had now turned to the Civil War, and when I observed that your lips set, your eyes sparkled, and your hands clenched I was positive that you were indeed thinking of the gallantry which was shown by both sides in that desperate struggle. But then, again, your face grew sadder, you shook your head. You were dwelling upon the sadness and horror and useless waste of life. Your hand stole toward your own old wound and a smile quivered on your lips, which showed me that the ridiculous side of this method of settling international questions had forced itself upon your mind. At this point I agreed with you that it was preposterous and was glad to find that all my deductions had been correct.'" Ever the diligent researcher, Doyle's writings make it crystal clear that he had studied the events of the American Civil War with a fine-toothed comb—and although he was distressed by the unnecessary loss of lives that each side had inflicted on the other, he never changed his opinion and remained convinced that the Union forces had deservedly triumphed over the Confederacy. And, of course, two years after his stint aboard the *Mayumba*, Doyle wrote *The Narrative of John Smith*, a less-than-subtle attempt to acknowledge Smyth's greatness (although it remained unpublished for a century until its discovery in 2011).

The notion that *all* Black lives matter was at the heart of a movement that originated in the 1800s with trailblazers of Garnet's and Smyth's ilk at the forefront. As proponents of the tenets expressed in the Civil War Constitutional amendments, they did the best they could to ensure that succeeding generations would not be relegated to their pre-Emancipation status. Unfortunately, the Jim Crow laws of the late nineteenth century exerted a negative effect on their newly gained freedom—and sadly, the ripples of these unjust mandates remain with us today. It is incumbent on us to bring the names of Henry Highland Garnet and John Henry Smyth into sharper cultural focus as a reminder of their courage and vision.

That one voyage aboard the *Mayumba* where Smyth was a passenger served as an epiphany for Doyle. As a white man, he came to see firsthand the true value of all peoples—regardless of their race, a credo predicated entirely on the basis of inner character over outer pigment. That chance meeting added to Doyle's tenacity when he stood up for his own religious and political beliefs. If he were to seek change in his time, he would have to be brave enough to speak up and to *write* about it—even if doing so left him vulnerable to attacks by his opponents. For the remainder of his life, Doyle would be a vociferous spokesman for Spiritualism, Britain's military campaigns, and groundbreaking public health measures—but a key catalyst of his fortitude and integrity came upon the open sea through those eye-opening talks with John Henry Smyth.

CHAPTER 5

Doyle and Medicine
Writing Prescriptions and Prose

Having already proven himself a talented and prodigious writer by his mid-twenties, it should come as no surprise that Arthur Conan Doyle continued to hone his writing techniques while also trying to establish a successful medical practice for himself. While the first of his stories, "The Mystery of Sasassa Valley" was being published—albeit anonymously—he was busy submitting original scholarly articles to the prestigious publications *The Lancet* and *The British Medical Journal*. And these were not mere fictional tales—they included case studies, self-experimentations, and various other types of groundbreaking research. Indeed, Doyle continued to dichotomize this natural gift for the rest of his life. At one moment, he might entertain the world with rich historical fiction and unique mystery thrillers—at the next, his name (followed by the professional letters "MD") might be found at the end of an editorial column in which he challenged anyone who dared not share his views on the day's public health issues and policies, current medical advances and conflicts, and political opinions or controversial stances.

Without question, Doyle was always strongly qualified to voice any number of opinions. After all, he was a highly trained doctor who had graduated from one of the world's finest medical schools. Moreover, he was not about to allow any ill-educated, ill-informed, or uncredentialed members of *his* community or country to endanger the health and welfare of his fellow citizens—no matter what the potential cost to him might be. In particular, it was his written views on such urgent health matters as vaccination, water contaminants, and even the spurious nature of a newly presented remedy for tuberculosis that helped set the stage for Sir Arthur Conan Doyle's worldwide success—not just as a top writer of detective fiction, but also as a strong and sometimes volcanic force that sought to empower all manner of growth and transformation in his world.

The year 2020 will be etched permanently in our collective memory as the time when Coronavirus-19 (COVID) was set loose across the four corners of the Earth. No group was immune from this scourge, which wreaked its most severe damage on the middle-aged, elderly, and the infirm. Research scientists around the world were confronted with the herculean task of finding an accelerated and accurate method that would stop the merciless virus in its tracks. By the end of 2020, Pfizer, AstraZeneca, Moderna, Johnson & Johnson—along with several other pharmaceutical companies—offered hope to humanity in the form of injectable vaccines. Not unexpectedly, anti-vaccination groups sprang up immediately and used social media websites as their main vehicle for steering people away from receiving "the jab."

A scenario like the one surrounding COVID—where a deadly disease caused by a virus was met with the discovery of a vaccine to counter it—took place back in 1796. This happened to be a landmark year for the field of medicine—an English country doctor named Edward Jenner extracted fluid from the blister of a young dairymaid whose skin was covered by the relatively innocuous cowpox virus, and dripped some of the fluid directly onto the skin of an eight-year-old child named James Phipps. Although only a single "pox" developed at the inoculation site, the young boy became the first person in history to be immunized and protected against *smallpox*, one of the most lethal diseases to have ever ravaged mankind. Despite Jenner's dauntless analytical nature, almost 200 more years would pass before smallpox would be eradicated through efforts made by the World Health Organization (WHO) in 1977. In an echo of the controversy that still surrounds immunizations, Jenner's vaccine saw its fair share of devoted proponents locked in battle with its staunch opponents. Among Jenner's detractors was Benjamin Moseley, a physician considered to be the world's first anti-vaccinationist. Dr. Moseley launched his campaign against vaccines by expressing his concern that they might have long-term untoward and unpredictable effects, and he sternly warned parents to protect their children from "becoming victims to an experiment." Several other noted physicians soon joined his campaign, and it was not long before anti-vaccination sentiments were written on placards and pamphlets throughout Great Britain. When several communities in the counties of Leicester and Gloucester refused to allow their residents to be inoculated against smallpox, they placed the entire country at risk. However, Jenner's side ultimately prevailed and in 1853, the Vaccination Act—which made it mandatory for all children under four months of age to receive the smallpox vaccine—became law. Any parent who refused to inoculate a child would face harsh financial penalties—and as money was often scarce, most families caved under the pressure of this Parliamentary decree. Yet there remained those who disputed the importance of the smallpox vaccination—a stance that often resulted in more harm than good for the people of Britain.

Over time, the Vaccination Act proved unable to silence the opponents of vaccines who viewed them as "potentially harmful." Those who objected used the press as their vehicle for making their opinions known to the public. In 1887, Lieutenant-Colonel Alfred Tritton Wintle of Southsea made front-page news when he refused to inoculate his own child against smallpox. Asserting that "vaccination meant the introduction of a poison into the system," Wintle told a public vaccination officer that "he and his wife had abstained from eating flesh, fish, fowl, or salt, and from drinking intoxicants for a number of years, and that as the child's blood was pure they did not intend to have it made impure by inoculation." Wintle was summoned to court for his violation of the law and was ordered to pay a hefty fine. In the courtroom, Wintle launched a verbal tirade against Magistrate Bouhant-Carter, accusing him of "administering the law, but not justice." Steadfast in his refusal to pay the fine, Wintle informed the judge that "he would rather go to prison." Once Doyle—still a solo practitioner residing in the Portsmouth suburb of Southsea—had read the details of the case, he took up his pen and proceeded to excoriate Wintle in the pages of the Portsmouth periodical *The Evening Mail*:

> "Sir, — From time to time some champion of the party which is opposed to vaccination comes forward to air his views in the public Press, but these periodical sallies seldom lead to any discussion, as the inherent weakness of their position renders a reply superfluous.

When, however, a gentleman of Colonel Wintle's position makes an attack upon what is commonly considered by those most competent to judge to be one of the greatest victories ever won by science over disease, it is high time that some voice should be raised upon the other side. Hobbies and fads are harmless things as a rule, but when a hobby takes the form of encouraging ignorant people to neglect sanitary precautions and to live in a fool's paradise until bitter experience teaches them their mistake, it becomes a positive danger to the community at large. The interests at stake are so vital that an enormous responsibility rests with the men whose notion of progress is to revert to the condition of things which existed in the dark ages before the dawn of medical science."

In his editorial, Doyle opens his argument by refusing to acknowledge the protestations made by anyone with the audacity to put forth public opinions without being properly credentialed. Although he claims not to be offended by these untrained propagandists, he certainly pulls no punches in his attack on Wintle, who he accuses of encouraging "ignorant people to neglect sanitary precautions"—and who, by so doing, further endangered "the community at large."

Doyle then offers his own synopsis of Wintle's platform. Classifying Wintle's first proposition as "immorality" and the second as "positive harmfulness," he goes on to attack Wintle's ethics by posing the following hypothetical questions:

"Is it immoral for a Government to adopt a method of procedure which experience has proved and science has testified to conduce to the health and increased longevity of the population?"

and

"Would it be immoral to give Colonel Wintle a push in order to save him from being run over by a locomotive?"

Doyle answers his own questions sardonically within the article by asking his readers, "If all these are really immoral, I trust and pray that we may never attain morality." Doyle then addresses Wintle's concerns about the efficacy of vaccines by reminding readers that the smallpox vaccination . . .

"has been before the public for nearly a hundred years, during which time it has been thrashed out periodically in learned societies, argued over in medical journals, examined by statisticians, sifted and tested in every conceivable method, and the result of it all is that among those who are brought in practical contact with disease, there is a unanimity upon the point which is more complete than upon any other medical subject."

Doyle, in a paraphrase of his literary hero (and notable British historian) Thomas Babington Macaulay, reminds his audience that, "The ravages made by smallpox in the days of our ancestors can hardly be realised by the present sanitary and well-vaccinated generation. Macaulay remarks that in the advertisements of the early Georgian era there is hardly ever a missing relative who is not described as 'having pock marks upon his face.'" He also warns his readers that "whole tracts of country were decimated" and points out that, because of the adoption of the smallpox vaccine, "there is many a general practitioner who lives and dies without having ever seen a case." And once again, Doyle poses another rhetorical question: "What is the cause of this amazing difference?" In a direct address aimed at the entire anti-vaccinationist community, he attempts to make them aware that their ". . . endeavour to account for the wonderful decrease of smallpox by supposing that there has been some change in the type of the disease . . ." is ". . . pure assumption, and the facts seem to point in the other direction."

In reference to a then-recent smallpox outbreak in Portsmouth, Doyle places the blame squarely on the "congenial uninoculated population upon which to fasten," and challenges Colonel Wintle's contention that the vaccine results in more harm than good. Doyle puts down this argument in no uncertain terms, stating, "they are to a very large extent imaginary. Of course there are some unhealthy children, the offspring of unhealthy parents, who will fester and go wrong if they are pricked with a pin. It is possible that the district visitors appealed to may find out some such case. They are certainly rare, for in a tolerably large experience (five years in a large hospital, three in a busy practice in Birmingham, and nearly six down here) I have only seen one case, and it soon got well." And just as in today's society, where vaccines are often blamed by parents and special interest groups as agents for inflicting harm on their children, Doyle repudiates the arguments of the anti-vaccination stalwarts with utter disdain—"Some parents have an amusing habit of ascribing anything which happens to their children, from the whooping-cough to a broken leg, to the effects of their vaccination. It is from this class that the anti-vaccinationist party is largely recruited"—before he concludes with the following:

> "I would say that the subject is of such importance, ancestors call and our present immunity from smallpox so striking, that it would take a very strong case to justify a change. As long as that case is so weak as to need the argument of morality to enforce it I think that the Vaccination Acts are in no great danger of being repealed."

Doyle's vivid description of his era's anti-vaccinationists parallels many of our own contemporary descriptions of the anti-vaxxer lobby. Unlike the late 19th century, where the editorial staff of newspapers and magazines had the final word on what was published, our modern-age social media platforms allow individuals to instantaneously spread fake news on a global scale. These false assertions can have devastating effects, especially when these harmful "pseudo-scientific posts" go unchecked in their fabricated claims that vaccinations contain deadly toxins or—even worse—implanted microchips.

Wintle, who was not won over by Doyle's words, sent a rebuttal to the local newspaper. Doyle read Wintle's response carefully and, having analyzed it, proceeded to pounce on the Colonel a second time:

> "Sir, — Colonel Wintle's second letter appears to me to contain a Jumble of statistics and quotations, some of which do not affect the question at all, while others tell dead against the cause which he is championing."

Doyle then explains that a diminution of pockmarked faces would have been expected to have occurred from 1815 to 1835, and that it is not a "mere coincidence" as Wintle suggests. Doyle then challenges the legitimacy of Wintle's thesis that England still suffered from occasional epidemics of smallpox, an implication that the system of vaccination had been unsuccessful. Doyle argues:

> "The most clinching argument in its favour is furnished by these very epidemics, for when their results come to be tabulated they show with startling clearness the difference in the mortality between those

who have and have not been vaccinated. The unvaccinated not only contract the disease more readily, but it attacks them in a far more virulent form."

He goes on to say that Colonel Wintle was under the false impression "that London and Liverpool are more afflicted by smallpox than any other towns and deduces from that an argument against vaccination"—but Doyle, with the gentle touch of a master logician, points out rightly that "[A] public vaccinator cannot eliminate smallpox in a large port with a constant influx of foreigners and seamen." As he did in his initial article, Doyle addresses the concerns of those who thought of vaccines as being poisons:

"Of course it is a poison. So is opium, digitalis, and arsenic, though they are three of the most valuable drugs in the pharmacopoeia. The whole science of medicine is by the use of a mild poison to counteract a deadly one. The virus of rabies is a poison, but Pasteur has managed to turn it to account in the treatment of hydrophobia."

Doyle then masterfully sums up this second article as follows:

" . . . there is no reason why Colonel Wintle should not hold his own private opinion upon the matter. But he undertakes a vast responsibility when, in the face of the overwhelming testimony of those who are brought most closely into contact with disease, he incites others, through the public press, to follow the same course and take their chance of infection in defiance of hospital statistics. Only the possession of an extremely strong case can justify a man in opposing medical men upon a medical point, and this is of all points the one which should be most cautiously approached, as the welfare of the whole community is at stake . . . The tendency of the scientific world, if we may judge from the work not only of Pasteur and Koch, but also of Burdon-Sanderson, Toussaint, and others, lies more and more in the direction of preventive methods of inoculation to check zymotic disease. In opposing that tendency Colonel Wintle, however much he may persuade himself to the contrary, is really opposing progress and lending himself to the propagation of error."

Doyle then encourages those readers who wish to learn more about the practice of vaccines to pick up "The Facts about Vaccination, published by the National Health Society, 44, Berners-street, London."

Doyle was unafraid to publicly champion his nation's legal mandate—that everyone should receive the smallpox vaccination. He was quite willing to place himself in the line of fire, using the power of his pen to convince those who might encounter a loudly squawking anti-vaxxer not to fall prey to their distortions and overall wrongheadedness. Doyle, a graduate of one of the world's most prestigious medical schools, had already provided hands-on care to people suffering from a wide array of illnesses. He acknowledged that not every affliction was treatable but added that he was unwilling to simply stand by and allow children or adults to succumb to any diseases—or equally harmful anti-science bunk—that were so easily preventable, and yet so markedly disputed. This would not be the only time Doyle would lend his influence and reputation to causes designed to increase the public's awareness of significant health issues.

On the eve of the twentieth century, Great Britain decided to go to war against the Boer republics in Southern Africa. Doyle, who had just turned forty years old, had stepped away from medicine almost a decade earlier in 1891 and had also retired (or, more accurately, killed off in 1893) his most famous character, Sherlock Holmes. By the time the Boer campaign officially commenced on October 11, 1899, Doyle was a household name around the world. Despite his age and global fame, Doyle volunteered his services to provide medical care for the ill and wounded soldiers of Her Majesty's Army. On February 28, 1900, Doyle sailed aboard the S.S. *Oriental* from the Essex, England town of Tilbury to the South African legislative capital of Cape Town. From there, he made his way to Langman Hospital in South Africa's judicial capital of Bloemfontein.

Within a day of his arrival on April 2, the local waterworks came under control of the Boers, the descendants of South Africa's original Dutch settlers. Soon after, British troops, who had no choice other than to drink water from contaminated local wells, soon became the victims of a deadly outbreak of typhoid fever. Doyle, quoted at the time by artist and writer Mortimer Menpes of *The Illustrated London News*, wrote that he was "'bound to work night and day'" taking care of the "'tremendous incursion of patients'" who were gravely ill with diarrhea and dehydration.

Luckily, Doyle had agreed before setting foot on South African soil to be inoculated against typhoid and therefore had the vigor to play "'football with zest and activity of a boy.'" Unfortunately, most British soldiers refused the vaccine. Doyle had a deep knowledge of waterborne diseases and their prevention. His former medical partner and friend, George T. Budd, was the son of William Budd, the physician who determined that diseases like cholera and typhoid were contagious in nature and could be spread via contaminated water. It was his research that became the basis for water filtration systems around the world. Furthermore, Doyle's childhood friend William K. Burton brought Budd's principles of contagious disease with him to Japan—where Burton engineered the state-of-the-art water filtration systems that put an end to that nation's deadly and continually repeated cholera epidemics. Burton's magnificent work enabled Japan to officially usher in the modern age on its own soil.

Perhaps Doyle should have given any one of his contemporaries who refused "the jab" a copy of his first Holmes story as required reading. Found in the third paragraph of *A Study in Scarlet* (1887) is Doyle's apt description of the plight of Holmes' trusted partner and colleague, Dr. John H. Watson, who—after completing his mandatory army field training at Netley—sailed to India and was then immediately reassigned to Afghanistan. Although he was shot in the shoulder—or perhaps his leg, as that is not made clear in Watson's own telling of the incident—the wound he sustained was *not* the event that brought a premature end to his professional military career. Watson tells us what followed in the aftermath of his battle wound:

> "Here I rallied, and had already improved so far as to be able to walk about the wards, [lending weight to the leg being the wounded extremity], and even to bask a little upon the verandah, when I was struck down by enteric fever, that curse of our Indian possessions. For months my life was despaired of, and when at last I came to myself and became convalescent, I was so weak and emaciated that a medical board determined that not a day should be lost in sending me back to England."

So, it was not a bullet that "struck down" Watson, but rather an insidious infection caused by a microscopic organism that was not yet preventable by immunization in his time. Had poor Watson served in the Anglo-Boer War instead, he would have found himself in quite a different situation.

For weeks on end, Doyle "lived in the midst of death—and death in its vilest, filthiest form," and sent off a letter to *The British Medical Journal* based on his personal observations, in which he tells its editorial board the following:

> "[T]here are three classes, as it seems to me, who have put in more solid and unremitting toil than any others. They are the commissariat, the railway men, and the medical orderlies. Of the three, the first two are the most essential, since the war cannot proceed without food and without railways. But the third is the most laborious, and infinitely the most dangerous."

Doyle goes on to declare ". . . the outbreak of enteric among the troops in South Africa . . ." as ". . . a calamity the magnitude of which had not been foreseen, and which even now is imperfectly appreciated." He then informs them "that in one month there were from 10,000 to 12,000 men down with this, the most debilitating and lingering of continued fevers. I know that in one month 600 men were laid in the Bloemfontein Cemetery. A single day in this one town saw 40 deaths." First, he praises the "efforts of the medical men and by the devotion of the orderlies." Although short-staffed, Doyle explains how each man has worked four times harder. Some orderlies, as Doyle observes, "were on duty for thirty-six hours in forty-eight, and what their duties were—how sordid and obscene—let those who have been through such an epidemic tell."

Doyle then points out the following key point on the topic:

> "[O]ne mistake which we have made, and it is one which will not, I think, be repeated in any subsequent campaign. Inoculation for enteric was not made compulsory. If it had been so I believe that we should (and, what is more important, the army would) have escaped from most of its troubles. No doubt the matter will be fully threshed out in statistics, but our strong impression, from our own experience, is that although it is by no means an absolute preventive it certainly modifies the course of the disease very materially. We have had no death yet (absit omen) from among the inoculated, and more than once we have diagnosed the inoculation from the temperature chart before being informed of it. Of our own personnel only one inoculated man has had it, and his case was certainly modified very favourably by the inoculation."

Here again, Doyle is a proponent of compulsory vaccinations. He was certain that if all soldiers received the typhoid (*enteric*) vaccine—one that the British military had available for its troops in 1899—there would have been considerably less morbidity and mortality, less loss of manpower, and—of course—a better military outcome.

If we set aside the brilliance of Doyle's article, he overlooks some of the differences between the century-tested smallpox vaccine and the embryonic state of the relatively new typhoid vaccine. Although the drawbacks associated with the smallpox vaccine were well-documented and known by then to the public at large, the potential safety, efficacy, and side effects of the typhoid vaccine were not well established. Doyle knowingly concealed the fact that it had taken him two days to recover after his typhoid inoculation, and that there were multiple strains of typhoid (caused by the bacterium *Salmonella Typhi*) and paratyphoid (caused by the bacterium *Salmonella Paratyphi*) disease that might be unaffected by the vaccine. Another problem that dogged the vaccine was that its therapeutic action was diminished considerably when it was exposed to heat—this became especially apparent when it was shipped, with long travel times, to the opposite side of the globe. Nevertheless, Doyle's writing was effective in focusing the public's attention on the methodology adopted to treat and prevent diseases—and it was this skill at writing that secured his standing on the highest rung of the medical profession's ladder.

Those same public health issues that Doyle encountered at the dawn of the twentieth century confront us once again in the twenty-first century. The COVID-19 vaccination was developed—and then approved—for emergency use in the US by the Centers for Disease Control and Prevention (CDC) and the Food and Drug Administration (FDA), despite scientists not knowing all its potential side effects. Western medicine must also deal with multiple evolving variants of COVID-19, some of which may prove to be resistant to the vaccines currently available to us. Additionally, the difficulty of properly storing certain brands of Covid vaccines—some of which presently require extremely cold temperatures—means that their overall effectiveness can be compromised. And as was the case when Doyle was vaccinated against typhoid, there is a small portion of the population that experiences moderate to severe after-effects from the COVID-19 vaccine. Nevertheless, Dr. Doyle—a *true* master of public health—put society above self by rolling up his sleeve and getting the vaccine. In addition, he soon afterward helped push to make vaccinations compulsory for the brave British troops serving in the South African campaign, which would help shield them from the invisible arrows of disease.

Although Doyle's outstanding work as an advocate for mandatory smallpox and cholera vaccination is to be commended, this was by no means his biggest "breaking news" public health and medical story. *That* article would be published in the years when Doyle was still living in Southsea, all the while finely honing his Holmes and Watson characters. Months after the publication of his first Holmes adventure in 1887, Doyle felt compelled to act on some free advice given to him after he graduated medical school by none other than George Budd: "There's a fortune in the eye. A man grudges a half-crown to cure his chest or his throat, but he'd spend his last dollar over his eye. There's money in ears, but the eye is a gold mine." Doyle phased out his general practice and switched to a more specialized career in the emerging field of ophthalmology. He was able to gain an apprenticeship under the aegis of Dr. Arthur Vernon Ford. Ford served as an attending physician at the Portsmouth and South Hants Eye and Ear Infirmary. He, in turn, introduced Doyle to Dr. John Ward Cousins, "senior surgeon to the Eye and Ear Infirmary," who had been "instrumental in founding the Portsmouth and South Hants Eye and Ear Infirmary." Soon, Doyle was then assisting Dr. Cousins in analyzing his data regarding his innovative treatment for perforated eardrums. It wasn't long before Doyle had become so proficient in the art of optical refraction that he swiftly gained a sterling reputation for his ability to properly evaluate and treat those of his patients diagnosed with an astigmatism.

Doyle found himself squarely in the right place at the right time. By the late 1880s, the field of ophthalmology was advancing rapidly—much of it due to Vienna ophthalmologist Carl Koller's revolutionary discovery that the drug cocaine can act as an eye anesthetic. Operations that had once been considered impossible to perform were now deemed child's play for skilled eye surgeons, all due to the "magical powers" of this newly isolated stimulant. Dr. Ford was quick to jump on the cocaine bandwagon—while he served as Doyle's preceptor, Ford published a review article of 150 cases of one specific type of eye surgery, a testimony to the volume of patients who had passed through his clinic. Concurrently, Ford developed a groundbreaking surgical technique that could replace opaque vitreous fluid (which fills the eye itself) with vision-enhancing clear vitreous fluid. Ford also authored a training manual pamphlet for eye surgeons—likely written with Doyle's uncredited assistance—entitled *Ophthalmic Notes*. There is no doubt that Doyle would have been preparing seven-percent solutions of cocaine—the medically appropriate concentration for use during an eye surgery—to be injected into Dr. Ford's patients through use of a hypodermic needle, which was stored by most physicians in a smooth leather morocco case.

At the same time that he was studying the eye under Dr. Ford's tutelage, Doyle was finishing up a historical novel to be named *Micah Clarke* (published in 1889). Once he had completed this lengthy book, he sent a letter to his sister Lottie that revealed what he envisioned his life would become should his self-proclaimed "masterpiece" be published by Blackwood Press:

> "{We} may then, I think, take it as proven that I can live by my pen. We should have a few hundreds in hand to start us. The next step would be to quietly sell the practice. For this I might get two or three hundred. I should then store the bedroom & drawing room furniture with Mrs Hawkins, sell the balance, possibly to the buyer of the practice, and so be off. I should go to London and study the eye. I should then go to Berlin and study the eye. I should then go to Vienna & study the eye . . . Having learned <u>all</u> there is to know about the eye I should come back to London and start as an eye surgeon . . . ."

When *Micah Clarke* was finally accepted for publication by Blackwood, Doyle did exactly what he had promised he would. In January 1891, he traveled to Vienna and attended a series of ophthalmology lectures at Krankenhaus Hospital. Soon after, he traveled by train to Paris where he completed his formal training. London would be his next stop—soon after settling down, Doyle opened a practice dedicated solely to ophthalmology on Upper Wimpole Street. Nonetheless, and despite his cutting-edge training, he found himself unable to compete with the firmly rooted and established eye physicians whose offices lined the nearby Harley Street. Within a few months, Doyle had no other option but to close the doors to his failed practice.

Still, he continued to write—and by the time of the publication of second Holmes tale, *The Sign of the Four* (1890), Doyle was ready to introduce readers to a Sherlock Holmes who occasionally partook of cocaine. Here, Doyle literally injected a portion of his own real-life medical training directly into the body of his fictional detective story. Moreover, he transforms this use of cocaine into a vice that his detective is unable to shed throughout the entirety of the Holmes canon. Doyle seems to have deprived his Dr. Watson character of important medical knowledge he should have possessed and which Doyle, himself, *did* have.

Having been portrayed as a former British Army medic, Watson should have had at least some limited knowledge—and exposure—to cocaine. Further, his statements regarding the properties of the narcotic seem shockingly ill-informed. In "A Scandal in Bohemia" (1891), Watson's direct-address narration explains to the reader that Holmes would frequently alternate "from week to week between cocaine and ambition, the *drowsiness of the drug*, and the fierce energy of his own keen nature." *[emphasis added]* Watson fails to realize that cocaine is a *stimulant*, not a sleep-inducing narcotic. In *The Sign of the Four* (1891), when Watson asks his roommate, "'Which is it to-day? . . . morphine or cocaine?,'" Holmes "raised his eyes languidly" and replies, "'It is cocaine.'" When Holmes raises his eyes in this lethargic-like manner, it makes no medical sense—after all, cocaine would produce a euphoric state, not one more likely to bring on sleepiness. In this scenario, Holmes was using the easily obtainable depressant morphine—and not cocaine—at that time, which begs the question as to why Holmes would have purposely lied to Watson. There is a strong possibility that Holmes was testing his partner's medical acumen—and Watson, by failing to spot Sherlock's trickery, failed the exam.

Doubtlessly, Doyle's thorough training in ophthalmology helped make his stories infinitely more colorful. In "The Adventure of the *Gloria Scott*" (1893), the evil sailor Mr. Hudson is described by Victor Trevor, Jr. as having "'two venomous eyes which uttered more threats than his tongue could do.'" In "The Adventure of the Speckled Band" (1892), Doyle intimates that the "fierce old bird of prey" Dr. Grimesby Roylott's "bile-shot eyes" can be traced to the man's chronic consumption of alcohol. Again, in "The Adventure of the Crooked Man" (1893), "yellow-shot, bilious eyes" are a feature of "'Mr. Henry Wood, late of India'"—and in "The Adventure of the Greek Interpreter" from that same year, Mr. Melas and Paul Kratidis are correctly described as having "swollen, congested faces and protruding eyes" after breathing in poisonous charcoal-gas (carbon monoxide). In

"The Adventure of the Empty House" (published a decade later in 1903), Watson pays particular attention to Colonel Sebastian Moran's "cruel blue . . . savage eyes" with their "drooping, cynical lids." By the conclusion of "The Adventure of the Dancing Men" (also published in 1903), it is Holmes who figures out that "'Mr. Hilton Cubitt, of Ridling Thorpe Manor, Norfolk'" lives out in the country, "far from the fogs of Baker Street" merely by gazing at his "clear eyes and florid cheeks." In the 1904 Holmes short story "The Adventure of Black Peter," Mrs. Peter Carey's "red-rimmed eyes, told of the years of hardship and ill-usage which she had endured." It is precisely these kinds of descriptive embellishments, strewn throughout the Holmes tales, that continue to enhance for readers just how vivid a picture of his characters Doyle remains—through the magic of *writing*—forever able to present.

Aside from the imaginative vision that continues to reside at the heart of his fiction, Doyle peppered throughout the Holmes stories even more details from his chosen field of ophthalmology. In "The Adventure of the Golden Pince-Nez" (1904), Doyle's knowledge of how to correctly fit spectacles is showcased. Holmes, having scrutinized "'a pair of glasses,'" states unequivocally "'that they belong to a woman . . . of refinement,'" adding that this female character had to have been "'well dressed'" as the glasses were "'handsomely mounted in solid gold.'" After analyzing its clips, Holmes states authoritatively "'that the lady's nose was very broad at the base'" and, of course, would have been "'a short and coarse one.'" After trying on these same spectacles, Holmes immediately infers that her "'eyes are set very near to the sides of the nose.'" Then, after examining the lenses themselves, Holmes states "'that the glasses are concave and of unusual strength. A lady whose vision has been so extremely contracted all her life is sure to have the physical characteristics of such vision, which are seen in the forehead, the eyelids, and the shoulders.'" Only someone with a combination of a vast knowledge of optometry and keen observational powers could have offered such a technical, yet pragmatic, description of a short-sighted person.

Doyle's profound medical knowledge—presented perfectly through the character of Sherlock Holmes—shines in the limelight once again in 1891's "A Case of Identity." Upon being introduced to a prospective client named Miss Mary Sutherland, Holmes immediately picks up on her short-sightedness and is audacious enough to suggest that she quit her job as a typist. Later in the story, Holmes states that Miss Sutherland's step-uncle has continued to take advantage of her affliction by disguising himself as a suitor, secure in the knowledge that her myopia will prevent her from seeing through the ruse. These, along with so many other fine details found in the Holmes adventures, would be nowhere near as rich and scrupulous in detail had Doyle been trained as a mere barber—or, for that matter, a butcher.

For any proper English gentleman in the Regency or Victorian or Edwardian eras, club membership was very much considered the thing to do. Although most clubs were open to members of the middle and upper classes, a few of them—housed chiefly on London's St. James and Pall Mall streets—restricted themselves to inviting only those gentry known to be extraordinarily wealthy or famous . . . or *both*. Although Doyle knew the workings of the exclusive Marlborough, Junior Carlton, and Regent Clubs, it was the Athenaeum—founded by and for men of science, literature, and art—whose intricacies he understood best. Indeed, his celebrated uncle Richard had suffered his fatal stroke as he regaled his fellow members within its hallowed walls. Soon after Doyle had achieved his initial fame, he immediately applied for—and received—membership to that same club. Now, when he sat down to write his Holmes tales, a template was available to him that allowed him to create in his literature a bevy of realistic and plausible organizations like the Tankerville, Cavendish, Anglo-Indian, and Bagatelle Card Clubs. Even Mycroft, Holmes' enigmatic brother, was a charter member of the "'queerest club in Britain,'" the Diogenes—where "'the most unsociable and unclubable men'" in London gathered. And, of course, when Doyle attained celebrity status, he was soon recruited by some of London's most prestigious organizations. "Our Society" was among those that Doyle joined, and membership in this secretive organization was soon to become the most highly sought-after of them all. The proceedings of their meetings were kept "top secret," and its strictly enforced code of silence added an extra layer of mystique to what contemporary reportage referred to as the "Murder Club." Nevertheless, there were those few occasions when its members regarded it as their unofficial obligation to share their opinions with the public. In those instances, certain members were asked to write cogent letters to the press to stir up sentiment for their "just" cause.

One of these causes was in support of a twenty-seven-year-old Farsi solicitor named George Edalji, who had been paroled—but not pardoned—after serving almost half of a seven-year sentence for horse, cattle, and sheep maiming. As his guilty verdict had not been officially overturned, Edalji remained prohibited from returning to his law practice. The Murder Club, having reviewed and analyzed his case in 1906, concluded that Edalji had been wrongfully convicted. Its members selected Doyle—by then with the added appellation of "Sir" in his name, after having been knighted in 1902—and literary critic John Churton Collins to initiate a letter-writing campaign designed to exonerate Edalji and, in the process, to bring about the establishment of a British Court of Appeals.

Doyle invited Edalji to meet him at a hotel in Birmingham where he was staying. When "former" ophthalmologist Doyle arrived there, he determined immediately that Edalji was myopic by the way he read his morning newspaper. When Edalji recounted the events of the night in question, he told Doyle he had not been wearing his prescription glasses that evening. Doyle later wrote in his 1907 article "The Case of Mr. George Edalji" that this revelation was "enough in itself to convince me both of the extreme improbability of his being guilty of the crime for which he was condemned, and to suggest some at least of the reasons which had led to his being suspected."

The following letter to the press, although attributed solely to Collins, was co-written with Doyle:

> "We are to assume that Mr. Edalji—this myope of six dioptres—found his way along a colliery tramway littered with obstacles at every step; crossed the main line of the L. and N.W. railway with its signal wires and fencings, over low rows of metals and sidings, points and sleepers; descended a steep flight of steps under an archway, made his way into the field, groping about till he found the pony; that he then—for this is what the police alleged—returned by another and equally difficult route over open country, where there were no paths of any kind, and where he would have to cross three or four ditches and find his way through several gaps in hedges . . . Now, let us picture to ourselves what must have been the state of his clothes on his arrival home after such an expedition, on such a night, and compare that to the actual condition of the clothes examined by the police about eight o'clock on the same morning."

Less than a year later, Great Britain's Committee of Inquiry ruled in Edalji's favor, having been won over by the inspired words of Doyle and Collins. A simultaneous push for a national Court of Criminal Appeal also gained momentum as a direct result of these two men's joint actions and statements. Their success spawned an entirely new layer of potential justice and mercy that, up until that moment, had been conspicuously absent from the English judicial system. Ironically, the creation of such a court would certainly have represented a devastating blow to Sherlock Holmes' ego, as it was the great detective himself who had boasted to Watson in *The Sign of the Four*, "'I am the last and highest court of appeal in detection.'"

As presented by Doyle in the first Holmes story *A Study in Scarlet*, Watson has never witnessed his roommate's use of cocaine during any lulls in his caseload. Watson's lack of knowledge about his partner's habit—that of injecting a seven-percent solution of the drug—is not at all due to Holmes hiding it; rather, it is because Doyle didn't impart Holmes with this potentially fatal character flaw at this juncture. However, when Doyle gave us the second Holmes tale, *The Sign of the Four*, he not only crafted a brilliant detective story, but one that also paid silent tribute to one of his favorite hometown authors, Robert Louis Stevenson. He made sure to create a scene in which Holmes stands at the entrance doors of Lyceum Theatre on a certain "September evening" in 1888. Two rather interesting things were happening around that time in the real world of London—the city was still reeling from the grisly "Jack the Ripper" murders committed there a month before, and the Lyceum Theatre had up on its marquee the title "Dr. Jekyll and Mr. Hyde." It just so happens that a play with that title—written by American novelist Thomas Russell Sullivan and based, of course, on Stevenson's world-famous Gothic novella published two years before—was being staged at the Lyceum. Stevenson's iconic tale concerns itself with a character named Dr. Henry Jekyll who, to firmly rid himself of the evil side of his personality, concocts a potion that transforms him into a hideous (and often violent) beast of a man named Mr. Edward Hyde. Eventually, Dr. Jekyll finds himself subdued and supplanted by his diabolical other half.

In *The Sign of the Four*, Doyle took Stevenson's theme of dual natures and weaved it directly into the Holmes persona. We first see this when Watson issues the following caveat to his drug-using partner:

> "'Count the cost! Your brain may, as you say, be roused and excited, but it is a *pathological and morbid process*, which involves increased tissue-change, and may at last leave a *permanent weakness*. You know, too, what a *black reaction comes upon you*. Surely the game is hardly worth the candle. Why should you, for a mere passing pleasure, risk the loss of those great powers with which you have been endowed? Remember that I speak not only to you as one comrade to another, but as a medical man to one for whose constitution he is to some extent answerable.'" *[emphases added throughout]*

In Holmes' situation, cocaine is the pharmacologic agent that elicits what Doyle has Watson call a "'black reaction'"—one that can take away Holmes' "'great powers'" and can also cause him "'permanent weakness.'" Drawing a parallel to *Superman*, a comic book hero first introduced to the world in the late 1930s, it can be said that cocaine is a form of "Kryptonite" for Holmes. The great detective refuses to heed Watson's warnings, though, and continues to use the potentially harmful stimulant intermittently throughout the entire canon. Doyle imparts Holmes with one vice, akin to an Achilles Heel—and in doing so, he pays homage to Stevenson's leitmotif that every human being, no matter who he may be, has some semblance of a *split* personality. Holmes is no exception to this rule, although to have that aforementioned "'black reaction'" manifest itself, he must *voluntarily* pull out a syringe, draw up a seven-percent solution of cocaine, and inject it into his vein.

We should not, however, misinterpret Holmes' occasional use of cocaine as something that taints his character as one whose intellectual prowess is reliant on drugs. Certainly, Holmes would have the willpower to "kick" any undesired habit at any time he wished to do so. We believe that Doyle mentions cocaine because he wanted to let his readers in on what he had been doing in medical practice back in 1888—the year in which *The Sign of the Four* takes place. During this time in his own life, Doyle was about to enter an ophthalmology fellowship in Portsmouth, where the use of seven-percent solutions of cocaine—as we established earlier in this chapter—was standard operating procedure when examining the eye. So, when he sat down to write this story, it seems inescapable that

Doyle was acknowledging one of his favorite writers, a man he held in the highest esteem—the great Robert Louis Stevenson. And what better way for Doyle to evoke Stevenson's conflicted dual characters of Dr. Jekyll and Mr. Hyde than to transform his brilliant eagle-eyed detective into a weak myopic creature whenever he introduces that telltale dose of potion into his body?

Although Doyle was a firm advocate for the benefits of a well-reasoned public health policy, he was also a realist. Seated at the helm of a seldom-visited medical office, Doyle found himself burdened with bills that had to be paid and a young but growing family that had to be fed. Although the occasional royalties he received for his stories supplemented his meager income early on in his career as a physician, they were insufficient to afford him a comfortable lifestyle. Soon, he would be forced to reconsider the career he had chosen for himself.

A rather peculiar episode ensued during Doyle's ophthalmology fellowship, when he read an article which intimated that the noted German physician and clinical researcher Robert Koch—one of the founding fathers of modern bacteriology—was going to announce he had discovered a cure for tuberculosis (consumption). Doyle became determined to be in Berlin when that official announcement was made. The details of Koch's groundbreaking treatment were scheduled to be delivered by Koch's right-hand man, the equally acclaimed German surgeon Dr. Ernst von Bergmann, on November 16, 1890. It had been arranged that von Bergmann be put in charge of selecting those members of the medical community who were to be invited to the symposium. Obviously, the virtually unknown Dr. Doyle's name was absent from von Bergmann's short list of medical luminaries. With the start of the conference only two days away, the ever-resourceful Doyle concocted a scheme that—if it worked—would secure him an invitation to attend. The thirty-one-year-old physician boarded a train from his Portsmouth home and headed straight to London. Once there, he paid a visit to William T. Stead, the editor of the scholarly periodical *Review of Reviews*, in the hope of convincing him that it was imperative that he be provided with proper letters of introduction to those in charge of the upcoming conference. The stars must have been in perfect alignment that day, for unbeknownst to Doyle,

Stead was somewhat desperate to find someone with sufficient medical and literary credentials to write a "character sketch" of Koch that would appear in his publication. Doyle's credentials were suitable enough for the assignment at hand, and Stead was pleased to provide his freelance reporter with two letters of introduction—one for Sir Edward Malet (the British Ambassador to the German Empire) and the other for Mr. Lowes, the European correspondent to Britain's premier newspaper *The Times*.

Although he claimed later in his 1924 autobiography *Memories and Adventures* that he had no particular interest in or experience with tuberculosis, that statement is not entirely truthful. His personal letters reveal that his first love, Elmore Weldon, had been diagnosed with consumption a full seven years prior to this conference and that Doyle had been quite involved in her medical care. At that time, he had gone so far as to declare himself an expert on the diagnosis, treatment, and management of tuberculosis—in an 1882 letter to his mother, he had the audacity to cast aspersions on Elmore's doctors, essentially denigrating them with the following words:

> "I got a letter from her yesterday in which she says that the Doctor at Solliat examined her most thoroughly; and pronounced that she had never had consumption. Now of course that is nonsense, but it at least shows that the symptoms are pretty masked now."

Perhaps the sad fact that Elmore—now a married woman with two children—was wasting away served as Doyle's motivation for making the trip to the Continent. Doyle must have had at least a subconscious, if not conscious, desire to come back as Elmore's knight in shining armor. Instead, his excuse for this hasty decision was ascribed to a "great urge" to be in the auditorium when Koch's people revealed their *magic bullet*. Up until then, it had been referred to simply as "lymph"—but that would soon change.

Armed with the proper documentation that confirmed he was a literary representative of the *Review of Reviews*, Doyle traveled by rail to the Channel crossing; ferried over the English Channel to France; and then jumped onto the Continental Express headed toward Germany (a journey eerily reminiscent of the one Sherlock Holmes takes right before his *feigned* death at Reichenbach Falls in Doyle's 1893 short story "The Final Problem"). Once Doyle arrived in Berlin, he immediately tracked down Sir Malet, who promptly gave him "a chilly reception" and "dismissed [him] without help or consolation." The greeting he then received from *Times* correspondent Lowes mirrored Sir Malet's discourteous response.

Despite having "no clear reason" for his actions and still in need of an admission ticket, Doyle dashed over to the headquarters of the Free Surgical Association, only to be told that there were absolutely no seats available to anyone who lacked an official ticket. In a last-ditch effort, Doyle decided to pay Dr. Robert Koch a visit at his home in the hope of coaxing a personal invitation out of him. Doyle got there just in time to see Koch's "mail arrive—a large sack of letters, which was emptied out on the floor of the hall, and exhibited every sort of stamp in Europe." Doyle perceived this mail delivery to be "a sign of all the sad broken lives and wearied hearts which were turning in hope to Berlin." While Doyle's unannounced and unappreciated visit failed to earn him a ticket, he held steadfast in his unwillingness to accept "No" for an answer.

The next morning—as he would himself explain in his article for the *Review of Reviews*—Doyle went over to the lecture hall where he successfully bribed a porter to grant him access to the lobby. As a clear path into the auditorium was still far from guaranteed for him, Doyle once again resorted to bribery—but this time, he was stopped "at the gate" while "people streamed passed {sic}" him. Just when the lecture hall was nearly filled, Doyle noticed Dr. von Bergmann making his way into the lobby. As the German doctor approached, Doyle—in a last-ditch effort to get a seat inside the auditorium—literally "threw" himself "across his path" and confronted him with the plaintive phrase, "I have come 1000 miles. May I not come in?" Von Bergmann condescendingly retorted, "Perhaps you'd like to take my place. That is the only one vacant," and continued with, "The first two rows of my clinik are entirely taken up by Englishmen."

Doyle, managing to hold his temper in check, replied in a "polite manner" by saying, "I wouldn't intrude if there is no room." Already aware that von Bergmann was lying—the only English physicians in the audience that day were Malcolm Morris and John James Pringle—Doyle had no other option but to simply walk away. But Doyle's measured words, in contrast to von Bergmann's crass evasions, prompted a member of von

Bergmann's entourage—an empathetic American physician named Dr. Henry J. Hartz of Michigan—to go over to Doyle and agree that von Bergmann had been out of line. Dr. Hartz then invited Doyle to meet him at the lecture hall at four that afternoon so he could show him the "full notes of the lecture." Even more astonishingly, Dr. Hartz offered to escort Doyle to von Bergmann's private wards the following day so that he could observe Koch's patients at their bedsides and, after that, pay a visit to Koch's "public laboratory" in the Kloster Strasse, a famed Berlin research hospital. Doyle gladly took Dr. Hartz up on both of his gracious offers.

The next day, Doyle was shocked to observe in von Bergmann's wards "a long and grim array . . . of twisted joints, rotting bones, and foul ulcers of the skin, all more or less under the benign influence of the inoculation." Afterward, Hartz brought him over to Prenzlauer Strasse where the clinical wards of a "Dr. Levy" were located, as well as those of Dr. Heinrich Adolf von Bardeleben at the Charite Hospital. After he perused the medical records of all patients included in Koch's study, Doyle had "the temerity to disagree with everyone and to come to the conclusion that the whole thing was experimental and premature." It is a distinct possibility that Dr. Hartz, a newly credentialed physician from Detroit, felt it his duty to expose Koch's results as lacking validity—and decided to grant an exclusive to Doyle as a reporter, and not as a physician. It wasn't long before Koch's hyped-up "lymph" was revealed to be nothing more than a good screening test for tuberculosis—certainly not a *cure*.

In response to this incident, Doyle pronounced that "madness had seized the world" and dispatched a "word of warning" to *The Daily Telegraph*, thus making it the first publication to present an article "on the side of doubt and caution" about Koch's flawed "cure."

Doyle also made good on his promise to write an article for Mr. Stead, one that appeared in the *Review of Reviews* under the title of "Dr. Koch and His Cure."

In its first section, Doyle writes of his failed attempt to converse with Dr. Koch:

"To the Englishman in Berlin, and indeed to the German also, it is at present very much easier to see the bacillus of Koch, than to catch even the most fleeting glimpse of its illustrious discoverer. His name is on every lip, his utterances are the constant subject of conversation, but like the Veiled Prophet, he still remains unseen to any eyes save those of his own immediate coworkers and assistants. The stranger must content himself by looking up at the long grey walls of the Hygiene Museum in Kloister Strasse, knowing that somewhere within them the great mastermind is working, which is rapidly bringing under subjection those unruly tribes of deadly micro-organisms which are the last creatures in the organic world to submit the sway of man."

In the next section of the article "The Recluse of Kloster Strasse," Doyle describes Koch as a trinity of "a student, a worker, and a philosopher," whose laboratory is a place where "some fifty young men, including several Americans and Englishmen, are pursuing their studies in bacteriology. It is a large square chamber, well lit and lofty, with rows of microscopes bristling along the deal of tables which line it upon every side. Bunsen burners, reservoirs of distilled water, freezing machines for the cutting of microscopic sections, and every other conceivable aid to the bacteriological student, lie ready to his hand. Under glass protectors may be seen innumerable sections of potatoes with bright red, or blue, or black, smears upon their white surfaces where colonies of rare bacilli have been planted, whose growth is watched and recorded from day to day. All manner of fruits with the mould and fungi which live upon them, infusions of meat or of sugar pled with unseen millions, squares of gelatine which are the matrix in which innumerable forms of life are sprouting, all these indicate to the visitor the style of work upon which the students are engaged, and the methods by which they carry them out. Here, too, under the microscope may be seen the prepared slides which contain specimens of those bacilli of disease which have already been isolated." This elegantly and exquisitely detailed description provided irrefutable proof to his readers, and to Dr. Koch, that Doyle had indeed gained direct access to this top-secret laboratory.

Doyle's article also offers readers a biographical sketch of Koch's early days as a student of the world-renowned German anatomist Friedrich Gustav Jakob Henle. It was Dr. Henle who had convinced the younger Koch to pursue twin careers in practical medicine and clinical research. In words that echo those found in his thesis, Doyle stated that Koch willingly "settled down to the humdrum life of a country doctor. He was then twenty-nine years of age, strong and vigorous, with all his great powers striving for an outlet, even in the unpropitious surroundings in which he found himself. To him it must seem but yesterday that he drove his little cob and ramshackle provincial trap along the rough Posen roads to attend the rude peasants and rough farmers who centre round the village. Never, surely, could a man have found himself in a position less favourable for scientific research—poor, humble, unknown, isolated from sympathy and from the scientific appliances which are the necessary tools of the investigator."

Despite the disadvantages that were part and parcel of rural life, Koch had overcome them and put forth his four postulates that, in turn, transformed microbiology into a more exact science. It was Robert Koch who developed the revolutionary oil immersion method, which enabled microbiologists to magnify objects without having to change lenses. Koch also appreciated and promoted the importance of staining microorganisms so they could be properly identified. Doyle then discussed the nature of the rivalry that developed between Louis Pasteur and Koch among the boondocks of Wollstein. Only at the very end of his article does Doyle allude to how Koch had "finally abandoned his country practice" to become an assistant at the University of Bonn, where he had isolated the tuberculosis bacillus and the comma-shaped cholera bacillus.

The final section of the article describes how the premature announcement of Koch's work by the International Medical Conference "was unfortunate . . . for it aroused such immense interest, and gave rise to so many circumstantial but fictitious rumours as to the efficiency of his treatment, that he was compelled, in order to prevent widespread disappointment, to give his discovery to the public rather earlier than he would otherwise have done." In all likelihood, Doyle was probably trying his best to protect Koch from public humiliation when he wrote, "It must never be lost sight of that Koch has never claimed that his fluid kills the tubercle bacillus. On the contrary, it has no effect upon it, but destroys the low form of tissue in the meshes of which the bacilli lie."

Doyle goes on to tell his readers the following:

"The remedy by which Dr. Koch effects his cures is at present a secret. According to the rule of the profession, no cures wrought by secret remedie can ever be examined into. All dealers in secret remedies are quacks. But Dr. Koch, as far as the retention of the secret of his remedy goes, is as much a quack as Sequah or Count Mattei. The faculty, however, ignored this defiance of their rules, and have poured to Berlin in thousands to witness for themselves the actual results of Dr. Koch's experiments. This puts an end once and for all to the non possumus with which the profession have hitherto opposed all attempt to compel them to subject the cures wrought by secret and patent medicines to competent, patient, experimental examination."

Doyle concludes his article with a favorable opinion of Koch:

"Whatever may be the ultimate decision as to the system, there can be but one opinion as to the man himself. With the noble modest which is his characteristic, he has retired from every public demonstration; and with the candour of a true man of science his utterances are mostly directed to the pointing out of the weak points and flaws in his own system. If anyone is deceived upon the point it is assuredly not the fault of the discoverer. Associates say that he has aged years in the last six months, and that his lined face and dry yellow skin are the direct results of the germ-laden atmosphere in which he has so fearlessly lived. It may well be that the eyes of posterity, passing over the ninety-year-old warrior in Silesia, and the giant statesman in Pomerania, may fix their gaze upon the silent worker in the Kloster Strasse, as being the noblest German of them all."

In "The Voice of Science," a short story published immediately after his return from Berlin, Doyle offered these words of praise to Koch: "Specimens of the flora and fauna of the Philippine Islands, a ten-foot turtle carapace from the Gallapagos, the os frontis of the Bos montis as shot by Captain Charles Beesly in the Thibetan Himalayas, the bacillus of Koch cultivated on gelatine—these and a thousand other such trophies adorned the tables upon which the two ladies gazed that morning."

Doyle's brilliant, though somewhat unethical, detective work led him to properly deduce that Koch's "lymph" was not the panacea that he had promised the world. Alas, it was only a screening test. It is more than likely that Doyle had been secretly praying that Koch could deliver a miraculous antidote capable of saving the person who remained closest to his heart—his first love and near-fiancée, Elmore Weldon. Doyle's exposé left thousands upon thousands of consumption victims in despair. To this day, no magical potion for the eradication of tuberculosis has materialized—only with the recent advent of the QuantiFERON gold blood test has there been any meaningful improvement in accurately screening for this dreaded global disease.

Drawing upon his hard-earned inner strength, Doyle ensured that Sherlock Holmes would inherit his creator's cunning and risk-taking behaviors, along with his habit of dropping in on people unannounced. This triad of traits is found in the 1923 short story of "The Adventure of the Creeping Man" when Sherlock Holmes matches wits with Professor Presbury, a physiologist of "'European reputation'" who has been behaving rather strangely and decidedly out of character for several weeks. Trevor Bennett, Presbury's professional assistant, attributes the professor's personality change to the presence of a mysterious item housed in a box that happens to originate from Koch's homeland—*Germany*. To determine what is inside it, Holmes drops in on the Professor, claiming that "'he had given us an appointment upon such a date.'" Holmes is certain that the Professor will view this forgotten "'scheduled visit'" as being due to a simple "'lack of memory,'" and *also* assumes that Presbury will pretend to have remembered summoning him there.

However, that is not the case at all. For if Bennett had not intervened on Holmes' behalf, a skirmish would surely have followed that would have placed Holmes' life in jeopardy. This scenario bears an uncanny resemblance to the events that transpired when Doyle sought to gain admission to von Bergmann's lecture armed with Mr. Stead's letters of introduction. As the plot of this Holmes short story continues to unwind, we are informed that—in a desperate attempt to make himself more attractive to his young fiancée—Presbury has been injecting himself with a serum that transforms him into a superhuman creature. The intended purpose of this magical substance is to restore the vim and vigor of the recipient in a manner analogous to the restorative waters of the legendary Fountain of Youth. The properties of this fictional restorative agent resemble Koch's proposed "lymph" curative for tuberculosis—a disease that, as we have established, literally consumed the body of the victim.

The subplots in both "The Adventure of the Illustrious Client" (1924) and "The Adventure of the Retired Colourman" (1926)—wherein Holmes snoops around a private residence or office while its owner is out—can be interpreted as being based on Doyle's own extraordinary German adventure. At the very moment when Professors von Bergmann and Levy were delivering their lectures, Doyle was sneaking into their wards and clinics. Once he had gained access to them, he had no reservation about thumbing through all their assembled data—including their patients' charts and figures. This is how, and *why*, Doyle weaponized his articles on Koch's alleged lifesaver—a greater good hung in the balance, which justified the exposé he wrote that essentially shattered Koch's flawed hypothesis. There was a mystery to be solved, and Doyle had *solved* it. And while his incendiary reportage on this occasion did little to launch Doyle's writing career, the series of Sherlock Holmes tales that would begin to be published only months later gave him the freedom to abandon his fruitless medical practice for a far more lucrative—and impactful—career as an author. The game of entertaining hungry readers with challenging detective stories was certainly afoot—and Arthur Conan Doyle was more than ready to play.

PART II

Becoming a World

CHAPTER 6

Something Borrowed, Something New

The Influence of Stevenson and Henley on the Writings of Doyle

As we have already established, Arthur Conan Doyle was born in Scotland's capital of Edinburgh. This city's stunning terrain, combined with an assemblage of magnificent Grecian-inspired architecture, would lead in the 1820s to Edinburgh first being called "The Athens of the North." Less than a century earlier, in the mid-1750s, Edinburgh had already joined the ranks of Europe's most literate metropolises. In addition to its growing league of intelligentsia, the citizenry worked in tandem with its politicians to evolve and move forward, transforming itself from a medieval city into a cultural mecca and beacon of affluence. By the time of Doyle's birth in 1859, the "New Town" of Edinburgh would symbolize freedom, hope, and prosperity for those fortunate enough to call this part of the city home. Bridges were built and roads constructed, water and sewage facilities were overhauled and modernized, and old and dilapidated homes were razed and replaced with sturdy, well-crafted dwellings. Soon, the world over would look to Edinburgh as a paragon of advanced urban engineering and infrastructure.

Another reason that Edinburgh was thought of so highly across the globe was an emphasis on the part of its populace on both acquiring and disseminating knowledge. The favorable political climate in the city at that time resulted in educational reform being given top priority, and the University of Edinburgh earned an international reputation as a bastion of higher learning. Visionaries and revolutionaries who attended the institution during that era included: famed evolutionist Charles Darwin; the inventor of the telephone, Alexander Graham Bell; economist Adam Smith; philosopher David Hume; and mathematician James Maxwell, among others.

During this "Golden Age," Edinburgh either itself engendered, or beckoned from nearby British regions, some of the most eminent and influential writers of all time—luminaries like James Hogg, Thomas Carlyle, the "Ploughman Poet" Robert Burns, and Sir Walter Scott, still widely regarded as the father of the historical novel. Doyle himself proudly followed Scott's lead and authored a few historical novels of his own, including *Micah Clarke* (1889), *The White Company* (1891), *The Refugees* (1893), and the 1906 work *Sir Nigel: A Novel of the Hundred Years' War*. Ironically—and in defiance of general assumption—it was for *these* stories, not the Holmes tales, that Doyle wished to be best remembered.

Additionally, Edinburgh was home to some of the world's finest medical schools and hospitals, with the University of Edinburgh Medical School and Royal Infirmary producing a great number of respected physicians. It was there, of course, that Doyle first encountered and worked under the tutelage of Dr. Joseph Bell, the exceptional professor whose mannerisms and powers of observation and deduction were transposed onto Doyle's most famous and enduring character—Sherlock Holmes.

Dr. Bell, however, was not just a prime influence on Doyle alone. He also helped shape the life of another Victorian Era writer, that being William Ernest Henley. Henley, best known for his enduring 1888 poem "Invictus," was born a decade before Doyle in the southwestern English city of Gloucester on August 23, 1849. An especially debilitating case of tuberculosis at age twelve left him with crippled feet and one nonfunctional hand. In his early twenties, Henley—whose left foot had already been amputated—was informed by London physicians that his right foot would also need to be removed to keep him alive. Henley was unwilling to submit to another excision without obtaining a second opinion from a certain surgeon. Despite not having a penny to his name, the twenty-three-year-old Henley departed from London and journeyed to Edinburgh, where he pleaded his case before the renowned "father of antiseptic surgery," Joseph Lister.

Although the invariably busy Dr. Lister certainly had no obligation and limited time to take on another patient, it appears that the young Henley's quick wit and fierce intellect intrigued the great man of science.

Among Lister's many questions to Henley during his initial examination was why he had literally risked life and limb to travel such a long way, while suffering from such a debilitating and potentially lethal condition. Lister was likely stunned into silence by Henley's response, which the doctor could never have anticipated: "The rest of the medical profession had declared that you [Lister] are totally incompetent." Won over by Henley's facetious quip, Lister agreed to enroll him as a private patient in his practice—it should be noted that there were very few who managed to secure this level of personal service. For the greater part of two years, Lister devoted himself to salvaging this promising young writer's remaining foot. During that same time frame, Joseph Bell was appointed attending physician at the Royal Infirmary, where he drew the assignment of working alongside Dr. Lister on Henley's case. Bell also found Henley to be thoroughly engrossing and became equally devoted to caring for the young man. This marked the beginning of what would become Henley and Bell's lifelong friendship.

During his two-year hospitalization and convalescence, Henley exercised his mind as much as he attended to his body. He immersed himself in poetry; taught himself three languages (German, Italian, and Spanish); and befriended Leslie Stephen, the editor of *Cornhill Magazine* and father of future legendary Modernist writer Virginia Woolf. Stephen was impressed by Henley's unique literary style and ability to move the reader with his passionate writing. As a result, he asked another of Edinburgh's native sons, Robert Louis Stevenson—who, although known, had not yet achieved the height of his fame—to pay Henley a visit.

Shortly after being introduced, Stevenson and Henley would go on to form their own powerful bond. In fact, Stevenson would years later model his iconic *Treasure Island* villain Long John Silver after Henley—complete with missing leg and volcanic temperament. In the preface to his most famous novel, Stevenson writes:

> "I then had an idea for John Silver from which I promised myself funds of entertainment; to take an admired friend of mine (whom the reader very likely knows and admires as much as I do), to deprive him of all his finer qualities and higher graces of temperament, to leave him with nothing but his strength, his courage, his quickness, and his magnificent geniality, and to try to express these in terms of the culture of a raw tarpaulin."

Stevenson would later describe Henley as possessing a "leonine head and a splendid torso," and voiced great respect for his "maimed strength and masterfulness under acute and crippling pain." Meanwhile, Stevenson's stepson Lloyd Osbourne, a notable author in his own right, remembered Henley as: "[A] great, glowing, massive-shouldered fellow with a big red beard and a crutch; jovial, astoundingly clever, and with a laugh that rolled like music . . . [H]e had an unimaginable fire and vitality; he swept one off one's feet." And in a May 1883 letter to Henley, Stevenson wrote: "I will now make a confession. *It was the sight of your maimed strength and masterfulness that begot John Silver . . . [T]he idea of the maimed man*, ruling and dreaded by the sound, *was entirely taken from you*." In another letter, written concurrently to one of their mutual friends, Sidney Colvin, Stevenson joyfully wrote, "They would instantly dub Henley 'the *Father of the Wooden Legs*.'" *[emphases added throughout]*

In 1884, Henley and Stevenson teamed up to write four theatrical dramas—*Deacon Brodie*, *Beau Austin*, *Macaire*, and *Admiral Guinea*. The last was written specifically for Henley's own brother, E. J. Henley, to perform on stage. *Admiral Guinea* even featured *Treasure Island*'s Admiral Benbow Inn, along with its central characters Pew and Long John Silver. Unfortunately, none of these works were well-received by audiences or critics. The two playwrights—demoralized, and with their association now somewhat strained—were left with no choice but to revert to their earlier writing styles.

By 1887, however, their once-robust relationship became severely strained when Stevenson decided to leave Britain for America's fabled healing water and medicinal air of Saranac Lake, New York. To fill the void created by Stevenson's absence, Henley surrounded himself with up-and-coming authors—most notably *Peter Pan* creator James M. Barrie and Rudyard Kipling of *The Jungle Book* fame—to serve as his muses. Henley's friendship with Barrie was especially strong. Not only was Barrie a frequent visitor to the Henley household, but the avuncular Barrie was absolutely adored by Henley's toddler-age daughter, Margaret. Henley introduced Barrie to his daughter as "This is my friend," and she began referring to the amiable playwright visitor as "Friendy." Her childhood speech pattern made the word "friendy" sound more like "Wendy." And although Margaret died sadly from cerebral meningitis at the tender age of five, she would achieve literary immortality when Barrie conferred the slightly mispronounced nickname that Margaret had given him onto the principal female character of Wendy Darling in his *Peter Pan* stories.

A few years would then pass before Doyle himself was granted the opportunity to secure admission to Henley's inner circle. In 1892, when Doyle came up from London to revisit his home city, Henley invited the newly famous creator of Sherlock Holmes to join him for lunch. Doyle, in a letter to his mother, would subsequently describe Henley as "the most savage of critics, and to my mind one of our first living poets." This budding friendship gained momentum the following year, when Henley and Doyle both joined news correspondent Harold Frederic's exclusive Ghouls Club—a monthly dining and social gathering, at which members willingly endured good-natured roasting about each other's lives, publications, and adventures. Doyle was constantly inspired by Henley's words, describing himself after one of these meetings as follows: "You left his presence, as a battery leaves a generating station, charged up and full." Doyle digested everything Henley had to say, "whether it be prose or verse," and praised him as "a remarkable man, a man who was very much greater than his work, great as some of his work was."

Equally remarkable in Doyle's estimation was the aforementioned James Barrie, with whom Doyle also established a friendship. Although they did not know each other during their time at the University of Edinburgh—Barrie would eventually become the university's Chancellor—Barrie invited Doyle in the 1890s to play for The Allah-Akabarries, a cricket team he owned. Doyle jumped at the chance to show off his athletic prowess. Off the field, the two would collaborate on an ambitious but ultimately unsuccessful play titled *Jane Annie*. In 1891, Barrie's "My Evening With Sherlock Holmes" appeared anonymously in a magazine called *The Speaker*—though recognized as such after the fact, publication of this piece brought him the distinction of being the first person ever to write a pastiche dedicated to Doyle's great detective. In that short story, Barrie designated Doyle, and *not* Dr. Watson, as Holmes' "biographer." By the turn of the century, Doyle was very much a part of the established literary cognoscenti in his country—and in his time. He had arrived and was counted among the top tier in this rarefied group of agile creative minds—and he was thrilled to have achieved that kind of associative link with his contemporaries.

We have demonstrated—through the example of Dr. Joseph Bell—that Doyle drew directly from factual elements of his life to adorn the multiple facets of his fiction. This is further bolstered by the conspicuous impact on his work derived from William Henley. We shall now explore in greater depth the influences exhibited by Doyle's writing style and creative imagination that are attributable to Robert Louis Stevenson—and, in particular, his masterwork, *Treasure Island*.

"'I was able to refer him to two parallel cases . . .
which have suggested to him the true solution.'"
– SHERLOCK HOLMES, SPEAKING TO DR. WATSON
IN *THE SIGN OF THE FOUR* (1890)

Although Doyle and Stevenson both graduated from the University of Edinburgh, there was an eight-year gap between their attending the school that precluded any rubbing of shoulders. By the time Doyle achieved public acclaim in the early 1890s, Stevenson had already departed Scotland in favor of the gentler climate of the South Pacific.

Nevertheless, there was a single incident in the mid-1880s that created a brief association between Stevenson's name and one of Doyle's works. In 1884, the relatively unknown Doyle—still trying to make a name for himself—submitted a ghost story for consideration to *Chambers Magazine* entitled "J. Habakuk Jephson's Statement." The magazine's publisher, James Payn, gave his full approval for Doyle's mystery to be printed in an upcoming issue—but only anonymously, as that was the magazine's strict policy. Loosely basing his tale on the real-life 1872 disappearance of the American-registered mercantile vessel *Mary Celeste*, Doyle manufactured a supernatural scenario. It was designed to fill in the gaps of what might have taken place from the time the ill-fated ship set sail from America, up to when its abandoned hull was found aimlessly adrift off the Portuguese coast of the Azores. Doyle's imaginative yet realistic style of storytelling would quickly result in public uproar.

Doyle purposely presented "J. Habakuk Jephson's Statement" to contemporary readers in the form of an eyewitness account—an early ancestor, perhaps, of the "found footage" style of cinema epitomized most popularly by the first version of *The Blair Witch Project* when released to movie theaters in 1999. The piece would later find its way into Doyle's 1890 short story compilation, *The Captain of the Polestar and Other Tales*, along with the earlier published multiple-author, three-volume series *Dreamland and Ghostland* and 1922's *Tales of Pirates and Blue Water*. Doyle successfully persuaded many readers that the fourteen-years-past tragic mystery had finally been solved. Even the well-respected *Boston Herald* in the United States had reprinted "Jephson's Statement" as breaking news. There were others, however, who held firm in their belief that the purported account by "Dr. Jephson" was indeed a sham.

Among the skeptics was Frederick Solly-Flood, who had served as principal investigator of the ship's disappearance for Her Majesty's Advocate-General of Gibraltar back in 1872. After reading the narrative, Solly-Flood sent off a scathing telegram to London's Central News Agency, in which he declared that Dr. Jephson's statement was "a fabrication from beginning to end," and excoriated James Payn's decision to publish it. Payn was unmoved—he justified his decision to print Doyle's work as originally presented by declaring it an example of superior modern fiction, something that he was proud to have personally selected for his magazine.

This episode did far more than merely grant the still marginally recognized Doyle a degree of notoriety and respect. As Hugh S. MacClauchlan wrote at the time in his 1896 *Windsor Magazine* article "Doyle and His Stories," Doyle's "weird tale . . . formed the foundation of a steadfast friendship with Mr. James Payn." Having now established a professional affiliation with Payn, who was widely seen as one of the most influential publishers in Great Britain, Doyle was well on his way toward achieving a finer literary cachet.

In the aftermath of the "Jephson" article, "critic after critic" began to attribute Doyle's writing style and command of language to the direct influence of Robert Louis Stevenson, whose seafaring classic *Treasure Island* had been published to great acclaim only a year earlier in 1883. Doyle would proudly recount in his 1893 article "Juvenilia" that he was "overwhelmed" by the "compliment" of being compared in any way to Stevenson, and these plaudits certainly gave him the confidence to continue to pursue his chosen avocation. We also assert that six years later, in 1890, Doyle produced his own well-disguised and modernized version of Stevenson's tale—never revealing to a soul that he had done so and, up to now, never having been detected. But to uncover those unacknowledged tributes so craftily embedded within *The Sign of the Four*, we need to first disassemble both Doyle's novel and Stevenson's *Treasure Island* into their component parts. Only after such deconstruction can we fully appreciate Doyle's gift and talent for retelling a story in such a way that readers are convinced it is his own wholly unique creation.

While Stevenson's pirate yarn is relatively devoid of romance, Doyle inserts a budding love affair—serving to camouflage his ultimate purpose—right at the start of *The Sign of the Four*. In the opening chapter, Holmes is commissioned by Miss Mary Morstan—a woman with whom Dr. Watson finds himself instantly smitten. But the two novels share an important central theme—one that is illustrated by the very last paragraph of each respective tale. In *Treasure Island*, Jim Hawkins realizes that, should he take the contents of the treasure chest with him, he would be doomed to only pain and torment. And so, to ensure his happiness, he chooses to leave it buried. Note that this identical idea can be found in the dialogue between Mary Morstan and Watson at the conclusion of Doyle's novel. The passage reads as follows:

> "'The treasure is lost,' said Miss Morstan, calmly.
>
> As I listened to the words and realized what they meant, a great shadow seemed to pass from my soul. I did not know how this Agra treasure had weighed me down, until now that it was finally removed. It was selfish, no doubt, disloyal, wrong, but I could realize nothing save that the golden barrier was gone from between us. "'Thank God!'" I ejaculated from my very heart.
>
> She looked at me with a quick, questioning smile. 'Why do you say that?' she asked.
>
> 'Because you are within my reach again,' I said, taking her hand. She did not withdraw it. 'Because I love you, Mary, as truly as ever a man loved a woman. Because this treasure, these riches, sealed my lips. Now that they are gone I can tell you how I love you. That is why I said, "Thank God."'
>
> 'Then I say, "Thank God," too,' she whispered, as I drew her to my side. Whoever had lost a treasure, I knew that night that I had gained one."

By story's end, both Watson and Mary Morstan recognize that recovering the treasure would have resulted in a life filled with perpetual sadness. Only when they both know that the priceless gems will remain forever at the bottom of the River Thames does Watson find the courage to confess his love for Mary—and to ask for her hand in marriage.

In his later book *Through the Magic Door* (1906), Doyle points out what he felt was a flaw in Stevenson's fiction—namely, Stevenson's decision to picture "only one side of life" without the perspective of "female interest." Even alluding to his first novel *A Study in Scarlet* from within the text of his second novel *The Sign of the Four*, Doyle uses his own character creations to point out this same perceived defect, exemplified when Holmes reprimands Watson about the quality of his work: "'You have attempted to tinge it with romanticism, which produces much the same effect as if you worked a love-story or an elopement into the fifth proposition of Euclid.'" And by the time of *The Sign of the Four*'s publication in 1890, Doyle deliberately chose to avoid what he saw as Stevenson's story-structure pitfall—doing so by incorporating the subplot of the triumphant love affair between Watson and Morstan.

Doyle also playfully inserts his own take on some key features and personages from Stevenson's *Treasure Island* into his second Holmes novel. Both tales feature characters with the same first name—Long *John* Silver from Stevenson, and *Jonathan* Small from Doyle—whose respective appellation or surnames are opposites of each other ("*Long* John" vs. "Jonathan *Small*"). Both novels feature a particular literary device, the invention of which Doyle attributes to Stevenson—that being "the mutilated villain." While Stevenson's antagonist, Long John, is described as "intelligent . . . very tall" and lacking a left leg, Doyle's Jonathan Small is the "mirror" version, characterized as "poorly educated . . . small" and lacking a *right* leg. It should be apparent that both Stevenson's and Doyle's one-legged men are modeled after William Henley—with both authors making a point of emphasizing the strengths of their wooden-legged characters far more than their faults. And lest we forget that fellow inner circle friend and associate James Barrie, when creating the characters for his equally famous *Peter Pan* adventures, conjured up a one-handed pirate named Captain Hook. This character *also* pays homage not only to Henley's defective hand, but also to a character from Doyle's *The Sign of the Four*. How do Captain Hook and Jonathan Small both lose their missing appendages? By amputation—each due to the chomp of a hungry crocodile.

The Sign of the Four and *Treasure Island* both feature named narrators—John Watson and David Livesey, respectively—whose purpose is the recounting and chronicling of events for the reader. Not only are Watson and Livesey each depicted as being physicians with "side jobs" in law enforcement—Watson is the partner of a consulting detective, while Livesey doubles as a magistrate—but both are said to have been wounded while defending Her Majesty's honor. In the separate tales, we learn from Doyle that Watson has fought at the 1880 Battle of Maiwand, while Stevenson has Livesey serve more than a century earlier in 1745 at the Battle of Fontenoy. Both novels contain plots that center around a search for a treasure chest—one of them has been buried (*Treasure Island*), while the other is hidden above ground and stowed in a hidden attic. At the beginning of each book, we are greeted with an account of a sea captain's death—William Bones in Stevenson's piece, and Arthur Morstan from Doyle's story.

In *Treasure Island*, Stevenson gives us a captain who goes to his grave as a result of the search for the treasure that had been taken from him—and reversing this take, in Doyle's *The Sign of the Four*, we read of a major who possesses a treasure chest that he refuses to tell anyone about, even as he lays on his deathbed. And both characters live in mortal fear of wooden-legged men. In *Treasure Island*, Captain Bones pays Jim Hawkins to keep his "'weather-eye open for a seafaring man with one leg.'" While in *The Sign of the Four*, we are told that Major Sholto "'actually fired his revolver at a wooden-legged man, who proved to be a harmless tradesman canvassing for orders. We had to pay a large sum to hush the matter up.'" Even the way these two characters meet their respective deaths is similar—each of them pass away after rising from a chair, and then falling to the ground from a standing position. Stevenson's character Captain Bill (who buried his loot) and Doyle's Major Sholto (who hid his jewels in an attic) allude to their concealed treasures while in their respective beds, and neither disclose the ultimate location of each.

The effect on the demeanor of the two captains when they encounter people who they know are aware of the existence of treasure is also analogous. William Bones (in *Treasure Island*) immediately turns "old and sick" during breakfast time when he sets eyes on his "'old shipmate'" Black Dog, while Major Sholto (in *The Sign of the Four*) "'nearly faint[s] at the breakfast-table'" after he opens and reads a letter written by an old acquaintance. And much like Captain Bones in Stevenson's work, Doyle writes that "'from that day he [sic Sholto] sickened to his death.'" Major Sholto speaks about his treasure chest from the confines of his bed, while Captain Bill informs Jim Hawkins about Black Spot's significance from his own bed.

When the major's son, Thaddeus Sholto, tells Holmes about the events that surrounded the premature death of Captain Morstan, he begins with, "'Early in 1882 my father received a letter.'" This correlates precisely with the year in which the final chapter of the serialized version of *Treasure Island* that appeared in *Young Folks Magazine* was published. And at *Treasure Island*'s end, the sought-after buried treasure is unearthed for everyone to share—while in Doyle's final scene of *The Sign of the Four*, the treasure contained in the chest is cast into the River Thames, to lie buried at the bottom for all eternity.

The Sign of the Four and *Treasure Island* also contain parallel murder scenes. When Stevenson's Long John Silver furiously hurls a tree branch at a sailor named Tom, its impact breaks the man's back "on the spot." Before Tom (now lying paralyzed on the ground) has time to regain his bearings, "Silver, agile as a monkey even without leg or crutch, was on the top of him next moment and had twice buried his knife up to the hilt in that defenseless body." Doyle recreates this scene in his own story, having Jonathan Small fire his gun at the messenger carrying the Rajah's treasure. Once the bullet penetrates his body, the messenger collapses to the ground and breaks his neck the instant he hits the floor. Unable to even right himself, Small's Sikh accomplice "'buried his knife *twice* in his side.'" *[emphasis added]* Both tales feature characters who, having been struck in the back (one by log, one by bullet), break their spines and are then stabbed to death—not just once, but twice.

Both authors employ the distinctive stench of tar to evoke in the reader's mind a particular olfactory ambiance. In *Treasure Island*, upon Jim Hawkins' arrival in Bristol, he immediately detects "[t]he smell of tar and salt." And in *The Sign of the Four*, when Watson and Holmes enter Sholto's chemical laboratory, Watson promptly observes that, "One of these [vials] appeared to leak or to have been broken, for a stream of dark-colored liquid had trickled out from it, and the air was heavy with a peculiarly pungent, tar-like odor." Stevenson and Doyle also notably utilize red crosses as symbols in their respective tales. In *Treasure Island*, the red crosses that appear on the treasure map "explain the cause," while in *The Sign of the Four*, a treasure map's four crosses correspond to Jonathan Small, Mahomet Singh, Abdullah Khan, and Dost Akbar—the quartet who purloin the treasure. Once Holmes subjects that treasure map to his double-lens magnifying glass, he can make out the numbers "'3.37 from left'" of the crosses. When the map from *Treasure Island* is subjected to magnification, those very same numbers—7/3/3—are found to the left of the small crosses. This can hardly be considered coincidental.

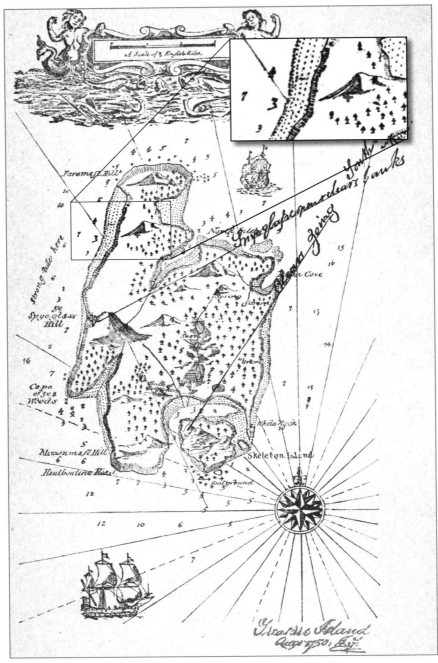

Numerical echoes between Doyle's *The Sign of the Four* and
Stevenson's *Treasure Island* (as shown in the map close-up above).

Here again, Doyle furnishes another correlation to *Treasure Island* as he lays out this challenging clue for the reader to decipher:

"'Before I left I bethought me that if I ever met my Sikh friends again it would be a satisfaction to know that I had left some mark of our hatred; so I scrawled down the sign of the four of us, as it had been on the chart, and I *pinned it on his bosom*. It was too much that he should be taken to the grave without some token from the men whom he had robbed and befooled.'" *[emphasis added]*

Once these words, spoken by Jonathan Small, are properly interpreted and decoded, it becomes evident that Small, with purpose and intent, pinned that note onto the *dead man's* (that is to say, Major Sholto's) *chest*. We recall that in *Treasure Island*, the pirates aboard the *Hispaniola* are prone to sing with great enthusiasm the now-immortal line, "'Fifteen men on the dead man's chest.'"

Doyle's character Tonga, and Stevenson's Ben Gunn, also share some unexpected equivalency. Doyle describes Tonga as being on the verge of death, fortuitously found in the woods by Jonathan Small—who then nurses him back to health. Although Tonga belongs to a tribe of cannibals, upon his miraculous recovery he becomes "'devoted to'" Jonathan Small, "'and would do anything to serve'" him. Similarly, *Treasure Island*'s Jim Hawkins finds himself confronted in the woods by a man with "dark and shaggy" hair and skin "burnt from the sun." Jim immediately assumes he is face-to-face with a cannibal. Fortunately, this ostensible "savage" is an Englishman named Ben Gunn, who had been left to die on the island. When Gunn encounters Jim, he "threw himself on his knees and held out his hands in clasped supplication," as Tonga had done with Small.

Both Tonga and Ben Gunn happen to be proud owners of hand-crafted boats—which, of course, are presented diametrically to each other. According to Jim Hawkins, Ben Gunn's "home-made" craft "was extremely small, even for me, and I can hardly imagine that it could have floated with a full-sized man." Tonga's tribe can rightfully "'claim the distinction of being the smallest race upon this earth'"—therefore, Tonga himself is likely quite diminutive. Yet his canoe is described by Small as "'big'" and "'roomy.'"

Immediately after Tonga's death, Doyle writes that Holmes and Watson's boat traverses the *southern bank*, heading into "a wild and desolate place . . . with pools of stagnant water and beds of decaying vegetation."

This equates to Jim Hawkins' description of the island in Stevenson's novel as a "desolate place" with "a peculiar stagnant smell . . . of sodden leaves and rotting tree trunks." And, of course, Jim first steps foot on the island at its *southern* tip.

Jim Hawkins and Tonga also share the unfortunate experience of having been treated like circus animals. In *Treasure Island*, Long John Silver compels Jim Hawkins to follow him by affixing a rope around his waist, as if he were "a dancing bear." Doyle expands upon Stevenson's description, affixing his own spin. Jonathan Small earns his living "'exhibiting poor Tonga at fairs and other such places as the black cannibal.'" And like the dancing black bear of old, Tonga earns a daily hatful of pennies by performing his tribal war-dances for eager onlookers. Doyle even goes so far as to have Sherlock Holmes disguise himself at one point as an "aged man, clad in seafaring garb, with an old pea-jacket buttoned up to his throat." This ancient mariner "leaned upon a thick oaken cudgel [and] his shoulders heaved in the effort to draw the air into his lungs. He had a colored scarf round his chin, and I could see little of his face save a pair of keen dark eyes, overhung by bushy white brows, and long gray side-whiskers. Altogether he gave me the impression of a respectable master mariner who had fallen into years and poverty." The elderly pirate, clad in scarf and sporting a stick, represents Doyle's tribute—in the form of a composite—to the graying salts Stevenson features in *Treasure Island*. Ben Gunn and Pew each carry a walking stick with them; Flint sports a colorful scarf; while old Billy Bones, donned in "an old blue coat," breathes "loud and hard." Doyle transforms Holmes into someone who could have stepped out of the pages of *The Sign of the Four*, and right into *Treasure Island*—fitting in seamlessly with Stevenson's own sailors.

Both Stevenson's and Doyle's adventures feature brief sections devoted to the narrators discussing, for the one and only time in the work (or in Doyle's case, the series), the deaths of their respective fathers. In *Treasure Island*, Jim Hawkins' father dies suddenly, and then is never spoken of again. While in *The Sign of the Four*, we learn of Dr. Watson's father's death, a character who is then never mentioned again anywhere else in the extensive Holmes canon.

Both stories feature chapters specifically including the word "Barrel" in their titles. Doyle's *The Sign of the Four* features "The Episode of the Barrel," and in Stevenson's *Treasure Island*, we find "What I Heard in the

Apple Barrel." In the former, the subject chapter features Doyle transitioning the novel from a land adventure to a sea voyage, while in the latter, Stevenson gives us the exact opposite—the chapter begins with the *Hispaniola* sailing across the ocean. At its end, the characters disembark on Skeleton Island—with the last two words being "'Land ho!'" Additionally, the way the authors present the use of the barrels in these chapters mirror each other. In *Treasure Island*, Jim Hawkins conceals himself within the barrel, while in *The Sign of the Four*, Toby the sleuth dog climbs on top of—but not inside—the barrel.

Interestingly, several of the locations that Doyle includes in *The Sign of the Four* are an unstated yet clear tribute to another of Stevenson's legendary masterworks. As an example, Doyle has Dr. Watson send off a telegram from a non-existent "Wigmore Street" post office, and not from the more authentic branch that actually existed at Number 66 Baker Street. It seems to us that Doyle, who wrote with great deliberation, explicitly chose to use this fictional address, rather than one based in real-life London. Doyle opens his adventure with Watson muddying his shoes at this site because he wanted to place him in close proximity to Wigmore Street's famous Cavendish Square. After all, this is the fictional location of the home office of one Dr. Lanyon—the venue at which the story of Stevenson's *The Strange Case of Dr. Jekyll and Mr. Hyde* commences.

The next shared location featured in *The Sign of the Four*, introduced shortly after Holmes takes on Mary Morstan as a client, is the Theatre District. Miss Morstan receives a letter commanding her to "be at the third pillar from the left outside the Lyceum Theatre to-night at seven o'clock. If you are distrustful, bring two friends." Of course, she brings Holmes and Watson along with her to the meeting. As this was "a September evening" in 1888, the words on this particular theater's marquee would have read, "Dr. Jekyll and Mr. Hyde," as a production adapted for the stage, derived from Stevenson's enduring work, was running at the Lyceum at that very time.

And it is not a random coincidence that both Sherlock Holmes and Henry Jekyll self-medicate with concoctions that bring out their worst tendencies. Jekyll's potion, as we know very well, turns him into a creature without conscience. In *The Sign of the Four*, Holmes injects himself with intravenous cocaine, leaving Watson no choice but to issue this warning:

"'Count the cost! Your brain may, as you say, be roused and excited, but it is a pathological and morbid process . . . You know, too, what a black reaction comes upon you.'"

Doyle doesn't limit himself to only drawing parallels and contrasts between his own work and those presented by *Treasure Island* and *The Strange Case of Dr. Jekyll and Mr. Hyde*. He also helps himself to the contents of other Stevenson stories, to create additional scenes that enhance his second Holmes tale. One case in point is taken from Stevenson's *The Rajah's Diamond*, a series of four short stories that revolve around the second most valuable diamond on Earth. Despite the stone's enormity, Stevenson's spectacular gem—which had once belonged to a Rajah from Northern India—goes unappreciated by those who view it. *The Sign of the Four* features the Great Mogul diamond, once the treasured possession of a Rajah from Northern India. And after Doyle's Rajah has been overthrown, "'no one had any particular interest in'" the priceless gem. Doyle's Rajah, "'being a careful man,'" opts to split his treasure into two parts: all gold and silver were to remain locked inside the palace vaults, while "'the most precious stones and the choicest pearls that he had he put in an iron box.'" It is that iron box, full of precious stones and choicest pearls, that Jonathan Small takes possession of during Doyle's story. The cache of riches that Jim Hawkins and his comrades acquire in Stevenson's tale, on the other hand, is limited strictly to gold and silver—in the form of money. Their treasure chest has not a single precious stone or pearl within it—and was wrought from wood, not iron.

Doyle also pays subtle tribute to Stevenson's novel *The Wrong Box* (1889) in the opening of *The Sign of the Four*'s second chapter. There, Miss Mary Morstan informs Holmes about a telegram she has received from her father upon his being granted leave to return to England. She tells Holmes, "'In the year 1878 my father, who was senior captain of his regiment, obtained twelve months' leave and came down at once, giving the Langham Hotel as his address.'" *The Wrong Box* features a character who dispatches an urgent telegram from that same hotel:

"'A telegram, very laconic.' Speedily the wires were flashing the following important missive: Dickson, Langham Hotel."

Doyle also lifts some of the elements found in Stevenson's powerful short story "The Pavilion on the Links" (1880) and transports them a decade into the future in *The Sign of the Four*. It makes sense that Doyle would do this, since he had once chastised his own mother for telling him that his "Cloombers is as good as the Pavilion." He went on to admonish her further by stating, "Never let your kind maternal feelings cloud your critical judgment. The Pavilion is far the better." And in *Through the Magic Door* (1907), Doyle wrote that Stevenson's powerful dramatic narrative had:

> "Stamped itself so clearly on my brain when I read it in Cornhill that when I came across it again many years afterwards in volume form, I was able instantly to recognize two small modifications of the text—each very much for the worse—from the original form. They were small things, but they seemed somehow like a chip on a perfect statue. Surely it is only a very fine work of art which could leave so definite an impression as that."

So exactly what did Doyle borrow from that story? Upon further inspection, *The Sign of the Four* and "The Pavilion on the Links" both feature characters trying to solve the mystery of how a burglar might enter a house with locked doors, inaccessible windows, and capped chimneys. Both characters come to the same conclusion: That the intruder had gained entry through the roof of a laboratory—one chemical, the other photographic.

And what are those parallel cases so casually mentioned to Watson by Holmes in *The Sign of the Four*? It turns out that Doyle has created for the story two cases identified by Holmes as "'the one at Riga in 1857, and the other in St. Louis in 1871.'" But if we view them through the lens of Doyle's imagination and in reverse order, it becomes clear that Doyle was providing readers with a hint as to whom *The Sign of the Four* was dedicated—the "R" in Riga being the first initial of **R**obert, the name "Louis" for **Louis**, and "St." for the first two letters of **St**evenson.

After the publication of *The Sign of the Four* in 1890, Doyle sent letters and books to Stevenson at his home in Vailima, Samoa. Perhaps Doyle was waiting to see if Stevenson—one of his biggest contemporary literary idols—might be able to pick up on the similarities between their stories. Although Stevenson was able to decipher that Sherlock Holmes was greatly influenced by Dr. Joseph Bell (as we have established), he was seemingly unable to spot his own characters and plots hidden within Doyle's second Holmes novel. Amazingly, on July 12, 1893, Stevenson, in a letter advising Doyle on how to travel to Samoa to pay him a visit, wrote, "Here is what you will have to do. Leave San Francisco by the down mail, get off at Samoa, and twelve days or a fortnight later, you can continue your journey to Auckland per Upolu, which will give you a look at Tonga and possibly Fiji by the way." Stevenson mentions the island of Tonga but still fails to piece together the clues and tie its significance to the character of Doyle's creation. Again, we consider this to be a testament to Doyle's transcendent and formidable abilities.

In retrospect, Robert Louis Stevenson's 1882 preface to his *New Arabian Nights* could be construed as an appropriate dedication to Doyle: "I must prefix a word of thanks to the gentleman who condescended to borrow the gist of one of my stories, and even to honour it with the addition of his signature." This is a perfect description to apply to *The Sign of the Four*—in essence, Doyle borrowed the basic building blocks of plot and character from *Treasure Island*, and reimagined and remolded it into a detective story. Nevertheless, Doyle's interpretation of Stevenson's treasure hunt is not at all a typical pirate's tale, replete with seafaring vessels and talking parrots. Instead, it is from start to finish a polished and elegant mystery, featuring a scientific/forensic detective carefully searching for clues, with a budding romance weaved throughout the storyline for good measure. *The Sign of the Four* still retains its standing as a Victorian-era magnum opus. But it is vital to recognize the key antecedents in literature—and in life—that Doyle resculpted into separate pieces and forged together anew in order to sire his own singular and fascinating work of art.

CHAPTER 7

Sherlock Holmes
Wanted Dead . . . *Then Alive?*

As imagined and written into existence by Arthur Conan Doyle, the fictive Sherlock Holmes is a superb early testimonial to the real-life benefits of genetic engineering. The great detective's DNA might be construed as having been spliced together with meticulous precision from the chromosomes of at least six Edinburgh physicians—Joseph Bell, William Rutherford, Thomas Richard Fraser, Alexander Crum Brown, Henry Duncan Littlejohn, and, of course, Doyle himself. Holmes' most remarkably recognizable traits and talents have nearly all been derived from this assemblage of brilliant medical men. Let's consider for a moment the many stellar attributes that Doyle so deftly wove into his own creation from this same shared source:

- A keen intelligence, physical strength, extraordinary athleticism, and uncanny acting prowess

- A deep and varied knowledge, which encompasses familiarity and experience with the poisonous properties at play in plant-based Belladonna alkaloids, snake venom, and tobacco ash

- A strong and, at times, sentimental attachment to violins (which is in frequent view throughout many of the tales that comprise the Holmes canon)

- An encyclopedic mastery of complex specialized areas including anatomy, chemistry, toxicology, forensic science, and all manner of British law

- And, above all, seemingly boundless powers of observation and intuition.

Despite possessing these innate gifts, there were occasions when Doyle conjured up plots that put his master detective into unfamiliar, and potentially deadly, situations. This necessitated the modification of some of Holmes' already-stated superior abilities. Fortunately, Doyle's supple imagination was able to work in tandem with his ample network of exceptional friends, to allow Holmes to troubleshoot in times of need. One of Holmes' most significant and life-altering traits was derived from one of Doyle's friends who was living in a faraway place.

When Doyle first introduces his readers to Sherlock Holmes in *A Study in Scarlet* (1887), his chosen narrator Dr. Watson is quick to determine—and then enumerate—the exceptional abilities with which Holmes is endowed as "an expert singlestick player, boxer, and swordsman." In Doyle's second Holmes novel *The Sign of the Four*, readers learn from an ex-prize fighter named McMurdo that Holmes' pugilistic talents were on par with England's top boxing contenders. While Holmes was able to defend himself against the many formidable adversaries who appear throughout the stories, these aforementioned fighting skills were of little use when it came to tracking down and cracking down on the criminal activities of his fiercest nemesis, Professor James Moriarty—the man Holmes referred to as the "'Napoleon of crime.'"

The nefarious character of Moriarty first appears in the 1893 short story "The Final Problem," where he masterminds a plot that lures Holmes out of London, across the English Channel, and eventually to locations across the European continent. Doyle, reflecting upon a trip he had taken earlier that year with Reverend William James Dawson from Meiringen to Rosenlaui in Switzerland, decides in this story to bring his master detective to Switzerland's picturesque Grand Falls of Reichenbach, where, by story's end, he engages Moriarty in a battle to the death. It is at this point that Holmes' destiny as a fictional character is challenged in what at the time must have seemed irreparable. In a way, it can be said that the Holmes character becomes the unknowing victim of his creator's wrath—a similar predicament to the one that befell the children of the mythical Greek god Cronus who, in order to maintain his own power, was compelled in the tale to devour his own offspring. As both a physical and intellectual match for Moriarty, Sherlock Holmes—as written by Doyle—has no choice available to him other than to await the moment when Doyle elects to have him sacrifice his own life by diving off one of the Reichenbach cliffs into a watery abyss—with the evil professor in tow.

By studying the historical records left behind by Doyle, we can be sure that he had no intention of giving his readers a Thomas Hardy-like cliffhanger story where "The Hero" somehow manages to survive. Instead, "The Final Problem" evidently represents a deepfelt effort by Doyle to rid himself—once and for all—of the character who he believed was ruining his life. Although Doyle clearly did appreciate the great commercial success that Holmes had bestowed upon him, at the same time he regarded the Holmes stories as a real stumbling block—a millstone around his neck that prevented him at that point in his life from receiving what he felt should be his due fame as a writer of erudite historical and biographical works. In an 1891 letter to his mother, he made the following declaration: "I must save my mind for *better* things, even if it means I must bury my pocketbook with him." And in another letter home from that time, he shared the following thought with her: "I think of slaying Holmes . . . & winding him up for good & all." As we have shown, Doyle eventually acted upon those very words when he wrote "The Final Problem." In order to prepare his mother (who had pleaded with her son not to kill off Holmes), Doyle decided to write her a letter in which he stated, "I am in the middle of the last Holmes story, after which the gentleman vanishes never to return! I am weary of his name."

The public, of course, felt otherwise. Thousands of by-now fiercely loyal Sherlock Holmes fans refused to accept the character's demise, and desperately petitioned Doyle to perform a literary resurrection of the detective who so famously wore a deerstalker cap and smoked a briar pipe. Initially, Doyle was totally unwilling to grant such a request—yet nine years later, he settled on giving hopeful Holmes fans a novel-length adventure entitled *The Hound of the Baskervilles* (1902). Though it was a new Holmes story, Doyle structured things so that the tale takes place *before* Holmes' reported demise at Reichenbach. But this was *still* not good enough for Holmes aficionados—they wanted Holmes alive and well in his Baker Street apartment. It wasn't long before Doyle gave in to this overwhelming public pressure and wrote a short story in 1903 called "The Adventure of the Empty House," a tale in which Holmes makes a miraculous return from the dead. It is in this tale that we learn that it was in fact Moriarty *alone* who "'splashed into the water,'" unaccompanied by Holmes. Apparently, Holmes had been able to defeat his enemy that day back in early May 1891 because of his training in "'baritsu, or the Japanese system of wrestling.'" It was this martial art that gave Holmes the edge he so desperately needed to slip out from the grip of the evil mathematician, and to ascend the slippery slope of the Falls of Reichenbach.

This leaves us with one problem that needs to be solved, though—the English translation for the "Japanese system of wrestling" is *not* "baritsu." That word is the more familiar term *sumo*. Could Doyle have erred here? Or did the term "baritsu" hold a poignant and perhaps *secret* meaning to him? Might he have been paying homage in "The Adventure of the Empty House" to a recently departed *best* friend? If we explore Doyle's past, while simultaneously taking a closer look at the Sherlock Holmes canon of stories, the answers to these questions shall stand before us.

To decipher the true etymology of the word "baritsu," we must first look ahead a bit at Doyle's 1924 short story, "The Adventure of the Illustrious Client." A vital clue to solving this mystery can be found in the section of the tale where Holmes hands Watson a visiting card imprinted with the name "Dr. Hill Barton." Holmes then informs his partner that *he* will need to masquerade as a sophisticated collector of highly valued Chinese pottery. The name that Holmes assigns to Watson is actually a play on the name Dr. John Hill Burton, an influential and revered friend to the Doyle family.

Dr. Burton was a prominent advocate-lawyer who, in 1867, was appointed Historiographer-Royal for Scotland by Her Royal Majesty Queen Victoria. It is very possible that Burton, the author of *Narratives from Criminal Trials of Scotland*, was a major influence on Doyle's own fascination with sensational crimes. Dr. Burton also enjoyed a reputation as "an indefatigable pedestrian, thinking nothing of a walk of fifty or even sixty miles in a day, over any tract of country and in any kind of weather." Surely the long journey that Holmes began after his feigned death at Reichenbach would have borne a marked resemblance to one of Burton's many arduous hikes. And so, we feel it necessary to add this seventh doctor to Holmes' remarkable genetic code.

In 1866, Burton's *Political and Social Economy for Use in Schools* (1849) was translated into Japanese by Fukuzawa Yukichi—one of the early formative architects of modern-day Japan. That book went on to become a bestseller and helped convince that then-feudalistic and isolationist nation to open up its borders to free trade and to implement diplomatic relations with the Western world. The Burton family had other strong ties to the East. Dr. Burton's youngest son, Cosmo Innes Burton, immigrated to China in 1890 after having received an appointment as the first Professor of Chemistry at the Polytechnic Institution of Shanghai. Sadly, just after he had prepared his initial course syllabus and assembled a laboratory dedicated to metallurgy, mining, and mineralogy, he succumbed to the complications of malignant smallpox and died at the age of twenty-eight.

Burton's eldest son, William Kinninmond Burton, was one of Doyle's few childhood friends. As a youngster, Doyle had many opportunities to explore his friend's haunted Old Craig House, where an alleged resident ghost (referred to within the family as "The Green Lady") appeared to have been given free reign over the entire strangely appointed mansion— except for its well-stocked library. In an attempt to shelter her child from the emotional and physical abuse inflicted on her son by her alcoholic husband Charles, Mary Doyle would send young Arthur to live "free of charge" as a boarder at Liberton Bank House, the home of William Burton's beloved aunt—the noted suffragette and educational reformer Mary Burton. It was from this residence that Doyle would walk to Newington Academy to receive his first experience with formal education.

Unlike the ill-fated Cosmo, William would go on to have an impressive career. After a five-year apprenticeship at the prestigious Brown Brothers and Company's Rosebank Ironworks in his home city of Edinburgh, William moved to London and joined his uncle's engineering firm to help design a water filtration system for the cholera-plagued city. William, who had rapidly acquired expertise in the emerging field of modern photography, soon began to submit articles to the *British Journal of Photography* and *The Photo News*. In 1882, his pieces "Tables of Exposures" and "Twelve Lessons on Dry Plate Photography" earned him a stellar reputation among amateur photographers. He then managed to find time to author the textbooks *The ABCs of Modern Photography* (1884), *A Practical Guide to Photographic and Photo-mechanical Printing Processes* (1887), *The Processes of Pure Photography* (1889), *Photographic Optics* (1891), and *The Manual of Photography* (1895). Both William Burton and Doyle were frequent contributors to the *British Journal of Photography*, and there were more than a few occasions when Doyle came to the defense of some of his friend's more controversial research. In light of Doyle's and Burton's shared embrace of all things photographic, it is fitting that Doyle's third Holmes tale, "A Scandal in Bohemia" (1891), would center on a tell-tale cabinet photograph as a chief piece of evidence.

In 1887, while Doyle was writing *A Study in Scarlet*, William was recruited by the Japanese government to supervise an engineering project slated for completion within a year's time. His first two months were spent in Tokyo, adjusting to what was for him a completely new alien culture and stifling climate. He wrote a letter to the *Photographic Times* in which he complained about the "very nondescript" food that was served to him inside teahouses, where "gaishes" (known to the West now as "geishas") danced around him. He boasted that "hard boiled eggs and very green and unripe apples formed, for several days, pretty well all I could get that was to me eatable." He further wrote—in a different letter to *Photographic Times* editor Irving Adams—that "It has been a month since I have had a chair to sit on . . . a table to work at, or a bed to sleep on, and I have had to manage all my eating with chopsticks." Over the next six weeks in 1888, Burton occupied his time "making a tour of the Northern towns of Japan, in company with a medical doctor, an executive member of the Sanitary Bureau, and a graduate of the college of engineering." His assignment was to "evaluate the sanitary conditions of these towns," and he was required to pay close attention to "sewer disposal and of water supply."

Nevertheless, Burton adapted quickly to his new surroundings, and soon fell in love with Japan and its people. He learned its language and its customs; acquired a taste for "salic" (Japanese wine); and enjoyed musical tunes performed on the "samishe" (a type of banjo). Within a year after his arrival, he decided that Japan was where he wanted to spend the rest of his life. In the five years that followed, William joined the Freemasons of Tokyo and Yokohama; helped charter the Photographic Society of Japan; and fathered a child with, and eventually married, a Japanese woman named Matsu Arakawa. Unlike other Englishmen in Japan, William was permitted to have an official wedding ceremony at the British Consulate, presided over by Joseph H. Longford on May 19, 1894.

Although he was a foreigner, William soon caught the attention of Japan's most accomplished academics, and was named the first Professor of Sanitary Engineering and lecturer in Rivers, Docks, and Harbours at the prestigious Imperial University of Tokyo. His expertise in irrigation and water filtration made him the government's top choice to design and supervise over a new water and sewage system for Tokyo and its surrounding towns. The success of this project put an end to the cholera epidemic that had plagued his adopted land for decades. In 1890, William designed Japan's first skyscraper—the octagonal twelve-story Ryoun-kaku Building. Located in the city of Asakusa, this engineering marvel, nicknamed "Fu-ni-kai" (Japanese for "The Twelve Stories") housed Japan's first elevator and the "Beauty-show," one hundred photographs "of the most famous of the *geisha* of all parts of Tokyo." Unfortunately, the Great Kanto earthquake of 1923—which was the most powerful earthquake to ever hit Japan—resulted in irreparable structural damage that later necessitated this landmark's demolition.

While all of these achievements are impressive in their own right, Doyle's character of Sherlock Holmes would surely have regarded William Burton's 1894 descriptive and illustrated book *Wrestlers and Wrestling in Japan* as being the most significant of them all. It was this book that introduced the Western world to the ancient ritualistic art form of sumo. Found within the pages of Burton's book were photographs of its most-celebrated practitioners, engaged in demonstration of the proper techniques required for competition. Sumo, which is officially "the Japanese system of wrestling," was regaining popularity during the Meiji era, which began in 1867 to restore imperial rule in Japan. Japanese wrestling also happens to be the exact fighting style that Holmes tells Watson—in Doyle's 1903 "return to form" short story "The Adventure of the Empty House"—he drew upon when he battled Moriarty in Switzerland. Holmes was not willing to rely *solely* on the principles of sumo wrestling—he also employed the techniques of the Japanese martial art of *jiu-jitsu*, which focuses on using the attacker's energy and force against him. And so, it was *both* of these ancient Japanese fighting styles that Doyle had Holmes use during his death match with Moriarty.

So how are these little tidbits related to one another? Before that question can be answered, we must address the popular misconception that Holmes was skilled in *bartitsu* (a word that has *two* letter ts in it). First, bartitsu is a totally *English*—not Japanese—martial art form that was first introduced by Edward William Barton-Wright in the year 1898. As Holmes' purported death off Reichenbach Falls occurred in the year 1891 in Doyle's "The Final Problem" (1893), and Holmes personally states in the 1903 "The Adventure of the Empty House" that he had become proficient "'in baritsu'" several years *prior*, there is no possibility whatsoever that Sherlock defended himself using a fighting style that did not yet exist.

Additionally, and for the most part, bartitsu is a combination of boxing and cane fighting and is not strictly based on the elements of Japanese wrestling. Doyle has Holmes vividly recall in "The Adventure of the Empty House" that Moriarty "'drew no weapon,'" but rather "'rushed at'" and then "'threw his long arms around'" him. This is Doyle's way of letting us know that boxing and single-sticking were not involved here. Doyle has Moriarty *grappling* Holmes—one of the critical maneuvers of sumo wrestling. Therefore, Doyle was not referring to bartitsu when he described how Holmes had managed to slip through Moriarty's grip. Instead, Doyle makes sure that Holmes utilizes an ancient martial art form that *predated* Barton-Wright's boxing / cane fighting methodology.

And so, the most likely origin of Sherlock's *baritsu* (as opposed to *bartitsu*) is that Doyle first substituted the "u" in *Burton* for an "a" (as he did when he would later have Watson don the disguise of "Dr. Hill Barton" in 1924's "The Adventure of the Illustrious Client") to make the name **Barton;** then replaced the first three letters from the word *jiu-jitsu* ("jiu") with the "Bar" of Barton; and this then yielded the heretofore unknown and totally fictitious martial art *baritsu*—based solely on the elements of sumo wrestling and jiu-jitsu.

This was *not*, as some have theorized, an inadvertent misspelling by Doyle of the aforementioned *bartitsu* fight style created by Barton-Wright five years after "The Final Problem" was published. To the contrary, Doyle wanted to make it crystal clear to his readers that Holmes was able to return from the dead by resorting to an *ancient* Japanese art form. To ensure that it was regarded as something separate and *distinct* from his already established strong boxing and single-stick abilities, Doyle has Holmes differentiate it when he tells Watson, "'I have some knowledge, however, of baritsu, or the Japanese system of wrestling, which has more than once been very useful to me.'" These words imply that Holmes' survival did not depend upon boxing, fencing, or single-sticking at all—it was all centered on sumo. Since William Burton wrote the book *Wrestlers and Wrestling in Japan*, and Holmes was able to survive the Battle of Reichenbach Falls only because of his knowledge of baritsu, it follows that William Burton was indirectly responsible—and also tacitly acknowledged—for the scenario wherein Doyle made the decision to retroactively, via *fiction*, save his Holmes character from a premature and permanent death.

As we will now further demonstrate, this was not to be the *only* time a member of the Burton family indirectly lent assistance to the Holmes character during one of his more difficult assignments. In 1891's "A Scandal in Bohemia," Holmes is commissioned to retrieve a cabinet photograph from the American-born soprano Irene Adler. Although he does know it has been hidden somewhere in her Bijou villa, he does not know its exact location. To solve the mystery, Sherlock devises a scheme aimed at tricking

Irene into revealing the secret chamber that houses the picture—a scheme that would depend upon Watson launching a "'plumber's smoke-rocket, fitted with a cap at either end to make it self-lighting'" into Ms. Adler's apartment. The plan, of course, works—but how does this detail of plot rendered by Doyle in his fiction relate to the Burton family?

Based on what existed in the 1800s, this type of sewer rocket would have contained gunpowder—a type of design that would have owed its genesis to Cosmo Innes, William Burton's uncle and mentor. A rocket of this type would have emitted smoke—and *not* a volatile liquid—for up to ten minutes in order to help detect defects in sewer pipes. Holmes' improvised smoke bomb was refitted to clear out a room—but if it hadn't been for Cosmo Innes' real-life ingenuity, Doyle's fictional Sherlock would never have learned the whereabouts of Irene Adler's compromising photograph.

When Doyle was seeking technical information regarding the complexities of hydraulic presses for 1892's "The Adventure of the Engineer's Thumb," he knew exactly who to turn to for advice—none other than his close childhood friend, William Burton. Doyle planted a secret tribute to William in this short story by disguising Burton's name in the form of the mad Colonel *Warburton*. Doyle had already *officially* acknowledged William Burton in his non-Holmes novel *The Firm of Girdlestone* (1890), where he wrote the following as his dedication page:

> "*To my old friend*
> *PROFESSOR WILLIAM K. BURTON*
> *Of the Imperial University, Tokyo,*
> *Who first encouraged me, years ago,*
> *To proceed with this little story,*
> *I desire affectionately,*
> *to dedicate it.*"

Sadly, in 1898 while William was performing surveying work for the Japanese government on the island of Formosa (now known as Taiwan) he contracted a debilitating case of dysentery, commonly associated with inflammation of the liver. He was taken back to Tokyo to receive appropriate medical attention. When his sister Mary received word of his grave condition, she left Scotland immediately and traveled to Japan to be with her brother in an attempt to nurse him back to health. Initially, William appeared to be on the road to recovery—and while convalescing, he gathered up the strength to write an article for the March 3, 1899 issue of *Photography Magazine*. Things soon would turn for the worse, though—on August 5, 1899, William died in his adopted city of Tokyo at the age of forty-three.

It wasn't long before the grateful nation of Japan acknowledged Burton as one of their national treasures. The water purification sand filtering system that he engineered has remained fully operational in the city of Shimonoseki after more than a century. The labels printed on the water bottles produced and sold by this facility once featured Burton's portrait—and there are still dozens of Burton-designed water filtration systems found throughout Japan, including plants based in Tokyo, Nagasaki, Osaka, Okayama, Kobe, and Hiroshima. In addition, the members of the Engineering Society of Japan still pay an annual visit to William Burton's gravesite to honor his enduring contributions to the health and welfare of his adopted land. It seems fittingly ironic that William Burton, who we have shown was ultimately responsible for Doyle's decision on how to save Holmes from drowning in water in "The Final Problem," was also the man who helped prevent the people of Japan from dying by drinking contaminated water.

As previously mentioned in this chapter, Doyle was not averse to separating himself from the character that had brought him fame and fortune if he were to fulfill his goal of being recognized as a legitimate author of noteworthy historical tales. Yet, there may have been other reasons for Doyle wanting Holmes dead and buried. After all, he had spent fourteen years studying and practicing medicine without gaining any recognition from his peers. And for most of those years, he was forced to supplement his income by submitting story after story to magazines that did not pay well at all. In his autobiographical 1893 article "Juvenilia," Doyle painfully confessed that "During ten years of hard work, I averaged less than fifty pounds a year from my pen." Not only had his medical and literary careers appeared fruitless to him, but his family situation was not any better. Certainly, if the Sherlock Holmes character had been granted the opportunity to investigate the details of his own fictive murder, he would have easily determined that his creator's medical and literary careers had subjected him to emotional distress, and that an inordinate number of deaths had befallen his creator's family, friends, business partners, and even lovers. It is possible that the stress imposed on Doyle by the deaths of the following people in his life weighed so heavily on his mind that it led him to finally put down his pen and declare an end to Holmes, and all things related to his imaginary world—at least for a certain period of time.

The Eccentric Inventor: George T. Budd, MD

On the last day of February in 1889, Doyle's medical classmate and former partner, George T. Budd, died from a "cerebral abnormality" at the age of thirty-four. His premature death plunged his young widow and their four children into a dire financial situation. Doyle had been Budd's business partner a decade earlier, and Budd had taught him the intricacies of what we now call *concierge medicine.* In Budd's own "large private practice," patients were required to pay a pre-set fee for "unlimited medical care." Although the Budd-Doyle partnership ended badly, Doyle still held strong feelings for Kate and George Budd as a couple. In fact, just two years after writing Holmes' "death," Doyle published *The Stark Munro Letters* (1895), a novel that doubles as a semi-autobiographical account of Doyle's adventures with the Budds.

The Governess: Annette Doyle

On February 13, 1890, Doyle's beloved older sister Annette died at the age of thirty-three from pneumonia, the result of "a virulent attack of influenza." Although it first gained worldwide notoriety as the Spanish Flu in 1918, this scourge was already present during Victorian times when it had been dubbed the "Russian epidemic." Annette, as the oldest of the Doyle family's female siblings, and Arthur, as the oldest male sibling, had seen their relationship strengthen over the years. When Annette accepted a job as a governess in Portugal, Doyle became saddened by the thought of a prolonged separation from his beloved older sister. When she fell ill, Doyle felt compelled to make the voyage to Portugal so he could direct her care, but his own mother Mary rejected such a thought, stating that he "could do no good, as two good doctors were in attendance." Hypocritically, Mary Doyle then decided to attend to her daughter and have Arthur see her off at the London piers. One year later, Doyle had a battle of his own with influenza, and described himself as being "weak as a child and as emotional." Convinced that he would soon be following his sister to the grave, he sold off all of his medical equipment and took down the brass plate from what had been his office door. Fortunately, he was able to make a full recovery, and by the Christmas season of 1891, he found himself entertaining his brother Innes and sister Connie by reading them one of his brand-new Sherlock Holmes stories—one that would have had a different ending for Holmes, had their mother not intervened. Mary warned her son that killing off his master detective would be literary suicide and would put his career in jeopardy. Doyle wrote the following letter to his mother, in which he thanks her for her wise advice: "During the holidays I finished my last Sherlock Holmes tale, 'The Adventure of the Copper Beeches' in which I used your lock of hair, so now a long farewell to Sherlock. He still lives however, thanks to your entreaties." Lingering grief about Annette's demise still cast a dark cloud over Doyle at this time, which is reflected in the words Holmes voices on behalf of his creator: "'I should allow no sister of mine to accept such a situation'" as a Governess.

The Art Collector: Henry Edward Doyle

During a span of just two years—1892 to 1893—all of Doyle's talented and accomplished uncles began dying off in quick succession. The first of them to go to his grave was Doyle's uncle Henry Edward Doyle, who died suddenly on February 17, 1892. This talented man had served as commissioner for the Papal States to the London International Exhibition and had been the recipient of the Order of Champion of the Bath for his services to Queen Victoria. Revered as a "great judge of old paintings," he had been named director at The National Gallery of Dublin in 1869. His keen eye helped the museum become the possessor of one of the world's finest and most meticulously curated art collections. Doyle lent some of his Uncle Henry's abilities to the Holmes mystique by imparting his fictional detective with his uncle's uncanny abilities to appreciate and evaluate the market value of fine works of art. In *The Valley of Fear* (1915), Sherlock Holmes lectures Inspector McDonald about the importance of a certain work of art that is mounted behind Moriarty's desk. Holmes tells him that there is no way a man making "'seven hundred a year'" could possibly afford a "'forty thousand pounds'" Jean Baptiste Greuze masterpiece.

The Historian: James William Edmund Doyle

The next to meet his end was James Doyle, a noted historian perhaps best remembered for having "written and illustrated" *The Chronicles of England: B.C. 55- A.D. 1485*, a massive historical tome that he began to compile in his youth. James revised it each year, and it wasn't long before his masterful work attracted the attention and approval of the most influential people in Britain, among them "His late Royal Highness, the lamented Prince Consort." James also spent thirteen years researching and writing the book *The Official Baronage of England showing the Succession, Dignities, and Offices of Every Peer from 1066 to 1885*. Unlike Doyle's other uncles, James did *not* share their belief in fairies, sprites, and unseen worlds. He died on December 3, 1892. Notably absent from the funeral service was James' younger brother Charles, who was then serving a prison sentence inside an insane asylum.

The Tropical Beauty: Elmore Weldon-McElroy

Doyle was struck with another great blow in September 1893, when his first love, Elmore Weldon-McElroy, succumbed to tuberculosis. Doyle had first met her in Lismore, Ireland twelve years earlier, while paying a visit to the Foley side of his family. Shortly after he was back in England, he decided that one day she would become his wife. That thought caused him concern as he thought that the two of them might become mired in a "long engagement" because he was financially unstable. When he began to set up his medical practice in Southsea a year later, he wrote his mother that if he "could marry" Elmore, "it would fetch the practice up with a rush" of patients—and with it, a sufficient amount of money. But that winter, Elmore ended their long-distance courtship. Although Doyle begged her to reconsider her decision, she rejected his proposal while informing him she had more important things to think about as she had been recently diagnosed with consumption and was on her way to Davos, Switzerland to seek medical therapy.

After they broke up, Doyle penned the anonymous short story "Heiress of Glenmahowley," where he issued a sort of confession about what had motivated him to pursue Elmore at all. When he first met her, Doyle was paying a visit to his Irish cousins—an event that mirrors an incident that takes place in this story's opening sentences. Here, we find two second cousins (Bob Elliott and a Doyle-like Jack Vereker) engaged in conversation in the Shamrock Arms Hotel. The innkeeper mentions an eighteen-year-old Ms. Clairmont, "'the purtiest girl in the county'" who happens to be worth "'five and twenty thousand pounds.'" Upon hearing this revelation, the two cousins decide to compete for the rich girl's affections, each of them coming up with a plan of their own.

Jack's scheme has him running down a private road, climbing over a ten-foot wall, and—although he injures himself in the process—continuing onward through woods laced with "bloodhounds," "spring-guns," and "mantraps." Not much later, Ms. Clairmont spots him and walks over to him. As she gets closer to him, Jack assesses her as being "one of the most lovely girls" he had ever laid eyes on, "not at all the doll-like sort of beauty . . . but a splendid, well-developed young woman with a firmly set lower jaw and delicately moulded chin which would have been almost masculine in their force had they not been relieved by a pair of pensive blue eyes and a sweetly sensitive mouth." This rather odd description represents a somewhat feeble attempt by Doyle to imbue Elmore in his veiled remembrances with at least some favorable physical attributes. It was also his way of telling his readers (and possibly her, if she had read it) that it had been her money he had been after, and her looks were of secondary importance. Nevertheless, Doyle viewed Elmore as being loyal and true, with sufficient wit and personality to escort him to social gatherings. He also assumed that she would be willing to lend her full support to any of those endeavors in which he chose to engage—and that she would always be at his side. Fortunately, Elmore was able to find happiness five years later in the form of Henry McElroy and had two daughters with him.

Apparently, Elmore's passing continued to occupy Doyle's thoughts as he wrote in the Holmes short story "The Final Problem" of a woman "in the last stage of consumption" who had "wintered at Davos Platz." Here, the conversation between Watson and Holmes is centered on the "sudden hemorrhage [that] had overtaken her" and continues with "It was thought that she could hardly live a few hours, but it would be a great consolation to her to see an English doctor."

The Artist: Charles Altamont Doyle

And then came the *coup de grace* in Doyle's prolonged season of loss. Less than three weeks after Elmore's death, Doyle's father died on October 10,

1893 at the age of sixty-one. Although his father had resided in insane asylums for more than a dozen consecutive years, Doyle continued to hold his father in great esteem. Charles, whose income was derived mainly from his position as a draftsman for the Scottish Office of Public Works, was also able to supplement his salary through the pencil sketches and watercolor paintings he designed for a slew of publishing houses. In his 1924 autobiography *Memories and Adventures*, Doyle confesses that he had "unfilled schemes" to collect as many of his father's original watercolors as he could in an effort to put them on exhibit in London, "for the critics would be surprised to find what a great and original artist he was—far the greatest, in my opinion, of the family." A few months later, Doyle made good on his resolution when the Brook's Gallery in London featured his father's illustrations. Charles Doyle's illustrations garnered considerable praise from many of the era's notable critics including George Bernard Shaw, who stated that Charles' work was worthy of a special room in a national museum.

Although a devout Catholic, Charles Doyle had no ethical or religious conflict about illustrating *The Anglican Alphabet*. He was an absolute favorite of the influential James Hogg, the publisher who commissioned him to illustrate some of the most sought-after artistic projects of his time—among them a new edition of John Bunyan's 1678 classic *The Pilgrim's Progress* and Jean Jambon's *Alice in Wonderland*-inspired story, *Our Trip to Blunderland* (1877). *Scotsman Magazine*'s review of *Blunderland* singled out Doyle's illustrations, declaring, "it is impossible to speak in terms too laudatory . . . the book in consequence, apart from its literary merits, may be safely called one of the prettiest and most enjoyable we have seen for many a day." Charles also illustrated Hogg's books for young readers and adults, among them *Pictures of Heroes* (1859), *Men Who Have Risen* (1861), *The Queens of Society* (1862), and *The Steady Aim* (1863).

Arthur Conan Doyle owes a special debt to the rock-solid relationship that was forged between Hogg and his father. When Doyle was doing his best to get his earliest works published, Hogg—taking a chance on the somewhat exotic theme of "The American's Tale"—put the short story into print anonymously. Hogg advised the budding writer to abandon his pursuit of medicine altogether and suggested that he would be better off if he devoted himself to becoming "one of the coming men in literature."

Doyle regarded his father Charles as a uniquely skilled, though unconventional, artist. When contemporary readers leaf through Charles

Doyle's sketchbook, they will observe watercolors indicative of a highly skilled professional—as well as glimpses into the artist's insanity. Squirrels nursing lost children, fairies using umbrellas for shade, Cupid rescuing sprites—all a depicted part of Charles' weird *reality*. Although Doyle knew all too well that his father's "thoughts were always in the clouds and he had no appreciation of the realities of life," he felt it was an honor to commission him to draw the six illustrations that appear in the first Holmes tale, *A Study in Scarlet*.

After Doyle had resurrected Holmes from a literary grave in "The Adventure of the Empty House," he was given one more opportunity to pay homage to his father. In "His Last Bow" (1917), Doyle gave us a disguised Sherlock Holmes who successfully foils an international spy ring using the alias "Altamont"—which was his father's middle name. As described by Watson, he perceives "Altamont" as a sixty-year-old Irish American with a "horrible goatee" who is also "a wonderful worker" with "a nice taste in wines"—characteristics that bear far more than a coincidental resemblance to the father that Doyle so admired. And while a love for his father and the grief that surrounded his sad demise may certainly stand as one of the prime reasons for killing off Holmes, there was one other special person in Doyle's life who was about to receive bad news.

The Lover: Louisa Hawkins

After all of this dying, Doyle could be forgiven for just wanting some peace and healing. But this was not forthcoming. Soon after his father's funeral, Doyle and his wife, Louisa Hawkins Doyle ("Touie"), went on a much-needed vacation. Upon their return home, Louisa began complaining "of pain in her side and cough." Although initially Doyle was not very concerned about her ailment, he did call in a physician to evaluate Louisa. To his "surprise and alarm," he was told that his wife's "lungs were very gravely affected" and "there was every sign of rapid consumption"—her condition was described as "a most serious one with little hope." Ironically, Louisa's terminal diagnosis coincided with her thirty-four-year-old husband's meteoric rise to fame. While dealing with this dreadful situation, Doyle was also receiving a growing tide of invitations to join London's most exclusive literary and social clubs. Worse still, he had already scheduled a multi-city book tour around Great Britain from which he could not extricate himself without tarnishing his reputation. He was aware that once his time on the lecture circuit was over, he would have to forgo any other engagements and attend to his dying wife. In a woeful letter to his mother written from inside the Reform Club, he told her the following:

> "on or about Dec. 10th when my lectures are finished Lottie Touie & I will start for Moritz—which is rather higher than Davos. If Touie does well there we might have a run to Egypt in the early spring and come back by sea to England when the weather is warm . . . That is, I think the best course we can adopt."

His final sentence says it all: "What with Connie's wedding, Papa's death, and Touie's illness, it is a little overwhelming."

The Detective: Sherlock Holmes

Then it happened. Two months later—precisely six years after the literary birth of Sherlock Holmes—Doyle put forth "The Final Problem," whose opening paragraph has Watson saying, "I have endeavored to give some account of my strange experiences in his [Holmes'] company from the chance which first brought us together at the period of the 'Study in Scarlet.'" Could these words—and, in particular, "his company"—have represented a cryptic reference, not to Holmes and Watson as is commonly assumed by most readers, but rather to Doyle's late father, illustrator of the first Holmes book?

Dr. Watson continues with, "It was never my intention to have stopped there, and to have said nothing of that event which has created a void in my life which the lapse of two years has done little to fill." Could these words have been a tribute in memoriam to George Budd, Elmore Weldon, and the entire Doyle clan? And could the reappearance of Sherlock's brother, Mycroft, in "The Final Problem" reflect Doyle's own longing for connection when so many in his own life had gone?

Apparently, Doyle understood from an early age that one day he might become obliged to turn against one of his own literary creations. As a sixteen-year-old Stonyhurst student, he wrote the following in a letter to his mother: "It is said that a mother ever loves best the most distorted and deformed in her children, but I trust the saying does not apply to the feelings of an author toward his literary child, otherwise it bodes ill for the poor foundling." At the age of thirty-four, Doyle would act upon these very words and kill off the character that had so swiftly made him into a household name throughout the world. Perhaps the act of murdering his Holmes character had been a catharsis for Doyle—he may even be said to have developed a taste for it by then. Ripping down the Holmes myth allowed him the freedom he needed to go on with his life after he had experienced so much sorrow in such a short period of time. In the decade that followed, Doyle did move on with his life, and gave us some of his best works, among them *The Refugees* (1893), *The Parasite* (1894), *Rodney Stone* (1896), and *Uncle Bernac: A Memory of the Empire* (1896).

And yet, the character who resonated best with Doyle's reading public continued to haunt him—and would do so until he was left with no choice but to bring him back from that precipitous fall that had seemingly consigned him to his grave.

CHAPTER 8

Rule Britannia, O Canada
Doyle's "Empty House"
and The Works of Grant Allen

"Well, sir, if it isn't too great a liberty,
I am a neighbour of yours . . ."
—SHERLOCK HOLMES, DISGUISED AS A "STRANGE OLD BOOK-
COLLECTOR" WHILE SPEAKING TO AN UNSUSPECTING DR. WATSON IN
THE SHORT STORY "THE ADVENTURE OF THE EMPTY HOUSE" (1903)

By 1890, the success of the first three Sherlock Holmes stories had transformed the thirty-one-year-old Arthur Conan Doyle from an aspiring writer into an international sensation. He became a regular on the lecture circuit, and even co-wrote the comic opera *Jane Annie; or, The Good Conduct Prize* with famed *Peter Pan* playwright James "J. M." Barrie—the show made it to London's West End Savoy Theatre in May 1893, but closed after only two months. Even though his biggest renown came from his solitary work as the creator of Sherlock Holmes, being a team player actually came easily to Doyle. Even before his meteoric rise to stardom began, he had played in Southsea's bowling, cricket, and football leagues; had been appointed a Brother in the fraternal order of the Freemason organization; and was regarded as a prominent member of the Portsmouth Literary and Scientific Society. Doyle had already gained a reputation as a man about town even *before* the success of Sherlock Holmes, and he was more than willing to stand in the limelight. Yet he never allowed his celebrity status to go to his head, a trait that explains why his friends sought him out in their times of trouble. Among the foremost beneficiaries of Doyle's innate good will was fellow novelist Grant Allen.

Born to the name Charles Grant Blairfindie Allen in 1848 in the Canadian province of Ontario, Allen immigrated to England in his early teens. After he had graduated from Oxford's Merton College in 1870, Allen was appointed the position of Classical Master at Brighton College on the English Channel. Three years later he would then leave England and travel to the Caribbean island of Jamaica, where he taught logic and philosophy to the all-Black student body at Queen's College. After another three years, he made the decision to abandon teaching, and *returned* to England to embark on a career as a full-time writer. His output was pro-lific, as he had expertise in an assortment of fields—among them were natural history, evolution, sociology, psychiatry, religion, travel, theology, science, and botany. His literary style was just as diverse and multifaceted as his range of knowledge, all of which served Allen in the same way that Doyle's prodigious gifts as a writer had served *him*.

Doyle and Grant Allen met for the first time in 1883 at a "Smith, Elder & Co's full-dress dinner" party held at Greenwich's Ship Tavern. Their introduction to each other must have a brief one—in a letter he sent to his mother immediately after the event, Doyle stated he had met "Allen Grant the botanist." Twelve years later, Allen—who had learned that Doyle's first wife Touie had become a victim of tuberculosis—sug-gested that the Doyles relocate to the village of Hindhead. Allen was proud to tell Doyle that the town's soil and air quality had "cured" him of that same affliction some years earlier. Doyle, who was always in search of a more favorable climate for his wife, immediately purchased a plot of land just down the hill from the Allen home. This purchase served to make two great intellectuals into friendly neighbors as well. Their cama-raderie, cemented with weekly bicycle excursions through the Surrey countryside, also afforded Doyle and Allen the opportunity to engage in long and thought-provoking conversations on a wide variety of topics. During this same period of time, both men were constantly submitting new works to their shared publisher George Newnes' popular periodical, *The Strand.*

Then in 1899, with just two chapters left to complete in his detective story *Hilda Wade*, Grant Allen became gravely ill with what was diagnosed as liver cancer. He was compelled to ask a favor of Doyle—that he be kind enough to complete his last novel for him. After Doyle had agreed to the dying man's request, Allen provided him with his outline for the remainder of the story. Doyle then masterfully—and unselfishly—completed the last two chapters of *Hilda Wade* for his colleague and friend. Unfortunately, on October 25, 1899, Grant Allen died.

The successful completion, and subsequent publication, of Allen's *Hilda Wade* would *not* be Doyle's final gesture of respect toward one of his generation's most beloved writers. Four years later, Doyle's short story "The Adventure of the Empty House" (1903) was published. By this time, Doyle had caved in to public demand and brought Sherlock Holmes back to literary life in the immensely popular novel *The Hound of the Baskervilles*. Although he had given the world another Holmes story, Doyle coyly set that first new story as taking place three years before he had killed off Holmes in his 1893 short story "The Final Problem." With "The Adventure of the Empty House," however, Doyle revealed just how Sherlock Holmes had somehow *survived* his purported fall off the cliffs at Reichenbach. The chief objective of Doyle's new story was to explain how Holmes narrowly escaped an ambush arranged by Professor Moriarty and his minions in "The Final Problem." What Doyle did not disclose to his readers was that he also had scattered several intriguing references throughout this new Holmes story. Each of them serves as clues that further illuminate—and celebrate—some key elements of the life and legacy of the late Allen.

In "Empty House," Doyle recycled several names of characters who appear in Allen's own works, and also some of the places Allen had written about or visited during the course of his long and illustrious career. The story opens with Watson as he briefs the reader about a decade-old case that involved "the murder of the Honourable Ronald Adair under the most unusual and inexplicable circumstances." Watson tells us that, at the time of Adair's assassination, he had shared a home with his mother and his sister, Hilda. The use of the name "Hilda" will immediately strike a chord with any Allen fan who has read the serialized novel that Doyle had helped Allen complete—the aforementioned *Hilda Wade*. In "Empty House," the Adairs reside in the posh London district of Kensington at "427 Park Lane." In Allen's 1899 mystery novel *Miss Cayley's Adventures* (which *also* opens in Kensington), we learn about the "**Park Lane** murders," while in his *Hilda Wade*, the residence of the character Sissie Montague's love interest is established early in the book as "**427**, Staples Inn." Doyle's choice of the Christian name "Ronald" for the Adair character is also significant, as it is the first name of the protagonist in Allen's debut novel *Philistia* (1884). In Allen's story, Ronald le Breton's older brother Ernest was engaged to "Miss Edith" Oswald; in Doyle's "Empty House," Ronald Adair is engaged to a **"Miss Edith"** Woodley. In Doyle's tale, Ronald Adair is identified as being the second son of the Earl of Maynooth. Interestingly, Maynooth is a municipality in the Canadian province of Ontario, which—as we have previously noted—is where Allen was born. And like Allen, Ronald Adair was a second-born child.

It also turns out that the primary motive of the man who kills Ronald Adair in "Empty House" matches perfectly with the one employed by the murderer in *Hilda Wade*. In the Doyle adventure, Ronald Adair partners with Colonel Sebastian Moran at cards. When Ronald realizes that the large sums of money that had been won by them have been obtained by the Colonel having resorted to underhanded methods, Adair considers it his duty to disclose Moran's lack of ethics to the fellow members of their exclusive clubs. Moran remains steadfast in his refusal to have his reputation tarnished in any way—and has no qualms at all about calling upon his specialized air-gun, with its imperceptible bullet, to do away with the idealistic Ronald. Similarly, in Allen's *Hilda Wade*, when Professor Sebastian learns of Dr. Yorke-Bannerman's humane experiment—one designed to provide a cure for an unnamed tropical disease by using the virtually untraceable chemical *aconitine*—he unilaterally modifies things in an attempt to determine the plant-derived agent's toxic dose. Professor Sebastian has no reservations blackmailing the pharmacist charged with preparing this promising medicinal and strong-arms him to increase the strength of the drug until it reaches its ultimately lethal level. This is what causes the unsuspecting patient's eventual demise. When Dr. Yorke-Bannerman realizes what had transpired on the ward, he issues a threat to Professor Sebastian, telling him that he will notify the authorities about what has gone on for the so-called sake of humanity. An unkind stroke of fate causes Dr. Yorke-Bannerman to suffer a fatal heart attack, which enables his partner to elude the hands of justice.

While Sebastian Moran and Professor Sebastian are regarded by their peers—and society at large—as the most honorable of men in their chosen professions, each of them is in fact a *sociopath*. Doyle's Colonel Moran is a soldier of fortune who is always prepared to murder anyone who might stand in his way, while Allen's Professor Sebastian is willing to violate the rules of society in the name of science. Indeed, Dr. Sebastian is a paradigm of the maxim voiced by Sherlock Holmes in 1892's "The Adventure of the Speckled Band"—"'When a doctor does go wrong he is the first of criminals. He has nerve and he has knowledge.'"

Doyle goes on to deftly incorporate several other books into "The Adventure of the Empty House"—books that are tied inextricably to the works and interests of Grant Allen. Doyle accomplishes this feat by creating the following scene: Dr. Watson is strolling down the streets of Kensington and "accidentally" collides with a book-carrying "elderly deformed man." This character conforms to the physical characteristics of the erudite Allen, a man often referred to as a "bibliophile." Doyle's new Allen-like character becomes irate when his precious books are knocked from his hands and lay scattered on the ground in disarray. Among those fallen treasures are "The Origin of Tree Worship" and *The Attis of Catullus*—the first of them an essay authored by Allen, and the second a Greek mythological work that he translated. In fact, in his introduction to his translation of *The Attis of Catullus*, Allen wrote, "It is nearly twenty years ago that I read Catullus's masterpiece with my class of students in an abortive little Government College in Spanish Town."

Another of the "old man's" fallen books in Doyle's scene is *British Birds*, a tribute to one of Allen's earliest published essays, "English Birds and their Haunts," which appeared in the 1880 issue of *The Magazine of Art*. This can also be seen as Doyle's nuanced way of alluding to Allen's reputation as the respected ornithologist who had authored the 1881 book *Vignettes from Nature*—a work in which much of the material is focused on *English* birds. Watson tells the bibliophile (who will soon be revealed as Holmes, in disguise) that "'Maybe you collect yourself . . .'"—here again, a reference to the book-hoarding habit of Allen. The fourth book that then falls on the pavement, *The Holy War*, stands as an unacknowledged reference to Allen's first novel, *Philistia*. Known in present-day as a region that intersects across Israel and Egypt along with Palestine, Philistia was hotly contested during the medieval period Crusades—or, as most historians refer to that time, the "Holy Wars."

Soon after this exchange in the London streets, Doyle reveals to his readers another unexpected and far more exciting development: The elderly gentleman whose books have been strewn about the pavement is none other than Sherlock Holmes—in *disguise*. Once Watson recovers from his initial shock at this revelation, Holmes readily explains how he managed to escape death in Switzerland. This scenario is a perfect fit for the title of one of the two *Hilda Wade* chapters that Doyle completed for Allen—"The Dead Man Who Spoke." Holmes' travels, during what would now become known to readers as the fictional detective's "long hiatus," offer Doyle's embedded tribute to Grant Allen's own substantial works and journeys. Holmes discloses to Watson that a week after he made his escape from Moriarty's henchmen at Reichenbach Falls, he was able to make his way to Florence. The choice of Florence as a starting-point city was not made by accident—after all, Allen wrote several historical travel books, one of them being his popular historical guide from 1897 entitled *Florence*. Holmes then tells Watson about his strange journey to distant Tibet, where he spent "'some days with the head Llama.'" Again, this ties in with what we know Doyle contributed to *Hilda Wade*. That book's eleventh chapter—"The Episode of the Officer who Understood Perfectly," the first written completely with Doyle at the helm—begins exactly where the Allen-penned *tenth* chapter "The Guide Who Knew the Country" left off: The characters Hilda Wade and Dr. Cumberledge are granted an audience with the "'head of all Lamas'" in exotic Tibet.

As an aside, Holmes' fictitious audience with the Dalai Lama—followed by his looking "'in at Mecca'"—provides us with further insight regarding his profound knowledge of two of the world's major religions. As described in Allen's *Hilda Wade*, any Westerner who makes even the merest attempt to enter Tibet—let alone one of its sacred Buddhist monasteries—will meet with immediate execution. The sole reason that allows the characters Hilda Wade and Dr. Cumberledge to make it out alive from their unplanned trespass into Tibet rests chiefly on Hilda's familiarity with the tenets and customs of Buddhism—and her flawless performance of some of its sacred rituals. We can assume that Holmes' knowledge of Buddhism must have been equal to—or perhaps even *exceeded*—that of Hilda Wade's. After all, Holmes spent not one day but *many* days with the Dalai Lama. Holmes also confesses to Watson that he had been able to enter Mecca—the holiest place on the planet, according to Islamic belief. Even today, only those who are *proven* Muslims can enter the city—all others who are *not* devout worshipers of Allah and adherents of the Koran are redirected to the highway that surrounds the area. And yet—in homage to nineteenth century pioneering British scholar, explorer, and multilinguist Sir Richard Francis Burton—Doyle ensures that Holmes must *also* have been proficient in Arabic, as it remains the only language permitted to be spoken in Mecca. It stands to reason that Holmes must have been able to convince everyone with whom he came in contact during his pilgrimage to Mecca that he was a practicing member of the Muslim faith.

Holmes then continues to share with Watson the details of his extensive and in-depth tours of Asia, Africa, and Europe—all of which serve as Doyle's sly tip of the hat to Allen, who was declared in the 1890s by the British journal *Review of Reviews* "an inquisitive explorer of continental cities." Holmes' peripatetic odyssey ends in the southern France city of Montpellier, the region where Allen had spent his winters coping with health-related issues beginning in the autumn of 1879. In Allen's books *The Evolution of the Idea of God* (1897) and *Historical Guide to Venice* (published in early 1900, just two months after his death), he writes about the holy man of St. Roch of Montpellier, who issued a firm warning to his countrymen that poor sanitary conditions were what promoted the spread of the plague. Of note, the Irish journalist and short story writer Frank Harris described Grant Allen in *Contemporary Portraits* (1923) as a "chemist"—a profession applicable to Holmes' time spent in a Montpellier chemical laboratory, as Doyle tells it.

In "Empty House," Holmes also masquerades as a Norwegian explorer named "Sigerson." There was in fact an actual Dr. Sigerson who had written favorably about Allen's series of science fiction-oriented books known as the "Hilltop Satires" ("Hilltop," of course, being the name of Allen's home). Just where Holmes traveled using the "Sigerson" alias is not exactly known, but Doyle *does* tell us that his exploits made the newspapers—and that Holmes was quite proud of his achievements. It is likely that Holmes/"Sigerson" was a member of the Norwegian expedition that sailed to Greenland with the illustrious American explorer and naval officer Robert Edwin Peary. It follows that Doyle may have been making subtle reference to his own personal adventures aboard the *Hope*, where he had served as ship's physician and as a valued member of this whaling vessel that sailed out of Peterhead (the northeastern-most point on the Scottish mainland). On his six-month stint aboard the ship, Doyle traveled above the Arctic Circle and hunted whales and seals off the Greenland coast. Nevertheless, once Holmes sheds his "Sigerson" disguise, he fills Watson in about the superficial details of how he had happened to wend his way to southern France—after pausing for a few stops in the Middle East and North Africa. And this contrived plot of assuming false identities may have been an undeclared tribute to Allen's Holmes-like character Maisie Yorke-Bannerman—a.k.a., Hilda Wade—who had appeared in the novel of that same name.

Of added interest is not only that the name Doyle gave to his "Empty House" villain (Colonel Sebastian Moran) is a close match to Allen's Professor Arthur **Sebastian**—it is that both the Colonel and the Professor are University of Oxford graduates who share remarkably similar physical *and* intellectual characteristics. Both men are described by their creators as elderly and brilliant, and both sport "grizzly" mustaches. Notably, both Doyle's Sebastian Moran and Allen's Thomas Cumberledge (the father of *Hilda Wade*'s narrator) had served in the late 1870s as colonels in India's large metropolitan Bangalore region.

In both "The Adventure of the Empty House" and *Hilda Wade*, murders are carried out in a very similar manner. In "Empty House," Ronald Adair meets instant death inside his locked room when a bullet penetrates his head. In *Hilda Wade*, the character Jan Willem Klaas is murdered outside his home by a bullet that pierces his left temple. And lest we forget, it is Colonel Moran who fires an expanding bullet that penetrates the forehead (the **temple** region) of Holmes' "bust in wax."

In Allen's *Miss Cayley's Adventures*, the title character is declared a *shikari* (a word used in India to describe hunters or trackers) after her rifle accidentally blasts a tiger right between the eyes. Holmes deems Colonel Moran a shikari, which stands as a direct reference to the **tiger-hunting** skills that *he* had displayed while serving in India. In *Hilda Wade*, we learn that Professor Sebastian has spent "three years in Africa"—in "The Adventure of the Empty House," Holmes tells us that Colonel Sebastian had authored a book entitled "*Three Months in the Jungle.*"

Holmes then proceeds to berate Watson, reprimanding him for his ineffective search efforts after his near-death experience at the hands of Professor Moriarty and his gang. Holmes goes on to deride Watson with these cutting words—"'There I was stretched when you, my dear Watson, and all your following were investigating in the most sympathetic and inefficient manner the circumstances of my death'"—and concludes his diatribe with "'At last, when you had all formed your inevitable and totally erroneous conclusions, you departed for the hotel and I was left alone.'" This statement makes it quite clear that it is Holmes' perception that Watson is no more than a rank amateur—an "'unprofessional detective'"—and it also happens to line up with a chapter from *Miss Cayley's Adventures* titled "The Unprofessional Detective."

The final pages of "Empty House" find Holmes as he waxes poetic on the subjects of evolution and natural selection:

"'There are some trees, Watson, which grow to a certain height and then suddenly develop some unsightly eccentricity. You will see it often in humans. I have a theory that the individual represents in his development the whole procession of his ancestors, and that such a sudden turn to good or evil stands for some strong influence which came into the line of his pedigree. The person becomes, as it were, the epitome of the history of his own family.'"

This statement, which students of biology have turned into the axiom "ontogeny recapitulates phylogeny," might well have been uttered by Grant Allen—a noted naturalist and evolutionist in his own right, who was also a biographer of Charles Darwin and the close friend of Herbert Spencer (coiner of the phrase "survival of the fittest").

When Doyle was writing "The Adventure of the Empty House," it would seem that he decided to add a few hidden tidbits related to his good friend, the noted humorist and publisher James Payn. Right before Doyle began working on the last two chapters of Allen's *Hilda Wade*, Payn died suddenly at his home on March 23, 1898. Not only was Payn in the same social class as Grant Allen, but he also "had a passion for whist," a very popular card game during the late nineteenth century. James Payn frequented the exclusive card clubs of London, including, as Doyle declared in his autobiography *Memories and Adventures*, the Baldwin—the same one mentioned in "Empty House." Had Colonel Moran been based on an actual person, he would certainly have been seated at the same card tables as Payn. And in Payn's own novel *A Woman's Vengeance* (1894), an altogether different Adair family is put forth as the story's central figures.

Doyle acted abstractly as Sherlock Holmes' "personal physician" by taking a character who had been pronounced "dead" and then recalling him back to literary life. And this *was not* just any old character—this brilliant consulting detective, as enamored of his violin as he was of his preferred "'seven-per-cent solution'" of cocaine, was destined to reach iconic status for more than a century . . . perhaps *forever*. What Doyle did is perhaps best summed up in the first chapter of Grant Allen's *Hilda Wade*, when Dr. Cumberledge asks, "'What nobler object can a man propose to himself than to raise *good* men and true men from the dead, as it were, and return them whole and sound to the family that depends upon them?'"

Doyle's considerable skills at hiding clues within the fabric of his works are most pointedly evident within "The Adventure of the Empty House." Having gone through the biographical details here, it must now be obvious that Grant Allen was much more to Doyle than just a neighbor. He was a novelist that Doyle held in greatest admiration. While Doyle's Holmes would go on to become a definitive symbol of the detective novel, so too did Grant Allen's *Hilda Wade* help pave the way for generations of female detectives devised by both British and American writers—among them Dame Agatha Christie's sophisticated Miss Marple; Edward Stratemeyer's juvenile whiz kid Nancy Drew (the stories of which were attributed to a nonexistent woman writer named "Carolyn Keene"); Sue Grafton's alphabet-solving Kinsey Millhone; and Jeffery Deaver's street-smart police officer Amelia Sachs.

CHAPTER 9

——————

A Tale of Two Countries
Doyle and Holmes
in the New World

*"Arthur was the most single-minded,
chivalrous, patriotic man upon earth."*

—Miss Westbury, talking with Sherlock Holmes
about her fiancé in "The Adventure of the
Bruce-Partington Plans" (1908)

Successful fiction writers often draw upon events in their own lives
to craft stories, and then use the characters they create as a vehicle
through which to make their opinions, concerns, and hopes known
to the public at large. In this way, Arthur Conan Doyle called upon his
most iconic characters Sherlock Holmes and John Watson to broadcast
his ideas—and *ideals*—to a wide and receptive audience. That Doyle was
loyal to England is beyond question, as was his belief that Britain had an
obligation to join forces with her former overseas colony—the United
States of America. A firm determination on Doyle's part to help restore
a bond between the two nations can be found scattered throughout his
stories and his letters to the press.

Although there were no immediate members of his family with established roots in the United States during his lifetime, Doyle had from his
youth "been greatly interested in American history and fiction." Unable
to "tumble about in an American library, he tumbled about with American
books, and his Americana were among the very best." As a young aficio-
nado of all things literary, Doyle was enthralled by American novelist

James Fenimore Cooper's entertaining land and sea adventures. Years later in 1893, Doyle would deliberately emulate Cooper's writing style in his novel *The Refugees*—he even had his tale take place in upstate New York, the same setting used by Cooper in his best-known works *The Last of the Mohicans: A Narrative of 1757* (1826) and *The Deerslayer, or The First War-Path* (1841). Doyle also gravitated early on to the works of New Englander Nathaniel Hawthorne, whose writings he admired for their "individuality and their quality." Doyle regarded Hawthorne's *The Scarlet Letter: A Romance* (1850) as "the greatest novel yet written in America." One might argue he may have been unconsciously influenced by the title of Hawthorne's masterwork when he decided to change the name of his first Sherlock Holmes novel from *A Tangled Skein* to *A Study in **Scarlet***.

Doyle was also fascinated by the subtle genius of American poet and short story writer Bret Harte, who weaved "finely-conceived bits of psychology" into characters who possessed both "heroic and criminal qualities." Here again was a writer from across the Atlantic who did much to influence and populate Doyle's own imaginary world set to pen and paper. In many of the sixty remarkable Sherlock Holmes stories, Doyle frequently endows his characters with dual personalities—a reliable literary device with which Doyle could humanize them more effectively. In one of the later stories "The Adventure of the Illustrious Client" (1924), Doyle presents the dashing Baron Adelbert Gruner as a man who "has an artistic side" yet is simultaneously a philanderer and a "murderer." In this adventure of extortion, the reader also has the opportunity to witness the usually law-abiding detective allow one of Gruner's near-victims to take revenge by hurling an open container of acid into the Baron's face, which leaves the man blinded and disfigured.

Doyle creates a similar scenario in his 1904 tale of blackmail and retribution, "The Adventure of Charles Augustus Milverton." In this tale, Holmes intentionally permits a woman who has been scorned by the titular Milverton to fire—at point blank range—a fatal fusillade of bullets into him. Worse still, Holmes displays a relatively shocking lapse in ethics when he prevents Watson from stopping the murder. Had Watson been able to intercede, Holmes could have brought Milverton to the proper authorities. He *doesn't*. Once the deed has been done and Milverton is dead, Holmes decides to ransack the villain's safe and then flees the scene of the crime—coming dangerously close to being apprehended by Milverton's henchmen in the process. It is this internal conflict between good and evil impulses that continue to make Doyle's characters so lifelike for readers.

Although ever the archetypal British writer, Doyle's imagination seemed to be possessed by what then-groundbreaking Austrian psychoanalyst Sigmund Freud termed the "id"—a kind of hidden darkness that lay at the center of the human soul, an unbridled madness within the heart of a brute. In the late 1880s, as Doyle was making a name for himself as the creator of Sherlock Holmes, he walked about the London streets that were being terrorized by "Jack the Ripper." At around the same time, in the Midwestern city of Chicago, Illinois, a confidence man named Herman Webster Mudgett was at work turning himself into America's first serial killer "H. H. Holmes." While Doyle was undoubtedly an English loyalist, the new society that was emerging in the United States also held a special resonance for him. Indeed, there always was the wayward pull of Yankee blood flowing through his veins. And over the course of time, with each of his American adventures, Doyle's work became increasingly evolved and more refined.

Doyle's longtime appreciation of contemporary American authors is shown to have continually rekindled his desire to be accepted and appreciated in both British and American literary circles. The year 1880 in particular marked Doyle's first *written* effort to convince his countrymen how important it was to reunite Great Britain with the United States. His anonymously published short story "The American's Tale" tells the story of Joe "Alabama" Hawkins, who goes missing after an altercation with an Englishman named Tom Scott. The patrons at Simpson's bar, who come to assume that Scott has killed Hawkins, decide to take justice into their own hands. These vigilantes round up Scott, put him into a cart, and take him out to be hanged in the Mojave Desert that stretched across the Arizona/Nevada border. Along the way, they come upon Hawkins' partially decomposed corpse rotting away within a gigantic Venus flytrap plant. This chance discovery serves to exonerate Scott—and by story's end, Jack Sinclair asks Jefferson Adams (a name that Doyle arrives at through combination of the United States' second and third presidents, respectively) the question, "'And what became of Scott?'" Adams' reply is a casual, "'Why, we carried him back on our shoulders, we did, to Simpson's bar, and he stood us liquors round. Made a speech too—a darned fine speech—from the counter. Somethin' about the British lion an' the 'Merican eagle walkin' arm in arm for ever an' a day.'" By linking these two symbols of Great Britain and the United States, it was Doyle's intent to show that if these two great nations were willing to join forces, a state of perfect harmony might easily be achieved.

Seven years later, in *A Study in Scarlet*, Doyle conjured up images of the American frontier by placing his focus on the dangerous trek undertaken by the Mormons to the city of Deseret—the site of present-day Salt Lake City, Utah. Although he had not as yet visited the US, Doyle was already a fervent reader of stories written by America's most popular fiction writers—men like Mark Twain, Edgar Allen Poe, and Bret Harte among others. The knowledge he had gained by reading these stories filled Doyle with enough confidence to profess that he knew the landscape of the Midwest and the Rockies like he knew his "own garden." *A Study in Scarlet* offers further evidence of his detailed knowledge of the Mormon Church, as well as his familiarity with the geography and topography of the Sierra Nevada Mountains and the Great Salt Lake—despite not having seen it in person.

Even with an appreciation of American locales and characteristics strewn throughout his fiction, this was not enough to ensure Doyle's success with his newly created detective. When the next Holmes tale *The Sign of the Four* (1890) was a financial flop, Doyle decided to take a brief hiatus away from his new characters. Instead, he delved into historical research on the Hundred Years' War between France and England during the 14th and 15th centuries. He then transformed that material into a historical adventure novel entitled *The White Company*. Since it remained a priority for him to help forge an inextricable bond with America at this time, Doyle dedicated the novel "To the hope of the future, the reunion of the English-speaking races." Soon after, he received a letter from pioneering British gynecologist Dr. Lawson Tait in which he encouraged the struggling new writer to provide the world with more of his Holmes stories. Doyle acted quickly on that sound advice, inspired at once to pen both "A Scandal in Bohemia" and "The Red-Headed League" within a year. It was the rapid succession and growing success of these three works—*The White Company*, "A Scandal in Bohemia," and "The Red-Headed League," together with the US publication of *A Study in Scarlet* in 1890—that first conferred official stardom on Doyle. By 1892, Sherlock Holmes, Dr. John

Watson, and Doyle were household names on two continents—Europe *and* North America.

It should serve as no surprise that Doyle made certain America was prominently represented in those next two Holmes tales that followed *A Study in Scarlet* and *The Sign of the Four*. In "A Scandal in Bohemia," his prima donna contralto character Irene Adler hails from New Jersey—and this American performer isn't just *anybody*. As Watson explains to us in his narrative, Holmes uncharacteristically bestows a nickname upon Adler— he calls her "*the* woman." And in "The Red-Headed League," the charter money received by the title's organization was a "'bequest of the late Ezekiah Hopkins, of Lebanon, Pennsylvania, U.S.A.'" Clearly, Doyle—a master of wordplay—was in search of a town that held an association with the color red without being too obvious about it. In support of that point, just down the road from Lebanon in the state of Pennsylvania is the small city of Reading—pronounced as "**RED**"-ing.

Doyle knew that his newfound reputation granted him an opportunity to voice his sentiments about what he saw as an urgent need for Britain to reclaim America. In a literary voice that echoed that of his real-life creator, Sherlock Holmes also began to petition for the unification of these two giant English-speaking nations. In "The Adventure of the Noble Bachelor" (1892), we observe as Holmes tells Mr. Moulton, a wealthy Californian gold miner, "'Then I trust that you at least will honour me with your company . . . It is always a joy to meet an American, Mr. Moulton, for I am one of those who believe that the folly of a monarch and the blundering of a minister in far-gone years will not prevent our children from being some day citizens of the same world-wide country under a flag which shall be a quartering of the Union Jack with the Stars and Stripes.'" Doyle, within the guise of Holmes, informs his readers in "Noble Bachelor" that King George III and his Prime Minister Frederick North, 2nd Earl of Guilford, had acted "'stupidly'" when they declared war on the American colonies. Doyle—placing not a scintilla of guilt on Sam Adams and Patrick Henry, along with the other masterminds of the American Revolution—has Holmes offer a prediction to Mr. Moulton about how it would be only a matter of time before the two countries would again share the same flag.

As 1892 came to a close, Doyle followed this up with a letter—signed in his own name—that was published in the prestigious, highly influential, and widely read *London Times*. The letter appeared as follows:

"TO THE EDITOR OF THE TIMES.

Sir, — A graceful act of courtesy may do more than the most elaborate statecraft. A capacity for such actions has never shown itself to be part of our national genius. Such a proceeding, for example, as the presentation of the Statue of Liberty by France to America is, as far as I know, unparalleled in our annals. *And yet if there are any two races upon earth between which such courtesies should prevail they are our own and our kin of the United States.*

At present their heart is set upon making their exhibition a success, and any help which we might give them in achieving this *would be very welcome to them.* Much after-dinner oratory has been expended upon both sides of the water upon our *common origin and common sympathies.* Our Government has an opportunity now of showing some practical sign of good will.

The German Government has just refused to the Americans the use of any of their military bands. It would be a graceful action upon the part of our authorities to offer, say, three of our own crack regimental bands, including one of the Guards, to play in the British section of the exhibition. If, in addition to this, a squadron of our Life Guards was sent over to take part in the opening procession the compliment would be the greater. German and French regimental bands have played in London exhibitions and American regiments have visited Canadian towns, so that the idea has no claims to novelty. It appears to me, however, to be just one of those occasions for cementing international friendship which seldom present themselves and which are too valuable to neglect.

Yours faithfully,
A. Conan Doyle
Reform Club, Pall Mall, S.W., Dec. 22." *[emphases added throughout]*

Doyle's representation of himself here is that of England's duly appointed ambassador to the United States. He recommends that Great Britain send a lavish gift to the people of Chicago—something akin to France's Statue of Liberty being offered to the US a few years earlier in 1886—to help make the American World's Fair "a success." He *further* states that any present would be "welcome," although he lacked the authority to make such a claim. Doyle, who had not been asked to act as an ambassador for either the United States or Great Britain, also had no reservations about using the London-based Reform Club's prestigious address to impress others in his letter's closing signature. His final suggestion is that a British military band be sent to the World's Fair in order to highlight how Germany had insulted the United States when it refused to permit its own military band to perform there at The Columbian Exposition.

A few days later, after reading an article in the *Leeds Mercury* publication that ran contrary to his stance, Doyle took it upon himself to then defend in a letter the right of Great Britain to send a "regimental band" over to the United States—in the hopes that his words would convince Britain's leaders to rise to the occasion and to send more than a token group of musicians overseas to Chicago. What he wanted most at this point was an official statement that would attest to Britain's loyalty to— and friendship with—the people of the United States:

"TO THE EDITORS OF THE LEEDS MERCURY

Gentlemen, — As the 'Leeds Mercury' is the only provincial paper of note which has contained any adverse criticism of the suggestion that British regimental bands should be offered to the Chicago Exhibition for use in the British section, you will perhaps allow me to say a word in defence of it. Your London Correspondent bases his objections on the assertion that our bands have never before been used in this fashion. *I submit, Gentlemen, that even if this were true, it would surely not be a very grave objection, since it would be the more creditable to our generation if they took a new and more generous departure* . . . And then as to what your correspondent says about reciprocity of courtesy, that is very true, but the balance of reciprocity lies at present against us. *We have never, as far as I know, done any generous deed for the United States, but several might be mentioned which they have done for us....* If we have individual enemies across the water, surely there is the more reason that we should show ourselves courteous and sympathetic. Your Correspondent cannot mean to maintain that it is a good thing for a nation to have enemies, and an evil one to take steps to disarm them.

Yours faithfully,
A. CONAN DOYLE.
12, Tennison-road, South Norwood, Dec. 29th."
[emphases added throughout]

In this correspondence above, Doyle does his best to persuade all who read it that the American nation has for more than a century gone out of its way to help Great Britain, as opposed to his own country's having not reciprocated with as much as a single "generous deed" for them.

The March 16, 1893 edition of *The Daily Chronicle* features Doyle's suggestion yet again concerning the World's Fair in the US in the article "A World's Fair Suggestion" as shown below:

> "Dr. Conan Doyle writes to the *Daily Chronicle* to urge the Government to send special representatives to the World's Fair. He says:—All plans for the future of our race which omit the United States are as vain as the planning of an arch without the keystone. *No difference of government or manners can alter the fact that the largest collection of people of Anglo-Celtic descent in the world is to be found upon the other side of the Atlantic.* If, therefore, the race is destined (as I firmly believe that it is) to become more homogeneous in the future, it is certain not only that this vast block of people must be regarded as a factor in the problem, but that their wishes will have a great deal to do with its solution. The centre of the race is shifting ever westward, until the British Isles represent its extreme fringe on one side, as Australia does on the other. If these world-wide communities are not to eternally oppose and neutralise each other, they must sooner or later be organized into a union of commonwealths which shall be founded upon no artificial treaty, but upon the permanent basis of common blood, and in the main of common traditions. But if this ideal is to be reached, then no opportunity should be lost of reminding the world that, in spite of the one great rift of the last century, the Anglo-Celtic rare is mindful of its common origin. The coming Chicago Exhibition affords an admirable opportunity for doing this . . . If four regimental bands, representing English, Scotch, Irish, and Welsh corps were to go, together with representatives of the Cape Mounted Rifles, or of the Victoria Rifles, or any other Australian corps, and of the Canadian Militia, it would, I think, meet the case." *[emphases added throughout]*

Doyle boldly predicted that Great Britain and America would reunite, and further asserted that once that had been accomplished, this *new nation* would have every right to rule the world. The end of that year came with heartbreaking news for both Doyle—and, by extension, his loyal fans. Following the death of his father in October 1893, Doyle decided to take a quick trip throughout the European mainland with his first wife, Louisa ("Touie"). On their way back home to London, however, Touie began to complain of "pain in her side and cough." Doyle called swiftly for a "good physician," who promptly diagnosed Touie with a terminal case of "rapid consumption." A few days later, in the December 1893 issues of the *Strand Magazine*, "The Final Problem" was published in serial format—and almost immediately, readers were stunned to learn that their beloved consulting detective had met his described death in Switzerland. Ironically, Doyle and Touie raced off to Davos, Switzerland around this same time—their shared hope was that the region's anticipated therapeutic air and pure mountain water might bring forth a cure for her dire condition. It was there at Davos that Doyle would write his semi-autobiographical novel *The Stark Munro Letters* (1895). America seems still to have been on Doyle's mind during this time, as this new story's narrator sends his letters of correspondence to a former classmate named as "Herbert Swanborough, of Lowell, Massachusetts."

It was also at Davos where Doyle wrote to "American impresario" Major James B. Pond and asked him "what the price of a lecture tour of the Eastern States for one month next autumn would be." Although he thought a lecture tour might furnish him with enough money to at least cover his travel expenses, Doyle claimed that "the main object of his visit to America, in fact the only object (for his lectures are incidental) is the necessity of finding a place where his wife could regain health and strength." Major Pond jumped at the chance to represent Doyle in America and booked thirty venues throughout that country for his lectures. In mid-September 1894, Doyle was still not sure whether he would extend his maiden trip to the US so he could visit "Colorado Springs (the American Davos)." If his speaking tour were successful, then Doyle would return in the spring of 1895—and this time, with his wife.

On September 27, 1894, Doyle—accompanied by his younger brother, Innes—made a transatlantic journey aboard the S.S. *Elbe*, which arrived in New York City less than a week later on October 2. After checking in at the upscale Adine Club (located at 75 Fifth Avenue and known for its well-respected literary membership), Doyle and his brother enjoyed two days of sightseeing throughout Manhattan. One of the highlights of touring Manhattan was taking a ride in an elevator—referred to by Doyle in a speech around this time as a "dynamite gun"—which may be seen as a subtle reference to J. T. Maston's fictitious gunpowder-fueled gun at the center of Jules Verne's 1865 novel *From the Earth to the Moon*—to the top of the Manhattan Life Insurance Building, which at that time was the city's tallest skyscraper. From its rooftop, Doyle looked out upon the "noble" Brooklyn Bridge, and "the magnificent city's . . . two rivers crowded with shipping." Doyle's first public appearance on American soil was as a guest at Manhattan's Lotus Club on October 4—and on October 10, he gave the first lecture of his tour at the Calvary Baptist Church. He even put away time to play a round of golf in the nearby suburb of Yonkers with the writer of the popular "Editor's Drawer" column in *Harper's Magazine*, the American satirist John Kendrick Bangs.

Following in the footsteps of his literary idol Robert Louis Stevenson, Doyle then set off to explore New York's Adirondack Mountains and the nearby "mountain regions of the New England States"—all in search of a perfect therapeutic climate for his wife. When he was not scouting for real estate, he was dutifully meeting the terms of his lecture tour agreement with Major Pond. He was still able to deliver one or two lectures a day, the majority of them "reminiscences and literary comments, largely personal, and two or three readings from" the assembled Sherlock Holmes works; his newly published historical novel *The Refugees: A Tale of Two Continents* (which takes place in the Colonial New York cities of Albany and Schenectady); and then one or another "from miscellaneous stories." And it was in America that Doyle offered his first public hint—revealed in a *New York Daily Tribune* article published in November of that year—that although the great Sherlock Holmes was "probably dead," there was a possibility that he "might escape, and be revived."

By October 15, Doyle headed further west to Indiana, where he addressed a large audience comprised chiefly of physicians. On that evening, he began his lecture by speaking about himself—how the famous *Vanity Fair* novelist William Makepeace Thackeray "held him for a moment . . . upon his knee" when he was four, and how he had, as a young lad, devoured "the entire series of novels" written by legendary Scottish author and "The Great Wizard of the North, Walter Scott." At the end of that discussion, Doyle had the opportunity to speak with the American writer James Whitcombe Riley, best remembered as the "Hoosier Poet" because of his work's frequent reference and embrace of all things Indiana. Doyle *also* met at that same event with noted dermatologist F. W. Hayes and

Indiana Medical College's anatomy professor L. D. Waterman. Doyle was able to prove "that his interest in medicine was real and not perfunctory," and went on to inform Hayes, Waterman, and Riley "when he has financially established himself he [would] open an eye infirmary in London, ophthalmology claiming his special interest." Apparently, he reneged on that night's promise.

Prior to his transatlantic voyage, Doyle had deliberately contacted two members of the current literati then based in America who he wanted to meet in person. Both of them resided in New England—Boston, Massachusetts-based Dr. Oliver Wendell Holmes, and the India-born British author Rudyard Kipling who now resided in Brattleboro, Vermont. Unfortunately, by the time Doyle arrived, Dr. Holmes had died. Yet, when Doyle gave a lecture in the Boston area, he made sure to pay a visit to Mount Auburn cemetery where the lamented Holmes had been laid to rest. "And as an accredited member and representative of the Society of English Authors of London," which Doyle had written in a letter home to his mother at this time, he "decorated the grave of the physician literateur. The memorial consisted of a number of palms tied with purple ribbon and ornamented with large bunches of English violets, bride roses, and asparagus vines. The card attached read: 'From the Society of Authors (London). A token of our reverence and our love. A. Conan Doyle.'" He also had time to see the tombstones of "Longfellow, Channing, Brooks, Agassiz, Parkman, & ever so many more."

Luckily, Kipling remained alive and well, and was eager to welcome Doyle and his brother to his home in late November. The origins of Doyle and Kipling are remarkably similar in certain respects. Kipling had been fostered out to England from his birthplace of India when he was six, while Doyle was fostered out to Mary Burton at Liberton Bank House at the same age. Both men were recognized for their precocious brilliance in their adolescent years, and they each achieved celebrity status while they were still in their twenties. And as some critics had attributed Doyle's anonymous magazine article "J. Habakuk Jephson's Statement" to Robert Louis Stevenson because of its technical mastery, so too had Kipling's inspirational poetry won the critics over, earning him the nickname "The New Tennyson" in direct homage to the celebrated British poet Alfred, Lord Tennyson who preceded him. In fact, following Tennyson's death, Kipling received an invitation to become his nation's Poet Laureate—a distinction that, along with two offered Knighthoods from the British Crown, he elected to politely decline. However, he *was* willing to accept the Nobel Prize for Literature, making him the first British author to receive that honor.

Similarities aside, there were also some notable *differences* between the two men. While the athletic Doyle was "a fine looking man of thirty-five, very tall and well-proportioned," Kipling was described as "an undersized, near-sighted lad" who "did not shine on the athletic field." Doyle was keenly aware that Kipling's views on America and its people ran totally counter to his own. Several days before his visit to Kipling in Vermont, Doyle wrote to his mother that American "children are very bright & pretty," and "the race as a whole is not only the most prosperous, but the most even-tempered, tolerant and hopeful that I have ever known. They have to meet their own problems in their own way, and I fear it is precious little sympathy they ever get from England in doing it."

On the other side of the coin, Kipling had nothing but disdain for the "spitter of tobacco-juice," the uncouth gentlemen who "pick their teeth" with a "pitchfork or a chestnut rail," and "other defects in American character." Still a diehard British imperialist to the point of outright aggression, Kipling especially enjoyed deprecating the American culture—first, by buttering it up and then, by pouncing on it with cutting and skeptical phrases like, "But I love them, and it is because I love them that I point out their defects." When Doyle eventually laid eyes on that deflating statement, his diplomatic retort was, "Love should be patient of faults. A nation is not born in a day. It has to learn many things, and to unlearn more. Give it time and it will grow; but it will not help its true growth to be perpetually irritating a nation with a caustic satire."

Ironically, Doyle did experience an unpleasant incident during a banquet held in his honor in Detroit, Michigan, one "marred by one of those waves of *anti-British feeling* which sweep occasionally over the States, and which emanate from their own early history . . . ." *[emphasis added]* Doyle became convinced that his host that evening had anti-British sentiments stoked by news reports he described as "being exaggerated and inflamed by the constant hostility of Irish pressmen and politicians," and the mishaps and misunderstandings that had taken place during the hotly contested America's Cup. Doyle wrote that someone had spewed out a venomous tirade against the British Empire. Taken aback by these damning comments, Doyle issued the following reply:

"You Americans have lived up to now within your own palings, and know nothing of the real world outside. But now your land is filled up, and you will be compelled to mix more with the other nations. When you do so you will find that there is only one which can at all understand your ways and your aspirations, or will have the least sympathy. That is the mother country which you are now so fond of insulting. She is an Empire, and you will soon be an Empire also, and only then will you understand each other, and you will realize that you have only one real friend in the world."

Doyle prophesied that only after the United States had become an empire of its own would the country allow bygones to be bygones, and be able to finally shift back into an alliance with its only true friend—Great Britain. Nevertheless, the actual source of that night's animosity had nothing to do with what Doyle called the "Lord Dunraven yacht-race" incident at the American Cup. Instead, it had much to do with the escalating border dispute between two South American nations—the English colony of British Guiana, and the independent nation of Venezuela.

In 1895, US Secretary of State Richard Olney declared that by virtue of the Monroe Doctrine—introduced in late 1823 by President James Monroe as the cited policy with which Europe was to end its colonial encroachment across the Western hemisphere—America was now granted the authority to act as an intermediary in the negotiations between these two geopolitical entities. Great Britain adamantly rejected Olney's claim, which triggered a tsunami of anti-American sentiment that even included a call for war against the United States. Rudyard Kipling pointedly lent his voice to the crusade against any US interference in South America—and even as the crisis began to cool down, Kipling did not. Rather, he quickly became disenchanted with America, packed up his belongings, and returned to Great Britain accompanied by his American-born wife Caroline Starr Balestier Kipling.

At each of his appearances during that first lecture tour, Doyle continued to place emphasis on tightening up the relationship between his country and the United States. He loved America, its people, and its potential for greatness. And when at the podium at New York's Lotos Club on November 18, Doyle told his audience of over 200 members and guests the following:

"There was a time in my life which I divided among my patients and literature. It is hard to say which suffered most. But during that time I longed to travel as only a man to whom travel is impossible does long for it, and, most of all, I longed to travel in the United States. Since this was impossible, I contented myself with reading a good deal about them and building up an ideal United States in my own imagination. This is notoriously a dangerous thing to do. I have come to the United States; I have traveled from five to six thousand miles through them, and I find that my ideal picture is not to be whittled down, but to be enlarged on every side."

Doyle's impression of America was generally a favorable one. He enjoyed the upstate New York Adirondack region, the "beautiful Hudson" River, the horse shows, and charming country inns, "where you can have your hair dressed by a barber at the same place where a century ago you might have been left with no hair to dress." Although he did find Washington, DC "interesting," he was put off when the "letter" of introduction he was carrying with him was rejected by President Cleveland who was apparently in no mood for visitors just one day after an unsuccessful election year. And Doyle drew a "very poor audience" at his lecture because General William Booth, the founder of the Salvation Army, was holding "a rally in Convention Hall." Doyle was amazed by the city of Chicago's rapid development, which seemed "to spring straight into a full growth of every modern convenience, but where, even among the rush of cable cars and the ringing of telephone bells, one seems still to catch the echoes of the woodman's axe and of the scout's rifle."

He was met and greeted by some well-known key members of the Windy City's literati at the Twentieth Century Club. Among them was twenty-three-year-old Herbert S. Stone, founder of the H. S. Stone & Company publishing house that became one of the era's most innovative publishing houses with a roster of writers that included Henry James, Arthur Morrison, and Kate Chopin. Three years later, Doyle sent a letter to Stone that included a diagram that showed Chicago bypassing New York City and communicating directly with England via transatlantic cable and high-speed sailing vessels. So enamored was he of Chicago that when he wrote the Sherlock Holmes spy story "His Last Bow" (1917), Doyle gave the alias of "Mr. Altamont of Chicago" to his great detective. And in the final Holmes novel *The Valley of Fear* (1915), the Pinkerton detective

John Douglas is a native of Chicago. During his visit to Chicago, Doyle also met Eugene Field (the American writer often referred to as the "poet of childhood" and still known for his poems "Wynken, Blynken, and Nod," "Little Boy Blue," and "The Duel"), a devoted crusader against pirated books and strong supporter of the United States International Copyright Bill. That bill—which was designed to protect the works of French, Belgian, Swiss, and British authors—was turned into law on March 3, 1891, but not before thousands of copies of Doyle's works were published without his permission . . . and without him receiving a royalty. Because of Field's efforts, sales of American editions of his works would send Doyle's "income up a good deal." At their meeting, Field slyly handed Doyle an unauthorized copy of *The Sign of the Four* for him to autograph. Doyle, quickly spotting the United States Book Company's trademark, dutifully obliged with the request, and then proceeded to dedicate the following poem to Field (indicating that he understood why he handed the book to him in the first place):

> "This bloody pirate stole my sloop
> And holds her in his wicked ward.
> Lord send that walking on my poop
> I see him kick at my main-yard."

On this first American tour, Doyle ranked Philadelphia, Pennsylvania as his favorite place of all—"in spite of its city buildings." He told the *New York Sun* that he "found the Philadelphians more homogenous with the English character than any other" place he had visited, and made it a point to tell the reporters that the "men were built better there and seem to have more of the free open life so anxiously sought by the Englishman." While in the "city of brotherly love," Doyle stayed as a guest for two days at the "palatial house" of Craige Lippincott, a revered local figure whose company became the first in America to publish an authorized copy of *The Sign of the Four* in February 1890. Doyle even got a chance to be a spectator at a Princeton Tigers / Penn Quakers college football game. To Doyle's surprise, the contest wasn't played at "the slow pace he had heard it called." Doyle must have seen the Federal Mint Building, for he made a reference to the facility twenty years later in "The Valley of Fear." And when he makes mention of a "sawed-off shotgun" in that story, he has the rifle manufactured at the "Pennsylvania Small Arms Company."

Doyle also ventured into Canada, and was especially looking forward to the Toronto leg of his lecture tour where he could personally thank the city's news critics for being the first journalists in the world to write a "favourable review" of his historical novel *Micah Clarke* published five years before in 1889. Although Doyle confessed that he was unable to recall the time when that laudable review had appeared in the local Canadian magazine *The Week*, he did state that "he date[d] his success" as a writer "from its publication."

Unfortunately, after exploring much of America's Northeastern and Midwest regions, Doyle still was unable to find a suitable place for proper treatment of his wife's illness. And so, making good on his promise that he would be back home to celebrate Christmas with his family, Doyle returned to Manhattan's Aldine Club for a farewell dinner held in his honor. Immediately after the event, the Doyle brothers sailed back to England on December 8 aboard the Cunard Liner *Etruria*, foregoing a trip to Colorado that had initially been planned.

In the end, Doyle's lecture tour of America failed on two separate levels. First, he did not find a therapeutic climate capable of restoring his wife's health. He was left with no choice other than to traipse from place to place throughout the Middle East and Europe, in continual search of a magical spa that might help prolong his wife's life. Secondly, the tour proved to be an economic fiasco. Doyle claimed that "the margin left over, after his expenses are paid, is probably a less sum than he could have easily earned in his own study." According to Doyle, he made roughly "$125 a night, from which the agent's commission and travelling expenses had to be deducted," as well as having to pay for "his double-passage money." Doyle summed up his tour with the complaint that "the business" of giving lectures "is not what it is cracked up to be," and unlike "Dickens, and Thackeray"—each of whom returned to England with "huge bags of good American gold"—he barely broke even.

The contemporary magazine *The Critic* concurred with the author's assessment, stating, "Dr. Doyle hits the nail on the head, when he says that another Thackeray or Dickens would make money by lecturing in America . . . Give us a really great author, and we will pay our money to hear him, or even see to him." *The Critic* then continued to deride him on that occasion with what can only be interpreted as a middling dismissal: "Dr. Doyle has created a popular character in Sherlock Holmes, but Sherlock Holmes is not known to this generation as well as Detective Buckett was to a previous generation. It was not by one character that Dickens and Thackeray were known, but by a whole library full . . . The characters of Dickens and Thackeray are intimately associated with the greater part of our lives, but with Sherlock Holmes we have little more than a bowing acquaintance." As Doyle's own literary idol Charles Dickens wrote in his *A Tale of Two Cities* some years earlier, "It was the best of times, it was the worst of times . . . ."

Immediately upon his arrival back in England on a "midwinter, pouring rain" day, Doyle set about an active campaign for uniformity in "the great interest in literature." He boldly suggested the following in a *New York Times* article dated February 10, 1895:

> "[I]t would be a very excellent thing to have an international congress for the determination of the correct spelling of our *common language*. When an Englishman reads such a sentence as 'Taking an ax in one hand and a saber in the other, he left his plow, and dove from the center of the bridge,' he can hardly realize that 60,000,000 of people accept that as true spelling of the English tongue. If the tendency goes on increasing we shall only know each other's literature by the help of a translation." *[emphasis added]*

Doyle, a strong proponent of a "universal spelling," sought to eliminate the necessity of having two distinct dictionaries—one for the United States, and the other for Great Britain. In his view, a *single* English dictionary was a key element for moving toward a united two-nation empire. Kipling, ever the skeptic, remained diametrically opposed to Doyle's mission. He voiced his stinging opinion that Americans "delude themselves into the belief that they talk English . . ." and "stole books from across the water without paying for 'em." This was his cynical explanation for why "they talk a foreign tongue to-day." And in his 1889 book *American Notes*, Kipling incisively wrote, "The American has no language. He is dialect, slang, provincialism, accent, and so forth. Now that I have heard their voices, all the beauty of Bret Harte is being ruined for me . . . ."

To reinforce his desire to create a uniform lexicon, Doyle wrote "The Adventure of the Three Garridebs" (1924), where slight spelling variations between English and American words prove helpful to Holmes and Watson as they aim to crack a case. Doyle has his sleuthing characters look over an English advertisement that reads as follows:

Howard Garrideb
Constructor of Agricultural Machinery
Binders, reapers, steam and hand plows, drills,
harrows, farmers' carts, buckboards, and all other appliances.
Estimates for Artesian Wells
Apply Grosvenor Buildings, Aston

After having scrutinized the notice, they both realize that "'the word "plough" was mis-spelt,'" and "'it was bad English but good American.'" Holmes then tells Watson that the "'printer had set it up as received,'" and that the word "'buckboards . . . is American also.'" Holmes goes on to say that "artesian wells are commoner with them {sic. Americans} than with us. It was a typical American advertisement, but purporting to be from an English firm.'" It was this established familiarity with Americanisms that permits Holmes to solve a counterfeiting case, but not quickly enough to prevent a former convict from Chicago from shooting poor Watson in the leg.

A year later, Doyle shared his lingering infatuation with the United States in print, this time writing a response dated January 7, 1896 to the editor of the *London Times* from his hotel room in Cairo, Egypt:

"An Englishman who travels in the United States comes back, according to my experience, with two impressions, which are so strong that they overshadow all others. One is of the *excessive kindness* which is shown to individual Englishmen. The other is of the bitter feeling which appears to exist both in the Press and among the public against his own country. The feeling is always smouldering, and the least breath of discussion sets it in a blaze. I believe, and have long believed, that the greatest danger which can threaten our Empire is the existence of this spirit of hostility in a nation which is already great and powerful, but which is destined to be far more so in the future. Our statesmen have stood too long with their faces towards the East. To discern our best hopes as well as our gravest dangers they must turn them the other way . . . To understand the American's view of Great Britain one must read such an American history as would be used in the schools, and accept the statements with the same absolute faith and patriotic bias which our own schoolboys would show in a British narration of our relations with France. American history, as far as its foreign policy is concerned, resolves itself almost entirely into a series of wrangles with Great Britain, in many of which we must now ourselves confess that we were absolutely in the wrong." *[emphasis added]*

Doyle admonished Britain that it must "lose no opportunity of doing those little graceful acts of kindness which are the practical sign of a brotherly sentiment. Opinions may differ as to the value of Bartholdi's Statue of Liberty as a work of art, but there can be no gainsaying that as a visible sign of French friendship it carries its message to every American who enters New York Harbour. We have our opportunities occasionally of showing a friendly feeling." And in an allusion to an article written in the *London Times* several years before, Doyle wrote, "The chance was missed, but others will arise. Above all I should like to see an Anglo-American Society started in London, with branches all over the Empire, for the purpose of promoting good feeling, smoothing over friction, laying literature before the public which will show them how strong are the arguments in favour of an Anglo-American alliance, and supplying the English Press with the American side of the question and vice versa. Such an organization would, I am sure, be easily founded, and would do useful work towards that *greatest of all ends, the consolidation of the English-speaking races.*" *[emphasis added]*

During this time, Doyle continued to place the entire blame for the "chronic state of sensitiveness and suspicion" on Great Britain, and absolved the United States of any responsibility. Doyle then called for the establishment of an Anglo-American society—not so much to create an "Era of Good Feelings," but rather to affect a reunification of the two nations. Doyle was convinced that if Great Britain continued to look toward India and Eastern Asia for trade purposes, it would aim itself in the wrong direction. That same sentiment bore a strong resemblance to Kipling's maxim that "East is East, and West is West, and never the twain shall meet."

And then things changed.

It was at this critical juncture that Britain sent its troops over to South Africa to enter into a war against the Boers, the Dutch settlers who were seeking to establish their dominance in that country's Cape Province region. With this, Doyle's interests and energies dramatically shifted to a place of *defense* in terms of his native country's political agenda. Virtually overnight, his plea for reunification with America ended. Instead, Doyle now rallied to the sole support of his nation's colonial policies—all of which signaled a mindset that cared not one whit about merging with its former cadre of Yankee colonies.

The response from his countrymen was strong and immediate. On October 24, 1902, Doyle was officially dubbed "Sir Arthur"—not for his Sherlock Holmes stories, but rather in recognition of the role he had played in advocating Britain's policies of colonialism and imperialism. At first, he was a bit reluctant to accept this honor, but soon acquiesced after some not-so-gentle prodding by his proud mother. His mixed feelings about knighthood were made public over time, and *indirectly*, with his Holmes short story "The Adventure of the Three Garridebs" (1924). In the tale, we read as Watson recalls an event "very well, for it was in the same month Holmes refused a knighthood for services which may perhaps some day be described. I only refer to the matter in passing, for in my position of partner and confidant I am obliged to be particularly careful to avoid any indiscretion. I repeat, however, this enables me to fix the date, which was the latter end of June, 1902, shortly after the conclusion of the South African War."

Although Doyle was not ever to witness an official merger between the United States and Great Britain, he did receive the opportunity to further forge a friendship with Kipling. Both men had their differences, but there existed between them an especially *British* bond of respect. When Doyle was interviewed by *The Churchman* magazine in 1895, he stated that Kipling "represents the greatest political power in fiction, and is the only writer except Dickens who ever achieved a stable place in literature so young, besides claiming an almost unrivaled brilliancy in the department of short stories." Today, both of these great writers are still remembered for their newspaper editorials that lent support to the British cause in South Africa—and both have achieved literary immortality.

Harried by the incongruent political realities of his day, Doyle decided eventually to abandon his scheme to link Britain with the United States under one flag. The best he could do was to have British and American detectives work in tandem in his stories. In "The Adventure of the Red Circle" (1911), Doyle's Scotland Yard's Inspector Gregson tells Holmes and "'Mr. Leverton, of Pinkerton's American Agency'" that it would benefit the case at hand "'if New York can't help us to keep'" a potentially dangerous member of a "Neapolitan society" known as the Red Circle (the equivalent of the modern-day criminal term "Mafia") in England so they can bring him to trial. And in "The Adventure of the Dancing Men" (1903), after he figures out that his chief suspect is American, Holmes cables his "'friend, Wilson Hargreave, of the New York Police Bureau'" to lend him assistance. With Hargreave's input, Holmes brings the case to a successful conclusion.

Nonetheless, Doyle still had plans in mind that would include the erasing of political and geographic borders for maximum mutual benefit. Doyle was of the opinion that technology had become sufficiently advanced to permit England to connect itself to its trans-Channel neighbor, France. In 1843, England had become the first country in the world to construct a tunnel under a navigable river (the Thames Tunnel, linking Rotherhithe to Wapping). A half-century later, Doyle was certain that his homeland could engineer just such a larger-scale modern day marvel. As Doyle began to promote this project, he also kept a careful eye on the political unrest that had by then enveloped the European mainland. At first, he served as a voice of reason regarding the atrocities that were then taking place in Portuguese prisons. He then shifted his focus over to Germany, which, according to the claims of several of his friends, had set about on a course designed to bring it world domination. Initially, Doyle rejected the thought of Germany as a potential threat to anyone; rather, he went about seeking to improve "the relations between the two countries," even going as far as becoming a member of the Anglo-German Friendship Society. But after he had read the notorious "book on Germany and the next war" by General von Bernhardi (a man recognized as being "one of the most noted officers in the German army"), Doyle's viewpoint went through a radical change. He was now convinced that "Germany, intoxicated by her success in war and by her increase of wealth, has regarded the British Empire with eyes of jealousy and hatred," and was correct in his assessment that the "building of the German fleet" was being forged as a weapon to be wielded directly against England. Kaiser Wilhelm made sure he could easily advance the German fleet up to the English Channel by widening the "Kiel Canal, by which the newer and larger battleships would be able to pass from the Baltic to the North Sea." Then, in 1911, Germany "stirred up trouble by sending a gunboat to Agadir, and pushed matters to the very edge of war." These provocative actions inspired Doyle to call upon his vivid imagination to formulate a sophisticated plan that would allow England to protect itself and its citizenry from a hostile German takeover. He was well aware that the ability to successfully deploy soldiers and military vessels—along with the transportation of food, munitions, and other war supplies—was of critical importance to the survival of Britannia in the event of war.

In 1913, Doyle warned the English public in the March 11 edition of the *London Times* that the English Channel was their nation's Achilles heel—and that any thoughts of mobilizing ships from the Naval bases at Portsmouth and Plymouth would be fraught with danger and potential disaster. In an ominous prediction, he declared that "the greatest danger" to his nation during times of war would be if a foreign nation gained control of the vital English Channel waters. He became convinced that if such a catastrophe occurred it would be accompanied by a critical "diminution" of the food supply, a consequence that would put all English subjects at risk for "starvation." He expressed his grave concern that if German strategists were as insightful as he was, the British Navy's fleet would become doomed sitting ducks. He reminded his Nation that "recent years have seen the development of a new great European navy"—and with it, the improved technology that would turn the submarine into the dominant component of warfare. He made this dire prediction—"that a single defeat at sea might entail our {sic. Great Britain's} absolute surrender."

To prevent such a grim scenario from taking place, Doyle engineered a plan that appeared in *The Fortnightly Review*, where he stated that a "Channel Tunnel is essential to Great Britain's safety." He asked rhetorically "Could an enemy in any way destroy it in time of war?" and responded with, "It would, as I conceive it, be sunk to a depth of not less than two hundred feet below the bed of the ocean. This ceiling would be composed of chalk and clay. No explosive form above could drive it in. If it were designed on a large scale—and, personally, I think it should be a four-line tunnel, even if the cost were doubled thereby—no internal explosion, such as might be brought about by secreting explosive packets upon the trains, would be likely to do more than temporarily obstruct it."

Doyle was willing to field questions related to the risks involved in creating an underground land bridge from Dover to the northern coast of France. To those who voiced their concerns about the inherent "danger of invasion through the tunnel," he suggested that fail-safe measures such as "destroying the tunnel in case of need" could be easily implemented by the nation's engineers. In a preemptive statement, he professed "in the unlikely event of a quarrel with France it is surely not difficult to seal up our end." Once the First World War had actually begun in 1914, he declared that "a whiff of poison gas down the tunnel would destroy any army within it."

Unfortunately, the onset of war doused any serious thoughts that Parliament may have had about implementing such a massive project. Still, Doyle adamantly refused to stop pushing for it. From the beginning of the conflict with Germany, Doyle was sending letters to "the War Office, the Admiralty, and the Council of National Defence, pointing out how essential a tunnel was" for his Nation's domestic security. He reiterated his trepidation about the dangers posed by submarines, and how a tunnel would circumvent them. One of his main points was that if a tunnel existed, British "lines of communication would be safe in all weather," and could free up the measured convoy of warships.

Despite the victory of the combined Allied Forces by war's end in 1918, Doyle continued to refute the opinions of those naysayers who believed that had a Channel tunnel been constructed prior to the war, Great Britain would have fallen to the Germans. In a letter to the editor of the *London Times*, he wrote:

> "Sir, — Mr. Skeus discusses in your columns the question of what would have happened had we had the Channel Tunnel during the war, and raises the bogy that it would have been seized by the Germans.
>
> Surely we have sufficient information at our disposal to show us that the German right wing was very nearly cut off by stretching itself as far as Amiens, and that, if it had extended to the coast, it could hardly have got away. The end of the tunnel would, of course, have been fortified, and a comparatively small garrison could have held it secure, for it would constitute a fortress unique in the history of war — a fortress into which reinforcements and supplies could always be introduced, and from which wounded could be evacuated. With

the smooth fields of fire which lie everywhere in that chalk country, it should be impregnable. If the very worst had happened, the cost of a destroyed tunnel would be less than that of a week of war.

On the other hand, so long as the tunnel existed, we could pass over reinforcements to France in all weathers with no danger of sub-marine attack, we could pass stores and munitions without breaking bulk, we could save all the shipping and all the escorts which were used in the Channel, and we could bring back our wounded swiftly and without discomfort. In money alone it is impossible to compute how much was wasted by our insane policy of obstructing the boring of the tunnel in pre-war days. We came badly out of the Suez Canal business, but our mistakes there were venial compared with those which we have made over the Channel Tunnel.

Now the matter has, as it seems to me, ceased to press. The mischief is done. It was only in view of a great Continental war that it was of really vital importance."

Doyle perceived the Channel tunnel to be a protective measure during times of war, and as an economic booster during times of peace. He insisted that such a tunnel would "be a source of great profit to the country" by encouraging "Continental traffic, and it would bring very many thousands of tourists to our {sic. Great Britain's} shores who are at present deterred by the sea voyage." He then made another prediction related to the Channel Tunnel; namely, that "actual trade" would "gain a great advantage, since merchandise need not break bulk."

And in "His Last Bow" (1917), a tale that begins on August 2, 1914— just two days before Britain declared war on Germany—Holmes puts his life on the line when he assumes the identity of an Irish-American spy named Altamont. Employing the story's dialogue as a vehicle for commu-nicating his beliefs, Doyle was able to alert the British public—through the conversations between his German agents von Bork and Baron von Herling—that "England is not ready" to engage in a war against the Kaiser. Doyle points out that the "docile" English "folk" have been "not very hard to deceive," and goes so far as to mention Germany's "special war tax of fifty million, which one would think made our purpose as clear as if we had advertised it on the front page of the Times, has not roused these people from their slumbers." Doyle goes on to caution his readership, "that so far as the essentials go—the storage of munitions, the preparation for submarine attack, the arrangements for making high explosives—nothing is prepared." To further worsen matters, the two German officers boast that their country has been orchestrating the "Irish civil war" that has become such a source of unrest on British soil. Doyle then points out some of Britain's more glaring weaknesses, ones that the Germans could and would exploit during the Great War—among them "Fords," "Harbour-defences," "Portsmouth forts," and, of course, "The Channel." Doyle sought to convince France and England that the ability to defend the English Channel would always be a key element in the protection of Europe, and extends this basic precept of constructing a tunnel beneath the Channel. At that point in time, the message of this spine-chilling Holmes tale was not sufficient to persuade his nation, and France, to invest in a project that might have ensured the freedom of subsequent generations.

Nearly a century later in 1994, Doyle's dream of connecting Britain to Continental Europe finally did come to fruition when the Channel Tunnel (also referred to as the "Chunnel") allowed trains to rumble through heading eastward from Folkestone in England to Coquelles in France. On the other hand, Sir Arthur's blueprint for bridging North America to Britain has yet to make it off the drawing board.

After Britain's less-than-stellar performance in the 1912 Olympic Games, a disappointed Doyle suggested a new strategy designed to restore his nation's international prestige. Borrowing, or perhaps stealing, the method used by the United States to "very wisely and properly send Red Indians, negroes, and even a Hawaiian amongst their representatives," Doyle put forth his idea for "a British Empire team instead of merely a British team." He was certain that if the British government addressed the issue "with tact," it could be represented by "one united team in which Africans, Australians, and Canadians" would be absorbed into the country's current team "under one flag and the same insignia." He further proposed that the Empire team recruit "Ceylon or Malay swimmers, Indian runners, and Sikh wrestlers . . ." because such a unified team was "of the highest political importance, for there could not be a finer object lesson of the unity of the Empire than such a team all striving for the victory of the same flag." He remained critical of those who might object to what he perceived as a perfect solution to the problem, deeming it unfathomable that "anyone conceive a meaner position than to say that the Sikh, the

Ghoorka, or the Rajpoot may fight for the Empire in war, but may not play for it in peace." Apparently, what was of overriding importance to Doyle was winning at any cost, and so, he had no qualms about resorting to any measure to achieve victory.

Arthur Conan Doyle was a flawed but truly *sincere* visionary, uniquely endowed with an uncanny ability to see what was necessary for the survival and expansion of the British Empire. If he hadn't lent his full support to the Crown's military agenda, the world might not look like it does today. Although Doyle is best remembered for his literary characters, he was also a "patriot, physician, and man of letters" who unashamedly and fearlessly shared his beliefs, no matter how strange they might have appeared, with the entire world. In the end, it was Doyle's unshakable belief that there exists a sphere beyond the corporeal world of flesh and bone and blood—a *spiritual* realm—that reveals the full and final story about Doyle's art and his life.

CHAPTER 10

Spirits and Spiritualism
Caught Between Doyle's World and the Afterworld

"You can't, as a man of science, defend such a position as that."
—FROM SIR ARTHUR CONAN DOYLE'S *THE LOST WORLD* (1912)

Even though Arthur Conan Doyle was a man who favored practical and observable scientific precepts—with extensive training in medicine prior to his fame as the creator of Sherlock Holmes—he also had a lifelong belief in the unseen world. Specifically speaking, he was transfixed by the realm of spirits and fairies, and remained firmly rooted for much of his life with an unshakable faith in what the Western imagination calls the "afterworld." The basic tenets of Spiritualism—a belief system that originated in New York in the 1840s—were an integral part of Doyle's life nearly from his birth. His father Charles had been entirely convinced, for many years prior to his own death in 1893, that he lived his life surrounded by any number of invisible spectral life forces. The senior Doyle's published illustrations—especially the artwork that he created in 1877 for Jean-Jambon's book *Our Trip to Blunderland*—reflected his own bizarre take on his perceived reality. However, Charles was *not* the only Doyle possessed of both artistic talent and a decidedly warped inner life. There were others—including, of course, his own imaginative and richly famous son.

Charles Doyle's older brother, Richard (often referred to by his nickname "Kitkat") gained fame and public acclaim as an illustrator of fantasy books that rose in popularity by the mid-nineteenth century. Examples of Richard's work could be seen in such contemporary titles as James

Robinson Planché's *An Old Fairy Tale Told Anew (Sleeping Beauty)* (1865); Mark Lemon's *Fairy Tales* (1868); and William Allingham's *In Fairyland: A Series of Pictures from the Elf-World* (1870). Richard, a firm believer in ghosts and goblins, claimed to family and friends alike that he possessed "insider" information about all aspects of so-called "supernatural" culture. As evidence of that knowledge, he declared the following:

> "[F]airies, sprites, elves, and goblins are not troubled with a pressing sense of the responsibilities of existence, but take life in a desultory, devil-may-care sort of fashion. Nothing like settled business casts its shadow over them. None of them appears ever to have kept a shop or a counting-house, or to have contributed in the least degree to the cultivation of soil. The utilitarian doctrines not only do not prevail, but do not exist among them.
>
> Their state of affairs are entirely ceremonial. They never had a legislative assembly, though the waste of time, idle talk, foolish jest, and absence of common-sense, which prevail in such places, would not be foreign to their habits."

Clearly, Richard Doyle's ability to project his own strongly held delusional beliefs so artfully to paper made him one of the most well-known fantasy book illustrators of his generation—and his legendary nephew was all but destined to inherit this trait.

The Witches of Stonyhurst Mountain

> *"You would certainly have been burned,*
> *had you lived a few centuries ago."*
>
> —Dr. Watson, in discussion with Sherlock
> Holmes from "A Scandal in Bohemia" (1891)

As he first entered the world of formal education, Doyle's relationship to religion was largely strained and chaotic. His time at the Jesuit-run and affiliated Stonyhurst College left him confused about his religious orientation. The administration's strict approach to matters of discipline caused him emotional and physical torment. Instead of rectifying his behavior, this painful and sudden pole vault into the rigors of ritual and dogma only made Doyle that much more "slovenly," "uncivilized," and "quarrelsome" in temperament. And yet, the punitive measures laid on him for his transgressions did not keep him from participating in several "long walks"—school-mandated hikes along the rivers, hedges, cliffs, and ditches of the nearby Pendle Mountain. During these treacherous and fatiguing treks (often more than twenty miles in length), the guides assigned to the students tried their hardest to scare the boys by spinning yarns derived from a vast bounty of local legends and folklore—a heady brew of imagination that seemed to almost float across the fog-enshrouded English moors toward the petrified students as they heard the stories. Tales about witches, phantoms, monsters, spirits, and ghosts surrounded Doyle on a near-daily basis while at Stonyhurst—and he soon grew to *like* them.

Named within these scary yarns was the terrorizing ghost known as the "Boggart," who derived a special glee from frightening young children and spooking horses; a plethora of evil witches and warlocks who were all executed in the late 1500s by order of Queen Elizabeth; Old Mother Cuthbert, whose power of mind control was said to have forced innocent people to commit all manner of Satanic acts; and, most importantly to Doyle's later life, the Skriker, who—according to local tradition—showed itself to those who were soon to meet their death.

Although it was believed that Skrikers could take on the appearance of cows and horses, they most frequently appeared in the ominous form of a gigantic black hound dog with broad feet, shaggy hair, drooping ears, and saucer-sized eyes.

It was said that these beasts could not only walk backwards at great speed without losing sight of their target—they were also able to sink slowly into the earth or vanish into thin air. The name "Skriker" was attributed to the *shrieks* it made whenever it would render itself invisible to others. Furthermore, any weapon raised in combat by someone foolish enough to fight a Skriker would simply pass right through the creature's body—without causing the phantom even the least bit of harm. When one reads the often grisly story at the heart of the 1902 novel *The Hound of the Baskervilles*—which remains almost universally recognized as one of the most entertaining and *chilling* tales in the entire Holmes canon—one can almost *feel* how terrified Doyle must have been when he first heard about the Skriker, and also how excited he must have been to bring his story to his adoring public.

The "Dark Walk" and the "Skriker." Local folklore learned
in Doyle's youth inspired *The Hound of the Baskervilles*.

The Hound of the Sherburnes

Stonyhurst itself had a legend all its own, which the older students were eager to share with the underclassmen. It was their local resident, the "Sherburne Ghost"—an apparition who haunted the Dark Walk, an area named as such because it was situated in one of the most remote sections of the school's campus. This "grand and magnificent avenue of trees, full of shadowy beauty and overhung by the richest foliage" was considered one of the finest avenues in all of Lancashire. It was *also* the customary place where young Doyle stole away to "smoke his pipe" with some of his other equally rebellious classmates beneath its majestically silent arch of "yews." All of the Stonyhurst students—Doyle included—were well acquainted with the macabre tale of eight-year-old Richard Francis Sherburne, heir of the school's original owner. Legend had it that after having lost his way among the bushes and trees that lined the Dark Walk, the naive boy pulled down tree branches and ate some easily reachable—and highly *poisonous*—"yew berries." It wasn't long before the toxin within the fruit took effect. Young Richard experienced a fatal seizure—and with his death, the Sherburne dynasty came to an end.

The Dark Walk served as the gateway for students who wanted to sneak off-campus and go into town to purchase "tobacco" for themselves. This covert operation required these rule breakers to make their way to the end of the pastoral lane, only to then veer off its wide dirt avenue toward a narrow path that led to the kennels of the elite upperclassmen. The kennels of these "gentleman philosophers" housed "well-fashioned, well-bred, *hound-like creatures . . . which can make ever so much noise.*" *[emphasis added]*

Doyle's exposure to the legends of the Skriker and the Sherburne Ghost heavily influenced the complex plot he created when he wrote *The Hound of the Baskervilles*. The novel opens as Dr. Mortimer tells Holmes that Charles Baskerville's "'favourite walk was down a path between two hedges of yew trees, *the famous Yew Alley of Baskerville Hall*.'" There "'he went out for his walk to think and to *smoke his usual cigar*.'" As envisioned by Doyle in his story, this yew-lined walkway is where Baskerville's dead body is discovered. This plot point mirrors the location where Richard Sherburne's body was found—Dr. Mortimer goes on to tell Holmes that "'In the months before his death, Sir Charles was a very worried man . . .

He often asked me whether I had seen any strange animal or heard the cry of a hound on the moor at night.'" And then Dr. Mortimer informs Holmes that "'It looked like a small *black cow*,'" except "'they were the footprints of a *huge hound!*'" [*emphases added throughout*]

Notably, only a single gate "through the hedge" was present along the paths of both the actual Stonyhurst Hall and the *fictional* Baskerville Hall. Dr. Mortimer also makes a point to tell Holmes that those who have seen this terrifying entity claim it had the appearance of "'an enormous hound . . . which shone with a strange light like a ghost . . . a supernatural hell-hound.'" And so, just as Richard Sherburne became the final male heir of his family's dynasty, so too does the equally young character Sir Henry become "the last of the Baskervilles."

Volcanoes in Ireland

After completing his preparatory year at Stella Matutina in July of 1876, Doyle decided to make a slight detour to Paris on his way back home to Scotland. His initial plan was to go sightseeing and to meet with his godfather, Michael Conan. Conan was also Doyle's great-uncle, and the only person who had thus far recognized and acknowledged his nephew's artistic and literary talents. Michael Conan had once been a London-based drama critic for *The Morning Chronicle*—and he remained so highly regarded within the city's writers' circle that he was able to secure a position as an illustrator/caricaturist for his nephew, Richard Doyle, at *Punch Magazine*. In 1854, Conan moved to Paris and purchased a home just a few blocks away from the iconic Arc de Triomphe monument just off the Avenue des Champs-Élysées. It had, in fact, been Michael Conan who advised Doyle's mother to enroll Arthur in a Jesuit school to begin with—on this impromptu visit, Doyle was eager to provide his great-uncle with a keen demonstration of his academic and literary achievements.

Doyle would have had easy accessibility to all that Paris had to offer during this three-week visit—after having been taken to his great-uncle's enormous library, which was to serve as his "bedroom" during his stay, he was like a kid in a candy shop. This library served as Doyle's own beloved bookworm haven—here, he pored over scads of old and original editions of works written by his literary heroes Scott, Poe, Carlyle, Burns, and Macaulay that were randomly stacked and strewn all over the place.

Instead of touring the City of Light, he was to cement his relationship with his great-uncle by engaging him in detailed conversations on genealogy, Arthurian legends, and heraldry alongside the mystic arts and the occult. As they conversed together, Doyle found himself overwhelmed by his great-uncle's wide breadth of knowledge and his natural storytelling ability. Conan educated his great-nephew in the Conan family's distinguished lineage, tracing it back all the way to the Dukes of Brittany. As a result, a fascinated Arthur learned everything he needed to know about his brave and splendid ancestors, which included the *original* Arthur—the heroic young thirteenth-century Duke who—as dramatized by Shakespeare in his late sixteenth-century history play *The Life and Death of King John*—was killed trying to escape from his ruthless reigning uncle.

When he wasn't engaged in spirited discussion with his great-uncle, Doyle happily stayed within the confines of the library, feasting on the treasure trove of books that lay before him. Although his great-uncle had by then a reputation as being "a mild-mannered and unobtrusive man who was more disposed to listen than to talk" and "rather averse to thrust his opinions upon others," Arthur did not find this to be the case. Whenever he was around Arthur, Michael Conan became an entirely different man. According to Doyle, his uncle was "a dear old volcanic Irishman" who had made it a point to steer him away from popular subjects and divert him toward more esoteric ones. He was given rare manuscripts and occult literature to read, the products of the most respected scholars and religious authorities from the previous two thousand years. And as he explored these many titles, Doyle was taken aback when his great-uncle voiced his own serious misgivings about some of the viewpoints of the Society of Jesus and the Holy Roman Church. When Michael Conan expressed his skepticism about the validity of Christian doctrine, Arthur's own doubts were magnified, and he immediately began his personal journey toward the embryonic philosophy of Spiritualism.

Michael Conan took his job as an art and drama critic seriously—he felt it was his duty to educate and guide the public, and his devotion to teaching his great-nephew resulted in Arthur gaining insights that others had never obtained. Doyle drew comfort in knowing that his great-uncle had been willing to abandon many of the doctrines he once held as being absolute, and comfortably embraced many concepts that would not have previously been associated with him—among them, the mystical, the occult, and the supernatural.

Doyle viewed his great-uncle as a kindred spirit who was willing to ingest, absorb, and finally accept unorthodox ideals—and *ideas*. When Arthur left Paris and returned to Edinburgh later that summer, he was from that point on inextricably tied to his great-uncle and proudly declared he was "built on the lines of body and mind of the Conans rather than the Doyles." Doyle paid further homage to Conan years later in his short story, "The Leather Funnel," whose first line reads, "My friend, Lionel Dacre, lived in the Avenue de Wagram, Paris . . . It was here that Dacre had that singular library of occult literature, and the fantastic curiosities which served as a hobby for himself, and an amusement for his friends." Dacre was a "wealthy man of refined and eccentric tastes . . . [who] had spent much of his life and fortune in gathering together what was said to be a unique private collection of Talmudic, cabalistic, and magical works, many of them of great rarity and value." Another reference to Michael Conan's hospitality occurs when the Lionel Dacre character extends an invitation to an unnamed friend to use his "'one spare couch'" in his library. The narrator describes this chamber as "a singular bedroom, with its high walls of brown volumes, but there could be no more agreeable furniture to a bookworm like myself, and there is no scent so pleasant to my nostrils as that faint, subtle reek which comes from an ancient book." Doyle's narrator and the Dacre character engage in a discussion that has at its center a "'torn and lacerated'" leather funnel. When Dacre asks, "'Have you included the psychology of dreams among your learned studies?'" the narrator replies, "'I did not even know that there was such a psychology.'" It is at this point that Dacre tries to convince the narrator that the study of dreams is "'a science in itself,'" but his efforts are rebuffed with his friend's retort of "'A science of charlatans.'" The professorial Dacre then fires back, and says the following:

"'[T]he charlatan is always the pioneer. From the astrologer came the astronomer, from the alchemist the chemist, from the mesmerist the experimental psychologist. The quack of yesterday is the professor of tomorrow. Even such subtle and elusive things as dreams will in time be reduced to system and order. When that time comes the researches of our friends in the book-shelf yonder will no longer be the amusement of the mystic, but the foundations of a science.'"

This semi-autobiographical recollection informs us that Doyle had been attracted to—and made himself knowledgeable about—all things charged with mysticism, magic, and Spiritualism at that very moment in his life when he was living under the roof of Michael Conan.

Joseph Cook's Boston Lectures

Upon Doyle's return to his home city, he had the good fortune to be granted admission to the University of Edinburgh to study medicine. Two years later (during the 1878 spring semester), he sent his resume over to those alumni who had expressed an interest in training future physicians at their offices. A Sheffield general practitioner named Dr. Charles Sidney Richardson accepted Doyle as his temporary assistant, but summarily dismissed Doyle just days later, ostensibly for looking "too young." After being sent packing, Doyle took the train down to London and wandered its East End docks and streets. Soon after, Doyle was given a second chance, this time in the rural Northwest English village of Ruyton-XI-Towns to train under the aegis of Dr. Henry Francis Elliot. His impression of Doyle was largely the same as Dr. Richardson's and, after getting into a heated argument over "capital punishment" for a second time, Doyle was dismissed. Three was to be the charm, however—in June 1879, Doyle landed an assistantship in Birmingham, where his preceptor and his family appreciated Doyle's talents as a natural-born storyteller.

During the time he spent with Dr. Reginald Hoare in the Birmingham suburb of Aston Villa, Doyle had ample time for rest, relaxation, and recreation, and took full advantage of this opportunity to hone his boxing skills, write and submit short stories—among them "The Haunted Grange of Goresthorpe" and "The Gully of Bluemansdyke"—and read in the public library. He also attended "a couple of lectures" not related to medicine. Although he described the first lecture as "a soft affair," it had actually evolved into a heated discussion about the controversial viewpoints of Reverends Thomas Dale and Richard Enraght. Each of these religious figures ·had been thrown in jail due to their thwarted attempts to reinstate several outlawed Anglican Church rituals back into the Church's liturgy.

Doyle described the second lecture as being "Capital." The guest speaker was Joseph Cook, a New England transcendentalist trained in the manner of Oliver Wendell Holmes and Ralph Waldo Emerson.

Cook, a "defender of the fundamental truths of the Christian religion against the open attacks of scientific materialism," had already made quite a name for himself as an apostle of transcendentalism, America's first great intellectual movement. At his Tremont Temple in Boston, Cook's fiery sermons worked crowds into full and unfettered arousal and that reputation preceded him across the Atlantic to the United Kingdom. This "Boston Monday Lecturer" drew a "standing room only" crowd that was eager to hear him philosophize on the perennial question, "Does Death End All?" Cook educated his audience about the meaning of the term *metaphysics*, which he defined as "an articulate knowledge of the necessary implications of axiomatic truths, and is not only a very clear and exact science in itself, but is the mother of all the other sciences." He continued by stating the following:

> "[I]f matter is a double-faced unity, having a spiritual and physical side, and is the only substance that exists in the universe, then in matter, spiritual and physical qualities must not only inhere, but co-inhere, in the same substratum. It must be true of every atom of matter that it has a spiritual and a physical side. In every atom, therefore, spiritual and physical qualities must be found so inseparably conjoined, that the one side cannot be conceived to be taken away without carrying the other side with it. If this be the true character of matter, then the physiological activities of the atoms must be at least co-extensive with the psychological activities displayed in connection with those atoms; that is *both the psychical and physical sides of the one substance-matter must go together, and if the latter be removed from any grouping of atoms, the former must go with them.*" [emphasis added]

Cook wrapped up his lecture by informing his audience that life does not end when one dies—and furthermore, that the writings of Carlyle, Macaulay, and the American transcendentalist Ralph Waldo Emerson are all praiseworthy. The young and impressionable Doyle, who idolized this particular literary trio, must have felt an instant connection with Cook.

Although Doyle wrote to his mother that Cook's words were "not convincing," his activities in the near-future—and indeed, throughout the rest of his life—indicated otherwise. The evangelical fervor of the event inspired Doyle to seek a suitable alternative to Roman Catholicism. And despite any of his words to the contrary, Doyle had become one of Cook's disciples, and that evening's agenda bent him toward a new theology.

The University of Edinburgh Medical School

After his preceptorship at Dr. Hoare's, Doyle returned to Edinburgh to finish the academic portion of the medical school curriculum. He soon learned that some of the school's most brilliant faculty members had been drawn into the occult, with William Rutherford devoting his leisure time to "metaphysical speculation and a study of Oriental [Asian] religions" and Joseph Bell working with Fleeming Jenkin (the inventor of the cable car) to determine whether certain geometrical intersections yielded the proportions of the ancient Doric order. They laid claim to having decoded the *mystical equation*, but—for the time being—Bell and Jenkin were keeping it to themselves. While Bell stated that "these intersections were in some way connected with, or symbolic of, the antagonistic forces at work," Jenkin stood at odds with him and vehemently opposed the notion that mysticism was involved.

Joseph Bell also believed that "the soul passes through no sudden or great change when it leaves the body, but simply continues the life it led on earth in a pure atmosphere beyond the reach of all temptations, and that enables it to progress in a manner of spiritual goodness." He thought that "in some dim way our dead were allowed to hear us at times, even visit us." Doyle soon followed in Dr. Bell's footsteps, employing his own brand of scientific methodology to delve into the metaphysical.

General Alfred W. Drayson

Several years later, Doyle put down roots in the Portsmouth suburb of Southsea. To his dismay, his fledgling practice failed to flourish, and he was doing his best to evade the revenue agents who constantly knocked at his door to collect, of all things, a "poor tax" from him. The concerns related to his practice, however, were actually exceeded by his fear of being labeled a social outcast. Despite his recent marriage to Louisa Hawkins, which provided him with the comforts of home life and companionship, Doyle was still missing the mental stimulation more readily available from within the intellectual world.

To fill those gaps, he joined the Portsmouth Literary and Scientific Society, the central meeting place for the intelligentsia and literati of this sophisticated and populous coastal area. After listening to a "not so scholarly lecture on Australia" (as he reported in a letter to his mother around this time), Doyle must have realized that he could easily deliver a superior talk on the fauna of the Arctic based on his 1880 voyage aboard the S.S. *Hope*. So speedily was his offer to speak accepted that he was caught off-guard. He hurriedly put his "Arctic Seas" seminar in order, and surreptitiously got a hold of thirty stuffed birds indigenous to the Arctic region from a local taxidermist. He convinced a beguiled audience that "he" had been the skilled hunter who had "bagged the lot"—and with the help of his sister Connie (who had contacted some of her Edinburgh friends and urged them to donate some of their old clothing to her brother), he enhanced his "performance" with an English Dandy gentleman look in homage to George Bryan "Beau" Brummell himself. His new vestments were complemented by an ebony and silver crutch stick, and Doyle began to consider himself quite the man about town. In a letter home, he wrote, "I am a dude- which is an Americanism for the masherest of mortals."

His lecture on his Arctic adventures earned him an immediate reputation as an intellect, and attracted several of Portsmouth's most prominent public figures to him. One of them, Major-General Alfred W. Drayson, became an important part of Doyle's life. Drayson, who had gained recognition for himself in the field of battle, authored books on billiards and the then-popular card game called "whist"—and was largely known as an authority on astronomy. Doyle was well-versed on the cosmos as a result of having attended Stonyhurst College, which had a large planetarium of its own run by an internationally famous faculty. What is surprising is that in the first Holmes novel *A Study in Scarlet*, Sherlock is described as being totally "ignorant of the Copernican Theory and of the composition of the Solar System." And yet, six years later, Doyle then reworks his Holmes character so that the brilliant-minded detective is then fully aware of all the details within Drayson's recent works. In Doyle's short story "The Adventure of the Greek Interpreter" (1893), Holmes and Watson are enjoying their free time "after tea on a summer evening, and the conversation, which had roamed in a desultory, spasmodic fashion from golf clubs to *the causes of the change in the obliquity of the ecliptic*, came round at last to the question of atavism and hereditary aptitudes." *[emphasis added]*

This is an affirmation of the Major-General's discovery, as conveyed in his books, that he had:

> "[D]iscovered the second rotation of the earth, and that by this fact properly grasped thirty thousand years of the earth's past history can be understood, especially in regard to the extraordinary changes of climate. According to him, it is not the whole axis of the earth which traces a cone, but the two semi-axes, a result of a second and slow rotation, and that the axis traces a circle round some point not the pole of the ecliptic, and that the decrease in the *obliquity of the ecliptic* is not owing to the lateral or the movement towards the pole of the heavens, but to the second rotation. If this is so, it is curious that astronomers should have missed such a discovery by so little, and that little compelling them to use perpetual corrections, and making, according to the author, a grand revolution of the equinoxes 31,682, instead of 25,868 years." *[emphasis added]*

Alfred Wilks Drayson was also an expert on the occult, a topic that was bathed in controversy at that time—and yet, Doyle willingly became Drayson's most devoted adherent and student.

Freemasons

On January 24, 1887, Major-General Drayson took Doyle to a table rapping demonstration, the origins of which dated back to March 31, 1848, when the teenaged Fox sisters of Hydesville, New York in the United States first popularized spirit communication. Like a pair of magicians, each of them would slyly "crack" their toes, ankles, and knee joints to convince their audience that the sounds they were hearing emanated directly from spirits eager to communicate with them. A multitude of the era's celebrities—among them James Fenimore Cooper, P. T. Barnum, Sojourner Truth, Horace Greeley, William Cullen Bryant, and William Lloyd Garrison—were attracted to the Fox girls' version of Spiritualism. Suddenly, *mediums*—those who purportedly had the power to summon up apparitions from the beyond—were springing up all over the country, and it wasn't long before Spiritualist associations were being established on both sides of the Atlantic.

To promote their *new revelation*, Spiritualists published and distributed magazines and brochures that spread their *vital message* far and wide. The American-born but London-based Daniel Dunglas Home (who became the subject of a biography edited by Doyle) was thought to have a singular ability to defy the gravitational pull of the Earth, and to speak and work directly with the dead. General Drayson was fortunate enough to have been a frequent attendee at Home's séances. And even though Margaret Fox, with her sister Kate at her side, publicly confessed at the New York Academy of Music on October 21, 1888 that they were both nothing more than charlatans, Doyle would continue to defend what he maintained was their mystical powers until his death in 1930. In his 1926 double-volume book *The History of Spiritualism*, Doyle wrote, "The skeleton of the man supposed to have caused the rappings first heard by the Fox sisters in 1848 has been found in the walls of the house occupied by the sisters and clears them from the only shadow of doubt held concerning their sincerity in the discovery of spirit communication." Certainly, he strongly advocated on behalf of their beliefs and abilities and was there to defend them whenever they were attacked in the press.

Just two days after having attended that table-rapping session with Drayson in 1887, Doyle joined Phoenix Lodge number 257, which had been housed for fifty years in an impressively columned two-storied temple in Old Portsmouth, High Street. Although General Drayson had been Doyle's mentor in all things occult, it was William David King, Portsmouth's mayor, who nominated him for membership—and it was John Brickwood, a prominent local brewer and frequent soccer teammate of Doyle's, who seconded the motion. Fifty other pillars of the community were in attendance on the evening of Doyle's induction. Once he had been confirmed by Worshipful Master W. P. G. Gilbert, Doyle dedicated himself to study the teachings of the "ancient Order." In less than two months, Doyle was able to rise up the ranks to become a full-fledged and third-degree Mason.

Doyle's underlying motives for joining the lodge and working so diligently to garner the organization's prestigious degree remains shrouded in mystery. He was probably in a type of subconscious, or even conscious, rivalry with the Freemason's poet laureate, Bryan Waller, the man who had become the majordomo of his parents' household and had also "stolen" his mother's affections away from his father. As we have established earlier in this book, Dr. Waller convinced Mary Doyle to leave Edinburgh and live with him in his country estate at Masongill, taking with her Doyle's two youngest siblings. Doyle might have thought that by learning the "craft," he would be able to add to his already vast knowledge of the occult and then incorporate it into his stories. Then again, his motivation to join could have been something entirely different and more practical. Only with third-degree Mason status could he have entered any of the lodge's many houses throughout the realm without the risk of having his name revealed to anyone.

Phoenix Lodge no. 257—as were most other Masonic lodges—was known for its charitable works, and when Doyle had risen to the ranks of third degree, the lodge was in the process of raising funds on behalf of a local hospital. This should have been very appealing to a young physician like Doyle, who was still trying to make a name for himself. On the contrary, though, he never involved himself with this effort. Doyle went on to allude to both the secret rituals and good works performed by the Freemasons in many of his Holmes stories. In *A Study in Scarlet*, Inspector Gregson directs Holmes' attention "'to a litter of objects upon one of the bottom steps of the stairs'" and tells him precisely what was in that cache:

> "'A gold watch, No. 97163, by Barraud, of London. Gold Albert chain, very heavy and solid. Gold ring, with masonic device. Gold pin—bulldog's head, with rubies as eyes. Russian leather card-case, with cards of Enoch J. Drebber of Cleveland, corresponding with the E. J. D. upon the linen. No purse, but loose money to the extent of seven pounds thirteen. Pocket edition of Boccaccio's "Decameron," with the name of Joseph Stangerson upon the fly-leaf. Two letters—one addressed to E. J. Drebber and one to Joseph Stangerson.'"

In the final Holmes novel, *The Valley of Fear* (1915), Doyle returns to the style he employed in *A Study in Scarlet* nearly thirty years earlier—the "tale within a tale" technique. In it, he offers a detailed depiction of a coal mining–dependent community of Freemasons gone bad. These corrupted Freemasons force everyone in the town to abide by their rules and regulations, and they issue the sternest punishments for those who dare defy their laws. When a boarding house keeper evicts the Jack McMurdo character merely for being a member of the Masons from another town, McMurdo replies, "'What's wrong with the order? It's for charity and good fellowship. The rules say so.'" Doyle also incorporates his own directly honed knowledge of the Freemasons' "members only" jargon and hand signals in that same story when he presents a scene where McMurdo engages in secret and intricate hand grips and arm movements with a fellow member. After having successfully completed this ritual, the two converse in a secret language that only "brothers" would comprehend.

In Doyle's 1891 short story "The Red-Headed League," Holmes casually tells a client named Jabez Wilson that he knows he is a Freemason. When Wilson asks him how he was able to deduce that information, Holmes simply replies, "'I won't insult your intelligence by telling you how I read that, especially as, rather against the strict rules of your order, you use an arc-and-compass breastpin.'"

Holmes repeats this feat of being able to evince personal and even *secretive* information about a potential client just by gazing at him in Doyle's 1903 short story "The Adventure of the Norwood Builder." Holmes, in a disarming statement to Mr. John Hector McFarlane, instructs him to relax and to "'sit down in that chair and tell us very slowly and quietly who you are and what it is that you want. You mentioned your name as if I should recognize it, but I assure you that, beyond the obvious facts that you are a bachelor, a solicitor, a Freemason, and an asthmatic, I know nothing whatever about you.'" Doyle's manner of presenting this implies that the great detective can read McFarlane's mind through a kind of thought transference or *telepathy*—a basic tenet of Spiritualism that was wholly embraced by Holmes' literary creator.

Years later in "The Adventure of the Retired Colourman" (1926), Holmes is somehow able to tell Watson that the man who had been on a train with him—and who had tried to follow him back to 221 B, Baker Street—had surely worn a Masonic tie-pin, although Holmes had been in the apartment the entire time. In the especially popular short story "A Scandal in Bohemia" (1891), Holmes tells Watson how he had gone about gathering information about a blackmailer by turning himself into a lowly groomsman. He informs his partner in crime solving that, "'There is a wonderful sympathy and freemasonry among the horsey men. Be one of them, and you will know all that there is to know.'" By using the term "freemasonry" on the written page with a lowercase "f" rather than the usual uppercase "F" format, Doyle strives to make the reader aware that an unwritten, but unbreakable, code of loyalty rules this society of horsemen—one marked, as it turns out in life, by an obligation *never* to divulge any secrets to non-members.

Perhaps getting closer to the mysteries of Freemasonry than in any other Holmes tale, Doyle's "The Adventure of the Musgrave Ritual" (1893) features a scene that depicts a family's long-held tradition that is strikingly similar to one of the rituals at the heart of Freemasonry:

"Whose was it?"
"His who is gone."
"Who shall have it?"
"He who will come."
"Where was the sun?"
"Over the oak."
"Where was the shadow?"
"Under the elm."
"How was it stepped?"
"North by ten and by ten, east by five and by five, south by two and by two, west by one and by one, and so under."
"What shall we give for it?"
"All that is ours."
"Why should we give it?"
"For the sake of the trust."

A few months after having accompanied General Drayson to séances and Freemason meetings, Doyle decided it was now time to bare his soul and share with the world the reason why he joined the Spiritualist movement. In the July 2, 1887 edition of the periodical *Light: A Journal of Psychical, Occult, and Mystical Research*, Doyle wrote the following:

"I believe that it has been found a useful practice among revivalists and other excitable religionists of all types, for each member to give the assembled congregation a description of the manner in which they attained the somewhat vague result known as 'finding salvation.' . . . Some months ago I read Judge Edmonds' Memoirs, and I have since read Alfred Russel Wallace's book, Major-General Drayson's tract, and other writings on the subject. After weighing the evidence, I could no more doubt the existence of the phenomena than I could doubt the existence of lions in Africa, though I have been to that continent and have never chanced to see one."

At the very end of his letter to *Light*, Doyle goes on to pay tribute to Major-General Drayson, even though he had been his protégé for some time. Doyle also seems to have purposely employed the phrase "have since read" anachronistically, for he surely must have read the General's work some time earlier. As he continues in this article, Doyle then details how he "set to work to organize a circle of six, which met nine or ten times at" his Southsea home and had observed "phenomena such as messages delivered by tilts, and even some writing under control . . ." He claims he had not been "absolutely convinced" by these meetings, and that it hadn't been until he had been "invited by two friends to join them in a sitting with an old gentleman who was reputed to have considerable mediumistic power" that he knew it was the right time to help promote the movement. Doyle also claimed that as soon as the medium sat down at the table, he became clairvoyant and began to speak. He still was not entirely convinced that he wasn't the target of some sort of deception. But then "the medium took up a pencil, and after a few convulsive movements, he wrote a message to each of us. Mine ran: 'This gentleman is a healer. Tell him from me not to read Leigh Hunt's book.'" Doyle swore that no one at the meeting was aware that he came close to reading Hunt's 1840 book *Comic Dramatists of the Restoration* and that he had not referred to the book or author to anyone throughout that entire day. Doyle wrote, "I can only say that if I had to devise a test message I could not have hit upon one which was so absolutely inexplicable on any hypothesis except that held by spiritualists." The article then ended as follows:

> "Let a man realise that the human soul, as it emerges from its bodily cocoon, shapes its destiny in exact accordance with its condition.; that that condition depends upon the sum result of his actions and thoughts in his life; that every evil deed stamps itself upon the spirit and entails its own punishment with the same certainty that a man stepping out of a second floor window falls to the ground; that there is no room for deathbed repentances or other nebulous conditions which might screen the evil doer from the consequences of his deeds, but that the law is self-acting and inexorable. This, I take it, is the lesson which Spiritualism enforces, and all phenomena are only witnesses to the truth of this central all-important fact."

As we have already established, Doyle had been deeply intrigued by Spiritualism for many years before his so-called "confession" appeared in the *Light* periodical. Why, then, this dichotomy between what Doyle privately believed as opposed to what he professed to the public? In his 1883 "non"-Sherlock Holmes short story, "The Captain of the 'Pole-Star',"

Doyle chastises—through his fiction—the uncalled-for way in which British biologist Ray Lankester had gone about "unmasking" the noted American Spiritualist Henry Slade—a man who Doyle refused to disown. In the story, Doyle writes:

> "11.20 P.M.—Captain just gone to bed after a long and interesting conversation on general topics. When he chooses he can be a most fascinating companion, being remarkably well-read, and having the power of expressing his opinion forcibly without appearing to be dogmatic. I hate to have my intellectual toes trod upon. He spoke about the nature of the soul, and sketched out the views of Aristotle and Plato upon the subject in a masterly manner. He seems to have a leaning for metempsychosis and the doctrines of Pythagoras. In discussing them we touched upon modern spiritualism, and I made some joking allusion to *the impostures of Slade*, upon which, to my surprise, *he warned me most impressively against confusing the innocent with the guilty*, and argued that it would be as logical to brand Christianity as an error because Judas, who professed that religion, was a villain." *[emphases added throughout]*

A man of action *and* of words, Lankester had already stalked and bagged the elusive wild beast, American medium "Doctor" Henry Slade. Slade had been all the rage within Britain's Spiritualist movement throughout much of the mid-1870s. In 1876, Lankester attended a séance conducted by Slade, whose purpose it was to somehow communicate with a spirit that would manifest itself by writing words on a blank slate. Suspecting that Slade had tampered somehow with the slate prior to the séance, an already highly skeptical Lankester decided "to test my hypothesis . . . by [conducting] a crucial experiment." Once the slate was passed down to Slade, but before any writing implement could have made contact with it, Lankester snatched it out from Slade's hands and found that a message was already written upon its surface. Lankester contended that it was Slade's intention to cheat and defraud him, evidence that "would be convincing to persons not already lost to reason." A trial was then held at the Bow Street Police Court on October 1, 1876 before the eminent Magistrate Frederick Flowers, who sentenced Slade to three months at hard labor. Slade was eventually released from work camp on a technicality and immediately scrambled out of England. In one single stroke, Lankester became the Spiritualist movement's chief antagonist. This incident, and his use of it in his fiction, proves Doyle's awareness—and, likely, *acceptance*—of the more occult elements of Spiritualism at least a decade prior to his self-reported "initiation date" in 1887.

A Spirited Romp Through Spiritualism

Even though Doyle failed to attend a single meeting at Phoenix Lodge after receiving his Masonic Apron in 1887, he *did* manage to read everything he could get his hands on related to occultism, mysticism, and Spiritualism. The Edmund Gurney and Frederick W. H. Myers article "Cases of Thought Transference"—featured at the time within the pages of the magazine *Mind and Nature*—led Doyle to ponder whether he might be capable of projecting his *own* thoughts to the minds of others. He remembered those Stonyhurst "Old Mother Cuthbert" stories, and in particular that character's seemingly magical ability to project her thoughts to others. If Doyle was to be the "agent" transferring his thoughts, he would need a willing and open-minded "percipient" to receive them. And so, in 1888, he recruited his friend and fellow Mason, the noted architect Joseph Henry Ball, to act as his "catcher." According to Doyle's recollection in his later autobiography *Memories and Adventures*, the two met at Ball's home where "again and again . . . I have drawn diagrams, and (Ball) in turn has made approximately the same figure. I showed beyond any doubt whatever that I could convey my thought without words."

By the 1930s, Harvard University's noted "perceptual" psychology professors Karl E. Zener and Joseph Banks Rhine performed a variation of this experiment where they introduced the science of "card guessing." This is how it was done by them: With use of a sturdy fountain pen, they drew a circle, a rectangle, a plus sign, a star, and two wavy lines on what was to become known as the "Zener card"—the card is named, of course, after the aforementioned Dr. Zener who (along with his colleague Dr. Rhine around this time) coined the phrase "extrasensory perception" (ESP). Unbeknownst to Zener and Rhine, Sir Arthur Conan Doyle had already produced a similar set of cards a half-century earlier. It turns out that Rhine had actually attended a lecture during his undergraduate years at the University of Chicago, where Doyle spoke enthusiastically about communicating with the dead. Rhine wrote of Doyle's lecture that, "This mere possibility was the most exhilarating thought I had had in years." Three years later, however, when Rhine published a report that accused medium Mina Crandon of fraudulent activity, Doyle retorted to this perceived betrayal by taking out an advertisement in a Boston newspaper stating, "J. B. Rhine is a monumental ass."

Two separate conclusions might be drawn from Doyle's mind-reading experiment: Either Ball could actually *read* Doyle's mind, or Doyle was hoping he had actually transferred his thoughts to Ball. If the latter is true, then it is our contention that Doyle would have been delusional—a victim of what psychiatrists call "magical thinking." Had Doyle been slipping into some kind of madness at this point in his life?

In February 1889, just after this "successful" experiment in which he was aided by Ball, Doyle handed in an official letter of "demission" to his Masonic board. Going back once again to his autobiography *Memories and Adventures* (published in 1924 when he was sixty-five years old), Doyle seems to have entirely forgotten that he had ever been a practicing Freemason.

After he resigned from the Masonic order during that time, Doyle dashed off a letter to his friend Amy Hoare, in which he informed her that he would henceforth divide his "time between oculism, occultism, and my writing, with a little cricket as a corrective." Apparently, Doyle was working frantically at all of these things around that time, writing his mother that he was "still working hard at the Middle Ages and at the eye" (under the direction of Dr. Arthur Vernon Ford, head of ophthalmology at Portsmouth Eye Hospital).

In late September 1888, Doyle attended the inaugural meeting of the Hampshire Psychical Society and was elected its first Vice President. "The object of the Society" was reported by *The Hampshire Telegraph* as being "the investigation of various rare and obscure mental phenomena, such as those of hypnotism, thought-transference, and allied states." The Psychical Society encouraged men and women to share their accounts of "abnormal or supernormal mental phenomenon," and promised "to conduct their inquiries by experimental methods."

On April 1, 1890, the Portsmouth Literary and Scientific Society welcomed Dr. David Nicolson—the Deputy-Superintendent at Broadmoor Asylum—to the podium. Seven years earlier, he had written a series of articles for *The Journal of Mental Science* on the provocative topic of "Witches and Witchcraft." Nicolson presented his research to a "standing room only" crowd in Guildhall. His first order of business was to review several cases in which the nation's courts had handed down the death sentence to those convicted of being practitioners of what was deemed an especially diabolical form of magic. Dr. Nicolson reminded his audience that "these illustrative cases are of no ordinary import. They are not the mere verbal traditions of a country side, traditions which, however much they may be truthful echoes of national or local sentiment or superstition, nevertheless fail, as matter of fact, to satisfy the requirements of historical criticism. These cases are from the official registers of the law courts of the period, and they, therefore, carry with them all the weight of authentic records."

He then asked the attendees to respond to the following question—"Are such records to be looked upon as criminal charges or indictments written out by society against itself, or are they to be regarded as having a pathological significance, as affording indications in fact that Christendom had 'run mad upon a cruel and absurd delusion?'"—and continued with, "The belief in witchcraft, sorcery, and the like had far too real an influence on the social life and character to warrant any one in bringing the bearings of such a belief to a rough-and-ready ficus as 'stuff and nonsense,' and there dismissing the subject . . . Witchcraft was a crime created by society—a phantom born of superstition, ignorance, and the fiery jealousy of ecclesiasticism." Nicolson offered his own description of what was then the current-day definitions of "witch" and "magician" as the "outcome of superstition, credulity, and ignorance," and went on to warn his listeners that there were still those who believed that these unorthodox individuals actually had the ability to "cure and cause most diseases."

At the very end of Nicolson's lecture, Doyle—who had been in attendance the entire time—stood up and proposed a vote of collective thanks from the audience to their esteemed guest. Pleasantries aside, Doyle then proceeded to lash out at Nicolson verbally, stating for all to hear that "modern science, far from having destroyed the original idea underlying this topic, has gone a long way to confirm it." He then reminded Dr. Nicolson that "The original idea in regard to witchcraft was that certain people possessed powers . . ."—powers that Doyle labelled "preternatural" as opposed to *supernatural*—and maintained that "as a secondary consideration those powers might be used for a malevolent purpose." In order to lend support to his theory, Doyle quoted a recent article with the title "Charcot and other eminent continental scientists into the phenomena of mesmerism and clairvoyance." Doyle's hypothesis gained the immediate support of his longtime friend, Hugh MacLaughlan, who added "we were all superstitious more or less, and we would be rather dull and unimaginative creatures if we were not." Apparently, those gleefully sordid tales of the sorceresses of Pendle Mountain he had heard years earlier at Hodder and Stonyhurst remained deeply embedded in Doyle's imagination.

While little is known about Doyle's activities in the overlapping worlds of Spiritualism, mysticism, and the occult during the ensuing few years, he made more than a few references to them in the decade between 1886 to 1895. This period corresponds to the period when Doyle was emerging as one of England's foremost writers. In his 1894 novella *The Parasite*, Doyle has young Professor Austin Gilroy (a character based loosely on noted toxicologist Robert Christison) bear witness to the hypnotic powers of mesmerist Helen Penclosa. Her abilities evoke Gilroy's curiosity, and he willingly becomes her subject. Although he is skeptical at first, Gilroy quickly changes his mind about Ms. Penclosa's powers, stating, "At least, I have shown that my devotion to science is greater than my own personal consistency. The eating of our own words is the greatest sacrifice which truth ever requires of us." Fatefully, the more the professor studies the mesmerist, the more infatuated with him she becomes, to the point where she attempts to force him to fall in love with her. Gilroy, realizing that his position at the university is compromised, tells Helen to desist from invading his mind. Rather than granting a retreat, the spurned Ms. Penclosa commands the young professor to break into banks, to attack a colleague, and to ultimately kill his fiancée.

In his 1890 short story "A Physiologist's Wife," Doyle has the character Ada Grey implore her science-rooted brother Ainslie "'to turn to spiritual.'" His rebuttal to her request is, "'I have faith in those great evolutionary forces which are leading the human race to some unknown but elevated goal.'" Then in another short story from that same year, "The Surgeon of Gaster Fell," Doyle's John Upperton character informs us that, "All day I bent over the Egyptian papyrus upon which I was engaged but neither the subtle reasonings of the ancient philosopher of Memphis, nor the mystic meaning which lay in his pages, could raise my mind from the things of earth." And yet, up until the death of his uncle James in December 1892, Doyle had not made a full-fledged effort to voice his beliefs to the public.

On January 4, 1893, Doyle chaired a lecture on "Psychical Research" at the Upper Norwood Literary Society in his capacity as its president. The evening's guest speaker for that event was noted physicist Sir William F. Barrett, who "had the honor of proposing him [Doyle] as a member of the Society for Psychical Research, and he was elected the following month." Alas, the year 1893 ended on two significant sour notes for Doyle. On October 10, his father Charles died in The Crichton Royal Institution—and within a month, Doyle's wife Touie entered the terminal stage of tuberculosis. With the cold of the winter season near, and fearful that his wife would start to cough up massive quantities of blood in such harsh weather, Doyle took his wife to Davos, Switzerland because of its "famous high climate sanitarium for the treatment of this disease." The change of venue helped Touie for a while, and allowed Doyle to begin what would become his semi-autobiographical 1895 novel *The Stark Munro Letters*. While the Doyles were in Davos, the noted physicist and Spiritualist Oliver Lodge forwarded to Doyle "a charming piece of narrative" that he had published in the UK publication *Transactions*. The article contained Lodge's opinion about Leonora Piper, a medium who claimed she could communicate with the dead through a spirit named "Phinuit." Doyle was harsh in his criticism of Lodge, accusing him of failing to give enough weight "to the idea that since this entity was so correct about other matters it might also be correct in its account of its own genesis and individuality." Although Doyle did not yet consciously realize it at the time, he was steadily becoming the world expert in the doctrines of Spiritualism.

Doyle vs. Oddie

The turn of the century was an exciting time in Doyle's life. Shortly after receiving his knighthood in 1902, Sir Arthur was inducted into a group called Our Society, which was a quasi-secret organization that had been labeled as "The Murder Club" by the British press. Each member brought to the table an assortment of impeccable credentials that would qualify him as an expert on the inner workings of the criminal mind. An offer of membership to Our Society became one of the most sought-after prizes in the nation—the most anyone could reasonably hope for, regardless of social station, was to be allowed to be placed on the group's ever-growing waiting list. At these dinner club meetings, which were originally intended to be held only four times a year, Doyle tried to convert some of his fellow Anglo intellectuals to the ways of Spiritualism. In service to that goal, Doyle cultivated a special relationship with Dr. Samuel Ingleby Oddie. This former navy surgeon (turned City of London Chief Coroner) shared his tales of the sea with Doyle and proved more than willing initially to accompany his new friend to table-turning séances. Soon enough, Oddie became disenchanted with Doyle's "childlike faith in the genuineness of the ridiculous antics and trickery of certain spiritualistic mediums." What irked him most was that Doyle seemed to have abandoned his "robust common sense and shrewdness and his extraordinary mental acuity," and now believed in things "which ought not to have deceived a fairly intelligent and observant youth of sixteen."

There was, however, one incident that absolutely *angered* Oddie. Doyle had told him about a medium who seemed to possess the ability to communicate with the dead at will. Oddie happily joined his friend at the medium's next séance. He wrote about that evening in his 1941 autobiography *Inquest*, stating he had gone there with "a completely open mind, ready to consider any evidence which might be forthcoming." He also confessed that he had gone there prepared with a vial of a quick-acting sedative and a cardiac stimulant concealed in his coat pocket just in the event that he should be "carried away by the highly dramatized surroundings."

Oddie found it odd that the ten people who entered this North London home had to pay a "very large" ten-shilling entry fee. His medical background as a coroner was such that he had already been trained extensively to identify things that appeared to be out of place, which led him to make the following observations about this particular occasion: "[A]ll the windows were fitted with a special type of light-tight spring blind. These were released by catch and worked from below upwards . . . Taking further stock, I observed a curtain on a semicircular rod, leaving a space, enclosed by the curtain between it and the wall, and against another wall I saw a second railed-off space also surrounded by a curtain." The open-minded but ultimately rational Chief Coroner suspected that things were not quite right.

Next, an uninspiring male medium in loud creaking boots began moving back and forth in front of a semicircular curtain. At the same moment, the entire gathering was locked inside the room and instructed to sit facing the medium at a large round table. An organist who was out of view played hymns and the entire group began to sing along with the music. Every now and then, a curtain or blind sprung open, and the subsequent audible barrage of bangs, slams, and generally chaotic clatter throughout the room did much to rattle the guest's collective nerves. Then the lights dimmed, and the room was plunged into total darkness. The medium spoke as he walked and began blabbering about astral planes, his gibberish mixed with ponderous words seemingly devoid of any sense. After the attendees had joined hands and sung a few more hymns in unison, the medium abruptly stopped talking. The initial silence was soon replaced by "loud stertorous breathing and a few muffled groans and cries." Someone seated at the table whispered with excitement "that the spirits had arrived and that the medium was 'going under'." It looked to Oddie like there were suddenly several lights that had begun to flash and float in the darkness of the room, followed by a quartet of strange voices who spoke in mysterious tones. As they alternated from loud to soft, the phantom voices suddenly shot up in high volume—and just as suddenly fell to a whisper. With that, nervous anticipation filled the room as the audience in attendance awaited some sort of great revelation.

The usually composed Oddie admitted afterward that he had been frightened by thoughts of what might happen next. He reached for his secret vial and swallowed a sedative that allowed him "to work coolly and calmly to examine any further manifestations which might appear." As would soon prove the case, he did not have to wait very long.

The first spirit to "arrive" at the séance introduced himself as "Joey." Doyle recognized the distinctive timbre of the spirit's voice, and then told Oddie that it had once belonged to a popular English "Clown" named Joseph Grimaldi. Almost a half-century before, in May 1837, Grimaldi had died a broken alcoholic . . . not unlike Doyle's own father. A few seconds after its appearance before the assembled group, the spirit of "Joey" and Doyle engaged in a full conversation with one another. In Doyle's short story "Selecting a Ghost" (first published in the December 1883 issue of *London Society* magazine), the reader is told that this same Grimaldi had once been the "property" of Frederick Tabb, a medium who also was the "sole . . . proprietor of the spirits of Byron, Kirke White, Grimaldi, Tom Cribb, and Inigo Jones," and other nineteenth-century celebrities.

The next spirit to appear at the séance was "Abdulla the Afghan," whose yellow ghostlike face, according to Oddie, had been created "by the glow of a wooden board, smeared with phosphorus, which [Abdulla] held under his chin." This sort of trickery had been described in print years before by none other than Doyle himself in the aforementioned acclaimed Holmes novel *The Hound of the Baskervilles*. "Abdulla," donned in a turban and a white robe, caused the skeptical Oddie to write that "the tan of his face had quite obviously come out of a bottle . . . and that his whiskers had also been hired." He set off to see if he was observing

"Abdulla the Afghan" at the séance that caused a rift between Doyle and Dr. Samuel Ingleby Oddie, who did not believe in Spiritualism.

a real person or a spirit, moved out of his seat in the darkness of the room, and slowly made his way over to "Abdulla." Although a member of the medium's staff did his best to keep Oddie in check, he got close enough to observe the spirit's pupils alternately dilate and contract under a luminescent board. Oddie instantly concluded, as he wrote later, that "the eyes were those of a human being" and that he was "in the presence of plain imposture." Believing he was no longer in danger nor in a room full of souls from beyond the grave, Oddie stuck out his foot and kicked the Afghan spirit on his very tactile and decidedly non-spiritual shin. When "Abdulla" yelped in pain, Oddie was warned by the ushers that if he failed to demonstrate more reverence to the spirits, they would disappear from view.

The third and final spirit to arrive that evening was "Sister Agnes," who reportedly danced around while she held a luminous board under her chin. Although its light cast a ghostly look onto her face, Oddie's trained eye was able to make out a vast amount of white muslin plastered across the plain face of an obviously living woman. Oddie studied this new spirit's breathing patterns and observed a rise and fall of her chest, and a normal reaction of her pupils to light. At that moment, he determined that the evening's charade was definitely *over*.

And yet, Oddie was suddenly aghast when the woman seated next to him began to plead with the "spirit" to put her in touch with her recently departed spouse. "Sister Agnes" was quick to oblige—in a thick Cockney accent, the spirit was said to have stated aloud that the woman's "'usband was quite well and 'oped she was the same." Doyle was taken by complete surprise when Oddie got up and then simply excused himself from the séance. As Oddie recalled in his autobiography, the strangest and most shocking aspect of that evening had been just how easy it had been for the medium to dupe Doyle into believing that what he had witnessed during the séance had been authentic—which was diametrically opposed to Oddie's sentiments that what he had seen was nothing more than an utter hoax. Oddie, prompted by Doyle's naivete, felt compelled to write, "One would have thought that the inventor of Sherlock Holmes and Dr. Watson, both of whom seem pretty certain of immortality in English literature, would be the very last man to be taken in by imposture."

Another incident that impacted Doyle's experiences with spirits was described by Oddie as "a ghost adventure which he experienced with Mr. Podmore, a well-known writer on the occult." Years before, the research done by Frank Podmore had prompted Doyle and Joseph Henry Ball to expand on Podmore's experiments on thought transference. Doyle, who "could never resist an invitation . . . to investigate mysterious manifestations," had visited an old house in the English countryside where strange events had purportedly taken place. The house was occupied by a widow, her son, two daughters, and—a *ghost*, based on what Doyle was told. The widow had sent a letter to the Psychical Research Society that asked for their help in investigating the matter. The Society responded to her request by sending Doyle and Podmore to do some "ghost hunting."

Doyle and Podmore decided to stay at the "haunted house" for a few days. On their first night there, not long after they attempted to conduct a séance, they decided to stay up all night and wait for the mysterious spirit to show up. When nothing happened, the two ghost hunters realized that they had wasted their time. They packed their bags to leave, but at the last moment, they had a change of heart and opted to remain there for a *second* night. They "secured every door and window in the house with cotton thread which would break if disturbed by human agency," and came up with a plan of action in case they heard any strange sounds. Since there were two staircases that each led to the upstairs landings, they concocted a scheme where the two of them would immediately rush to the same spot, but they would take two different routes—one from the front, and one from the back. By doing so, they would be guaranteed to spot any person or persons playing tricks on them.

That night they conducted another séance—and once again, the rumored ghost failed to materialize. Then the two camped out in the dining room but decided not to put up a fire, which would have illuminated the house. At two o'clock in the morning, Doyle suggested they call it a day—but the eerie silence of the witching hour was "suddenly rent by an extraordinary uproar." Doyle later told Oddie it had been "unlike anything [I] had ever heard. It was unearthly—terrifying! It suggested immense power—a reverberating clanging which seemed to rock the house to its very foundations—as though some giant force were pounding some unknown metallic material."

Sticking to their plan, Doyle and Podmore rushed up the two staircases, but not a trace of anyone or anything trying to escape was observed by them. When they checked the doors and windows, they found that the cotton threads had been left undisturbed. They then meticulously re-examined each room, but neither doors nor windows had been touched. When the new day dawned, the two of them returned to town without any satisfactory explanation as to the source of the strange noises. Much later, Oddie would come to realize that there were significant differences between the two nights in question. On the first, the owner's son had stayed with Podmore and Doyle in the same room—but on the second more eventful night, the son had not been within their sight, even though he never left the house. It was Oddie's theory thereafter that the owner's son had somehow been able to create those preternatural noises, attributing his motives to his hope that his mother would abandon this lonely and unexciting residence for a newer house in a livelier neighborhood.

Doyle had previously shared his experience in a haunted house in the 1899 short story "The Story of the Brown Hand," in which he has his main character tell the reader that, "as a member of the Psychical Research Society, I had formed one of a committee of three who spent the night in a haunted house. Our adventures were neither exciting nor convincing, but, such as it was, the story appeared to interest my auditors in a remarkable degree."

Doyle vs. Jerome—A Duel

Doyle also failed to win over Jerome K. Jerome, a respected writer and charter member of the Murder Club, to the tenets of Spiritualism. In 1919, Jerome used the pages of *Common Sense* magazine to challenge Doyle to respond to queries about this "new religion" that Doyle claimed would be the "successor" to Christianity. Jerome led off by telling Doyle and his followers that "with gladness would I accept a new religion 'founded upon human reason on this side and upon spirit inspiration upon the other.'" But instead, he stressed one of its glowing weaknesses, that the only thing Spiritualism had to offer was a "darkened room, the ubiquitous tambourine, the hired medium (sometimes 'detected in trickery' and sometimes not), now tied into a chair, and now locked up in an iron cage; the futile messages, proved frequently to be 'concoctions,' vague prophecies of the kind that we can read in any 'Old Moore's Almanac.'" Jerome then hurled the following barrage of questions at Doyle:

"What does spiritualism preach? . . . Has spiritualism done anything—
is it doing anything—to help man to be less brutal, less hypocritical,
less greedy? Has it done anything—is it doing anything—to lessen
the appalling wickedness that is threatening, like some foul weed, to
poison the whole earth?"

Doyle was eager to pick up the gauntlet and, in a retort to Jerome's
questions, explained the necessity for darkened rooms, the rattling tambourine, the bound medium, and the so-called "puerile" messages. He
then invited Jerome to "examine the 120 books upon this subject" that
were in his private collection, many of them written "as high as mortal
brain can follow." Following his rebuttal, Doyle graciously offered to send
Mr. Jerome a copy of his own book *The New Revelation*, which had been
published the year before.

Jerome proceeded to present, "without prejudice" to *Common Sense*,
his perception of an accurate "picture of mental states accompanying"
Doyle's conversion to Spiritualism. He told his readers the following:

"Sir Arthur admits that before he became converted he would occasionally return from a seance 'puzzled and disgusted.' What he had
witnessed struck him as either fraud or folly so supreme as to render
the whole subject unworthy of attention. The 'explanations' by which
spiritualists sought to remove his skepticism did not satisfy him 'at
the time.' Before his conversion he admits having come across mediums whose performances imprest him, but who were later, detected in
trickery. After his conversion, he appears to have had no experiences
calculated to weaken his faith, while the 'explanations' that had before
this time appeared so unsatisfactory to him he is now able to regard
as 'a rough approximation to the truth.'"

Jerome's opening paragraph used Doyle's own words against him, and
represented an attempt to snap Doyle out of his hypnotized state. Jerome
went on to mention that a portion of Doyle's conversion was based on the
testimony of three "men of honor and repute" who claimed they had witnessed "Mr. Home, a medium, 'float out of the window and into another at
the height of seventy feet above ground.'" Jerome did his best to discredit
them, stating that "less than two hundred years ago men of 'honor and
repute,' men of intellect and education, kindly Christian gentlemen—were
attesting in open court that they had seen old women riding through the

air on broomsticks." Jerome closed his argument with a barbed statement that "the gradual rise of rationalism in Europe has cleared men's eyes so far as this particular delusion is concerned."

Doyle reacted as expected, calling out Jerome for his indecency of not having "examined these alleged facts." Doyle then alludes to the contemporary intellectuals who are staunch believers of the "New Revelation," a list that included Professor Lombroso, Professor Schrenck-Notzing, Sir William Crooke, and Dr. Crawford. He dares Jerome to be courageous enough to accuse them of faking their work. Doyle then addresses Jerome's reference to the Pendle witch trials, stating that he was "well acquainted with the history of witchcraft, and the main characteristics of the old trials were the illiteracy and general independability of the witnesses."

Although Doyle had been a follower of the Spiritualism movement for decades, his duel with Jerome K. Jerome in the pages of *Common Sense* marked a turning point in Doyle's life. From that point on, he would become the go-to man for responding to those influential skeptics who challenged the fundamental principles of his new religion. Over the next few years, he played an active role in the defense of mediums, occult research, mysticism, and fairies. And although in that retort to Jerome where he wrote that he "cared nothing about proselytising," he would be doing an abrupt about-face a year later.

The Cottingley Fairies

In 1920, Doyle was asked to validate a collection of photographs that had been taken by a sixteen-year-old from rural Yorkshire named Elsie Wright. She claimed she had captured images of playful sprites on film near a stream behind her home for the past four years. After Doyle had scrutinized the photos and had judged them to be genuine, he was quick to set off to the village of Cottingley and somehow managed to convince her skeptical father that it was the obligation of the Wright family to share this scientific breakthrough with the entire world. Mr. Wright, who was so impressed that a man of Doyle's celebrity would insist that Elsie's accidental discovery be publicized, adamantly refused to accept any financial compensation for them. With Doyle standing behind her, Elsie's pictures appeared in the December issue of *The Strand*, sparking a flame that would pit the Spiritualists against the non-believers.

Acting in the capacity of a self-appointed mediator, Doyle called upon the Kodak Company to weigh in on the issue at hand. Kodak, under pressure to accede to Doyle's request, began subjecting "The Fairies" to meticulous scientific study. After concluding its investigation, Kodak's technical staff was unwilling to issue a certificate of authenticity to the negative plates Doyle had submitted to them. Doyle was not at all pleased by their decision and immediately sought a second opinion from the Ilford Company. It didn't take long for Ilford to concur with Kodak's opinion. But Ilford went beyond Doyle's request, declaring that there had been "evidence of faking."

Somewhat ironically, Doyle's 1912 novel *The Lost World*—published eight years before the photos were taken—has Tarp Henry offering the following bit of advice to Edward Malone: "'If you are clever and know your business you can fake a bone as easily as you can a photograph.'" What most of the public had no knowledge of was that Doyle was an expert in the science of photography and had a column of his own back in the 1880s in the prestigious *British Journal of Photography*. When Elsie Wright's photos were first released, a boastful Doyle wrote, "The recognition of their existence will jolt the material twentieth century mind out of its heavy ruts in the mud, and will make it admit that there is a glamour and mystery to life. Having discovered this, the world will not find it so difficult to accept that spiritual message supported by physical facts which has already been put before it." There is no way of determining whether Doyle actually had sought to put one over on the public or whether he, himself, had been fooled. What *is* determinable is that Doyle was fully willing to take advantage of a situation that would offer proof that fairies, sprites, "brownies," gnomes, and exotic creatures were living among us.

Two years later, Doyle was defending his beliefs again in *The Coming of the Fairies*. The book's preface tells readers that they are "in almost as good a position as I am to form a judgment upon the authenticity of the pictures." An acerbic Doyle goes on to warn those who would dare doubt him "not to be led away by the sophistry that because some professional trickster, apt at the game of deception, can produce a somewhat similar effect . . ." In the book's first section, he lets the public in on a family secret—that this new species of fairies is "as numerous as the human race," and insists that the only reason we are sometimes unable to spot them is because:

"[W]e see objects within the limits which make up our colour spectrum, with infinite vibrations, unused by us, on either side of them. If we could conceive a race of beings which were constructed in material which threw out shorter or longer vibrations, they would be invisible unless we could tune ourselves up or tone them down. It is exactly that power of tuning up and adjusting itself to other vibrations which constitutes a clairvoyant, and there is nothing scientifically impossible, so far as I can see, in some people seeing that which is invisible to others."

Doyle was an apostle of his father's belief that there would come a time when "psychic spectacles . . . will be invented, and that we shall all be able to adapt ourselves to the new conditions." Doyle furnishes us with the precise dates when he had been told about these photos by Mr. David Gow, the editor of the periodical *Light*. In a chronologically ordered assortment of letters, Doyle wrote that he had subjected Elsie Wright's parents to separate interviews, and that Mr. Wright had told him he "was 'fed up' with the whole business, and had nothing else to tell." Captivated by Doyle's charisma, he then corroborated his wife's account, stating that his daughter had actually been able to capture images of fairies on film. Soon afterward, *Detective* Doyle interviewed Elsie Wright at her workplace at Sharpe's Christmas Card Manufactory. An unyielding Elsie told him that "she firmly believed that she and her cousin were the only persons who had been so fortunate" to see them and that "if anybody else were there, the fairies would not come out." So detailed were her descriptions of these "fine-weather elves" that Doyle dedicated a full section of his book to Elsie's fairies, goblins, elves, "brownies," gnomes, and water nymphs. Doyle reproduced an article he had written on this very subject prior to *The Coming of the Fairies*, where he had rambled on about subsequent cases of the existence of unseen worlds. He closed this section with a synopsis of the Theosophist viewpoint toward these creatures and agreed with their opinion that these magical beings are lighter than air, are linked to the plant kingdom, and have no food requirements. *The Coming of the Fairies* concludes with, "I have given the reader the opportunity of judging the evidence for a considerable number of alleged cases, collected before and after the Cottingley incident."

Sixty-three years later in 1983, Elsie Wright issued a confession to the British popular magazine *The Unexplained* admitting that all of her photographs had been nothing but *fakes*. She then revealed how she had been able to pull off that little prank. She and her younger cousin had made cardboard cutouts of fairies they had traced from *Princess Mary's Gift Book* (1914) and then had placed "wings and hatpins" on them. Too embarrassed to admit they had been able to pull the wool over the eyes of the great Arthur Conan Doyle, the two girls made up their minds to keep their little secret to themselves. As Elsie said, "Two village kids and a brilliant man like Conan Doyle—well, we could only keep quiet."

The Great Magician

In 1920, Doyle met the man regarded as the most powerful medium of all time—internationally acclaimed magician Harry Houdini. Doyle had already been corresponding with the master illusionist for some time when he learned that the great Houdini would be performing at Brighton's Hippodrome. He invited Houdini and his wife to an overnight stay at his Crowborough estate. When Houdini arrived, Doyle stood there in awe. In the weeks that followed this auspicious occasion, Doyle bombarded Houdini with newspaper clippings and articles related to the "religion" of Spiritualism for a period of months. But Houdini was not one to be won over easily, and so, when Doyle and his second wife, Lady Jean Leckie, traveled to America to preach on behalf of Spiritualism, Doyle made it a top priority to convince the Houdinis to vacation with him and his wife at the seaside resort town of Atlantic City.

Whether it was due to pure chance or careful orchestration, the Doyles and Houdinis *did* meet at the Ambassador Hotel on what would have been the eighty-first birthday of Harry Houdini's mother—June 17, 1922. The day began with the two couples lounging together on the beach, but in the mid-afternoon, Doyle excused himself so he could take a nap. Upon his return to the beach, he extended the following invitation to Harry: "Houdini, if agreeable, Lady Doyle will give you a special séance, as she has a feeling that she might have a message come through." Doyle then turned to Mrs. Houdini and said, "We would like to be alone. You do not mind if we make the experiment without you." Although Mrs. Houdini acquiesced to Doyle's somewhat strange request, she did have time to employ a secret spousal code that informed her husband that Lady Doyle had *already* interrogated her about Houdini's relationship with his mother.

Once the trio had entered Doyle's suite, Doyle "drew down the shades so as to exclude the bright light" and invited Houdini to sit down at a table covered with pencils and writing pads. Apparently, Doyle hadn't taken an afternoon nap that day, but rather had busied himself arranging the room for a proper séance. Once they all took their seats, the Doyles placed their hands upon the tabletop and Sir Arthur uttered a devotional prayer. Houdini had already made up his mind to observe the ceremonial rites objectively. He "excluded all earthly thoughts" and later stated that he would have been willing to embrace Spiritualism if the Doyles had provided him with evidence sufficient to shatter his doubts.

Suddenly, self-proclaimed medium Jean Leckie Doyle was "seized by a Spirit." Houdini offered this description of the events that followed:

"Her hands shook and beat the table, her voice trembled and she called to the Spirits to give her a message. Conan Doyle tried to quiet her, asked her to restrain herself, but her hands thumped on the table, her whole body shook and at last, making a cross at the head of the page, started writing. And as she finished each page, Sir Arthur tore the sheet off and handed it to me. I sat serene through it all, hoping and wishing that I might feel my mother's presence."

The letter that Lady Jean then handed to Houdini read as follows:

"Oh, my darling, thank God, thank God, at last I'm through- I've tried, of, so often- now I am happy. Why, of course I want to talk to my boy- my own beloved boy- Friends, thank you, with all my heart for this. You have answered the cry of my heart- and of his- God bless him- a thousandfold for all his life for me- never had a Mother such a son- tell him not to grieve- soon he'll get all the evidence he is so anxious for . . . -God bless you, too, Sir Arthur, for what you are doing for us- for us, over here- who so need to get in touch with our beloved ones on the earth plane- If only the world knew this great truth- how different life would be for men and women."

Houdini, who had hoped to find a serenity that never "materialized," wrote with disappointment that "there wasn't even a semblance of it. Everyone who has ever had a worshipping Mother and has lost earthly, knows the feeling which will come over him at the thought of sensing her presence."

The spirit from beyond must have misplaced the memo that informed her that although Houdini's mother "had been in America for almost fifty years, she could not speak, read nor write English." Astonishingly, each and every phrase and sentence that appeared on Lady Doyle's pads and papers had been written in perfect English and *not* in German. Harry Houdini, who had studied each and every aspect of Spiritualism for more than three decades, was totally aware that when "Spiritualists claim that when a medium is possessed by a Spirit who does not speak the language, she automatically writes, speaks, or sings in the language of the deceased." Although he now knew he had been the intended target of a cruel hoax, he decided to play along with the Doyles' game. Houdini picked up a pencil and asked Doyle, "Is there any particular way in which I must hold this pencil when I want to write, or does it write automatically?" Then, pretending he was receiving a message from the world of spirits, he "wrote the name of 'Powell,'" an appellation he had conjured up as a tribute to his old friend and fellow magician, Frederick Eugene Powell. When Doyle noticed Powell's name, he lost all control of himself and started to jump up and down, exclaiming, "The Spirits have directed you in writing the name of my dear fighting partner in Spiritualism, Dr. Ellis Powell, who has just died in England. I am the person he is most likely to signal to, and here is his name coming through your hands." This was to be the death stroke for Doyle.

On the day before Halloween of that same year, in an interview with *The New York Sun*, Harry Houdini stated unequivocally that he had *never* seen the claims of any medium validated. Doyle, aware that this was an intentional slight aimed at his wife, was quick to confront Houdini with a letter in which he wrote:

"You have all the right in the world to hold your own opinion, but when you say that you have had no evidence of survival, you say what I cannot reconcile with what I saw with my own eyes. I know, by many examples, the purity of my wife's mediumship, and I saw what you got and what the effect was upon you at the time. You know also you yourself at once wrote down, with your own hand, the name Powell, the one man who might be expected to communicate with me."

Houdini retaliated by informing Doyle that his mother had never spoken in, nor written in, the English language, and that he had chosen the name "Powell" simply because he was doing a "great deal of correspondence" with a man by that name around that time.

Two months later, Doyle sent off the following letter, reprimanding Houdini for participating in the Scientific American Committee's efforts to find an authentic psychic photograph taken under test conditions:

"My dear Houdini:

... I see that you are on the Scientific American Committee, but how can it be called an Impartial Committee when you have committed yourself to such statements as that some Spiritualists pass away before they realize how they have been deluded, etc? You have every possible right to hold such an opinion, but you can't sit on an Impartial Committee afterwards. It becomes biased at once. What I wanted was five good clear-headed men who can push to it without any prejudice at all, like the Dialectical Society of London, who unanimously endorsed the phenomena."

A few years later, Doyle came to the defense of Boston-based medium Margery Cranston in the editorial columns of various newspapers. Houdini, who had had enough of Doyle by this time, stood up in front of a packed audience at one of his well-attended lectures and derided Doyle as "a menace to mankind." Eventually, Houdini came to the conclusion that *all* mediums were to be looked upon as frauds and charlatans until proven otherwise. Doyle stalwartly refused to yield to Houdini's accusations and did his best to "turn the tables" on his former friend. He remained convinced that Houdini possessed "great mediumistic powers" and that his "feats are done with the aid of spirits." Houdini retorted that "Sir Arthur has told me time and time again that his whole life is based upon the subject of Spiritualism and that he has sacrificed some of the best years of his life to the betterment and spread of the cause, which, due to his sincerity, is a beautiful faith" and added, "But in my opinion it is no 'sacrifice' to convince people who have recently suffered a bereavement of the possibility and reality of communicating with their dear ones. To me the poor suffering followers eagerly searching for relief from the heart-pain that follows the passing on of a dear one are the 'sacrifice.'"

Doyle as Advocate for the Spiritualists

Early in 1917, Doyle began to speak out more often on behalf of Spiritualism. His timing was right, as the Great War—with its accompanying "enormous loss of life on the battlefield, the unfulfilled character of the lives thus abruptly ended, the hunger of those left behind for reunion with 'the loved and lost,'"—had caused many to lose their faith in society. Many members of the era's "Lost Generation" were hopeful that Spiritualism held the answer to solving "the problem of survival after death. Brothers, Sisters, Mothers, Fathers, friends, and spouses were desperately searching for a way to communicate to those that had died during the Great War, and Spiritualism promised them a way!"

In March 1917, Doyle addressed the London Spiritualist Alliance, and four months later he was asked by *The Strand* to defend the outspoken Spiritualist Sir Oliver Lodge's contention "that the Dead can communicate with the living." Doyle was responsible for the "Yes" column of this point/counterpoint article while noted anthropologist and biographer Edward Clodd picked up the gauntlet for the "No"s. Doyle offered nothing more than a recapitulation of his own experiences with Spiritualism that had "extended over thirty years." He did, however, encourage the public to read four books in the following sequence: Lodge's *Survival of Man* (1909), J. Arthur Hill's *Psychical Investigations* (1917), W. T. Stead's *After Death* (1905), and Lodge's other notable Spiritualist title *Raymond or Life and Death* (1916). These books all asserted that Spiritualism did not conflict with nor destroy religion, but, instead, would "enrich and revive each and all of them." Doyle made the bold statement that Spiritualism was "the greatest religious event since the coming of that Great Spirit Who brought, nearly two thousand years ago, the message of gentleness and tolerance from which the world seems to have profited so little." He then retraced the path he had taken, the one that had led him to fully immerse himself in the Spiritualist movement. He had begun his journey by reading a biography about Spiritualism convert Judge John W. Edmonds, and followed it with in-depth references to: Robert Browning's 1864 poem "Mr. Sludge, 'The Medium'"; a collection of varied police reports related to the exposure of fraudulent mediums; Alfred Russel Wallace's three essays entitled "Modern Miracles"; and Sir William Crookes' various experiments. He offered the details of his own friendship with General Drayson, "one of the pioneers of this movement in England," and closed with the statement that "all other religious systems have come from the East. Here at last is one from the West, not supplanting but clarifying and strengthening others. It is the very special glory of England that she has done far more than any other country to rescue this system from being a mere playing with Poltergeists, and to dignify it into a scientific system."

A month later, Doyle chastised his skeptical sister Ida for what he considered to be her flawed interpretation of the precepts of Spiritualism with these words:

> "Your views about the spirit land seem to me a little unreasonable. If Percy were called away which God forbid, you would not complain that he was 'hanging about clamouring to communicate with earth' merely because he wished to assure you that all was well with him. When people first pass over they have the desire, but after a little, and especially if they find no corresponding desire in those who are left behind, it soon passes . . . I am sorry you dont like the prospect but what you or I may like has really nothing to do with the matter. We dont like some of the conditions down here. But if you try to define what would satisfy you you will find it very difficult . . . Cheer up, its not so bad!"

On October 25 of that year, Doyle was in London delivering a speech on "The New Revelation," in which he stated that it was "the first attempt to show what the real meaning is of the modern spiritual movement." He offered a prediction that the clergy would soon be doing their best to use his words and sentiments against him. Three days later, he wrote his brother Innes, "I have a rather contentious life as I have two big subjects on which I seem, with no deliberate intention of my own to have become a leader, that of devil-made marriages, and that of the bearings of modern psychical research upon Christianity." A few days later, he sent a hopeful letter to Innes in which he wrote, "I seem to see a second Reformation coming in this country. The folk await a message, and the message is there. I hope some stronger & more worthy messenger than I may carry it but I should be proud to be a Lieutenant."

Although Doyle was traveling around England preaching in the name of Spiritualism, his own son Kingsley was not a ready convert. On January 22, 1918, Kingsley diplomatically wrote the following to his father:

"I was very interested by the talk on Spiritualism, though I must admit my feelings just grip me in the same old way . . . Also a thing I have always found instinctive is to pray for a person just as really after they have been taken from us as before. I could not believe that the future existence was without effort and striving, whatever else that might be there. But you must forgive me if I have seemed aloof in these matters but just lately I have sort of felt like a man who has had a vision which faded away and he is now watching the spot where it faded knowing that it will come back again."

On October 28, 1918, Doyle was once again forced to handle another tragedy in his life. This was the day that his daughter Mary had to inform him that Kingsley had become another victim of the Spanish Flu. That evening, Doyle went up to the podium and gave a lecture that promoted his newest book, *The New Revelation*. Later on, he was to state, "Had I not been a spiritualist, I could not have spoken that night. As it was, I was able to go straight on the platform and tell the meeting that I knew my son had survived the grave, and that there was no need to worry." He decided then and there to dedicate himself to communicating with the departed. The loss of his beloved Kingsley produced a noticeable change in Doyle's personality, and he informed his mother that, "I shall speak in every town of any size in Great Britain." He made good on that promise.

Doyle suffered another personal loss three months later when he received word that his brother Innes had died in Belgium, another of Doyle's family taken by complications of the Spanish Flu. Doyle arranged for an impromptu séance, whose purpose was to help him communicate with his dead brother. By this time, Doyle's fanatical devotion to Spiritualism had placed him in the crosshairs of trigger-happy critics and enemies—and, at times, even members of his own family. Some of his contemporaries suspected that Doyle had lost his mind, perhaps in a perverse echo of his doomed father's eventual fate. His mother remained at odds with him on this topic, and in a letter to her son, she wrote, "You are asking a thing which it is not my power to give. The best I could do would be to lie and what good could possibly come from that. I always hope that I have made you understand this but your letters show me that I fail. You still speak as if I were refusing you something which I could give you. This has never been so. Such letters disturb me deeply but I cannot see how they can alter that 'which is.'" Although a good deal of

Books for Booklovers.

IS CONAN DOYLE MAD?

By JAMES DOUGLAS.

WITH an ironical smile on my lips I began to read "The Wanderings of a Spiritualist," by Sir Arthur Conan Doyle. Maunderings or wanderings? For years I have regarded his writings about the dead with benign contempt. In private talk with men of letters I have assumed that on this subject he is mad. That is a very general assumption. One does not trouble to analyse the ravings of a madman. One shrugs one's shoulders, laughs, and forgets. But before I had read half the book I found myself in a quandary. Doyle, I reflected, is no fool. He is not only a novelist and historian: he is also a man of action. He is healthy in mind and body. He is direct and downright, prosaic and practical. He has plenty of vigorous common sense. If ever there were a well-balanced mind in a well-balanced body, it is his. He is also a medical man, and therefore not likely to fall a victim to hallucinations and neurotic delusions.

METHOD IN MADNESS.

Moreover, his world-famous character, Sherlock Holmes, is a master of the science of induction and deduction. Doyle could not have created Sherlock Holmes if he had not been deeply versed in the laws of evidence. In many other respects, too, Doyle is a pioneer, for he sees further ahead than most of his contemporaries. He foresaw the nature of the submarine war. Many other predictions that he made have been fulfilled. As an imaginative realist he rivals Mr. Wells. It is not easy to reconcile these facts with the hypothesis that he is stark, staring mad on the subject of the dead. It is possible, I thought, that there may be a method in his madness. He has established his right to be heard, and we may be wrong in refusing to hear him. There may be oceans of fraud and folly in Spiritualism, but there may be a grain of truth in it. It may be one of the great movements of the human mind, as yet in its early stage, but destined to struggle towards full and final victory.

TO MOCK IS HUMAN—

After all, man is a creature of prejudice. He mocks at every new thing. He derides every fresh discovery. Wireless telegraphy and aviation were at one time scoffed at as absurdities. They are now commonplaces. It may be that Spiritualism will become an ordinary fact and factor in human life. The ancient barrier between the living and the dead may be crossed. Intercourse between the two separated portions of the human race may be made possible. The mourner may cease to mourn. The continuity of personality may be proved beyond doubt. It may be possible to know as well as to believe. How can I rule out this vision of hope and joy? I certainly cannot prove that it is impossible.

Science has wrought so many miracles in our time that it is stupid to set a limit to its march. The earth has been explored. The stars have been analysed. The one great unknown region is the mysterious land of the living dead. Is it not possible that the spiritual universe may be explored as successfully as the material universe? And Doyle may be one of the precursors. He may be groping and fumbling on the threshold of a

miracle. His totterings and stumblings may seem comical to us, but they may be the first steps of the human infant. Reasoning thus, I grew ashamed of my cynical disdain. I opened my mind wide and sat down at the feet of Gamaliel in an attitude of respectful humility. I resolved to be critical without being contemptuous.

One thing this book proves—Doyle's intellectual honesty. He may be a dupe, but at least he strives to be fair and frank. He makes admissions which a rogue or a lunatic would not make. He deliberately weakens his own case by his exposition of its flaws. The working of his mind is candid. And he is a glorious evangelist. His fervour is splendid. After three years of polemical crusading

SIR A. CONAN DOYLE.

in this country, during which he often spoke five times a week, and addressed 150,000 people, he set forth on his mission to Australia, New Zealand, and Tasmania. There were difficulties. His wife and three children of tender age, a girl of seven, a boy of nine, and a boy of eleven, could not easily be left behind. A maid was necessary. A party of seven in all! A secretary was essential. A cheque for £1,500 was drawn for their return tickets, apart from outfit. At the end of the tour, after paying all expenses, Doyle handed the balance of £700 to the cause in Australia. A businesslike evangelist, surely!

The paradox pleases me. Doyle conducts his spiritualist campaign on sound business lines. His propaganda is hard-headed and matter-of-fact. He is a practical mystic, and there is nothing hectic in his altruism. He does not live on locusts and wild honey. He likes the good things of life. He can savour a glass of wine. This burly cricketer, with his robust frame, his interest in all phases of life, is no demented dervish or hysterical fakir. He is as solid and as serious as any man of business. He pounds away at his job as if he were paid for his aide. And he does not often pull out the sentimental stop. He believes in his

wares and he pushes them with all the energy and persuasiveness of a good salesman or commercial traveller. He is the drummer of the unseen.

He is not credulous. For example, he acutely analyses the mango-tree trick and explains it away. "My explanation is that by a miracle of packing the plant had been compressed into the little rag doll. I observed that the leaves were still rather crumpled, and that there were dark specks of fungi which would not be there if the plant were straight from nature's manufactory. That is Sherlock Holmes. I hesitate to suggest that our Sherlock Holmes does not honestly apply his unique powers of analysis to spiritualistic phenomena. It is only fair to assume that our Sherlock Holmes conscientiously exhausts every possibility of error before he accepts the evidence as conclusive proof.

DEATH OF FAITH.

"I asked for proofs," he says, "and spiritualism has given them to me. *I have done with faith.* It is a golden mist in which human beings wander in devious tracks, with many a collision. I need the white, clear light of knowledge." The age of faith, it seems, is dead. The war killed faith for many. There are few signs of its revival. Is it possible that the next great spiritual renascence of the soul of man may be wrought by an exploration of the other world? If the patient labours of these exploring moles can excavate evidence which will convince mankind that it survives death, surely the human race may be redeemed from the horrible materialism of despair.

Doyle says that he has seen and touched the mysterious stuff known as ectoplasm, psychoplasm, or ideoplasm. It is poured out of the medium's body. It can be built up into forms and shapes, first flat, and finally rounded, by powers which are beyond our sciences. "It was about six inches long and as thick as a finger. I was allowed to touch it, and felt it shrink and contract under my hand." This strange stuff has been photographed. Men of science were present when it appeared! One theory regards its shapes as thought forms. Another theory suggests that "what we see is never the thing itself, but always the reflection of the thing which exists in another plane and is made visible in ours." Well, I think of wireless telegraphy, of radium, of electrons, and I wonder.

EVE OF REVOLUTION.

Doyle asserts that "the human race is on the very eve of a tremendous revolution of thought, marking a final revulsion from materialism." He predicts that it will "give religion a foundation of rock instead of quicksand." I humbly suspend my judgment. But I claim a fair hearing for Doyle. Let us investigate instead of sneering. Let us examine all the evidence, all the witnesses, all the "cross-correspondences," all the "book-tests," and all the photographs. Let us sift and clarify, weigh and measure. The progressive Press, at any rate, ought to be on the side of reverent research and honest exploration.

"The Wanderings of a Spiritualist." By Sir Arthur Conan Doyle. (Hodder and Stoughton. 12s. 6d net.)

Doyle's ongoing fascination with Spiritualism wreaked havoc with his public image, as can be seen in the 1918 *Sunday Express* article above.

their ideological disagreements were fought out in private letters to each other, Mary still continued to support her son in public.

Doyle was always willing to use any means available to publicize and disseminate his new religion. Having convinced himself that he had the mandate of the people, he felt it was his obligation to act on *their* behalf in all matters great and small. Unfazed by the constant threats and taunts hurled at him, he merged his slick writing style with his charisma to disarm his critics and win public support on a slew of the day's social, economic, and political issues. All of his proselytizing on behalf of Spiritualism eventually exerted an adverse effect on his reputation—*especially* once he reached the age of sixty. He followed his *The New Revelation* with *The Vital Message* (1919), another book dedicated to Spiritualism that made the following claim:

> "[T]he soul is a complete duplicate of the body, resembling it in the smallest particular, although constructed in some far more tenuous material. In ordinary conditions these two bodies are intermingled so that the identity of the finer one is entirely obscured. At death, however, and under certain conditions in the course of life, the two divide and can be seen separately. Death differs from the conditions of separation before death in that there is a complete break between the two bodies, and life is carried on entirely by the lighter of the two, while the heavier, like a cocoon from which the living occupant has escaped, degenerates and disappears, the world burying the cocoon with much solemnity by taking little pains to ascertain what has become of its nobler contents. It is a vain thing to urge that science has not admitted this contention, and that the statement is pure dogmatism."

From Books to Bookshop

Early in 1925, Doyle came up with a plan to remedy "one of the weak points" of the Spiritualist movement—its lack of a central headquarters. The solution he offered was to open his own bookshop and library "in one of the most central positions in London." He leased a store just a stone's throw away from Westminster Abbey to serve as the "central depot for knowledge . . . to meet the fact that psychic literature, the most important literature in the world, found hardly any place upon the shelves of the ordinary book seller." He called upon the followers of Spiritualism to send him any of their spare books so that the store's shelves and showcases could be adequately stocked. Within a few months, "The World's Happiest Museum" opened in the basement of his shop. Once again, Doyle implored his devotees to send him any items they had that had an association with psychic phenomena. In an article written by Leonard Crocombe, "Through a Room of Miracles with Sir A. Conan Doyle," Doyle declared that "the core of every religion, and my little museum must be doing good work if it proves our survival of bodily death." Doyle saw himself as Spiritualism's Savior, and he lived in the hope that it would evolve into one of the world's major religions. He certainly was ready, willing, and able to be selected as its official leader. The choice of exclusive Victoria Street for the shop's location was no coincidence. Doyle had been meticulous and artful in conceiving this project of his but found himself "handcuffed" by the exorbitant seven-hundred fifty-pound yearly rent he had to pay. He was forced to reach into his personal assets in order to ensure that anyone who stood on the steps of Westminster Abbey would have an unobstructed view of his "Temple."

Visitors to his bookshop went there to thumb through its extensive collection of rare books on the twin subjects of Spiritualism and the occult. They were encouraged to spend their day looking at the exhibits in "the smallest museum in London" and to spend some time studying spirit writing, paintings done by mediums, the *actual* Cottingley Fairy photographs, genuine "gloves" cast from the hands of a spirit who dipped them into wax, and hundreds of other objects. But some visitors used their time there sharing their troubles with an accommodating staff that was always willing to listen to their stories and then offer them some spiritual advice.

In 1926—while serving as President d' Honneur de la Federation Spirite Internationale, President of the London Spiritualist Alliance, and President of the British College of Psychic Science—Doyle published a two-volume book, *The History of Spiritualism*. Here Doyle reaffirmed his conviction that this religion was equal to Christianity in its importance. Its preface reads, "It is indeed curious that this movement, which many of us regard as the most important in the history of the world since the Christ episode, has never had a historian from those who were within it, and who had large personal experiences of its development."

On July 7, 1930, Sir Arthur Conan Doyle died unexpectedly at the age of seventy-one of a heart attack, causing all of his Spiritualism activities to come to an abrupt halt. Doyle's daughter Mary had no choice but to close her father's labor of love—by year's end, the premises were vacated.

The legacy left by Sir Arthur Conan Doyle remains a complex one. Although the inscription on his tombstone reads "PATRIOT, PHYSICIAN, & MAN OF LETTERS," he was far more than that. He was a sportsman, religious figure, legal defender, artist, husband, grandfather, playwright, songwriter, prankster, and, of course, the unrivaled creator of some of literature's most recognizable characters. Now, almost a century after his death, a close study of all things Doyle brings forth a new set of clues not only about who he really was—but what other mysteries he may well have left in our midst.

PART III

Uncovering
a Hidden World

CHAPTER 11

Lost Doyle Stories—
Backstory

At the age of seventeen, Doyle gained acceptance to the prestigious University of Edinburgh Medical School. One of the benefits enjoyed by the students at the school was its preceptor program, where loyal alumni would invite them into their homes and offices to serve as clinical assistants. This perk provided them with free room and board while it also earned them credit toward their degree. Doyle would take full advantage of this opportunity, and early on in his third year of medical school, he began to send out applications to the many physicians who participated in this program. Soon he joined the ranks of those students lucky enough to be selected for one of these extramural clerkships.

Doyle's first two positions wound up only being temporary—not because of his skill level, but due to his rebellious and inflexible nature. His *third* mentorship was to be much more successful. That invitation came from Dr. Reginald Ratcliff Hoare, who ran a busy and lucrative urban practice in the Aston Villa section of Birmingham. Unlike Doyle's previous preceptorships, this one came with a generous stipend of two pounds per month. Hoare, the son of a well-respected Birmingham physician, had been married for almost a decade to Amy Jane Tovey when Doyle arrived in the city for the first time in June 1879. Doyle quickly became a favorite of the doctor's family and described his position there as "rather that of a son than of an assistant."

It was in Dr. Hoare's home that Doyle began his professional literary career in earnest. The inspiration for his first attempt at "truer-than-true" fiction was drawn from an unlikely source—two of his fellow assistants known to history only as "Dr. Smith" and "Dr. Hughes." When Doyle arrived at Dr. Hoare's, he was in the midst of a terrible headache—a debilitating condition that had afflicted him since his early teenage years. After being shown Dr. Hoare's well-stocked medical laboratory, with its multitude of chemical reagents and glassware, Doyle decided the time was right for him to medicate himself with *gelsemium* (a derivative of the deadly jasmine root). Doyle worked in secret during his free time to continually refine the powerful analgesic, and then began to ingest ever-escalating amounts of it each day. Doyle became more and more ill with each increasing dose. Fortunately, Drs. Smith and Hughes discovered what was behind Doyle's rapid decline in health and informed Dr. Hoare of it before something fatal might have occurred.

Angered by his new assistant's reckless behavior, Dr. Hoare delivered a scathing lecture to his wayward "son" in which he admonished Doyle about the dire consequences that might have accompanied his irresponsible self-experimentation had it gone further awry. Hoare's wife, Amy, joined the reproachment and ordered Doyle to write a confessional letter to his mother that detailed each of his thoughtless activities. The humiliation that accompanied this forced written admission of guilt evoked anger in Doyle against Smith and Hughes. Doyle was likely convinced that his two peers should have approached him directly about their concerns rather than going behind his back to their superior. This perceived insult to his honor was quick to set Doyle on a path aimed at exacting revenge on the "pestilent little quack . . . or rather a firm" who turned him in. Doyle's plan was to ruin the doctors' reputations by writing "a most preposterous case [about an eel] and sen[ding] it to the *Lancet* in [sic] Hue's name." Although Hughes' "letter" was received on June 28, 1879, the highly trained editorial staff of England's most prestigious medical journal rejected the submission outright due to its absurd content.

A few months later, articles written by Doyle would be published in medical and literary journals alike. In September 1879, the *British Medical Journal* would publish his findings on the effects and side effects of gelsemium in an article entitled "Gelseminum as a Poison" while Scottish publisher and political figure William Chambers' *Edinburgh Journal* would publish Doyle's first short story "The Mystery of Sasassa Valley"—each piece having been prepared by Doyle at Dr. Hoare's home. These were the first literary efforts that the public would read from the pen of Arthur Conan Doyle.

By December 1880, Doyle's "The American's Tale,"—a short story about a man-eating plant—was published anonymously in *London Society*.

Doyle was on a writing spree, one that would stay with him for the rest of his life. Just when "An American's Tale" hit the newsstands, the *British Medical Journal*'s "Communications, Letters, etc" department started receiving multiple letters signed by "R. R. Hoare," "R. Ratcliff Hoare," and "Mr. Reginald R. Hoare"—but it was to be a full year before the first of these "Hoare" commentaries were to appear in its pages. The reason behind "Dr. Hoare's" compulsory letter-writing campaign was so that Doyle could critique articles on the subject of gout written at the time by his former classmate, George Turnavine Budd. Published on Christmas Day 1880, the first letter by the purported Reginald R. Hoare, F.R.C.S. (Fellow of the Royal College of Surgeons) begins non-confrontationally, but quickly changes tone with its strong objections to Mr. Budd's "conclusive evidence" as being overly optimistic and "sanguine." "Dr. Hoare" goes on to suggest "certain objections to his novel theory," and then poses a few questions of his own that demand a response from Mr. Budd. "Dr. Hoare" then closes the letter in a conciliatory manner, stating that "Mr Budd has advanced a bold and original theory, and one capable of far wider application" if it were proven to be founded upon a "true scientific basis."

A week later, on January 1, 1881, in the "Clinical Memoranda" section of the *British Medical Journal*, George Budd defended himself against "Mr. Hoare's" criticisms, stating that he had every right to draw his "own deductions." He went on to conclude that "it is evident, before we attempt to comprehend the phenomena which tissues exhibit in disease, we should first ascertain the duties they perform in health."

It is virtually impossible that Hoare's letters would have been the product of his own pen, as he had not published a single article in any medical journal before this period and is never again credited with medical-related articles at any time thereafter. Evidence for this hypothesis can be found in a letter Doyle wrote to his mother a year later, in which he tells her that he will submit in writing "a rattling essay on 'Listerism—a success or a failure,' and sending it in Hoare's name." He further informed her that if it were to be printed, then he would expound upon its subject matter as the topic of his medical school thesis paper. Although that "rattling essay" was never published, the wording of his letter implies that Doyle's mother understood that her son had been engaged in such literary deceptions in the past. Apparently, Doyle was under the impression that his articles had enough merit to be published but had been rejected because of his lack of sufficient credentials.

Within a few months, Doyle would leave Hoare's office and venture out on his own, but not before he had already written the short stories "The Gully of Bluemansdyke," (published anonymously in December 1881 by *London Society*), "That Little Square Box" (also published in December 1881 by *London Society*, but under the name "A. C. D."), "An Actor's Duel," (also known as "The Tragedians" and first published in the magazine *Bow Bells* in August 1884), and "Crabbe's Practice," (published in December 1884 by *The Boy's Own Paper*). After his departure from Birmingham, Doyle remained in contact with Dr. Hoare—both in person and in letters—for the rest of Hoare's life. Doyle's writing career soon exploded across all literary genres—historical novels, letters to the press, poems, plays, and (most importantly) his Sherlock Holmes detective stories. It was while he was working for Dr. Hoare in Birmingham that Doyle was able to harness the power he needed to express his creativity on paper. Suspiciously, it was during Doyle's Birmingham stay that Dr. Hoare's name made its only appearance in published medical literature.

It would be another eighteen years before the name "Reginald Ratcliffe" or "Ratcliff Hoare" would be found in journals of any kind. When it finally *did* resurface, it was not in a medically-related paper—rather, it was found in two periodicals devoted exclusively to the art of fiction. In an ironic twist, these two short stories—one purportedly authored by Ratcliffe, and the other by Ratcliff Hoare—appeared immediately after Dr. Hoare's death on March 23, 1898, after a "long debilitating" illness had left him, in Doyle's words, "quite beyond work." Ostensibly, the two stories—"What the Moon Revealed" and "His Word of Honour"—were written by a man who was terminally ill . . . and both stories somehow found their way into two of England's most prestigious literary magazines, *Belgravia* and *London Society*.

It is our opinion that it was Arthur Conan Doyle, and not Reginald Ratcliff Hoare, who authored these two short stories. Looked at through our lens, Doyle seems intent here to confer a bit of immortality on the person he regarded as "the only man I have ever met who has no fault in his character—a plain straight forward jolly fellow without pride, affectation, or anything else." This unselfish gesture is reminiscent of the closing couplet in Shakespeare's Sonnet 18: "So long as men can breathe or eyes can see, / So long lives *this*, and this gives life to thee." *[emphasis added]*

Doyle's "this," like Shakespeare's "this" in Sonnet 18, was an effort to impart eternal life on a loved one through use of literature as a vehicle. And unlike his grandfather John Doyle, who chose in his own seventeen-page confession letter to Sir Robert Peel in 1843 to expose his identity as "HB," Doyle was more than willing to go to his grave with this secret.

Doyle's actions in the wake of Dr. Hoare's death closely resemble his later collaboration in 1899 with his friend Charles Grant Blairfindie Allen, the Canadian writer and evolution proponent. As he was in a losing battle with liver cancer at the time, Allen fought bravely to complete his *Strand*-serialized stories—known subsequently as the novel *Hilda Wade*. Unfortunately, Allen was too ill to complete the final chapters and called on Doyle to do it for him. Doyle, who had tremendous respect for Mr. Allen, worked on the last installments "The Episode of the Office Who Spoke Perfectly" and "The Episode of the Dead Man Who Spoke" unselfishly—and anonymously. Unlike his contributions to Allen's *Hilda Wade*, Doyle was on a solo mission when he wrote "What the Moon Revealed" and "His Word of Honour." The language used in these purported "Hoare" works precisely matches Doyle's own syntax, grammar, and overall writing style—which we shall endeavor to prove with the textual analysis that follows.

CHAPTER 12

Lost Doyle Stories—
Textual Analysis
of the "Dr. Hoare" Works

In volume 96 of the periodical *Belgravia* published in 1898, a story appeared that was attributed to a certain "Ratcliff Hoare" and which bore the title "What the Moon Revealed." The Shakespearean inscription that precedes the rest of the text—"A little, little grave; an obscure grave"—stands as a sentimental gesture made by a grateful disciple, and was deliberately designed to save his idol from the obscurity that would otherwise have accompanied his death that year.

The story's opening sentence—"It was rather a *stiff* climb up the old Worcestershire hill . . . and by the time we reached the top, Temple and I were hot and *breathless* with our exertions"—will be the first text that we will analyze. In his 1912 science fiction novel, *The Lost World*, Doyle describes the art of climbing as "A very *stiff* task"—and in his earlier historical novel *Sir Nigel* (1906), he employs the phrase, "Bleeding and *breathless*." The "Ratcliff Hoare" writing style mimics Doyle's sentence structure. [*emphases added throughout*]

A bit further on, "Ratcliff Hoare" continues with "'Would that I didn't,' he muttered, *sotto voce*." [*emphasis added*] Doyle uses that same term "and then *sotto voce*" in his 1884 short story "Crabbe's Practice." It seems odd that a relative novice like Ratcliff Hoare would have used that exact terminology to describe the speaking tone of one of his characters.

Just a few lines later, the "Hoare" story presents "an old man, with bright, cheery face like a *Ribston pippin*"—while in "The Adventure of Black Peter" (1904), Doyle uses those precise words to describe "The first who entered was a little *ribston-pippin* of a man, with ruddy cheeks and fluffy white side-whiskers." The "Ribston-pippin" is a reddish-orange apple that is native to England's Yorkshire area—and never had that image been used to describe a man's face and build, except for one other instance. In his 1895 novel *The Stark Munro Letters*, Doyle describes the character Dr. Horton—himself a fictional surrogate for Dr. Hoare—in the following way: "Ruddy cheeked and black eyes, with a jolly stout figure and honest genial smile. I felt as we clinched hands in the foggy grimy station that I have met a man and a friend." In a letter addressed to his mother, Doyle described Hoare as having a "jolly red face," while tacking on that Hoare's "nature meant him to be a healer." *[emphases added throughout]*

The next paragraph in the "Hoare" story has the Temple character, along with the tale's unnamed narrator, being offered food by their host. The meal consists of ". . . a *rasher* of home-cured, with some poached *eggs*." Let's compare these words with the text of Doyle's previously published 1892 Holmes short story "The Adventure of the Engineer's Thumb." There, Sherlock Holmes "ordered fresh rashers and eggs." The pairing of "rasher" and "eggs" alongside omission of the words "bacon" or "ham" (as was customary at the time) is absolutely unique. *[emphases added throughout]*

Next, let's consider the following sentence—"And he *started off along the* sunny road, and his *quick strides* soon took him out of our view"—which appears in the "Ratcliff Hoare" story "What the Moon Revealed." This phraseology was not at all typical of that era. Yet, just eight years later in his novel *Sir Nigel*, Doyle writes, "Then he crossed with a *quick stride* from the darkness into the light." In addition, Doyle's 1891 historical adventure *The White Company* uses the phrase "*started off along the* path," which so resembles the aforementioned sentence from the "Hoare" piece. Here again, the writing styles of the said "Ratcliff Hoare" and Doyle parallel one another, both syntactically and thematically. *[emphases added throughout]*

In his 1893 historical novel *The Refugees*, Doyle employs the phrase "Knitting his brow in thought" while "Hoare" writes "his strong black *brow knitted* together as he glanced at it" in "What the Moon Revealed." Once again, the manner in which the *two* authors describe things are virtually identical. *[emphasis added]*

We can now draw upon the following phrase taken from "What the Moon Revealed"— "After we had satisfied our *inner man*"—and compare it to words found in two of Doyle's published works. In his semi-autobiographical work *The Stark Munro Letters* (1895), Cullingworth (a fictional stand-in for Doyle's friend-then-enemy, George Budd) is depicted as follows: "But the *inner man*, after all, was what was most worth noting." And in Doyle's 1900 book *The Taming of the Jungle*, Doyle reuses "*inner man*" in the following sentence: "After Goor Dutt had refreshed his *inner man* and taken a place by the fire . . . ." [*emphases added throughout*]

Next follows a phrase that was rarely used in the literature of the day—with the exception, of course, in "What the Moon Revealed" and in Doyle's Holmes short story "His Last Bow: The War Service of Sherlock Holmes" (1917). The words used by "Hoare" are "What a fool to bolt like that and leave the *proof of his guilt* behind him," while Doyle uses it in the same context when he describes the stupidity of a criminal: "'Why on earth, then, should any criminal send her the *proofs of his guilt*?'" [*emphases added throughout*]

Another telltale piece in the chain of evidence, which suggests that "Hoare" was in actuality Doyle, revolves around the word "disremember." This verb is an Americanism—with origins in the Deep South—that then traveled eastward across the Atlantic as part of the vernacular spoken by the former slaves who began their lives anew in Liberia (the new African nation created by the United States in early January 1822). This unusual word can be found in *A Study in Scarlet* (1887), Doyle's first Sherlock Holmes story, where a man traveling across the Great Plains and up the Sierra Blanco mountains looks out on the vast desert that looms before him. He is convinced that, like most of the members of his original party, his end is near. He asks the little girl he is protecting if she would be willing to offer up her prayers for the day. She responds that "'it ain't night yet'" and then continues with, "'Why don't you say some yourself?'"

His reply is an embarrassed "I *disremember* them. I hain't said none since I was half the height o' that gun." This same colloquialism reappears in Doyle's 1890 novel *The Firm of Girdlestone*, when Von Baumser tells Tom Dimsdale and Captain Hamilton Miggs that "'Mr. Ezra Girdlestone is about to be married.'" Miggs asks him, "'Who's the gal?'" to which Von Baumser responds, "'I *disremember* her name.'" In the "Hoare" story, when Temple learns that his former love is now a widow, he goes to her in an attempt to rekindle their old flame. While bystanders are taken aback by his action, the old man in the story pieces together what is going on and deduces that Temple must have known her in the past. He says, "'I *disremember* now . . . that there was a talk of a young fellow, a hartist, a friend of the 'ed maister at the Grammar School, bein' sweet on this little governess . . ." Doyle—who served as ship's surgeon aboard the S.S. *Mayumba* in 1881—made it clear in his personal letters that he had listened in on and learned this, and *other* Americanisms, while in the port city of Monrovia. By way of comparison, it should be noted that Dr. Hoare had no known connection to Liberia—and it would have been extremely unlikely that he would have known to use the word "disremember" in his writing. [*emphases added throughout*]

Apparently, windows *also* appear to attract the dual literary interests of Doyle and "Hoare." In "What the Moon Revealed," an inn is described by "Hoare" as "a small, one-storied building, with tiny *latticed windows*, and [a] door standing invitingly open"—and in stories written under his name, Doyle repeatedly offers descriptions of windows. In his 1896 mystery novel *Rodney Stone*, he tells us that "a faint light stole through the *latticed window*"; in his 1898 tale "The Story of the Brazilian Cat," Doyle writes that "the *latticed windows* rattled and shook"; in the Sherlock Holmes short story "The Adventure of the Three Students" (1904), he paints a picture of a "long, low, *latticed window*;" and in his 1906 novel *Sir Nigel*, Doyle echoes this phrase with "rude *latticed windows*." It would be unreasonable to regard it as mere coincidence if two different writers would have come up with the same exact description of a window. [*emphases added throughout*]

In Doyle's 1899 novel *A Duet, With an Occasional Chorus*, the twentieth chapter ("No. 5 Cheyne Row") has Frank Crosse gently admonish his wife: "'I tell you, Maude, there were two sides to that. Don't be so prejudiced! And remember that no one has ever blamed *Carlyle* as bitterly as he has blamed himself . . . The success of *Sartor Resartus* encouraged them to the step.'" In the "Hoare" story, its unnamed primary character and his friend, Temple, observe a hat on display in a glass showcase. The two men come to the conclusion that the owner of that hat might be one of the "'admirers of *Sartor Resartus*'" and continue on with "'I often think how grimly amused *Carlyle* would be, could he see his old hat reposing under that glass case in his house in *Cheyne Row*.'" Doyle and "Hoare" both make allusions to the 1836 novel *Sartor Resartus*, which was written by one of Doyle's literary heroes—Thomas Carlyle. The odds are against the possibility that these two unrelated works would both focus on characters who chat about that *particular* work, especially when Doyle and "Hoare" happen to inform their readers of the precise townhouse address of Carlyle's residence on the Thames embankment. [*emphases added throughout*]

Offering further proof of the connection between Doyle and Carlyle, we present here an incident in *A Study in Scarlet* where Dr. John Watson informs the reader that "upon my quoting Thomas Carlyle, he [Sherlock Holmes] inquired in the naivest way who he might be and what he had done." By using this small bit of didactic literary trickery, Doyle was successful in immortalizing his favorite author. This was not the first time that Doyle referred to Carlyle in print, as on January 28, 1886—a full year before the publication of *A Study in Scarlet*—a blistering letter to the editor from Doyle appeared in Portsmouth's *The Hampshire Post*. It was written in response to a recent article that had savagely attacked the now-late Carlyle's reputation and literary standing. Doyle, picking up the gauntlet for the great Scottish writer, referred to the author of this negative piece about Carlyle as a small "jackal" taking "a snap or pinch" at "the old lion" who now "lay still and silent." By 1889—two years after *A Study in Scarlet* first appeared in print—Doyle delivered a public reading at the Portsmouth Jewish Literary and Debating Society of an interesting and exhaustively researched essay that he had entitled "Thomas Carlyle—The Man, The Writer, The Philosopher." The fact that he chose to present this celebratory piece about Carlyle's life and times is an indication that Doyle had already established a reputation as a reliable expert on the writer. If one were to make a wager as to who would author a story with detailed references to what Carlyle had accomplished as a literary artist, one would do well to place one's gambling chips on Doyle, and certainly not Reginald Hoare.

When drawing comparisons between the "Hoare" story and Doyle's, both writers have a shared tendency to use overly inflated vocabularies. An example of this can be found in the "Hoare" story "What the Moon Revealed"—when the unnamed main character answers the question "'[A]nd wot d'ye think 'e were a-doin'?'" with "'Setting a gin, I suppose, to trap some unwary creature,'" and continues with "'I said, rather impatient of the old man's *prolixity*.'" *[emphasis added]* This word choice is out of place here, as it does not conform to the spoken dialect that precedes it. Doyle employs this same esoteric word in both his semi-autobiographical novel *The Stark Munro Letters* (1895) and his 1907 nonfiction work *Through the Magic Door*, which is a commentary on the great enjoyment that reading provides.

Further parallels between these "two" writers are found in "What the Moon Revealed," where "Hoare" uses the phrase "if it will suit you" and its response, *"It will suit us down to the ground"*—as compared to Doyle's

A Study in Scarlet, where a delighted Sherlock Holmes tells his future roommate Watson that "'I have my eye on a suite in Baker Street . . . which would *suit us down to the ground.*'" It would border on incredulity to accept that these dialogues are not derived from the same author—and it seems unfathomable that Dr. Hoare, who had never been published before 1898, would have been able to write in such a sophisticated vein (and on his very first attempt, no less). There are limited possibilities here: Either Doyle was the sole writer of this story, or Hoare—a man who was physically incapable of lifting a pen by himself—was its author. Then again, perhaps we should entertain the unprovable belief that Reginald Hoare found a way to communicate with his former apprentice from the world beyond—a notion that may at first seem ridiculous to most, but which would have seemed to Doyle (an avid Spiritualist for most of his adult life) entirely plausible. [*emphases added throughout*]

In the other posthumously published "Hoare" story "His Word of Honour," we notice that Hoare's middle name—Ratcliff—is spelled with an incorrect final "e," making it read as "Ratcliffe." This "Ratcliffe Hoare" story, which also came out in 1898, was published by *London Society* rather than *Belgravia*. Unfortunately, we have no way of knowing whether Dr. Hoare's misspelled middle name was the fault of a typesetter or was due to an error made by the person who submitted the story. Curiously, when Doyle was about to leave Britain in 1875 for his preparatory year in Austria at Stella Matutina, he wrote a letter to his mother about his stay with the Rockliff family of Liverpool in which he had also added a final "e" to their surname ("Rockliffe"). Trivial errors of this type may have occurred as a result of the way Doyle thought words should be spelled—names that sounded like "cliff," for instance, were invariably spelled by Doyle with a final (and *silent*) "e."

We begin our textual analysis of "His Word of Honour" with the epigram that appears on the first page below the listed author's name of "Hoare." This epigram—penned by British Poet Laureate Alfred, Lord Tennyson—reads, "His honour rooted in dishonour stood." This phrase bears a striking resemblance to the title of Thomas Carlyle's 1836 novel *Sartor Resartus* (whose translated title is "The Tailor Retailored"). This is precisely the type of sophisticated wordplay that Doyle so thoroughly enjoyed and frequently employed in his writing. "His Word of Honour" begins not only with a modification of a Carlyle title, but also with a quotation taken directly from Shakespeare's Sonnet 18. Surely, the writer of "His Word of Honour" was profoundly influenced by Carlyle, Tennyson, and Shakespeare. When Doyle was a fifteen-year-old student at Stonyhurst College, his Aunt Annette—along with his uncles Richard and James—invited him to spend his Christmas holiday with them at their respective London townhouses. During his visit, Doyle had the time of his life as he visited the great city's most notable sites—The Zoo, The Tower of London, the city's many theaters, Madame Tussaud's Wax Museum, the Crystal Palace, and (most significantly) Westminster Abbey.

His fascination with, and appreciation of, the Abbey's "famous Poets' Corner" is demonstrated in a scene from his 1899 novel *A Duet, With an Occasional Chorus*, when Frank Crosse takes his wife, Maude, to Westminster Abbey for the first time: "'What an assembly it would be if at some supreme day each man might stand forth from the portals of his tomb. *Tennyson*, the last and almost the greatest of that illustrious line, lay under the white slab upon the floor.'" As the two of them stand in reverence beside Tennyson's grave, Frank tells his spouse, "'What lines for a very old man to write! I should put him second only to *Shakespeare* had I the marshalling of them.'" In this opening sequence, "Hoare" leaves no doubt as to the identity of two literary icons—Shakespeare and Tennyson. So it would be a surprise if both Doyle and "Hoare" shared the same degree of respect for these two authors. It remains unlikely that Dr. Hoare ever paid a visit to this particular section of Westminster Abbey. [*emphases added throughout*]

Two "Ratcliffe Hoare" phrases—"Throwing out his hands with a despairing gesture" and "*throwing out her hands* with a comic *gesture of despair*"—virtually mirror two phrases found in Doyle's stories. The first of them—"'Because,' he cried, throwing out his long arms with a passionate, *despairing gesture*"—appears in "The Man from Archangel" (1885). The second phrase—"She listened for an instant, *threw up her hands with a despairing gesture*, and vanished suddenly"—comes from the Holmes short story "The Adventure of the Engineer's Thumb" (1892). And in "The Story of the Jew's Breast-Plate" (1899), written in the same year as the "Hoare" stories, Doyle tells the reader through the character Jackson's narrative that "Professor Andreas saw him also, and stopped running, with a *gesture of despair*." These words are *identical* to those used by "Hoare." This repetitive pattern only reinforces our firm conviction that Doyle and the author of "His Word of Honour" are one and the same. [*emphases added throughout*]

In *A Study in Scarlet*, Sherlock Holmes utters "'Though I have quite made up my mind on the *main fact* . . .'" while "Hoare" gives us, "Now that you know the *main facts*." And the recurrent use of the adverb "curiously" is itself a curious thing. "Hoare" writes, "Constance looked *curiously* at her friend," and follows with "'Can you not?' looking at her, *curiously*. . . .'" Similarly, Doyle writes in "The Croxley Master" (1899) that "The two looked *curiously* at each other . . ." and describes in the 1898 novel *The Tragedy of the Korosko* that "They lisped *curiously* in their speech . . ." Further, Doyle tells readers of his 1893 short story "The Slapping Sal" about how "The lean lieutenant, who had reappeared upon deck with a cutlass strapped to his side and two pistols rammed into his belt, peered *curiously* at the ensign." [*emphases added throughout*]

A few other passages from "His Word of Honour" lend added strength to our hypothesis. One involves use of the word *paragon*, which appears in Doyle's *A Duet, With an Occasional Chorus*. Doyle writes: "'From which it follows,' said her husband, 'that Jemima must be a perfect *paragon*'" while one of the "Hoare" sentences reads, "He must be a *paragon* of a brother." [*emphases added throughout*]

The second of these passages centers on the phrase "*a lapse of two years*," which appears verbatim in Doyle's "The Adventure of the Engineer's Thumb" (1892). The similarities of a person's vocal qualities provide yet another example of the usage of shared recurring words. In "His Word of Honour," the "Hoare" character Brandon is described as speaking in a "*low, husky tone*" while Doyle's Sherlock Holmes novel *A Study in Scarlet* features the character Gregson's description of Madame Charpentier's voice as being of a "'*husky* unnatural *tone*.'" [*emphases added throughout*]

Another phrase that appears in the "Hoare" works is "two *laughing blue eyes* met her own, and the owner's thick *golden moustache*." Echoes of these words are voiced by Doyle's narrator in his 1891 historical novel *The White Company* when he tells us "The maid looked aslant at him with *laughing eyes*"—and again in his 1889 novel *Micah Clarke*, when that tale's narrator uses the words ". . . tall and slender, with a long *golden moustache* . . ." Both Doyle and "Hoare" use the phrase "wistful face" in their respective works. In Doyle's 1894 short story "Sweethearts," he writes, "All that is kindly was set stirring by that *wistful face*," while "Hoare" writes, ". . . looking up with a puzzled *wistful face*." [*emphases added throughout*]

"Hoare" is an equal match for Doyle when it comes to writing in the tone and jargon of a specific region's dialect. It is always a challenge for any writer to capture the essence and nuances of the general population in a particular place—and yet, somehow, a novice like "Hoare" mastered this difficult feat without any problems at all. What we should remember is that during his medical school years, Doyle was a prize student of the esteemed Dr. Joseph Bell and became proficient in the art of doing this very thing himself. Dr. Bell, in his 1892 interview for *The Strand* magazine, is quoted as saying:

> "'The student must be taught to observe. To interest him in this kind of work we teachers find it useful to show the student how much a trained use of the observations can discover in ordinary matters such as the previous history, nationality, and occupation of a patient . . . physiognomy helps you to nationality, accent to district, and, to an educated ear, almost to county.'"

Doyle was among Bell's fortunate students and, as evidenced by his Sherlock Holmes stories, he had been the ideal pupil. He had acquired the skills needed to understand and write in the vernacular—but Reginald Ratcliff Hoare possessed no such gift.

Other similarities between Doyle's works and the "Hoare" stories can be found in a side-by-side comparison between Doyle's anonymously published short story "Gentlemanly Joe" (1883) and "His Word of Honour." "Gentlemanly" Joseph Smith is keenly aware that the woman trapped by fire inside a building's upper floor is doomed unless someone is brave enough to come to her rescue. Gentlemanly Joe then describes to the reader, "How terrible it was to stand and wait for the end, powerless to *stretch out a saving hand.*" That same expression appears in the "Hoare" piece "His Word of Honour," when Dr. Hugh Clifford asks his wife, Constance, for permission to care for an attractive patient in their home. By doing so, he frees himself from any potential guilt his wife might place on him for looking after the beautiful young woman. Dr. Clifford leaves the fate of this "damsel in distress" in the hands of his spouse, and then feigns his inability to take action by saying, "'Of course I can do nothing without your consent, and if you feel that you cannot *stretch out a saving hand* to one of your own sex, why, there is nothing to be said. . . .'" As is typical in melodrama, Clifford's patient is saved from what appears to be

certain death at the very last second. Once again, the writing characteristics of the two authors cannot be separated from one another. [*emphases
added throughout*]

In the introduction to his 1906 novel *Sir Nigel*, Doyle writes, "I am
aware that there are incidents which may strike the modern reader as
brutal and repellent. It is useless, however, to draw the Twentieth Century
and label it the Fourteenth. It was a sterner age, and men's *code of morality*,
especially in matters of cruelty, was very different." In "His Word of Honour," the "Hoare" writer has two women discuss the new "'Social Movement for elevating and refining the minds of young women.'" During their
conversation, one of them says to the other "'Don't you think we women
are awfully hard on one another?'" and receives the reply, "'. . . but, I don't
see how we are to help it, so long as the ethics of the Western nations
are what they are, and yet, even among the harems of the Orientals, a
deviation from their *code of morality* is punished as severely, if not more
so, than with us.'" [*emphases added throughout*]

Doyle was raised in a household where the world of ghosts, pixies,
and sprites was considered an absolute reality. Not only did *he* "see" these
magical creatures, but so did his father and his Uncle Richard. Charles
Doyle gained quite a reputation as an illustrator of this "universe," but
Richard—whose fairy-themed illustrations appeared in *Punch* magazine
during the 1840s and 1850s—was the one to receive the plaudits of an
adoring public. It is not surprising that when a teenager named Elsie
Wright claimed in 1917 that she had captured images of fairies on photographic film at her Cottingley home, Arthur Conan Doyle would come to
her defense. As it turns out, the "Hoare" author appears to share this same
belief in Spiritualism—when his Miss Brandon invites Mary Hamilton to
"'see our fairy lake'" in "His Word of Honour," she prefaces it with, "'I
often fancy I can see ghost-like forms flitting about when the moon is at
the full as she is to-night.'" Having seen the lake, Mary says to Brandon,
"'No wonder Barbara called it a fairy lake, one could imagine fairy forms
flitting beneath those trees, and water sprites holding revels under the
lilies.'" These images are highly reminiscent of Charles Doyle's sketch
book that he kept while incarcerated at Sunnyside Mental Hospital—and
which was later published in 1978 as *The Doyle Diary*.

Flushed crimson faces are also a common theme in Doyle's works,
as the following cited examples will demonstrate. In his 1891 adventure
The White Company, the character Peter Terlake "*flushes crimson* in the

moonlight"; in *The Refugees* (1893), his character Louis' visage is *"flushed crimson"*; meanwhile, Nigel *"flushes crimson"* in 1906's *Sir Nigel*, while in *His Last Bow* the German spy Von Bork *"flushes crimson"* (1917). From the "Hoare" side of things in "His Word of Honour," we are informed that "Miss Hamilton *flushed crimson"* in the moonlight. Another repeated motif used by Doyle in his stories is an emphasis on violet eyes, an atypical eye color choice that is also used by "Hoare." Doyle gives us a character with violet eyes in *The Firm of Girdlestone* (1890). Within a year, he recycles it in "The Boscombe Valley Mystery" (1891)—and "Hoare" uses it as well in "His Word of Honour." Doyle also endows his main female characters with chestnut hair color in the Holmes short story "The Adventure of the Copper Beeches" (1892) and once again a few years later in his Gothic mystery novel *Rodney Stone* (1896). In "His Word of Honour," "Hoare" describes Dr. Clifford's female patient's hair the same way. [*emphases added throughout*]

Another similar word pattern—although a bit reversed—is found between the "Hoare" phrase *"Strove in vain"* (from "His Word of Honour") and Doyle's *"In vain he strove,"* which appears twice—once in his 1891 novel *The White Company* and a second time in *The Lost World* (1912). Another of these similar word reversals appears in the "Hoare" tale "His Word of Honour," where we find the sentence, "In the meantime the two who were being discussed were walking in *silence* under the trees, which threw quaint *shadows* on the winding walks which led to the lake." This cited language reflects text in Doyle's historical novel *The Refugees: A Tale of Two Continents* (1893), which reads ". . . he led them in a long curve through the woods, hurrying swiftly and yet *silently* under the darkest *shadow* of the trees." Three years earlier in the novel *The Sign of the Four*, Watson—just prior to issuing a reprimand to Holmes—tells the reader, "I sprang from my chair and limped impatiently about the room with considerable *bitterness in my heart*." The "Hoare" author reverses these same words in "His Word of Honour," when he has Brandon confess his love with the words, "'Mary, the *heart knoweth its own bitterness*.'" [*emphases added throughout*]

Other echoed phrases that stand out occur in the descriptions of sunlight as *"long shafts of* coloured light which shone through the stain glass windows" in Doyle's *Micah Clarke*, and the description of moonlight by "Hoare" in "His Word of Honour" as *"long shafts of* glistening radiance on the emerald surface of the water." And in 1923's *Our American Adventure*,

Doyle employs the French phrase "I was kept waiting for a *mauvais quart d'heure*" while "Hoare" repeats it exactly in "His Word of Honour" when he describes Brandon as "going through a *mauvais quart d'heure*." [*emphases added throughout*]

In "His Word of Honour," Brandon and Mary engage in a serious discussion on the subject of suicide by drowning. When Mary declares "'I can't understand anybody leaving this world, willingly, for the unknown one,'" Brandon poignantly replies, "'Can you not? . . . can't you realize the sudden impulse to put an end to everything when the past is a *hideous nightmare*, and the future a *daily dread*?'" In *Sir Nigel*, Doyle rather astonishingly uses that same rare alliterative term "*daily dread*" (itself a play on the Biblical phrase "daily bread" from the Lord's Prayer). Even more glaring is the "Hoare" phrase "*hideous nightmare*," which reappears twice in Doyle's works: first in Doyle's 1884 short story "J. Habakuk Jephson's Statement" as "I still see him sitting like a *hideous nightmare* at the end of my couch," and again six years later in *The Firm of Girdlestone* (1890) as "looking back at it now, it all seemed like some *hideous nightmare*." [*emphases added throughout*]

In 1898, the year of Dr. Hoare's death, Doyle wrote a short story that offered us a pivotal clue which allowed us to properly identify Doyle as the true writer of the "Hoare" piece "His Word of Honour." Published in December of that year by *Pearson's Magazine*, "The Retirement of Signor Lambert" depicts a sad episode in the life of Sir William Sparter, whose wife Jacky is thought to be having an affair with the world-famous tenor Cecil Lambert. The opera star, swearing that he is not an adulterer, goes on to plead, "'Sir William, I give you my word of honour'"—words that are an exact match for the title of the aforementioned "Hoare" story. Doyle also seems to be offering a tribute of sorts to Dr. Hoare's brother-in-law—the celebrated operatic tenor Cecil Tovey—when he chooses to name the ill-fated singer of this story *Cecil*.

Doyle's devotion to Hoare went far beyond mere gesture. Immediately following the premature death of his mentor and friend, Doyle supported Hoare's widow financially. After all, he regarded Amy Tovey Hoare as his "second mother." Even more daringly, Doyle was willing to take the risk of evoking his "first mother's" wrath when he angrily admonished her in French (possibly to conceal the contents of this letter from the eyes of others) with what is conveyed in the following translation from French into English:

"I'm surprised you gave advice to Amy Hoare on money affairs. If she loses the money we'll have to replace it. As if you knew anything about money matters! Leave such things, I implore you, to her family lawyer. It's very serious if the advice goes bad, and you know very well that that's always possible."

In conclusion, we have asserted here—armed with extensive textual analysis—that Arthur Conan Doyle willingly and lovingly disguised himself as Dr. Reginald Hoare when he put pen to paper and wrote two stories that he was happy to credit to Reginald Hoare. During this clandestine operation, Doyle drew his inspiration from events that had taken place in his own life and skillfully wove them into these short stories. In 1885, Doyle agreed to attend to a terminally ill patient named Jack Hawkins in his Southsea home office. "His Word of Honour" begins with Dr. and Mrs. Clifford locked in a heated debate as to whether it is proper for a patient to be cared for on a long-term basis in a physician's own residence. Furthermore, in 1881 Doyle met his first romantic interest, Elmore Weldon—a woman whom he at one point fully intended to marry—at a village flower show in Ireland. In "His Word of Honour," a story is told of a man who meets a beautiful woman at—of all places—a village flower show. The man seriously intends to marry this woman, until the vicissitudes of life bring an end to the relationship.

Meanwhile, in "What the Moon Revealed," Doyle creates two fictional towns—Persbeach and Apton. The names given to these villages strike us as Doyle's gentle nod to Amy Hoare's childhood home in *Pershore* ("-beach" being replaced by "-shore"), and to the Hoare residence in *Aston Villa* (the letter "s" in "Aston" here replaced by "p" to become "Apton"). This type of wordplay was a Doyle trademark, and it was included in many of his Sherlock Holmes tales. In "The Adventure of the Creeping Man," Doyle merges "Oxford" and "Cambridge" into the blended town name of "Camford"—while in his short story "Crabbe's Practice," the nearby cities of "Bristol" and "Portsmouth" become "Brisport." In *The Stark Munro Letters*, Doyle links "Avon" and "Portsmouth" to form "Avonmouth." A noteworthy element of Doyle's work is the profound depth with which he incorporated his words into his *world*. And in the "Hoare" stories, Doyle dexterously arranged some of the details of his own life—using the shielded veil of authorship as his vehicle for imbuing a kind of *immortality* upon the legacy of his beloved mentor and authority figure.

Perhaps the richest reward that can be gleaned from reading the "Hoare" stories is the artfulness and devotion with which Doyle wrote them. He was only willing to submit high-quality works that would have been cherished if he had written them under his *own* name. In the next section, when you read "His Word of Honour" and "What the Moon Revealed," we ask that you remain mindful of the backstory and textual analyses that will enable you to further appreciate the power and the *origin* of these tales. As ever, when it comes to the creation of some of the most memorable characters, dialogue, themes, and plots invented and devised in world literary history, all roads lead to Sir Arthur Conan Doyle.

CHAPTER 13

Lost Story # 1
"His Word of Honour"
London Society, vol 73, 1898

by Ratcliffe Hoare

"His honour rooted in dishonour stood."
—Tennyson

"How should you like a patient in the house, one that would pay well?" asked Dr. Clifford of his wife, one evening after dinner.

"I am sure I can't say—it would all depend upon the kind of patient. But why do you ask?"

"Because someone I know is anxious to send a friend of his to be under our care."

"A gentleman?" queried Mrs. Clifford.

"No, the individual is of your sex; but before you consider the matter, I had better give you the history of the affair. Two years ago, I was called in to attend a case, by a young fellow who seemed in great anxiety and trouble; when we reached the house, I was quite taken aback by the beauty of my patient, she was one of the loveliest creatures you can imagine, divinely fair, with wavy chestnut hair, dreamy *violet* eyes fringed by long black lashes, a perfectly chiselled nose, and a mouth like a cleft cherry. You understand the style of woman I mean?" said the doctor, tentatively.

"I understand; she was very beautiful," replied Mrs. Clifford, with a smile. "I didn't think you could describe a woman so well after the lapse of two years, Hugh."

"Well, you see, the case turned out differently to what I expected; I saw at once she was not a lady, and not the equal of the man who had surrounded her with every luxury, which she seemed to take as a matter of course, and her right; in fact she was a very exigent little woman, and a most trying, fretful patient. I felt awfully sorry for him; and one day, when she had tried our patience to the uttermost, he followed me downstairs, and in a sudden outburst of confidence, told me she was not his wife."

"What!" exclaimed Mrs. Clifford, "not his wife: how horrible!"

"I was not surprised," continued the doctor, "for I have noticed before, that when no marriage tie binds two people together, the woman—especially if she is beautiful—has far more power, and exercises it more selfishly than a wife does."

"Then how foolish men must be to put themselves in the power of such women."

"Very true, but as long as human nature is what it is, there will always be men foolish enough to go to the dogs for a pretty face. It seems he met this girl, who was a milliner, at a village Flower Show, and was attracted by her beauty; the acquaintance ripened, till the inevitable end came—inevitable, when one considers the girl's loveliness, and the man's passion and position. When the time came that she had to leave her employment, he took rooms for her here, and asked me to attend her; I did so, and after it was over, advised him to send her to school in Paris, where no one would know anything of her antecedents, and to put the child out to nurse."

"Did he take your advice?" asked Mrs. Clifford.

"He was very thankful for the suggestion, and carried it out. The child is dead—which is a blessing for the child—and the mother is anxious to come back to England, but unfortunately she has not improved as much as she ought to have done, in fact he tells me Madame Roubaud is extremely annoyed at her 'unpresentableness.' She, herself, objects to the discipline of a *pension*, and would like to go into a family where she thinks she would have no difficulty in learning how to speak and behave like a lady. Now you know the main facts, what do you say to trying the experiment?"

"Oh, Hugh! I couldn't have such a person here," exclaimed Mrs. Clifford, with wide-open eyes of disgust. "What would everybody say and think?"

"For the matter of that, no one takes any notice of the kind of patients a medical man has in his house; he may be treating them for hysteria, an incipient taste for indulging 'not wisely, but too well,' or for one of the thousand ills that flesh is heir to. But I don't wish to persuade you, Constance; even a charitable action requires consideration."

"Charitable?" echoed his wife.

"Yes, I think so," answered her husband. "Here is a case where the woman has been led astray, either through her love or her vanity, and has lost caste; the man wishes to make amends by marrying her, but feels it would be madness to do so till she is more fitted to take her place among his people as his wife. He thinks she would have more chance in a family than a school, and knowing that doctors do take patients sometimes, he has begged me to ask you to receive her. Of course I can do nothing without your consent, and if you feel that you cannot stretch out a saving hand to one of your own sex, why, there is nothing to be said, only I have heard you say what a pity it is that so few women help their weaker sisters, and that you would if ever you had the opportunity."

"Yes, I know I have," said Constance, uncomfortably; "but it is so easy to theorize, and so difficult to practice."

"Just so; then shall I write and say it is impossible for you to have Miss Read here?"

"No!" hesitatingly. "Can I have till to-morrow to think it over? It is a serious undertaking, and I don't know that I am equal to it," looking up with a puzzled wistful face into her husband's.

"Equal to it!" he exclaimed, stooping down and kissing her. "If you are not, I don't know who is; but there will be very little to do, except helping her, as you would a gauche girl to speak and behave like a lady."

"Then I will see what I can do; Mary Hamilton is coming in to-night, and I should like to ask her opinion. You know she has joined this new Social Movement for elevating and refining the minds of young women who have little time for self-improvement; so I shall not be surprised if she tries to persuade me to take in hand the training of this particular one."

❧

Mrs. Clifford was right in her conjecture, Miss Hamilton did her utmost to induce Constance to consent to receive Mattie Read.

"What was the good," she argued, "of expressing sympathy with erring people, if, when the chance came to help them, one stood on one side from a cowardly feeling of what the world might say?"

"It would be cowardly," murmured Constance; "at the same time it would be very unpleasant."

"All the more credit will be due to you, then, for undertaking it," said Mary, warmly; "it is strange," she went on, "but this very subject was brought up at Avonwood, the other day, where I have been nursing Barbara Brandon, who was down with influenza."

"I am sorry," said Mrs. Clifford. "Is she all right again? Influenza is such an uncanny disease, one never knows what complications may arise."

"She is much better, but her recovery would have been slower if it had not been for the care and attention of her brother. I never saw a man with such tact in nursing a fretful invalid, his patience was marvellous; I *did* admire him."

"You didn't fall in love with him, I suppose?" said Constance, quizzically.

"I think not," said Miss Hamilton, gravely: then, while a faint flush rose in her face, she added, honestly, "though he is just the kind of man I could love, there is something so manly and strong about him, at the same time he is very sympathetic and affectionate. He used to carry his sister up and down stairs, read by the hour to her, and never got impatient when she was cross and irritable."

"He must be a paragon of a brother," said Mrs. Clifford, with a comical look at her friend.

Mary laughed, and went on: "You needn't try to be sarcastic, Connie; it won't affect me; I consider Mr. Brandon to be a perfect brother, and I only wish I had one like him."

"Won't he do in another capacity?" asked Connie, wickedly.

Then as Miss Hamilton stooped for a cushion to throw at her tormentor's head, she cried, "Pal Mollie, sit down and tell me what the discussion at Avonwood was about."

"About this very subject—whether a woman ought to be helped to rehabilitate herself—it seemed to me rather a strange subject to talk over in a drawing-room."

"Oh!" exclaimed Mrs. Clifford, "since these Society plays have been the vogue, matters are talked about openly, that a few years ago would have been mentioned with bated breath in the privacy of one's boudoir."

"It seems so," with a sigh, "Mrs. Brandon thought that a woman's past could never be obliterated, and though she didn't suggest suicide," indignantly, "she seemed to consider that death 'à la Traviata' was the best thing that could happen."

"It is often, to some people, the only solution of a difficulty, but to me, there is always a suspicion of cowardice about 'felo de se.' What did Mr. Brandon say?"

"He said it was only women who hounded other women down, that if a man sinned, his fellow-men were always ready to give him a helping hand—unless they were troubled with a nonconformist conscience—but that women were like the priest and the Levite, instead of aiding the fallen, they passed by on the other side. I was astonished at the warmth with which he spoke, though I agreed with him. Don't you think we women are awfully hard on one another?"

"Yes, I suppose we are, but I don't see how we are to help it, so long as the ethics of the Western nations are what they are, and yet, even among the harems of the Orientals, a deviation from their code of morality, is punished as severely, if not more so, than with us. If laws exist, they have to be obeyed, and those who break them cannot expect to be treated just the same as those who keep them."

"That is true," gravely. "Still, we may severally do what we can to help individual cases."

"Perhaps so, though I have a hopeless feeling about this one. Isn't it Daudet who says it is utterly impossible to reform a woman who has once fallen? And do you remember how Tennyson girds at men who take back their wives to escape an open scandal? His words always make me shiver," and Connie looked disconsolately out of her brown eyes at her friend.

"They are terrible, but I imagine Tennyson meant them to apply more particularly to men in public positions, like King Arthur; it was impossible for him to hide Guinevere's sin; whereas, no one need know that this patient of your husband's has ever had a past."

"I hope not, indeed, for then it would be useless to assist her to retrieve it; however, you have given me courage to make the attempt, and I do feel grateful to you, dear child, for promising to help me," taking Mary's hands lovingly in her own.

"What nonsense! there is nothing to be grateful about," replied Miss Hamilton, with a funny little laugh, and a suspicious liquidness in her dark grey eyes. "I shall run in again very soon, as I leave Avonwood the end of this week," and a faint sigh followed her words.

Constance looked curiously at her friend, but some inward monitor made her refrain from saying anything more, so with a warm kiss they parted.

Ten days later, Mrs. Clifford was welcoming, with as much cordiality as her nervousness would allow, the girl whom she had consented to receive and help.

She had been prepared to find Mattie Read beautiful, but, even with that fore-knowledge, she was still astonished at the loveliness of face and figure which the young woman possessed, and also considerably surprised at the ease and indifference she displayed, considering her position.

A Tale of Two Ladies—Mary Hamilton and Mattie Read.

But it was not till they sat down to dinner, that Constance Clifford fully realized how gauche an uncultivated woman can be; the very way she unfolded her serviette, broke her bread, and used her knife and fork, set Connie's teeth on edge, and it was quite a relief when it was over, and she could retire to the drawing-room with her. As they entered, she said, pleasantly: "I expect you are rather tired with your journey, and will not care to look at photographs, or read."

"No, I never bother much about reading," was the unexpected reply, as the girl advanced, and calmly took possession of the sofa, adding, as she stretched out her tiny feet, clad in silk stockings and satin shoes, "and I feel too done up to-night to care about doing anything but snooze," throwing her head back on the silk cushion, and closing her eyes.

"Would you prefer to go to your room?" asked Connie, amiably, though feeling a decided inclination to tell the girl it was hardly the correct thing to lay herself out for a nap directly they left the dining-room.

"No," carelessly, "I am all right here," and she did not trouble to unclose her eyes.

Mrs. Clifford said no more, but picked up *Blackwood,* a magazine she religiously read through every month, and finished the political article without interruption.

When they were saying good-night, Constance received another small shock.

"We breakfast at nine," she was beginning, in a tentative manner, when the girl exclaimed:

"Oh! I always have mine in bed; I will ring when I want it," and with a careless nod to Dr. and Mrs. Clifford, she ran up the stairs, and disappeared in her bedroom.

Constance turned to her husband with astonishment and dismay in every feature.

"Decidedly cool!" said Dr. Clifford with an expressive shrug of his shoulders.

"Well, I could never have believed that a girl would behave so cavalierly, especially considering her position," said poor Connie. "I am sure I shall never be able to influence her, Hugh," throwing out her hands with a comic gesture of despair.

"Oh! yes, you will, but don't trouble yourself," putting his arm round her assuringly, "do the best you can and leave *the result in the hands of Providence.*"

Was it Providence, or chance, which led Mrs. Brandon to suggest the last evening that Mary Hamilton was with them—that Eric should take her to see the lovely effect of the moon on the waters of the lake which ran at the foot of their grounds, and was studded with myriads of water lilies.

Mrs. Brandon and her daughter, Barbara, speak with Mary over tea.

"Do so," said Miss Brandon, "it is the last night of your stay, and I should like you to see our fairy lake. I often fancy I can see ghost-like forms flitting about when the moon is at the full as she is to-night."

"Will you come?" said Brandon; then, seeing Mary hesitate, he said quickly, "perhaps you would rather not, or, are you afraid of the night air?"

"Take this, Mary," said Barbara, throwing her a soft wrap, which her brother took, and folded carefully round Miss Hamilton's shoulders, adding, as they left the room, "how I wish they cared for each other, it would be lovely to have Mary for a sister."

"Yes, I wish Eric would propose to her," replied Mrs. Brandon, "that is why I suggested this walk, water lilies and moonshine have a wonderful effect sometimes," and she laughed pleasantly, then added, "have you noticed how quiet and preoccupied he has seemed lately?"

"Yes, and I have wondered if he cared for Mary, and thought she didn't care for him."

"Well, let us hope they will come to an understanding to-night: and now let us finish that article by Z in the *New Review.*"

In the meantime the two who were being discussed were walking in silence under the trees, which threw quaint shadows on the winding walks which led to the lake. To Mary the air was full of pregnant suggestions, she had felt for some time that Mrs. Brandon and Bab looked upon her with affectionate regard, and now this plain coup of Eric's mother convinced her she was right; her pulses quickened, her cheek flushed, and she felt it impossible to begin any trivial conversation lest Brandon should guess how her heart was beating from the way in which she spoke. She did not deny to herself that she was indifferent to him, and the only fear which oppressed her was the fear that he might think she had too readily come with him for a téte-à-téte, otherwise her happiness in being with him was complete.

Brandon, on the contrary, was miserably uneasy, he knew perfectly well his mother's wishes, and would have given anything to have been able to carry them out, but, with his past staring him in the face, he knew the impossibility of asking Miss Hamilton to be his wife; unfortunately it did not prevent him falling in love with her, to an extent, which this unlucky stroll was to bring out in startling vividness. So absorbed were both that neither noticed the other's silence, till, as they reached the glittering water, the intense beauty of the scene drew from Mary the exclamation, "how lovely!"

"It is rather pretty," said Brandon, absently.

Mary and Eric Brandon, strolling the grounds before his "confession."

"Pretty!" indignantly, "I never saw anything so exquisite in my life, and what a funny little bridge," pointing to a slender shaft thrown across one end of the water, "what is it for?"

"It leads to a summer-house, shall we go across?"

"If it is safe," uneasily.

"Do you think I would let you go on it, if it were dangerous?" said Eric, with an unconscious note of tenderness in his voice.

Mary flushed, and moved hastily on to the narrow wood work as she said, "of course not, only it looks such a fragile structure."

By this time they had reached the centre of the bridge, and stopped, involuntarily, to admire the lovely scene. The water lay still and placid, except at the edge, where every now and then a faint ripple stirred the water lilies, as if they were lifting their silvery chalices to catch the night breeze as it floated softly by.

Grand old trees of bronzed birch, grey alder, and scented pine enclosed the lake as if with protecting arms, and the moon sailing aloft, as if it were running races with the fleecy white clouds, threw long shafts of glittering radiance on the emerald surface of the water.

"No wonder Barbara called it a fairy lake," said Mary, "one could imagine fairy forms flitting beneath those trees, and water sprites holding revels under the lilies."

"I couldn't fancy anybody holding revels here, the place always oppresses me," replied Brandon, folding his arms on the railing and looking gloomily down.

"Oppresses you! Why what have you to be depressed about? Surely nothing of any consequence," and she looked at him enquiringly.

"The heart knoweth its own bitterness," muttered Brandon, sotto voce, then added aloud, "I was thinking what an attractive power there is in water, and that probably that was the reason so many people committed suicide by drowning."

"Not by the attraction in the water, though, it must be an overpowering sense of misery that makes anyone take refuge in death; how unhappy they must be," shaking her head, "I can't understand anybody leaving this world, willingly, for the unknown one."

"Can you not?" looking at her, curiously, "can't you realize the sudden impulse to put an end to everything when the past is a hideous nightmare, and the future a daily dread?" Brandon stopped abruptly, as his companion turned to him with astonishment.

"Yes, I can understand the wish to have done with life, when life has nothing more to offer, but surely," after a pause, "few are in such straits; what could possibly make one's life a daily dread?"

"Many things, Miss Hamilton. But tell me," he went on, impetuously, "do you think one can ever be justified in breaking a promise?"

"No, certainly not," hastily, "at least most promises, for some must be extremely difficult to keep."

"Difficult!" throwing back his head and taking a long breath as if a thought were stifling him. "How if it spoilt your whole life?" gazing into Mary's grey eyes with nervous anxiety.

"I am afraid I shouldn't keep it," with a strained little laugh. She was getting decidedly uncomfortable, and racked her brains to think of something cheerful to say.

"Suppose," said Brandon, in a low, husky tone, "a fellow had—had fooled with a girl, and then promised to marry her, do you think he is bound to keep that promise if it will ruin his whole life?"

"I don't understand," stammered Mary, whose tongue seemed to have suddenly lost its power, while her heart beat with such sickening throbs that she grasped the wooden railing to steady herself. *What did Mr. Brandon mean?*

"Is a man justified in breaking his promise if he finds the girl utterly unfit by birth, education, everything in fact," throwing out his hands with a despairing gesture, "to be his wife?"

"Why did he make the promise?" in a constrained voice, with her face turned away.

"Because he was a fool, and lost his head over a pretty face."

"But no good woman would keep a man to his promise if she loved him, she would think of his happiness."

Brandon shivered slightly, and turned white as he said slowly through his clenched teeth, "but if she were not a good woman, if she were another 'Marguerite,' how then?"

Mary started as if she had been shot. "What," was all she could utter, for the conversation had taken such a different course to what she had fondly imagined, that the disappointment was bitter, and she had much ado to restrain her tears.

"Forgive me," went on Brandon, hurriedly, "but you are so unlike most girls, so much more in earnest over social questions, that one feels tempted to ask your advice when perhaps one ought not to: God knows I would not vex you for all the world."

"Thank you," said Miss Hamilton, gently, "please go on with what you were saying."

"Then do you think," gazing straight in front of him, with a shamed look on his handsome face, "that a man ought to marry a girl whom he has—he has," low and unsteadily, "ruined?"

The word was out, and Brandon waited in miserable incertitude, the verdict from the fair lips of the woman beside him, whose eyes he dared not meet.

Miss Hamilton flushed crimson, and her mouth for a moment curved with a faint suspicion of scorn, then her lips quivered, her cheeks paled to a ghastly whiteness, as she said in a faint whisper, "yes, I think he ought to marry her."

Just then the moon, which had been sailing gaily aloft, entered the edge of a thick black cloud, leaving them in darkest shadow, and mercifully hiding their faces from each other.

Mary was the first to break the silence which had become intensely painful, by saying, in a voice she strove in vain to render calm, "don't you think it has turned very cold? Perhaps it would be better to go back," trembling visibly as she spoke.

Eric turned without a word, and in utter silence they walked back to the house.

One glance at their faces was sufficient to prove to Mrs. Brandon that, as so often happens, "The best laid schemes of men and mice gang aft aglee."

With a hurried "good-night" Mary left the room, while Brandon flung himself into a chair and told Barbara he should not be able to drive Miss Hamilton to the station on the morrow.

"Not drive Mary to the station! Well! she will be disappointed," said his sister in astonishment.

"I can't help that," irritably, and with a hasty "good-night, mother," he followed Mary's example, and left the room.

"What can have happened?" exclaimed Bab in dismay. "Evidently something serious, but as we are quite in ignorance, it is no good discussing the matter; the best thing to do, is to go to bed," and they went accordingly.

☙

In the meantime Mary Hamilton was enduring agonies as she went over again the details of her conversation with Brandon, and tried to reason out the motives which had induced him to repose such confidence in her, for, that he was speaking from a personal standpoint she could scarcely doubt. Had he fancied she was in danger of falling in love with him, and so taken this means of letting her know it was useless? Mary writhed at the thought, and her face grew hotter and hotter as she tried to think if any action of hers had been open to that construction. But, no, she could remember none, she had always treated him in a calm, friendly manner, as she would any other man of her acquaintance.

What was it he had said, "that he felt tempted to ask her advice, because she was interested in social questions more than most girls." Evidently he trusted her, and her face brightened at the thought; then came the wretched suggestion, had she given him the best advice? Surely, yes, what other reparation could a man make than marrying the girl he had ruined. Ah! she had forgotten that, this man of whom she had thought so highly, as brave, manly, and true, was after all only of the same common clay as other men, had sown his wild oats, and been as sinful and reckless as others. She had put him on a pedestal, and with what a crash had her idol fallen! And Mary threw herself on the bed, and shed the bitterest tears her eyes had ever known.

Brandon also, as he paced up and down his bedroom, was going through a very "mauvais quart d'heure," while he wondered for the hundredth time why on earth he had mentioned the miserable affair to her; he went over and over again what he had said, and wondered if he had been brutally frank; he had felt the flash of scorn on her lips, and noticed her deadly whiteness when she answered his disagreeable question.

Well, it was all over now, any liking she may have had for him must be effectually quenched by what he had said, by his quasi confession; and he made up his mind to obey her dictation, and marry Mattie Read as soon as he decently could.

The resolution thus formed did not, however, seem to give him much satisfaction, and the last feeling he had that night was one of repulsion and disgust at the thought of marrying the lovely, lazy, sensuous creature, whose only idea was how to get the greatest amount of pleasure out of life; and a pang of self pity shot through him as he thought what happiness the future might have held for him, if he could have shared it with a woman like Mary Hamilton.

Mary is shocked to see Eric seated with Miss Read, lying back on the couch.

It was a good thing for Mary that she found plenty to occupy her mind and hands when she reached home, and was kept busy for several weeks in helping her father in parochial, and other matters.

At length one lovely afternoon in November, she found herself at leisure to make some calls, and started off to see her friend Mrs. Clifford, and apologize for not having been able to keep her promise with regard to Miss Read. As she entered her friend's drawing-room a smothered exclamation met her ear, and she saw, to her astonishment, Eric Brandon seated by the fire, while lying full length on the sofa was the figure of a lovely girl, dressed in a blue plush tea gown bordered with golden brown beaver, and having a cascade of creamy lace falling from the neck to the hem of the skirt, while from beneath the gown peeped two tiny feet in blue silk stockings, and bronze shoes.

Mary took this all in before she had presence of mind to utter a word, and Brandon started up with a look of dismay on his fine face.

In a sickening flash the truth entered Miss Hamilton's brain, and she turned, white and trembling, to leave the room. Brandon sprang forward to open the door, their hands met on the handle, and while Mary could not repress a faint shudder, Eric whispered, "forgive me, I did not——" but before he could finish the sentence, Mary was gone.

"Well, this is delightful," said Connie, as Miss Hamilton entered her friend's boudoir, "but what is the matter? You are as white as a ghost, and your face is quite cold," rubbing her cheeks fondly as she spoke.

"I—I—went into the drawing-room first," said poor Mary, in a dazed way, sitting down limply on the sofa, "and Mr. Brandon was there, with some strange lady——" impossible to go on.

"That is Hugh's patient; but why did that startle you? Oh! I forgot," as it dawned on her that Mary had not seen Miss Read, and knew nothing of her connection with Brandon, "you did not know that it was Mr. Brandon who asked Hugh to receive her; no doubt it came as a surprise after seeing him at Avonwood. He is a nice fellow, and I wish to goodness that girl was more worthy of him, and had a better nature."

"Why, what is her nature like? From the glimpse I caught of her, she is certainly very lovely."

"No doubt she is lovely, but she is lazy, selfish and extravagant," said Mrs. Clifford, gravely.

"What a pity; but are you sure you are not prejudiced against her, Connie?"

"Sure, my dear," emphatically, "she never gets up to breakfast, lies on the sofa half the day, reading novelettes, and the money she spends!" lifting up hands of righteous indignation, "it's perfectly wicked; Mr. Brandon will have to give her an allowance when they are married, and make her keep to it. I told her one day that it was a pity she didn't try and conform to English habits, but she only laughed, and said if Mr. Brandon expected her to live by rule, he would find himself mistaken."

"But if she loves him, she will want to please him," said Mary, bewildered by this new view of the case.

"Loves him! She doesn't smile and dimple when he comes, like she does when that Monsieur Mougé appears."

"Who is he?" asked Miss Hamilton.

"The brother of one of the girls at the French pension. He brought Miss Read a present from his sister, and asked to be allowed to call. I wonder how he came to know she was Hugh's patient. I don't like the man."

"Perhaps Miss Read wrote and told them she was here," suggested Mary.

"Most likely," assented Connie. "I shall be very glad when the wedding is over, and the responsibility taken off my hands," she added.

"Will it be soon? I thought it was not coming off for months," said Mary, with a wretched attempt at indifference.

"In a fortnight it takes place; by then, it is to be hoped, Miss Read will have completed her trousseau," with a laugh, "but," seeing Mary shiver, "you are cold, we will have a comfortable cup of tea, and leave Miss Read to her own devices."

In the meanwhile, a slight sparring match was taking place in the drawing-room.

Miss Read, who had looked Mary insolently over, said, sharply, "Who is that prim-faced individual who has just left the room? She looks as if she had only just come from a mothers' meeting, or some such exciting place. What a turn out! Good Lord!" throwing up her hands in disgust.

"I wish you would not use such expressions," shortly. "That is the rector of Comber's daughter, and I wish some people looked as much like a lady as she does."

"That is one for me, I suppose, but I don't mind, old chappie," slipping her feet indolently from the sofa and going up to the looking glass, "what I do mind is stopping in this 'deadly-lively' hole. Isn't there some place where we can go to-night?" looking down at him, crossly.

"No!" emphatically. "I don't care to go to the theatres here at present."

"Well, you needn't snap one's nose off if you don't. Oh!" stretching her arms above her head and yawning, "what would I not give to go and see Yvette Guilbert to-night, and hear her sing one of her screaming songs? Do you know," going up to Brandon with a wicked look on her lovely risque face, "Monsieur Mougé said I should make a splendid understudy for Yvette?"

"What on earth do you mean? and who the dickens is Monsieur Mougé?" angrily.

"The brother of one of the girls at Madame Roubard's. She very often allowed us to go to the theatre with the English governess— horrid old frump she was—and sometimes Monsieur Mougé would join us on the way, and persuade us to go to a cafe chantant instead."

"But surely you never went?"

"Didn't we though! And oh, what fun it was! I used to laugh myself black in the face at the frightened look on Miss Smith's; she couldn't understand half they said, but, as she remarked one night, in a horrified whisper, she was sure it wasn't refined, from their gestures. What a lark it was! There is no place like Paris for enjoying one's self," and she heaved a sigh of regret.

"What a beastly cad that Mougé must be," exclaimed Brandon. "What was he?"

"How should I know? He had heaps of money, and a lovely black moustache, curled up at the ends, great black eyes, and such a dapper little waist, and tiny feet," gazing at Brandon's very different personality, with a supercilious air.

The look and the remark were lost on Brandon, who was thinking of the contrast between this lovely, sensuous creature—whose every word and action jarred and irritated him—and the girl who had just left the room.

"Shall we go to Paris when we are married?" she went on. "I don't intend to moon about at the sea-side; I want to see some life," emphatically.

"No, I shall *not* go to Paris; London will have to give you all the excitement you crave," said Brandon, shortly, while he asked himself, could it be possible that he had given his promise to marry this frivolous, selfish girl? Was there no way out of it?

"I wish I had never left Paris. Monsieur Mougé begged me not to; he, at any rate, was jolly and charming."

"Look here," starting angrily to his feet, "I don't want to know whether your friend was jolly or charming—as you call it,—it is no use regretting that you left Paris; we shall soon be married, and there is an end of everything!" with a gesture almost of despair.

"That's just it," petulantly, "a married woman in England is boxed up, and never has any fun, scarcely, while in France they can go anywhere when married—at least, so Monsieur Mougé told me."

"D—— n Monsieur Mougé; what has he to do with it? If you want to draw back now," a ray of hope coming into his face, "it is not too late."

"No—no," hurriedly, as the thought of the lovely trousseau she would lose flashed through her mind, "only I hate the thought of having to be goody-goody all my life. Sometimes," sullenly, "I wish I had never seen you."

"I wish to God you never had," ejaculated Brandon, as he flung himself out of the room, banging the door furiously.

As it closed, the girl raised her "augmented fifths" to her dainty little nez, with a gesture of inimitable impudence, then with a faint "pouf," and a decided "I will," sat down to the writing-table.

જ્જ

A few hours later, and Mary was seated at her beloved Erard, vainly trying to distract her thoughts with Paderewski's exquisite "Melodie tirée des Chants du Voyageur." The intense yearning and passionate pain which seems to run through all its wonderful harmonics—as the out-pouring of a soul which has suffered and lost —thrilled the girl's being, and so absorbed was she in the music that she did not hear the door open, and started violently when the sigh, with which she let her hands drop from the keys, was echoed by someone standing behind her.

"Thank you so much," said Brandon; "and forgive me for startling you; the fact is," he went on, hurriedly, "I have been so wretched since I saw you this afternoon, that I felt I must see you, to offer some explanation. You looked so—so—," stumbling over the word, "disgusted and scornful, that I——"

"Indeed, I hope not," interrupted Miss Hamilton; "why should you think so?" with an attempt to appear indifferent.

"After our last talk," continued Eric, ignoring her question, "I felt the only thing to do was to get married as soon as possible; I was just beginning to grow callous, when the sight of you this afternoon blew all my callousness to the winds, and I determined to see you once more, and ask if there is any chance——"

"Chance!" exclaimed Mary, "of what?"

"That if I had not told you of my promise in the past, you might have learned to care for me; that you would—would— — ," but here Brandon stopped abruptly, for Mary rose to her feet, exclaiming indignantly:

"You have no right to imagine anything of the kind when I have told you what I think it is a man's duty to do," her face growing crimson, "to the woman he has—has injured."

"I know that, and I am trying to fulfill my promise; but if you only knew the awful struggle it is, sometimes I feel it is more than I can endure."

"Why should you feel so strongly about it now?" asked Mary, unguardedly.

"Because I love you! Oh!" as Mary shrank back involuntarily, "don't you see how much harder it is for me to marry this girl, now that I have met you, and learned to know what true, perfect love could be?"

"Perhaps," murmured Miss Hamilton, who had grown very pale; "but I did not know you loved me; if I had — —"

"Would you have given me a different answer?" taking her hands impulsively in his own.

"No; I hope I should have given you the same. Why should you think so meanly of me as to suppose that I would alter my opinions to please myself? It is unfair—unmanly to ask me such a question. What good can it do?" trying to draw her hands from his clasp. "It only makes matters worse. You are miserable, while I——," but she could say no more, and dropping into the chair behind her, she buried her face in the cushions, sobbing piteously.

Eric was on his knees in a moment beside her. "Don't," he implored, "don't cry; it makes me wretched to see you, and God knows I am wretched enough. I *will* break this promise—hundreds of men do, and why should not I? It would not break *her* heart," with savage emphasis. "Mary, if—if things could be arranged, would there be any hope for me—any chance that you would forget the past, and let me——."

Mary shook her head, and struggled hard for composure, as she said, slowly, "It is quite useless to talk any more on this subject; you cannot undo the past, and I cannot, in honour, change my convictions; when you think it over calmly, you will know I am right."

"Then you condemn me to a life of misery," bitterly.

"Certainly not; that," faintly, "lies in our own hands to a great extent."

"Will nothing alter your decision? Mary," throwing his arms round her, till she shook with the violence of his emotion, "think what it means to me—a future of wretchedness, years of misery. I can't believe you mean it, it is too cruel."

"It is *you* who are cruel, in trying to tempt me to do what I should regret all my life. Oh!" looking at him wistfully, "please say no more, I cannot bear it; leave me, at least, the recollection that, though it was bitterly hard to keep, you yet did not break your word of honour."

Brandon sprang to his feet, and walked to the window, biting his lips to control his agitation. At last he turned, and said, huskily, "I cannot thank you now; some day, in the years to come, when I have grown accustomed to my life, perhaps I may be able to do so," and with a murmured "God bless you," he was gone, while Mary stood gazing into the ruddy fire, with the tears raining down her cheeks, and a heart that felt like lead.

❧

The day dawned which had been fixed for the wedding, and Brandon entered Mrs. Clifford's drawing-room with a face the reverse of ecstatic, though, to do him justice, he did his best to look cheerful.

What was his surprise to see the doctor's wife alone, with an open letter in her hand, and a look of mingled dismay and delight on her face. "Oh!" she exclaimed, starting up as she saw him enter, "what do you think? Miss Read has gone—eloped!"

"Gone! Where to? With whom?" excitedly.

"To Paris, with Monsieur Mougé. Read this!" and she gave him the letter.

It was addressed to Mrs. Clifford, and the writer asked her to be good enough to tell Mr. Brandon that it was no good attempting to follow her, for she was going to marry Monsieur Mougé, with whom she could live in Paris, and have a good time. She had long hated the thought of a quiet country life, and meant to enjoy herself in the French capital, where she was sure her lovely trousseau would be much admired. She thought she was entitled to keep it for the trouble Mr. Brandon had caused her. She never wanted to see him again, but guessed he would marry the prim faced individual, whom he could tyrannize over to his heart's content!

As Brandon finished this cool effusion, he gave a low laugh of such relief that was pleasant to hear.

"I am glad the letter hasn't upset you," said Mrs. Clifford, laughing, "I never read such consummate impudence in my life; you have had a lucky escape."

"Yes, thank goodness! I hope that page of my life is blotted out, and may the leaves of the next chapter be brighter and purer."

"How glad Mary will ——," began his companion, and then stopped short, with a vexed look.

"Please go on," eagerly; "do you think Miss Hamilton will really be glad?"

"I think it is very probable, but it is hardly fair of you to ask," with a reproving smile.

"Don't say that. If you knew all you would understand my anxiety. May I tell you a little of what has passed between us?"

When he had finished, Mrs. Clifford wrote the following little note;

"Dearest Mary,—Do come and see me this afternoon, now it is all over. I want to have a chat with you very much. Yours ever,— CONNIE."

The short winter day was drawing to its close as Miss Hamilton stood looking into the blazing logs on the hearth in her friend's drawing-room, and thinking of the last time she was there; she wondered how far they had got on their journey. How glad she was she had helped him to keep his promise; how hard it had been; how she prayed she might never see him again.

She had got thus far in her meditations, when suddenly two arms encircled her waist, and a low voice said "Mary."

Wedding bells for Mary & Eric and Mattie & Monsieur Mougé.

For a moment, Mary imagined she had lost her senses, and that her thoughts had conjured up the presence of the man she loved, but as she turned her head in terror, two laughing blue eyes met her own, and the owner's thick golden moustache brushed the tip of her dainty ear.

"Mary, darling, don't be frightened," as she shrank from his embrace, with a pale, scared look, "it is not my ghost, but my very self, dying to tell you I am free—yes, free to say how much I love you."

"But where is your wife?" gasped Mary.

"Here, I hope," said Brandon, with a happy laugh, as he folded Mary in his arms, and told her of the dénouement of the morning.

As Mary realized the fact of Brandon's freedom, she lifted her head from his breast with a fervent "Thank God, you didn't break your promise;" and for once in this work-a-day world two people were completely happy.

CHAPTER 14

Lost Story #2
"What the Moon Revealed"
Belgravia, vol 96, page 235, 1898

by Ratcliffe Hoare

"A little, little grave; an obscure grave."
—SHAKESPEARE

It was rather a stiff climb up the old Worcestershire hill, and by the time we reached the top, Temple and I were hot and breathless with our exertions.

We were on a walking tour in the beautiful Vale of the Avon, and Temple—who in the last year or two had come to the front as one of the foremost landscape painters of the day—was sketching some of the exquisite views of hill and dale which lay around us.

"How far are we now from the old inn you mentioned?" asked Temple, lifting his hat from his brow with a sigh of relief.

"About a quarter of a mile; it lies there in the hollow," said I, pointing to a dip in the hill on the right. "Why, are you tired?" I added.

"No, not particularly; but I don't remember any inn about here," looking keenly at the prospect in front of him.

"It is hardly an inn in the proper acceptation of the term. I believe it was once the toll-gate house, when turnpike gates were one of the established orders of the day. Do you remember it? I thought you had never been here before."

"Oh! it is a long time ago, ten or twelve years, I should think," said Temple hurriedly, looking slightly confused.

"So long? Then no wonder you have forgotten the place."

The narrator and his friend Temple are welcomed with food
and drink by the old innkeeper, Jimmy Woollums.

"Forgotten!" he interrupted; "I remember every stick and stone, every gate and stile in every meadow," gazing round him: "Would that I didn't," he muttered, *sotto voce.*

Guessing that something painful was passing through the book of his memory, I said no more, and we walked on in silence till we reached the inn, a small, one-storied building, with tiny latticed windows, and door standing invitingly open.

As we entered, and threw down our knapsacks, an old man, with a bright, cheery face like a Ribston pippin, came forward, and asked what might be our pleasure.

"Something to eat and drink; your hills make it thirsty work walking," I replied.

"Aye, aye, so they does, Sir, but we can give you a cup of fine old cider, that'll beat your fizzy wine into fits; rare old stingo it be!" and his lips seemed to curl inwards, as if he were tasting its flavour, "and a rasher of home-cured, with some poached eggs; my missis be a fine 'and at poaching, if that'll suit you, maister."

"It will suit us down to the ground," said I, as I seated myself on the old-fashioned wooden settle which filled up one side of the room with its tall carved back, and outspreading arms, like wings on either side; while Temple flung himself into a big sag-seated chair, covered with patchwork, and pulled out his beloved black briar pipe.

The meal did credit to our host's missus, and if "the proof of the pudding is in the eating," we proved it to the full, by the empty dishes left on the table, after we had satisfied our inner man.

We had nearly finished our second pipe, and I was fast subsiding into a state of *dolce far niente*-ism, when Temple—who had seemed unusually restless and irritable—suddenly exclaimed, "What a queer idea to put a hat under a glass case; I wonder if it belonged to anybody special," getting up and peering into the case, which was placed on a bracket over the fireplace.

"Perhaps they took the idea from the admirers of 'Sartor Resartus.' I often think how grimly amused Carlyle would be, could he see his old hat reposing under that glass case in his house in Cheyne Row," said I; "but what is that written on the label?"

"'A would-be murderer's hat!'" read Temple, in an astonished voice.

"And so 'e wud 'ave bin, if by the marcy of Providence I 'and't 'ave stopped 'im," remarked old Jimmy Woollums, as he brought us our second

Old Jimmy shows his "hat under glass," and tells the tale of its origin.

mug of cider. "Many's the time I've bin blessed for that night's work," he added.

"How did you stop him, and who may he have been?" I queried, with not a little natural curiosity.

"Well, it's a bit of a story, Sir, and if, so be, as 'ow you'd like to 'ear it, maybe you'll not object to me a-sittin' down. I'm a trifle *roomaticky* betimes."

"By all means, sit down," I replied, "and let us have the history of the man and his hat."

And I looked at Temple with a smile, as much as to say, "We are in for a fine old rhodomontade."

To my surprise, he seemed lost in thought, and took no notice of my glance, so I turned to the old man, who had seated himself at the other end of the settle.

"It's nigh upon twelve years ago," he began, when Temple got up suddenly, and sat down in the window seat with his back to the light, "that this thing 'appened, and before the new line o' railway were laid, so the people 'ad to depend on the carrier's cairt, if they wanted to git from Persbeach to Apton, or if they 'ad any passels they wanted takin' to their friends. I druv the carrier's cairt then, and my boy Jim used to drop the passels at the 'ouses of our customers and 'elp the wimmin passengers to git in and out; for the steps were 'igh, and it were mighty okkard at times when ole Bess 'ad got her 'ead turned t'wards 'ome and wudna stan' still, an' many a neat ankle 'ave I seen in their nice white stockin's as they clumb up the step."

And the old fellow looked round with a chuckle.

"So you have an eye for a pretty foot," I remarked, laughingly.

"Right ye are for sure, Sir, and the gals be mostly 'clean in the pasterns' about 'ere. 'Owsomever, as I were a-sayin', it's about twelve years since this thing 'appened. It were on a lovely night in June, and I was on the road from Apton. We'd 'ad a good many passels to leave, and extry work, as theer were a big fair on in the next town, so it were gettin' on for ten, when we see the last milestone, which were a bran' new white one, in front of us, about fifty yards a'ead."

"Then was it a moonlight night?" I asked, "or how could you see the milestone?"

"Well, it were moonlight, sartainly, but there was 'eavy clouds aloft, and now and again the light were dim, and the road a'most invisible when the moon were in a cloud. That was why the murderer wanted a lantern. But before we saw the light, Jim ses to me, 'e ses:

"'Hi! feyther, wot be that a-dodgin' about the milestone?'"

"And when I lookt a bit for'ard, there were a figger a-jiggin' and a-wavin' its arms like mad; so I pulls ole Bess into the grass by the side of the road, and drives on slowly, and wot d'ye think it were, Sir?"

"The would-be murderer gone mad," said I.

"Na, na; we 'adna cum up to the light then. Well, it were Willum Bettums—and a fine drunkard e' were, but 'e drank no beer after that night—and, if you'll believe me, 'e were that muzzy tight that 'e niver 'eard us cum behind 'im, and we 'eard 'im say to the milestone, 'Who be you?' Well, in course, there was no answer, and Willum e' squares up to the milestone and shakes 'is fists in its face, and 'e ses, ses 'e, 'Look 'ere, my fine fellow, I've axed you wunst, and I'll ax you three times, and if you doan't answer me then I'll knock you into smithereens!' It were the funniest sight, and Jim and I nearly died with laffin' to 'ear 'im ax that milestone, 'Who be you?' three times."

"He must have been very drunk to imagine the milestone alive," I remarked.

"That 'e were, for sartain sure, though we thot, some 'ow, as 'e'd see that it were no man before 'itting out, but 'e didn't, and the next thing as we see were Bettums a-rammin' 'is knuckles agin that stone, and by gosh! 'e niver forgot it, for it smashed ivery one on 'em, and knocked im clean, 'ead over 'eels, on the grass. When Jim and I cud see for laffin, there were Willum, a-setten' on the ground, with 'is and to 'is mouth, a-roarin' like a bull of Bashum! 'Wot's up, Willum?' ses I, a-puttin' me 'ead round the end of the cairt, 'wot bist 'owlin' for?' 'Oh! Woollums,' ses 'e, 'I'm done for this time, for sure,' and 'e gets up, and stares wildly round him. 'Not a bit on it,' ses I; 'cum and git into the cairt, and I'll drive you 'ome; yer missus will do the rest for ye.' Well, 'e clambered up, as well as 'e cud, for 'is knuckles was all a-bleedin', and 'e'd got a fairly rough old shakin' tryin' to knock a milestone down."

"I should think it knocked him sober as well," I exclaimed, as the old man stopped to take breath.

"And it did for sure; 'owsomever we didn't say any more to him then, knawin' Mrs. Bettums were 'andy at that, for she'd got the tongue of a reddy reckoner, as one might say, so we put ole Bess into a trot, and jogged on till we got to the top of the 'ill. I was jest tightenin' the reins to go down, when Jim ses, 'Look at that light in the wood, feyther. Wot can anybody be doin' theer at this time o' night?' 'They'm up to no good,' ses I, a-standin' up in the cairt, and lookin' down into the wood which skirted the road for 'alf a mile or so on the left; jest then the moon shone out bright, and I cud see, down in the 'ollow, the figger of a man, movin' up and down as if it were diggin'.

"'Be they poachers, feyther?' ses Jim, in a whisper.

"'Dunno, I'm sure, but wotever they be, I'll 'ave a look at 'em. Take the reins, Jim,' ses I, and I got down, and I clambered over a gate—'ard work it were too, for it were a 'igh one—then I worked me way, very gingerly, on the inside of the 'edge, close to the bank, as I didn't want to step on a twig, or make a noise to disturb 'em. The moon went in agen, and it were pesky dark at times, but I cud see the glint o' light ivery now and agen. At last I got within a few feet of the figger, and wot d'ye think 'e were a-doin'?"

"Setting a gin, I suppose, to trap some unwary creature," I said, rather impatient of the old man's prolixity.

"''E wud a-trapped a little critter if I 'and't a-stopped 'er! Na, 'e were a-diggin' a grave, and it jest made me blood run cold to see it. This'll 'ave to be stopped thinks I, but 'ow can I fritten 'im away? If 'e thinks theer be only one, may'ap 'e may turn round and fetch me one on the cop with the spade. So I puts me fingers and thumbs to me lips, and gives a most unairthly yell, enou' to waken the dead, and shouts out, "Ere, Dick, Tom, catch the murderin' villin!' Well, 'e niver stopped to look behind 'im, but dashed through the wood and across the fields like blazes, and I knew it were no good to foller 'im; so I jest run for'ard, grabbed 'is 'at—that very one you see there—and 'is lantern. I didn't stop for the spade, which 'e dropped in the grave when he bolted, and made for the cairt as fast as my legs would carry me."

"What a fool to bolt like that and leave the proofs of his guilt behind him," I exclaimed.

"Na doubt 'e were a fule, but don't Shakespeare say somethin' about conscience makin' cowards of people? Any'ow it made a coward of 'e. When I gets back to the cairt I 'eld up the lantern to look at the 'at, and when I saw the name inside I fairly 'ooted, for it was the name of the squire's son, Maister Cotterill. 'Owsomever, it were no good savin' anything then, so I took the reins and druv on."

"Did you know Mr. Cotterill?" I asked.

"I knowed 'im for the biggest rip about these pairts, and 'e a-goin' on for nigh thirty. Theer wasn't a gal as 'e didn't make love to, and the last we'd 'eard 'e were a-foolin' round were the young 'ooman wot taught the passon's childern—a prutty little thing, with great blue eyes, black wavy hair, and a skin like a chaney doll, all pink and white; eh! she were prutty; s'pose that's wot took 'is fancy."

"What was her name?" asked Temple, abruptly.

"It were Miss Marsden, Sir; may 'appen you knawed the young lady?" looking at him suspiciously.

"Your description reminded me of someone I knew years ago," replied Temple, with an attempt at indifference; "but go on with your story, please."

"Well, we jogged on till we cum to the Three Springs, about a mile from 'ome, when, jest as we turned the corner, who should we a'most run over than this very young lady, a-goin' in the direction o' the wood. This'll niver do, thinks I; the murderin' villin may cum back, a'ter all, and do for 'er; so out I jumps, and without stoppin' to think ses, 'It's very late for you to be out, Miss.' She flushed up a bit and ses, shortly, 'That's my business.' 'Na doubt, but you maunt go any further along this yer road to-night,' ses I, a-placin' meself in front of 'er. 'You're a very rude man,' ses she; 'please to let me pass.' I saw she were gettin' angry, so I ses, sharply, 'D'ye knaw wot your young man were up to jest now?' 'How dare you?' ses she. 'What young man do you mean?' gettin' redder and redder. 'I mean Squire Cotterill's son,' ses I; 'e's a-diggin' a grave in Tiddesley Wood; leastways, 'e were till I frittened 'im away. If you doan't believe me ere's 'is 'at and the lantern 'e were a-diggin' by.' She gave a little cry and went as white as death. 'Oh! Mr. Woollums, don't try to frighten me like this,' says she, a-grabbin' me by the arm; 'it can't be true.' And she bu'st out cryin' and sobbed as if 'er 'eart wud break.

"'Tell me,' says I, 'was you a-goin' to meet him tonight?' She nodded 'er 'ead, for she cudn't speak—'er teeth was all a-chatterin' and she shook all over.

"'Well, then, it's a blessed good job as I seed 'im,' ses I, 'or a dead corpse you'd be by this time.'

"'Oh! but it must be a mistake,' she cried. 'He was to meet me at the top of the hill with a carriage and drive me to his father's house. He has told him we are married and he has promised to receive me.' And she wrung 'er 'ands, an' lookt as if she'd faint.

Old Jimmy spies "Squire Cotterill's son" digging a grave in Tiddesley Wood.

"'So you're married, are you?' ses I. 'Well, I'm mighty glad to 'ear it.' And I lookt down at 'er figger, which weren't as slim as it 'ad bin, by no means.

"'We were married six months ago, and he has promised, week after week, to take me home—and now you tell me this. Oh! what shall I do? What shall I do?' And the poor girl lookt as if she was going to die.

"'Well, Miss, it do look very 'spicious! Theer beant any kerridge on the 'ill, and if so be as 'e meant to bring one, why should 'e be a-diggin' of a grave at this time o' night, and then run away when I 'ollowed at 'im? Men doan't dig graves at night for fun, and you mun own that it do look black agen him.'"

"The damned scoundrel!" muttered Temple, dropping his beloved pipe suddenly with a crash.

"'But he couldn't be so cruel as to want to kill me. Oh! if I could only see him, it would be all right,' she cried. 'He loves me so much,' and she looked at me so piteously that I felt, if I'd got me'and on 'is neck, I could 'ave scragged the villin.

"'P'raps so,' ses I, 'but I 'eard in the town to-day that 'e's going to marry Lady Barbara, the Earl of Draycourt's daughter, and the lawyers be drawin' up the settlements; so if you be married, as you say, 'e either means to commit bigamy, or to put you out o' the way; 'e can't 'ave two wives, legal.'

"I thowt it best to be plain, for I cud see she were a-ankerin' to go on up the 'ill.

"'What!' ses she, 'marry Lady Barbara'—and she giv' a little click in 'er throat, and fell agen me in a dead swound.

"I picked 'er up, and hefts 'er into the cairt, and Jim 'eld 'er up, and took care on 'er; she were no more trubble than a babby, and when we got 'ome, my missis she put 'er to bed, and axed no questions, for the poor thing seemed dazed like.

"The next morning, without sayin' a word ta anybody, I just saddled ole Bess, and went and told the squire the same as I've told you. 'E were a decent ole gentleman, tall and dignified, and me 'eart sank in me boots when the butler showed me into the libry, but it were no good 'emmen' and 'awin', so I up and telled 'im all—that I 'ad 'is son's 'at with 'is name inside, and 'is lantern, and if 'e didn't see 'is way to receive graciously 'is son's wife, I should make it my business to make things pretty 'ot for the young squire.

Old Jimmy reveals to Squire Cotterill what he saw the night before.

"I felt sorry for the ole gentleman, for 'is face went as white as ashes, and 'e put up 'is 'and, and ses, 'I think you mean well, but I shall be glad if you'll say no more; I will call on the young lady this afternoon'; which 'e did, in his grand ole-fashioned kerridge, and took 'er away with 'im to 'is big 'ouse, Rednor Hall."

"And what became of the Squire's son?" asked Temple, eagerly.

"Killed in a steeplechase; 'is father wudn't 'ave anything to do with 'im after the tale of 'is wickedness cum out, but they brought 'im 'ome, and berried 'im in the family vault, quite respectful! The ole squire died soon after 'is son was killed, and so the little babby cum into all the estate, and lives with 'is mother at the ole 'all now."

"It was lucky for the young lady that you were on the road that night, or no doubt she would have been murdered," I said. "Where on earth are you off to?" I added, in astonishment to Temple, who had risen hastily, put on his soft round hat, and, with his stick in his hand, was making for the door.

"To Rednor Hall, to see Lily Marsden. I—I mean Mrs. Cotterill," stammered Temple, with a heightened colour. "Wait till I come back, old man—I won't be long."

And he started off along the sunny road, and his quick strides soon took him out of our view.

"That's curious now," said the old man. "Spose 'e knew the young lady years ago," looking at me, inquisitively.

"It seems like it," I answered, "or he would scarcely march off in that fashion. He is evidently gone to renew his acquaintance with her."

"I *dis*remember now," said Woollums, knitting his brow in thought, "that there was a talk of a young fellow, a hartist, a friend of the 'ed maister at the Grammar School, bein' sweet on this little governess, and 'ow he were awful cut up when the tale cum out, and left the place at wunst. P'raps this be 'e."

And "'e" it proved to be; for just as the sun was setting in a golden glory, and the sky was flushed with brilliant opaline tints of rosy pink and faint emerald green—while I forgot the flight of time in watching the lights and shadows over the Malvern Hills—a groom appeared, driving a spanking roan in a high dog-cart.

He brought me a letter from Temple, written rather hurriedly, from which I gathered he was going to remain at Rednor Hall for a short time, and asking me to join him there. He also enclosed a dainty little note from

Mrs. Cotterill, inviting me to join my friend; but, remembering the old adage that "two's company and three's none," I decided to decline the invitation and returned to London the next day.

A few months afterwards, at the quaint old church of St. Agnes-on-the-Hill, I had the pleasure of acting as best man to my friend Temple; and when I caught the glance of intense love which lit up his usually sombre face as he saw his bride enter and the look of quiet happiness with which she met his gaze, I felt there was every chance of their future being a bright and happy one, and blessed the lucky accident which had made us choose Worcestershire instead of Devonshire for our walking tour that summer.

Temple and Lily Marsden ("Mrs. Cotterill"), newly married.

Afterword

This book—or more accurately, the *idea* of it—was really born twenty-seven years ago, while I (Daniel) was sitting in my medical school library. I was a third-year student at that time, studying for my upcoming Board Examination. For no particular reason (well, truthfully, there *was* a reason—to give my exhausted brain a brief respite from the academic grind), I pulled out an old issue of *The Journal of the American Medical Association (JAMA)* and happened upon a random article devoted to Arthur Conan Doyle's 1885 medical school thesis.

As I read, the first thing that struck me was that the creator of Sherlock Holmes and I shared a common bond—that each of us had attended medical school (news to me at that moment, as my knowledge of Doyle's background was cursory). But as I came across the topic of Doyle's thesis—written when he was twenty-five years old, my exact age at the time—the more intrigued I became about his career outside of the world of writing.

I was so impressed by Doyle's article on *tabes dorsalis*, a neurologic condition caused by syphilis, that I felt compelled to quickly dash off an email to the University of Edinburgh's librarian in Scotland, requesting that she please send me a copy of Doyle's actual thesis in its entirety. The pages arrived in my mailbox a few weeks later, and I immediately pored over the work. When I'd finished, I felt strongly that Doyle had composed a literary masterpiece—one that was well-researched, filled with vignettes articulated in the most colorful way, uniquely transcending a typical scholarly composition. To say I was utterly humbled would be an understatement.

Over the course of the next three years, my medical and academic obligations as an intern and resident didn't afford me much leisure time to focus on Doyle—at least, until I began regularly frequenting the medical library once again to prepare for my Pediatric Board Examination. And to my surprise, I would come across additional articles about Doyle in the journals—every one of them fascinating. Among these were his probable association with the "Piltdown Man Hoax," his failed attempt to sneak into an international medical symposium in Germany, his defense of Britain's Contagious Diseases Act (which allowed for the incarceration of any woman whom the authorities believed harbored syphilis), and his impassioned crusade to mandate the typhoid vaccination for British troops dispatched to South Africa to fight in the Boer War.

Every one of these articles opened a new road for me to travel when it came to learning about Doyle's life. But there was so much about him that, to me, still remained a mystery. I began to wonder about what other surprises I might encounter when it came to his accomplishments. This small sampling of articles had already revealed the man to be a fearless risk taker, global adventurer, public health advocate, and even an unrepentant prankster. I needed to see the *full* picture. That was the moment when I decided in earnest to begin my research, with the endgame of putting together as complete a composite as possible of the real Sir Arthur Conan Doyle. This has now become, much to my surprise, a decades-long process of writing and discovery, during which I have been fortunate enough to be joined step by step by my father and fellow pediatrician, Eugene.

In our first book, *The Strange Case of Dr. Doyle*, my father and I worked tirelessly to scrutinize and reconstruct Doyle's first thirty years. By arbitrarily limiting ourselves with the immovable end-year of 1889 for that book, we were left with untouched files representing the next forty years of Doyle's life. To that end, *Doyle's World* stands as an extension of our research on all things Doyle, with a greater focus on his life from thirty years old to his death in 1930 at the age of seventy-one. Unlike *The Strange Case of Dr. Doyle*, this book has enabled us to reveal and elaborate on our discoveries pertaining to the legendary characters Sherlock Holmes, Dr. John Watson, and Professor Moriarty, and also to write about Doyle's vigorous campaigns related to Spiritualism, the Boer War, and the unification of the United States with Great Britain among other topics.

Even now, after all the time and distance, we find ourselves just as enthralled—and, at times, equally frustrated—by Doyle as we were when we first set off upon this journey at the turn of the twenty-first century. Doyle passionately integrated himself into every facet of the world around him—nothing was off-limits, and he was often a study in dichotomy. He could defend divorce rights for women one minute; and in the next, campaign against a woman's right to vote. He could preach about his unshakeable faith in the ability to commune with the dead, while he simultaneously wrote an adventure story featuring a detective who was devoted entirely to rationalism and scientific method. But these contrasts only serve to make him all the more captivating.

In the lead-up to the publication of *Doyle's World*, we have been invited to contribute dozens of articles to various "Sherlockian" and "Doylean" magazines and journals around the world. Much like our subject, we have *also* had the honor of giving lectures at libraries, museums, and universities nationwide. And we've enjoyed being featured guests on programs like the globally popular "Coast to Coast AM" and the top-rated "America Unearthed" with forensics expert/host Scott Wolter. And through it all, we have been able to return to the world of Sir Arthur Conan Doyle for insight, inspiration, ideas—and, ultimately, for the clues to decrypt what powered the engine of this especially gifted man.

For us, and for *you*, the game of Doyle remains forever afoot.

Annotated Bibliography

BOOKS

Adams, W. H. Davenport. *The Steady Aim*. London: James Hogg and Sons, 1869. Includes eight illustrations by C. A. Doyle.

The African Repository. Washington, DC: The American Colonization Society, 1883. Notes that the new ambassador to Liberia, Henry Highland Garnet, sails aboard the steamship *Nubia*, not the *Mayumba*. The departing ambassador, John Henry Smyth, boards the steamship *Mayumba* on the first leg of his return to America.

Ainsworth, William Henry. *The Lancashire Witches*. London: Henry Colburn, 1849. Popular tales of the Pennine district that would have been familiar to the boys at Stonyhurst.

Allen, Grant. *The European Tour*. London: Grant Richards, 1899. Travel guide that highlights Paris, French towns, Venice, Florence, and Rome.

—. *Historical Guide to Florence*. Boston: Page and Co., 1901. Travel guide to the landmarks of Florence (the Bargello, the Pitti Palace, and the Etruscan Museum). **N.B.:** After his fall off Reichenbach Falls in Doyle's "The Final Problem" (1893), readers learned a decade later in "The Adventure of the Empty House" that Sherlock Holmes had then traveled to Florence.

—. *Historical Guide to Venice*. New York: A Wessels Co., 1902. Travel guide to the landmarks and museums of Venice.

—. *Hilda Wade*. London: Putnam's Sons, 1900. Doyle authored the last chapters as a favor to his friend and neighbor. He has Hilda Wade escape from Tibet.

—. *Miss Cayley's Adventures*. London: Grant Richards, 1899. Story about a clever young woman who regards the world as her playground. She successfully shoots and kills a tiger in India.

—. *The Evolution of the Idea of God*. New York: Henry Holt and Co., 1897. Allen writes of the Holy man from Montpellier.

Atlay, J. B. *Famous Trials of the Century*. Chicago: Herbert S. Stone & Co., 1899. Discusses the Tichburne case, the Madeleine Smith case, and the Burke and Hare case.

Baines, Edward. *The History of the County Palatine and Duchy of Lancaster*. London: John Heywood, 1891. Describes the origins and architecture of Stonyhurst College.

Baker, Michael. *The Doyle Diary: The Last Great Conan Doyle Mystery*. London: Paddington Press, 1978. Brief biography and sketches drawn by Charles Doyle while he was confined in an asylum.

Baring-Gould, Sabine. *Devonshire Characters and Strange Events*. Plymouth: William Brendon and Son, 1908. Insights into George T. Budd from his relative, John Wreford Budd.

Bell, Joseph. "Some Hints by a Medical Examiner." *Transactions of the Insurance Society of Edinburgh*. Edinburgh: H. & J. Pillans & Wilson, 1904. A primer on the proper performance of insurance physicals, with special emphasis on occupation, hereditary disease, vices, and environment.

The Bengal Catholic Expositor. Calcutta: P. S. D'Rozario and Co., 1840. An overview of Stonyhurst College that mentions its most illustrious graduate, Charles Waterton.

Bennett, Arnold. *Books and Persons*. New York: George H. Doran, 1911. Includes an obituary of John Churton Collins.

Bunyan, John. *The Pilgrim's Progress*. London: James Hogg and Sons, 1860. Twelve illustrations by Charles Doyle.

Burton, John Hill. *The Book-Hunter*. New York: Sheldon and Co., 1863. Biography of Burton; contains description of his famous library.

—. *Narratives from Criminal Trials*, London: Chapman and Hall, 1852. Description of some of the most sensational trials of the early 19th century.

—. *Political and Social Economy for Use in Schools*, Edinburgh: William and Robert Chambers, 1849. It was this book that helped feudalistic Japan transform into the modern country it is today.

Burton, William K. *The A.B.C. of Modern Photography*. London: Piper and Carter, 1886. Innovative photographic techniques devised by Doyle's best friend, William K. Burton. **N.B.:** Burton died in 1899 while serving as a visiting professor at the University of Tokyo.

—. *A Practical Guide to Photographic and Photo-mechanical Printing Processes*. London: Marion and Co.,1888. Guide to transfer images onto paper, glass, canvas, and fine china.

—. *The Processes of Pure Photography*, New York: The Scovill and Adams Co., 1889. Wonderful account of the history of photography, and review on how to make gelatin emulsions.

—. *Photographic Optics*, New York: The Scovill and Adams Co., 1891. Textbook for professional and amateur photographers.

—. *The Manual of Photography*, Bradford: P. Lund and Co., 1895. Practical guide in the technical aspects of photography.

—. *Wrestlers and Wrestling in Japan with an Historical and Descriptive Account by J. Inouye*, London: Low, 1895. Depicts the form of many noted wrestlers of Japan. Only problem was that, as these photographs were staged, "the gyofi or umpire" looked at the camera.

Burton, William, and John Milne. *The Great Earthquake of Japan*. London: Sampson, Low, Martson, and Co., 1891. Burton captures twenty-nine terrifying pictures of the aftermath of an earthquake.

—. *The Volcanoes of Japan*. London: Sampson, Low, Martson, and Co., 1891. Photographs of Japan's many volcanoes.

Byrne, Mrs. William Pitt. *Gossip of the Century*. London: Ward and Downey, 1892. The identity of H.B. is known only to John Doyle's daughter, Annette, until Doyle reveals it to former Chief of Police Robert Peel.

Carlyle, Thomas. *History of Friedrich II of Prussia*. London: Chapman and Hall, 1888. The name "Sherlock" is featured in *Afternoon and Evenings*, Chapter 5, "A Chapter of Miscellanies."

Carr, John Dickson. *The Life of Sir Arthur Conan Doyle*. New York: Harper & Bros., 1949. "Novelized biography" of Sir Arthur Conan Doyle.

Carson, William English. *The Marriage Revolt*. New York: Hearst International Library Co., 1915. Notes that Arthur Conan Doyle helped found the Divorce Law Reform Union.

Cavanagh, F. J. L. *Cavanagh's Phrenology*. Toronto: Cavanagh [self-published], 1895. Doyle's superior athletic skills are conveyed in detail here.

Chesnutt, Charles W. *Frederick Douglass*. Boston: Small, Maynard and Co., 1899. John Smyth gives a speech at the unveiling of the Frederick Douglass Monument in Rochester, New York.

Chiene, John. *Looking Back, 1907–1860*. Edinburgh: Darien Press, 1908. Notes that Doyle is Joseph Bell's favorite student.

Christison, Robert. *The Life of Sir Robert Christison*. Edinburgh: William Blackwood and Sons, 1886. The controversial Robert Christison refers to William Rutherford and Arthur Gamgee in performing liver research.

Comrie, John D. *History of Scottish Medicine, Vol. II*. London: The Wellcome Historical Medical Museum, 1932. Discusses Joseph Bell's ability to lecture to large classes.

Cook, Joseph. *Life and the Soul*. London: Ward and Lock, 1892. Doyle attends one of Cook's famed Boston Monday Lectures while living and working with Dr. Reginald Hoare in Birmingham.

Culp, Daniel Wallace. *Twentieth Century Negro Literature*; Atlanta, Georgia; J. L. Nichols and Co., 1902. Biography of (and article written by) Professor John H. Smyth.

Diver, Ebenezer. *The Young Doctor's Future*. London: Smith, Elder, and Co., 1881. Doyle accepts the position as ship's surgeon aboard the *Mayumba* after failing to find other viable work opportunities.

Doyle, Arthur Conan. *The Adventures of Sherlock Holmes*. New York: Harper and Bros., 1892. Four of the twelve stories in this collection are some of Doyle's favorite Holmes tales.

—. *The Captain and the Polestar: And other Tales*. London: Longmans, Green, and Co., 1892. In the story "The Great Keinplatz Experiment," Doyle describes a case of taking "a man's soul out of his body." Mentions syphilologist von Althaus, whose book on spinal cord diseases was critical to Doyle's medical thesis on locomotor ataxia.

—. *The Case of Oscar Slater*. New York: George H. Doran Co., 1912. Doyle pleads for the full pardon of the man convicted of murdering Marion Gilchrist with a hammer.

—. *The Case for Spirit Photography*. New York: Doran Co., 1923. Doyle defends the scientific principles behind spirit photography after having returned from a tour of America.

—. *The Coming of Fairies*. New York: George H. Doran Co., 1922. Doyle provides a spirited and bizarre defense of alleged photographs of sprites and fairies.

—. *The Field Bazaar: A Sherlock Holmes Pastiche*. Summit, NJ: Pamphlet House, 1947. Sherlock Holmes deduces that "Doctor" Watson had been asked to help raise funds for Edinburgh University's cricket field just by analyzing the contents of an envelope.

—. *The German War: Some Sidelights and Reflections*. London: Hodder and Stoughton, 1914. Doyle tries to convince his nation to enter the war against Germany.

—. *The Great Boer War*. London: Smith, Elder, and Co., 1900. Doyle explains Britain's stance in the Boer War.

—. *The Haunted Grange of Goresthorpe*. Ashcroft, British Columbia: Ash Tree Press, 2000. Despite its evocative title, this early ghost story by Doyle is unsophisticated.

—. *His Last Bow: A Reminiscence of Sherlock Holmes*. A. L. Burt Co., 1917. This collection features Sherlock Holmes doing undercover work in the United States and Ireland in an effort to assist his government. Holmes suffers from rheumatism and is studying the habits of bees.

—. *The Hound of the Baskervilles*. New York: Grosset and Dunlap, 1902. A gruesome, creepy tale about a demon hound; this story was able to "resurrect" Holmes after his purported death off Reichenbach Falls by bringing him back to solve a mystery taking place in 1888—five years *before* Doyle killed off his most widely recognized character in "The Final Problem."

—. *Letters to the Press*. London: Secker & Warburg, 1986. A collection of letters written by Doyle that appeared in England's newspapers, literary periodicals, and medical journals.

—. "Life and Death in the Blood." In *Good Words for 1883*. London: Isbister & Co., 1883. An article written from the perspective of a traveler microscopically placed inside the human body.

—. *The Memoirs of Sherlock Holmes*. New York: Harper and Bros., 1894. A collection of stories that introduces readers to Mycroft Holmes and Professor Moriarty.

—. *Memories and Adventures*. Boston: Little, Brown, 1924. Doyle's autobiography; does not discuss his medical school thesis, Freemasonry, or father's battle with mental illness.

—. *Micah Clarke*. Leipzig: Bernhard Tauchnitz, 1891. Moving away from the Holmes stories, Doyle writes this well-received historical novel.

—. *The New Revelation*. New York: George H. Doran Co., 1918. Doyle's writings on Spiritualism, psychic experiences, the afterlife, and other metaphysical topics.

—. *The Refugees: A Tale of Two Continents.* London: Harper and Bros., 1893. Historical novel that deals with colonial America.

—. *The Return of Sherlock Holmes.* New York: Wessels Co., 1907. First collection of Holmes stories after the detective's purported death off Reichenbach Falls. We learn that Holmes traveled to Florence, Tibet, and France during the great hiatus.

—. *The Sign of the Four.* London: Spencer Blackett, 1890. Second Holmes novel that features Jonathan Small, a man who lost his foot to a crocodile.

—. "The Silver Hatchet." In *My Friend the Murderer and Other Mysteries and Adventures.* New York: Lovell, Coryell, and Co., 1893. Contains reference to Thomas De Quincey.

—. *The Stark Munro Letters.* New York: D. Appleton and Co., 1895. A semi-autobiographical account of Doyle's years immediately following his graduation from the University of Edinburgh Medical School.

—. *A Study in Scarlet.* London: Ward, Lock, Bowden, and Co., 1892. The first story to feature Sherlock Holmes and Dr. John H. Watson.

—. "The Third Generation." In *Round the Red Lamp.* 1894. Reprint. Richmond, VA: Valancourt Books, 2007. A case of congenital syphilis is described as having been passed down for three generations, according to the basic tenets of Lamarckian theory.

—. *Through the Magic Door.* New York: McClure Co., 1908. Doyle discusses his enjoyment of books and what it takes to be a skilled biographer.

—. *The Valley of Fear.* New York: A. L. Burt Co., 1914. Sherlock Holmes helps solve a mystery that relates to a group of American Freemasons.

—. *The Vital Message.* New York: George H. Doran Co., 1919. Doyle's thoughts on the Second Coming.

—. *The Wanderings of a Spiritualist.* New York: George H. Doran Co., 1921. Doyle uses the words of Teddy Roosevelt to open his book, "Aggressive fighting for the right is the noblest sport the world affords."

—. *The War in South Africa: Its Cause and Conduct.* New York: McClure, Phillips, and Co., 1902. Contains Doyle's defense of Britain's involvement within South Africa.

—. *The White Company.* Leipzig: Bernhard Tauchnitz, 1891. Historical novel set in England, France, and Spain during the Hundred Years' War.

—. *The Works of A. Conan Doyle.* New York: D. Appleton and Co., 1902. A compilation of some of Conan Doyle's greatest literary works.

Doyle, James. *The Chronicles of England, B.C 55–A.D 1485.* London: Longmans, Green, and Co., 1864. Written and illustrated by James Doyle, chronicling the notable events that had taken place in England.

—. *The Official Baronage of England showing the Succession, Dignities, and Offices of Every Peer from 1066 to 1885.* London: Longmans, Green, and Co., 1886. A book written to assist in learning English history.

Doyle, Richard. *A Journal Kept by Richard Doyle in the Year 1840.* London: Smith, Elder, and Co., 1886. Journal written and illustrated by Richard ("Kitkat") Doyle when he was 15.

Drayson, Alfred Wilks. *The Art of Practical Whist.* New York: George Routledge and Sons, 1879. While living in Southsea, Doyle is taken under the wing of this eccentric British polymath.

—. *The Gentleman Cadet.* London: Griffith and Farran, 1875. While living in Southsea, Doyle was taken under the wing of the author, a noted polymath. This book chronicles Drayson's adventures at the Royal Military Academy at Woolwich, a school that Doyle's brother Innes would attend before launching his outstanding military career.

Edwards, David. *Modern Scottish Poets.* Brechin: D. H. Edwards, 1893. A book that emphasized Doyle's many literary accomplishments outside of his detective stories.

Elderkin, John. *A Brief History of the Lotos Club.* New York: Club House, 1895. Doyle's speech while attending a gala in New York is transcribed here.

An Evening From Among the Thousand

Evenings Which May Be Spent with Punch. London: Bradbury, Agnew & Co., Ltd., 1900. Describes Richard Doyle's work and his rationale for leaving *Punch*.

Farmer, John. *The Public School Word-book*. London: Hirschfield Bros., 1900. "Dark Walk, The (Stonyhurst)." A long avenue of tall yew trees in the garden. Tradition says the last of the Sherburne was poisoned by eating some of the berries from these trees.

Feasey, Henry John. *Westminster Abbey Historically Described*. London: George Bell, 1899. Reverently describes those who are commemorated in the Abbey's Poets' Corner.

Fitzgerald, Percy Hetherington. *Stonyhurst Memories*. London: Richard Bentley & Son, 1895. A contemporary of Doyle shares his recollections of his life as a student at Stonyhurst College.

Fraser, Norman. *Student Life at Edinburgh University*. Paisley, Scotland: J. & R. Parlane, 1884. Mentions the table at which Napoleon Bonaparte dined during his final exile on St. Helena.

Fry, Danby. *The Lunacy Acts*. London: Knight and Co., 1864. Lists Bryan Waller Procter (Bryan Charles Waller's uncle) as one of the appointed Commissioners in Lunacy.

Fry, Herbert. *London in 1880*. London: David Bogue, 1880. A description of the London of Doyle's youth.

—. *London in 1887*. London: W. H. Allen, 1887. A description of the London of Doyle's youth, accompanied by maps of Whitechapel.

Gale, Rachel. *After Taps*. Boston: Baker and Co., 1891. The detective skills of Sherlock Holmes are alluded to during this drama in three acts.

Gambier, James. *Holiday Adventure*. London: Hames Hogg and Sons, 1860. Includes eight illustrations by Charles Doyle.

Garnet, Henry Highland; *A Memorial Discourse*; Philadelphia: Joseph M. Wilson; 1865. Sermon given by Garnet to the House of Representatives, making him the first African-American individual ever to do so.

Geddie, John. *The Water of Leith from Source to Sea*. Leith, Scotland: W. H. White and Co., 1896. Describes John Hill Burton's home and its centuries-old specter, the Green Lady.

Gerard, John. *Centenary Record. Stonyhurst College, Its Life Beyond the Seas, 1592–1794, and on English Soil, 1794–1894*. London: Marcus and Ward and Co., 1894. Although Doyle describes a Mr. Chrea as being a Stonyhurst prefect, no such person appears in the college's registry.

Graham, Richard. *The Masters of Victorian Literature, 1837–1897*. Edinburgh: James Thin, 1897. In a section devoted to Arthur Conan Doyle, Graham claims that Sherlock Holmes was based on Dr. Joseph Bell.

Grant, Alexander. *The Story of the University of Edinburgh*. London: Longmans, Green, and Co., 1884. Summarizes the first three hundred years of the University's history. Also includes short biographies of the medical school's outstanding faculty members.

Grant, James. *Cassell's Old and New Edinburgh*. London: Cassell, Petter, Galpin and Co., 1880. Contains references to the Morningside Asylum and to John Hill Burton's Craigshouse, with its library and "Green Lady."

Greene, Joseph M. "In the Interests of Humanity, Should Vivisection Be Permitted, and If So, Under What Restrictions and Limitations?" In *Vivisection: Five Hundred Dollar Prize Essays*. Boston: American Humane Education Society, 1891. Attests to the worldwide influence of Dr. William Rutherford, the leading vivisectionist of his time.

Gruggen, George, and Joseph Keating. *Stonyhurst: Its Past History and Life in the Present*. London: Kegan Paul, Trench, Trübner, and Co., 1901. "The Dark Walk—a grand and magnificent avenue of trees, full of shadowy beauty, and overhung with the richest foliage." Also mentions that Stonyhurst has devoted a special room for the teaching of gymnastics, fencing, and boxing.

Hardwick, Charles. *"Traditions, Superstitions, and Folklore."* London: Simpkin and Marshall and Co., 1872. "Skriker" is described as having the appearance of "a large dog, with very broad feet, shaggy hair, drooping ears, and 'eyes as large as saucers.'"

Henley, W. E., and John Stephen Farmer. *A Dictionary of Slang and Colloquial English*. London: George Routledge and Sons, 1905. Jargon of the Victorian and Regency eras.

Hewitson, A. *Stonyhurst College: Its Life Beyond the Seas, 1592-1794, and on English Soil, 1794-1894*. London: Marcus Ward and Co., 1894. Refers to the legend and ghost of Richard Francis Sherburne, a student at Stonyhurst who inadvertently ate some yew-berries and died. Also mentions the Gentlemen Philosophers' dog kennel—perhaps the inspiration for *The Hound of the Baskervilles*.

—. *Stonyhurst College: Its Past and Present*. Preston: Chronicle Office, 1870. Richard Francis Sherburne was born "December 3rd, 1693, who died suddenly, June 8th, 1702. Tradition has constantly related that he died from eating poisonous berries in the garden, which story has been embellished with various touches of local colouring, it being now commonly believed that he lost his way in his father's labyrinth, and in his hunger fed on the yew-berries he found growing there. It is, however, very improbable that the labyrinth had been finished, and quite certain that there were no yew-berries at the beginning of June."

Hogg, James. *De Quincey and his Friends*. London: Sampson Low, Marston and Co., 1895. "Thomas Papaverius," written by Thomas De Quincey's friend, John Hill Burton. Features a not-so-veiled reference to the use of opium, which Doyle has Sherlock Holmes use occasionally throughout the canon.

—. *Men Who Have Risen*. New York: Townsend and Co., 1861. Contains illustrations by Charles Doyle.

Holden, Edith. *Blyden of Liberia*. New York: Vantage Press, 1967. Notes that ambassador Henry Highland Garnet arrived in Monrovia on December 22, 1881, on the English steamer *Nubia*.

Hole, Samuel Reynolds. *A Little Tour in America*. London: Edward Arnold, 1895. Chapter twenty-two of this book mentions Doyle's 1894 American adventure and tour.

Home, Daniel Dunglas. *D. D. Home: His Life and Mission*. London: Kegan Paul, Trench,

Trübner, and Co., 1921. Doyle wrote the introduction to this edition to pay tribute to influential medium and spiritualist Daniel Dunglas Home.

Houdini, Harry. *"Margery" the Medium Exposed*. New York: Adams Press, 1924. Houdini chastised Doyle's role in defending mediums within this book.

Hugh, Goldie. *Memoir of King Eyo VII of Old Calabar*. Old Calabar: United Presbyterian Mission Press, 1894. Notes that Doyle violated King Eyo VII's decree by firing a gun on the Sabbath. Doyle also violated international maritime law by bringing a gun onto his ship and by carrying it ashore.

Hutton, Laurence. *Literary Landmarks of Edinburgh*. New York: Harper and Bros., 1891. Discusses Professor Adam Ferguson's home at 2 Sciennes Hill; mentions that it was the location where Robert Burns ordained Sir Walter Scott.

Innes, Katherine. *Memoir of Cosmo Innes*. London: W. Paterson, 1874. Presents Cosmo Innes' then-progressive view that women should be permitted to attend law and medical schools.

Irving, H. B. *A Book of Remarkable Criminals*. New York: George Doran and Co., 1918. Irving recalls a conversation between his father, the well-known actor Henry Irving, and Great Britain's poet laureate, Alfred, Lord Tennyson.

Jack, Thomas. *The Waverley Handbook to Edinburgh*. Edinburgh: Thomas C. Jack, 1876. A guide to Edinburgh.

Jambon, Jean. *Our Trip to Blunderland*. Edinburgh: William Blackwood and Sons, 1877. Includes sixty illustrations by Charles Doyle.

Jerome, Jerome K. *My First Book*. London: Chatto and Windus, 1897. Arthur Conan Doyle contributes the piece "Juvenilia" to this collection of essays written by famous authors about their first works.

Jones, Rhys Bevin. *Spiritism in the Bible Light*, London: The Religious Tract Society, 1921. Makes a case both for, and against, Doyle's belief in Spiritualism.

Knott, George. *Trial of Sir Roger Casement*. Philadelphia: Cromarty Law Book Co., 1917. Contains Doyle's petition to the prime minister on behalf of Roger Casement.

Lambton, Arthur. *Echoes of Causes Célèbres*. London: Hurst and Blackett, Ltd., 1931. Dedicated to "My Fellow-Members of 'Our Society.'"

—. *The Salad Bowl*. London: Hurst and Blackett, Ltd., 1927. Discusses formation of the "Crimes Club," which counted Doyle, Max Pemberton, and John Churton Collins among its first members. Remarks upon exemplary memory of Collins.

—. *Thou Shalt Do No Murder*. London: Hurst and Blackett, Ltd., 1930. Acknowledges friendship with Doyle, research assistance by Doyle on essay "The Psychic in Crime." Also discusses case of Thomas Neill Cream.

Landsborough, David. *Arran: Its Topography, Natural History, and Antiquities*. London: Houlston and Sons, 1875. Details Arran as "Scotland in miniature" and describes a trek up Goatfell Mountain.

Lankester, Edwin. *Cholera: What Is It? And How to Prevent It*. London: George Routledge & Sons, 1863. Charles Doyle moved to Edinburgh just after the cholera epidemic of 1848–49. It was George Budd's family that had figured out who to decrease morbidity and mortality associated with cholera.

Lankester, Ray. *Science from an Easy Chair*. New York: Macmillan Co., 1911. Collection of articles and illustrations from the Director of the British Natural History Museum's "Daily Telegraph" column.

Lellenberg, Jon, Daniel Stashower, and Charles Foley. *Arthur Conan Doyle: A Life in Letters*. New York: Penguin Press, 2007. Selections from Doyle's correspondences; provides commentary and photos.

Le Queux, William. *The Crimes Club*. London: Evenleigh, Nash & Grayson, 1927. A record of the Crimes Club's secret investigations, written by Le Queux, a member of "Our Society."

Lloyd, WR. *Pictures of Heroes, and Lessons from their Lives*. London: James Hogg and Sons, 1869. Includes eight illustrations by Charles Doyle.

Lodge, Oliver. *Pioneers of Science*. London: Macmillan, 1893. Discusses Copernican theory of the revolution of Earth around the Sun; insults Alfred Drayson.

Lycett, Andrew. *The Man Who Created Sherlock Holmes*. New York: Free Press, 2007. Biography of Doyle.

MacGregor, George. *The History of Burke and Hare and of the Resurrectionist Times*. Glasgow: Thomas D. Morison, 1884. Presents the methods and reasoning behind two of Edinburgh's grave robbers (and murderers) from the 1820s.

Masson, David. *Edinburgh Sketches and Memories*. London: Adams and Charles Black, 1892. Biography of John Hill Burton.

Maunder, Samuel. *Treasury of Knowledge*. London: Longman, Orme, Brown, Green, and Longmans, 1840. Describes Old Town as resembling a turtle, with the castle as head, High Street as back ridge, the narrow lanes as sides, and Holyrood House as tail.

McLaren, Elizabeth. T. *Dr. John Brown and his Sister Isabella*. New York: Anson D. F. Randolph and Co., 1891. Mary Doyle's friend and confidant, Dr. John Brown, was the author of *Rab and his Friends*.

McLean, Thomas. *An Illustrative Key to the Political Sketches of H.B.:1829 to 1832*. London: Howlett and Brimmer, 1902. Analysis of HB's (John Doyle's) political cartoons.

Milwaukee County. *Proceedings of the Board of Supervisors of Milwaukee County*. Milwaukee: Ed Keough, 1894. Details of the conspiracy trial that used Doyle's "A Case of Identity" as a reference.

Mitchell, David. *The History of Montrose*. Montrose, Scotland: George Walker, 1866. Describes the Montrose Old Asylum and Sunnyside Royal Hospital, to which Charles Doyle was sent after a failed escape attempt.

Morrison, Arthur. *A Child of the Jago*. Chicago: Herbert S. Stone and Co., 1896. Novel functioning as a sort of survival guide to London's East End.

Moseley, Sydney. *An Amazing Séance and an Exposure*. London: Sampson Low, Marston and Co., 1919. Doyle wrote the introduction to this book, promoting the tenets of Spiritualism.

Natural History. New York: Appleton and Co., 1897. Discusses Thomas Richard Fraser and his views on snake poisons.

Oddie, Samuel Ingleby. *Inquest*. London: Hutchinson and Co., 1941. Oddie gives both favorable and unfavorable opinions of his friend, Doyle.

Oliver and Boyd's New Edinburgh Almanac and National Repository. Edinburgh: Oliver and Boyd, 1884. Contains official information and statistics on commerce, agriculture, law, chronology, and the government of Edinburgh. Reginald Hoare's name appears on the roster of the Royal College of Surgeons for the year 1879.

Owen, Reverend George Vale. *The Life Beyond the Veil*. New York: Doran Co., 1921. Doyle pens the introduction to this book regarding Spiritualism.

Pond, James Burton. *The Eccentricities of Genius*. London: Chatto and Windus, 1901. Includes chapter on Doyle, featuring several letters written by Doyle that discuss his lecturing tour in America.

"Portobello." In *The Topographical, Statistical, and Historical Gazetteer of Scotland*. Edinburgh: A. Fullarton and Co., 1853. A description of the seaside resort town where Doyle spent several of his early boyhood years.

Post Office Edinburgh and Leith Directory, 1859–1860. Edinburgh: Ballantyne and Co., 1859. Notes residence of the Doyles.

Post Office Edinburgh and Leith Directory, 1862–63. Edinburgh: Ballantyne and Co., 1862. Doyle's name spelled incorrectly.

Pritchard, Edward William. *Trial of Dr. Pritchard*. Glasgow: William Hodge and Co., 1906. Discussion of Henry Duncan Littlejohn's medico-legal contributions to the Pritchard murder trial, which took place in 1865.

Reekie, Auld [Crosse, Herbert W.]. *Lays for Leeches*. Norwich, England: A. E. Hunt, 1929. A *nom de plume* of Dr. Crosse of Norwich, who was a member of the 1905 "Jack the Ripper" Whitechapel tour with Doyle.

Ross, Janet. *Three Generations of English Women*. London: John Murray: 1888. Includes letters written by Doyle's uncle, Richard "Kitkat" Doyle.

Roughead, William. *Trial of Dr. Pritchard*. London: Sweet and Maxwell, 1906. Includes testimony by Douglas Maclagan and Henry Littlejohn, both professors at the University of Edinburgh Medical School.

Rules and Regulations and List of Members. London: Athenaeum Club, 1874. Lists Richard Doyle as a member of the Athenaeum; "Kit Kat" suffered a stroke after attending a meeting there and died a day later.

Rutherford, William. *An Experimental Research on the Physiological Actions of Drugs on the Secretion of Bile*. Edinburgh: Adam and Charles Black, 1880. Refers to vivisections performed by Rutherford and his associates.

"Rutherford and the Liver." In *Physiological Fallacies*. London: William and Norgate, 1882. The process by which the liver secretes bile is explained.

Scott, Walter. *The Pirate*. London: George Routledge and Sons, 1880. Describes the technique of seal flinching.

Shakespeare, William. *The Life and Death of King John*. New York: MacMillan and Co., 1890. This play features a character with the name of "Arthur," which Doyle connected to himself in a somewhat hidden way when writing home to his mother.

—. *The Tragedy of Othello, the Moor of Venice*. London: George Kearsley, 1806. The handkerchief serves throughout the play as a symbol of love and fidelity. Doyle drew on this reference when writing a letter to his mother, who he suspected of infidelity.

Sidney, James Archibald. *Alter Ejusdem*. Edinburgh: Maclachlan and Stewart, 1877. Includes illustrations by Charles Doyle.

Simmons, William. *Men of Mark*. Cleveland:

George M. Rewell and Co., 1887. Biography of Henry Highland Garnet.

Smith, Alexander Duncan. *The Trial of Eugene Marie Chantrelle*. Glasgow: William Hodge and Co., 1906. Discussion of the poisoning case that includes testimony from Dr. Henry Littlejohn, one of Doyle's teachers at Newington Academy. Includes a photo of Littlejohn.

—. *The Trial of Madeleine Smith*. Glasgow: William Hodge and Co., 1905. Dr. Littlejohn personally assisted the editor with the findings of this case.

Speight, Harry. *The Craven and North-west Yorkshire Highlands*. London: Elliot Stock, 1892. Describes Bryan Waller's family genealogy.

Stevenson, Robert Louis. *Edinburgh*. Philadelphia: J. B. Lippincott Co., 1905. Stevenson describes his home city.

—. *Letters and Miscellanies of Robert Louis Stevenson*. New York: Charles Scribner's Sons, 1900. Reprints letter addressed to Doyle, complimenting him on his Sherlock Holmes adventures and noting the resemblance of Holmes to "Joe Bell."

—. *New Arabian Nights*. London: Chatto and Windus, 1882. Doyle's "The Pavilion on the Links" can be found in this book. Doyle considered this story to be for himself "the very model of dramatic narrative."

—. *Treasure Island*. Boston: Roberts Bros., 1884. Pirate adventure that features Long John Silver, a one-legged pirate.

—. *The Strange Case of Dr. Jekyll and Mr. Hyde*. New York: Charles Scribner's Sons, 1886. A story whose theme is the dualistic nature of man.

Stevenson, Robert Louis, and William E. Henley. *Admiral Guinea*, New York: Charles Scribner's and Sons, 1894. Loosely based on *Treasure Island*.

—. *Beau Austin*. New York: Charles Scribner's and Sons, 1894. Play written by Henley and Stevenson.

—. *Deacon Brodie*. New York: Charles Scribner's and Sons, 1894. Play written by Henley and Stevenson.

—. *Macaire*. New York: Charles Scribner's and Sons, 1894. Play written by Henley and Stevenson.

Stoker, Bram. *The Watter's Mou'*. New York: Appleton and Co., 1895. The author of *Dracula* describes Peterhead, Scotland, the town from which the *Hope* departed.

Tales From Many Sources. New York: Dodd, Mead, and Co., 1885. Features Doyle's short story "Bones, the April Fool of Harvey's Sluice" appears on pg. 106.

Thin, James. *Reminiscences of Booksellers and Bookselling in Edinburgh*. Edinburgh: Oliver and Boyd, 1905. Memoir from the proprietor of one of Doyle's favorite bookstores.

Thom's Irish Almanac and Official Directory of the United Kingdom. Dublin: Alexander Thom and Sons, 1857. Lists Charles Doyle among members of the Office of H. M. Works.

Waller, Bryan Charles. *The Twilight Land, and Other Poems*. London: George Bell and Sons, 1875. A collection of poems written by Mary Doyle's border and friend.

Ward, Thomas Humphry. *The Reign of Queen Victoria*. London: Smith, Elder, and Sons, 1887. Includes a short sketch of Richard Doyle.

Warner, Charles Dudley. *A Library of the World's Best Literature: Ancient and Modern* 12. New York: The International Society, 1897. Biography of Doyle, and a reprinting of "The Red-Headed League."

Wells, Carolyn. *The Technique of the Mystery Story*. Springfield, MA: The Home Correspondence School, 1913. Investigates how crime writers, including Doyle and Gaboriau, create their characters.

Who's Who. London: Adam and Charles Black, 1910. Dr. Thomas Richard Fraser was not only an expert on snake venom and arrow-poisoning (both topics in which Holmes was proficient), he was *also* a member of Sir George Nares' Arctic Expedition of 1877.

JOURNALS

"A. Conan Doyle on America." *Bulletin of the American Steel and Iron Association* 30 (February 1895): 25. While staying at the Mena House in Cairo, Doyle wrote, "I believe, and have long believed, that the greatest danger which can threaten our Empire is the existence of this spirit of hostility in a nation which is already great and powerful, but which is destined to be far more so in the future."

"Account of the Family of Sherburne." *Gentleman's Magazine* 135 (1824): 515–517. "The family of Sherburne, a name long known and still remembered in the county of Lancaster, once possessed large estates and princely revenues in that Palatinate; but they have within this century dwindled into obscurity, and are supposed to be totally extinct."

Ad for Edward's XL Dry Plates. *Journal and Transactions of the Photographic Society of Great Britain* 7 (October 1882): xii. Includes endorsement of Edward's photographic plates by Doyle, who mentions taking them on trip to Africa, though none of the resulting photographs were ever published elsewhere.

"Advanced Writing Lesson." *Munson's Phonographic News and Teacher* 9 (1894): 261–262. "A. Conan Doyle's Address at a Lotos Club" is found in this passage.

"After Office Hours." *New England Medical Monthly* 18 (February 1899): 67. Doyle's newest work receives a chilly reception from his medical peers in the United States.

"The American Minister at Monrovia." *The African Repository* 58; 1883: 87–89. Henry Highland Garnet arrives in Liberia aboard "the English mail steamer *Nubia*, from Liverpool," (not Doyle's ship, the *Mayumba*).

"An Important Sanitary Fact." *Popular Science* (November 1876): 123. Quotes Dr. Littlejohn describing the old town of Edinburgh as overcrowded and unsanitary.

"The Architecture of our Large Provincial Towns—XII Edinburgh." *The Builder* (January 1898): 1–14. Review of all the landmarks of Edinburgh.

"Art and Music: The Death of Doyle and

Mario a Loss to both." *Toronto Daily Mail* (December 1883). Details how when *Punch* magazine attacked Cardinal Wiseman—a devout Roman Catholic who had assisted his older brother in the art field—Richard Doyle quit his job.

"Art Chronicle." *The Portfolio* 15 (1884): 24. Obituary of Richard Doyle. Mentions that John Doyle had "three sons, all more or less gifted in art." Charles Doyle is significantly not included in this description.

"At Dodsley's." *Gazette Montreal* (November 1892). "The new novelist is certainly Dr. Conan Doyle, whose 'Sherlock Holmes' has made a hit almost without parallel. The usual run of detective stories, like the usual run of detectives, is apt to be vulgar and stupid. The adventures of Sherlock Holmes are neither stupid nor vulgar. The ingenuity in working out details; the cultivated skill in observation; the remarkable exhibition of logical power— all contribute to make this new volume well worth attention."

"Author-Physicians." *Canadian Journal of Medicine and Surgery* (January 1922), 51: 17–19. Doyle is described as a physician who also is a poet, playwright, and novelist.

The Bee (April 1883): 3. John Smyth's wife crosses the Atlantic to join her husband in Liberia.

Bell, Joseph. "Somewhat Unusual and Complicated Case of Inguinal Hernia." *New York Medical Abstract* 2 (December 1882): 472–473. Bell notes that he makes a groin incision after chloroform has been administered to his patient.

Benham, Allen. "John Churton Collins: A Review." *Modern Language Notes* 24 (November 1909): 204–208. Obituary. Notes that Collins dies "under circumstances somewhat obscure."

Bishop, Joseph B. "Early Political Caricature in America." *Century* 44 (June 1892): 219. Claims that John Doyle was the "real founder" of the *Punch* political caricature style.

Black, James. "Ectoplasm and Ectoplasm Fakers." *Scientific American* 127 (September

1922): 162. "Doyle assures us that science knows absolutely nothing about ectoplasm."

—. "The Spirit-Photograph Fraud." *Scientific American* 127 (October 1922): 224. Doyle's views on spirit photography are questioned. Doyle declares that William Hope is "the leading psychic photographer of Great Britain."

—. "A Square deal for the Psychics." *Scientific American* 127 (December 1922): 389. Doyle is called out to be a "well-known spiritualist" who "specifically leaves open the religious significance of psychic phenomenon."

"Book Talk and Tattle." *The American Book-maker* 19 (November 1894): 149. "'Sherlock Holmes' has been more successful in banishing sleep from the eyes of terrified readers."

Boston Home Journal 55 (1899): 2. It is reported that Boston police have begun to adopt Doyle's methods to solving a poisoning case.

The Brooklyn Eagle (December 1884): 11. Garnet's ascension to the position of American diplomat was to be "the last appointment made by President Garfield."

—, (October 1881): 4. A farewell party was held in Garnet's honor on October 5 at Chickering Hall.

—, (November 1881): 5. Garnet sails aboard the S.S. *Egypt* from New York to Liverpool, England.

Brown, Crum. "On the Theory of Isomeric Compounds." *Transactions of the Royal Society of Edinburgh* 23 (1864): 707–719. An article written by the man who taught William Burton's younger brother, Cosmos, when he was a student at the University of Edinburgh.

Brownrigg, Henry. "Midnight at Madame T's." *New Monthly Magazine* (1837): 392–400. Includes reference to Madame Tussaud's "Chamber of Horrors," predating the so-called "original" use of that term by *Punch* magazine in 1846.

Burton, William. "Precipitation Methods and Green Fog—Alcohol in Emulsions." *British Journal of Photography* 30 (January 1863): 44–45. Burton introduces a method for eliminating green fog from photographic plates;

he thanks his friend Doyle for contributing information to his article.

—. "W. K. Burton." *Photographic Times* 17 (June 1887): 295–296. Includes a biography of Burton.

—. "A Letter From Japan." *Photographic Times* 17 (October 1887): 520. Burton describes his first few months in Japan.

"Celebrities at Home." *Sydney Morning Herald*. (December 1892). Doyle "prefers the historical novel to any other kind of romantic writing, although the 'Sherlock Holmes' style might be far more profitable."

"The Champaign Democrat." *Lippincott's Magazine*. (February 1890). Describes Doyle's writing of *The Sign of the Four* as follows: "Doyle must take rank as a leader in the line of such writers as Poe, or Gaboriau, or Anna Katharine Green."

"A Chat with Conan Doyle." *Idler Magazine* 6 (August 1894): 340–349. Doyle discusses the state of current literature.

"Chronicle and Comment." *Bookman* 22 (1902): 113–128. Biography of Doyle with photographs.

"Conan Doyle Weary." *Havre Plaindealer* (Montana) (December 1904). "Sherlock Holmes is tired and is to make his final farewell to the public next month. As he says of himself: 'For a long time he has nursed the idea of a country life, with its simple delights. He will take a little place and go in for bee-keeping.'"

"Conan Doyle's Impressions." *Book News* 13 (1895): 75. Doyle's arrival in America is mentioned, where he will lecture on "Facts about Fiction."

—. 212–213. Doyle declares that "the finest city in America by far" is Philadelphia.

"Conan Doyle's Rapid Work." *American Bee Keeper* 7 (February 1897): 62. Doyle was reported to be able to write a story in the time it takes for him to go on "a brisk walk" with a friend after a "vigorous game of cricket the early afternoon" to dining at eight.

"Conan Doyle's Rapid Work." *Phrenological Journal and Science of Health* 103 (April 1897):

198. Report on Doyle's uncanny ability to perform difficult tasks speedily.

"Conan Doyle's 'Sherlock Holmes.'" *Newark Sunday Call.* (October 1892): 14. Doyle is quoted to have confessed that Joseph Bell is the inspiration for Sherlock Holmes.

Cortie, A. L. "The Scientific Work of Father Perry, S.J." *Month* 68 (March 1890): 474–488. Discusses career and educational techniques of Father Perry, noted Stonyhurst teacher and astronomer.

Craig, J. M. "Observations on Impaired Lives." *Transactions of the Actuarial Society of America* 2 (1889): 52. The Gresham Life Assurance Society helped keep Doyle afloat financially.

The Critic 657 (1894): 196. It was reported that Doyle would sail to America aboard the "*Elbe*," represented by tour organizer/agent Major Pond.

"Current Topics." *The Week* 12 (November 1894): 4. An article in which Doyle thanked *The Week* for an early enthusiastic review they gave to his historical novel *Micah Clarke*.

—. (February 1895). It is reported that Doyle visits Mount Auburn Cemetery in Massachusetts, and places a memorial at the grave of fellow writer Oliver Wendell Holmes.

The Cyclopedic Review 8 (1898): 439–440. Doyle "protested against the persistent use of 'Anglo-Saxon,' with its seeming ignoring of the part played by Celtic blood in the development of the British-American power."

Damon, F. William. "Rambles in the Old World." *Friend* 29 (July 1880): 49–52. Contains detailed description of the capping ceremony at the University of Edinburgh Medical School.

Diogenes [*pseud.*]. "A Letter from the West Coast of Africa." *Fettesian* 4 (November 1881): 3–10. Describes a voyage aboard the *Mayumba* prior to Doyle's own journey a few months later.

Dolman, Frederick. "Two English Authors of Repute." *Ladies' Home Journal* 11 (October 1894): 7. Notes that Doyle's fame "bids fair to eclipse" that of his relatives.

Doyle, Arthur Conan. "The American's Tale."

London Society (1879): 185–196. An early short story written while Doyle was still a medical student displays his interest in and knowledge of America and of Americanisms.

—. "Crabbe's Practice." *Boy's Own Paper* (December 1884): 54–57. Doyle humorously describes the skills and skullduggery required to build a new medical practice.

—. "De Profundis." *McClure's Magazine* 3 (November 1894): 513–518. Discusses Ceylon tea fields, the family business of his friend James Ryan. Also mentions the Thames shipping towns of Gravesend and Falmouth. The story itself features elements of telepathy.

—. "Dr. Koch and His Cure." *Review of Reviews* 2 (December 1890): 552–560. Doyle tenders a harsh but respectful critique of Dr. Koch's purported cure for tuberculosis.

—. "The Edalji Case." *British Medical Journal* 1 (January 1907): 173. Doyle deduces that George Edalji, who gained notoriety in the cattle mutilation "outrage," could not possibly have been guilty of the crime as he suffered from myopic astigmatism.

—. "The Gully of Bluemansdyke." *London Society* 40 (December 1881): 23–37. The Wawirra, an Australian river, is referenced by Doyle in this short story, which was submitted prior to his employment on board the *Mayumba*.

—. "The Heiress of Glenmahowley." *Temple Bar* 70 (January 1884): 46–60. This short story by Doyle was first published *anonymously* in 1884.

—. "Is Sir Oliver Lodge Right?" *Metropolitan* 46 (September 1917): 20–21. Doyle explains his conversion to Spiritualism.

—. "J. Habakuk Jephson's Statement." *Cornhill Magazine* 2 (January 1884): 1–32. Published anonymously, and once assumed to be written by Robert Louis Stevenson, this short story is a fictionalized account of the ghost ship *Mary Celeste*. Mistakenly taken to be a true eyewitness record by many readers.

—. "Life on a Greenland Whaler." *Strand Magazine* 13 (January 1897): 16–25. Doyle records his adventures in the Arctic Seas; includes photos of Colin McLean, Captain

John Gray, Doyle, polar bears, walruses, and narwhals.

—. "Mr. Stevenson's Methods in Fiction." *Living Age* 69 (March 1890): 417–424. Doyle analyzes Stevenson's fiction, including *The Strange Case of Dr. Jekyll and Mr. Hyde*.

Doyle, Richard. "Madame Tussaud Her Wax Werkes." *Punch* 17 (September 1849): 112. Chamber of horrors and character sketches of Ye Celebrated Murderers—Oxford, Greenacre, Rush, Thom, Good.

"Doyle's Crowborough Home." *The Bookman* 36 (February 1913): 604–605. Contains a sketch of Doyle made by himself after receiving his medical degree. Includes the written words, "Licensed to Kill."

"Dr. Conan Doyle." *Mansfield Daily Shield.* (June 1894). Theory of Sherlock Holmes regarding the Whitechapel Murders. Doyle killed Holmes in self-defense. "At last I killed him, and if I had not done so I almost think he would have killed me." Prior to his lecture tour trip to America, he had planned not to speak about his own work.

"Dr. Conan Doyle." *Toronto Daily Mail.* (November 1894). Report of Doyle's visit to Massey Music Hall. During his lecture, he discussed his "'good friend Sherlock Holmes', whom he had treated very ungratefully."

"Dr. Conan Doyle's Impressions of Our Country." *Journal of Education* 41 (1895): 112. Doyle attends the Princeton-Pennsylvania football game. Enjoyed Philadelphia "in spite of its buildings."

"Dr. Joseph Bell's Introductory Address." *Edinburgh Medical Journal* 26 (January 1871): 577–590. Bell offers his views on the teaching of botany and natural history; also explains differences between medical school in London and medical school in Edinburgh.

Edwards, Duncan. "Life at the Athletic Clubs." *Scribner's Magazine* 18 (1895): 4–23. Doyle calls Philadelphia his favorite American city.

The Electrical Engineer 11 (March 1893): 324. "Dr. Conan Doyle tried his hand at introducing electricity in a short story a while ago, but if the truth be told, he made a sad hash of Ohm's law and electrostatics."

Ironically, Doyle's idea for a defibrillator is an integral component of today's medical armamentarium.

"Events of the Month." *Donohue's Magazine* 5 (January 1881): 93–94. Article that features the accomplishments of Henry Doyle.

F., H.G. "Reminiscences of School Life at Feldkirch." *Month* 81 (May 1894): 98–104. An alumnus recounts his life at Stella Matutina.

Farrar, C. B. "The Revival of Spiritism." *Archives of Neurology and Psychology* 5 (1921): 670–686. Discussion of Doyle's beliefs in Spiritualism. Makes mention that Doyle and Oliver Lodge each lost a son in the Great War (World War I).

"Fine-Art Gossip." *The Athenaeum* 3357 (February 1892): 282–283. Obituary of Henry Doyle, uncle to Conan Doyle, who transformed the National Gallery of Dublin from "a miserable to a respectable position."

"Foreign Intelligence." *Psyche* 5 (1925): 371–385. Clash between Harry Houdini and Conan Doyle is mentioned after the former publicly discredited "Margery" the Medium.

The Fourth Estate 12 (November 1899): 11. "Doyle as Trade Journalist." Hilarious article about Doyle's visit to "the first woman writers' club of London."

Friends' Review 35 (November 1881): 248. "Henry Highland Garnett, United States Minister to Liberia, sailed from New York for Liverpool. On reaching Monrovia, the capital of the Republic of Liberia, H. H. Garnett will be within twelve miles of the place from whence his grandfather was taken as a slave, while the grandson returns an educated Christian man, the representative of a nation of fifty millions of people."

Grant, W. J. A. "Cruise of the Yacht Eira." *Leisure Hour* 30 (1881): 213–220. A description of a wealthy gentleman who sponsored a research expedition whose objective it was to reach the North Pole.

Hatton, Joseph. "Revelations of an Album." *The Idler* 11 (1897): 293–295. About Doyle's first visit to Boston, where he is recognized by a cabman.

Hamilton Literary Monthly 29 (January 1895):

162. Description of when Doyle first attended the Fellowship Club meeting in Chicago.

"The Ice-Caves of Fuji." *Japanese Weekly Mail* (February 1895.): 183. William Burton describes the ice caves of Mt. Fuji.

"The Identification of Typewriting." *Illustrated Phonographic World* 10 (1895): 230. In which Doyle's "A Case of Identity" is referenced in solving a conspiracy to defraud Milwaukee.

Illustrated Phonographic Journal 52 (May 1895): 797. "A Case of Identity" is shown here, transcribed in shorthand.

"Immunity Against Snake Venom." *Public Health* 7 (September 1895): 441. Presents use of "anti-venom" for the treatment of snake bites in humans.

"In Memoriam of Thomas Irwin and Henry Doyle." *Donahoe's Magazine* 27 (1892): 446–447. Obituary of Doyle's uncle, noted for his role in establishing the National Gallery of Ireland.

Innes, Cosmo. "'Smoke Rockets' for Testing Drains." *Sanitary Record* 6 (February 1885): 385–386. With no concern for his own financial benefit, Cosmo Innes altruistically forgoes the copyright on his drain-testing invention, and instead gives it to society.

Irwin, Francis. "Stonyhurst." *Catholic Encyclopedia* 14 (1912): 309–310. Includes images of Stonyhurst from the western and southern fronts.

"It May Be Smyth." *The Bee* (November 1891): 1. Article about John Smyth.

"J. Doyle, Esq." *Gentleman's Magazine* 224 (February 1868): 251–252. The obituary of John Doyle fails to acknowledge his son, Charles Altamont Doyle, though it notes that "[t]he best character of himself may be found in the career of his children, all in different paths and careers, individual as artists."

Journal of Education (September 1890): 481. Adelaide Doyle (Conan Doyle's sister) is awarded Heriot-Watt College's Marshall Prize for being "first in elementary, theoretical, and practical chemistry."

Keith, Mercia Abbott. "Stately Edinburgh Throned on Crags." *Churchman* 90 (July

1904): 186–189. Photographs of Holyrood Palace, etc.

Laycock, Thomas. "Lectures on the Principles and Methods of Medical Observation and Research." *Edinburgh Medical Journal* 2 (December 1856): 550–553. "There is no such thing as an insulated fact in nature, whatever occurs is linked to something that came before and to something that comes after."

"The Late Mr. Cosmo Innes," *Industry* 10. (January 1891). Cosmo Innes dies in Shanghai from complications of smallpox.

"The Late Richard Doyle." *The Book Buyer* 1. (February 1884): 7. Obituary of Richard Doyle, uncle of Conan Doyle, who died as a consequence of apoplexy on December 11, 1883, while exiting the London's Athenaeum Club.

"Lecturing in America." *The Author* 6 (July 1895): 35. Doyle defends himself: "My own trip to America was one of the most pleasant experiences of my life, but if it had been the wish to earn more than I could have done at home which had attracted me thither, I should certainly have been disappointed."

"Literary Chat." *Munsey's Magazine* 12 (1895): 434. Doyle "has none of the charm, the magnetism, the sympathy, which keep a man's personality before the public . . . after hearing Dr. Doyle you have an uncomfortable feeling that he writes prescriptions for his novels and then carefully fills up the schedule: that his stories are compounded of various chemical ingredients. Brilliant imagination Conan Doyle has; but after you see him, you begrudge him the hidden gift as a personal possession."

Literature 83 (May 1899): 508. Doyle is described as having "the eagle eye of Mr. Sherlock Holmes."

Littlejohn, Henry Duncan. "A Case of Poisoning with Nitrate of Potash with Hints as to the Conduct of Medical Practitioners in Cases of Suspected Poisoning." *Transactions of the Medico-Chirurgical Society of Edinburgh* 4 (1885): 23–32. Article written by noted toxicologist and professor at the University of Edinburgh. Some elements of Sherlock

Holmes' personality and intellect are quite likely based on him.

Mabie, Hamilton, and Arthur Conan Doyle. "Literary Aspects of America." *Ladies' Home Journal* 12 (March 1895): 6. Doyle discusses his fascination with American authors, especially Bret Harte and Nathaniel Hawthorne. States that *The Scarlet Letter* is "the greatest novel yet written in America."

McCarthy, Justin. "Disappearing Authors." *North American Review* 170 (1900): 399. Stanley Weyman and Doyle should not be considered "old-fashioned because, although they sometimes dealt with old-fashioned subjects, they always treated them in a new-fashioned and up-to-date sort of way."

"The Medical Evidence and an Abstract of the General Evidence Adduced on the Trial of William Palmer, at the Central Criminal Court for the Alleged Wilful Murder by Poison of John Parsons Cook." *Lancet* 1 (May 1856): 563–585. A murder-by-poisoning case that Drs. Littlejohn and Maclagan were instrumental in solving.

"Medical News." *Edinburgh Medical Journal* 37 (September 1891): 283–285. Indicates that Crosse and Oddie were classmates at the University of Edinburgh.

"Medical Schools of Scotland." *Edinburgh Medical Journal* 26 (October 1880): 354–355. Describes Bryan Charles Waller's job as a pathologist.

Mee, Arthur. "Papers communicated to the Association. A Visit to Stonyhurst." *Journal of the British Astronomical Association* 13 (December 1902): 68–70. Discusses contributions to astronomy by Fathers Perry, Moore, and Sidgreaves at Stonyhurst College.

"The Method of Sherlock Holmes in Medicine." *Monthly Retrospect* 12 (1898): 959–960. Holmes uses "the method of Zadig."

Minutes of Proceedings of the Institution of Civil Engineers 139 (1900): 373. William Kinninmond Burton's obituary.

Moore, J. Murray. "The Hand as an Indicator of Disease." *Journal of the British Homeopathic Society* 10 (1902): 249–264. Quotes from Sherlock Holmes story noting characteristic

pyrogallic acid stains on the hands of the photographer. Doyle used pyrogallic acid to treat his psoriasis.

Morris, Malcolm. "Professor Koch's Remedy for Tuberculosis." *British Medical Journal* 1 (January 1891): 72–74. Koch's tuberculin therapy is doomed to failure.

Morrison, Sara Graham. "English Snap-shots of the American Women." *New England Magazine* 31 (1904): 271–278. Doyle and Kipling's differences toward American women are discussed.

"New Literary Star." *Toronto Daily Mail* (March 1893). "It now seems a certainty— that is, since the publication of the first installment of 'The Refugees' in *Harper's Magazine*—that Dr. Conan Doyle is destined to become very soon the chief luminary in the literary heavens."

"New York Letter." *The Author* 6 (June 1895): 11. "Dr. Conan Doyle, who has thus identified his name with but a single character in fiction, comes here and receives 500 dollars per lecture; whereas if Edgar Poe had gone to England, in his day, and had offered to lecture, he would have been fortunate if he cleared a profit of 3s 6d… It is impossible to see in this anything but a survival of that trade wind called colonialism."

"New York Letter." *The Literary World* (March 1894): 89. In which Doyle is said to have "decided to devote himself chiefly to story-telling" while traveling in America.

"News of the Week." *The Spectator* 56 (December 1883): 1607. Richard Doyle was "a great friend of Thackeray's."

"Notes and Queries." *American Practitioner* 29 (June 1900): 439. Obituary of Sir Andrew Douglas Maclagan, who was "a poet and a man of great and genial humor . . . His lays, or poems, or songs, were possessed of high artistic merit."

"Novels and Stories." *Glasgow Herald* (December 1887). "The piece de resistance is a story by A. Conan Doyle entitled 'A Study in Scarlet.' It is the story of a murder, and of the preternatural sagacity of a scientific detective, to whom Edgar Allen Poe's Dupin was a trifler, and Gaboriau's Lecoq a child."

"Obituary." *British Journal of Medicine.* (January 1920): 100–101. Obituary of Sir Thomas Richard Fraser, M.D., F.R.S. who had an "unexpected interest and even fascination, especially when he was considering tobacco, alcohol, and the arrow poisons and ordeal beans." **N.B.**: Sherlock Holmes wrote a monogram of tobacco ash.

"Obituary." *Magazine of Art* 15 (1892). Death of Henry Doyle, uncle of Conan Doyle and director of the National Gallery of Ireland.

"Obituary." *Medical Record* 97 (January 1920): 200. Dr. Thomas Richard Fraser's "name will be most closely associated is that having to do with his investigations into snake poisoning."

"Obituary: Henry Duncan Littlejohn, M.D." *Lancet* (October 1914): 913. "He was engaged in all the chief criminal trials of the last 50 years in Scotland, notably of Prichard and the Ardlamont case."

"Obituary: John Doyle." *Art Journal London* 7 (March 1868): 47. Obituary for John "HB" Doyle, Doyle's grandfather.

"Obituary Notices." *Journal of the Chemical Society* 59 (1891): 453. Obituary of Cosmo Innes Burton, William K. Burton's younger brother, who died of smallpox while living in Shanghai.

"Obituary Notices." *Musical Times* 21 (September 1880): 469. Notes death of Reginald Hoare.

"Obituary: Thomas Laycock" *Edinburgh Medical Journal* 22 (November 1876): 476–479. Thomas Laycock displayed the same powers of observation and deductive reasoning as did Joseph Bell, one of his students at the University of Edinburgh Medical School.

"The Original of Sherlock Holmes." *Book Buyer* 11 (March 1894): 61–64. Discusses Bell as inspiration for character of Sherlock Holmes; relates story illustrating Bell's prowess as a detective.

"Our Booking Office." *Punch* 125 (December 1903): 413. "The dedication being adorned with a fancifully imagined capital letter -T- as an initial, in red ink, designed by Richard Doyle."

"Our Forefathers' Books." *American*

Bee-Keeper 8 (March 1897): 91. Doyle is quoted as saying, "It would not be a bad thing now and again if we went into a retreat for a month or a year and swore off all ephemeral literature and turned back to the classics of our language."

Overton, Grant. "Have you Read." *Collier's* 75 (January 1925): 43. Doyle reaffirms that Holmes is based on Joe Bell and that Holmes' original name was supposed to be "'J. Sherringford Holmes' and Dr. Watson was first christened Ormond Sacker'."

"Personal Gossip." *Corbett's Herald* (December 1883). "The death of Richard Doyle, the caricaturist, who quitted *Punch* because the paper was then anti-papistical."

"Personalities." *Phrenological Journal* 108 (August 1899): 262–263. "When Conan Doyle was about four years old a big man took him to see a melodrama; the little fellow was thoroughly scared, but the big man clapped him on the back and told him it was all make believe. The big, cheery man was William Thackeray, the friend for so many years of Doyle's uncle."

"The Pictures of Richard Doyle." *Edinburgh Monthly Magazine* 137 (April 1885): 485–491. Author claims that if a poet is "the man who has been in hell," Richard Doyle could be considered "the man who had been in Elfland."

"Poisoning Cases." *Law Times* 72 (1882): 425–426. Notes expert testimony of Professors Penney, Christison, Maclagan, Littlejohn, Crum Brown, and Fraser in recent Scottish poisoning cases.

"A Protest from Conan Doyle." *Outlook* 48 (1893): Doyle talks about his pirated books that are being sold in the United States.

"The Real Sherlock Holmes." *Literary Digest* 43 (October 1911): 734–735. Joseph Bell's role in the creation of Sherlock Holmes.

"Recent Fiction." *Toronto Daily Mail* (June 1889). Possibly the article Doyle referred to when he addressed reporters during his visit to Toronto in 1894. This would have been his first favorable review. "'Micah Clarke' is a story of absorbing interest, replete with realistic situations, steeped in local colour, and charged to the full with the play and movement of its stirring time." The newspaper predicted "the century is to see another master story-teller arise who, like the great Magician of the north, will take the world by storm with his first book."

"Richard Doyle, Painter and Humorist." *Littell's Living Age* 161 (April 1884): 131–138. Tribute to the late Richard Doyle.

Richards, Grant. "The Book World." *Great Thoughts* 53 (April 1894): 27. Report of Doyle killing Holmes in "The Final Problem."

Richfield Shield and Banner (December 1904). Doyle sets out to prove that America "is menaced by a wave of crime and the evidence he offers is staggering." For example, he says "Americans are our own stock; they can have no more and no less tendency to lawlessness than we; yet, whether measured by murder, robbery, divorce or any other symptom, the irregular state of things in the United States not only exceeds European country, but bids fair to exceed all European countries combined."

Ringer, Sydney, and William Morrell. "On Gelseminum Sempervirens." *London Lancet* 4 (April 1876): 164–168. Doyle used gelseminum in a failed attempt to cure his chronic neuralgia.

Robinson, Fred Byron. "A Sketch of Mr. Lawson Tait and His Work." *Journal of the American Medical Association* 18 (January 1892): 129–133. Discusses Lawson Tait's reputation as a detective; notes that he consults in high-profile criminal cases, including the Whitechapel murders.

Rodin, Alvin, and Jack Key. "Arthur Conan Doyle's Thesis on Tabes Dorsalis." *Journal of the American Medical Association* 247 (February 1982): 646–650. Discusses Doyle's medical school thesis.

"Sealing." *Adventures Round the World* (March 1881): 88–93. Notes that the "molly" is a "sacred bird" and that "no sailor ever thinks of killing one."

"Sir Thomas Fraser." *British Medical Journal* 97 (January 1920): 200. Fraser and snake venom.

"Small Talk." *Sketch* 8 (January 1895): 474. "One specially bold thing Dr. Doyle did, and that was to express a distinct preference for one American city over all the others. His preference was for Philadelphia."

"Smoke Testing of Drains." *American Architect and Building News* 17 (January 1885): 46. Cosmo Innes' invention for using a smoke rocket, the same type of rocket used by Sherlock Holmes in "A Scandal in Bohemia."

"Society Life." *Photogram* (1896): 51–54. William Burton is discussed.

"Societies and Academies." *Nature* 48 (May 1893): 92. Preliminary notice on the arrow-poison of the "WaNyika" by Thomas Richard Fraser. **N.B.:** Sherlock Holmes had expertise in arrow-poisons.

"Stonyhurst Life." *Month and Catholic Review* 20 (1874): 325–336. Describes life at Stonyhurst; includes a brief section on noted alumnus Charles Waterton.

The Theatre 26 (October 1895): 250. Doyle "will be writing a play in collaboration with his brother-in-law, Mr. Hornung," and when it is completed, Doyle "may let Irving have it."

To-Day 2 (May 1894): 395. Description of W. E. Henley; "Miss Constance Doyle, the sister of 'Sherlock Holmes.'"

"A Typewriter as Detective." *Illustrated Phonographic World* 10 (1895): 214. Reportage of a conspiracy case, and how Doyle's "A Case of Identity" helped solve it.

"W. K. Burton." *Photographic Times* 17 (June 1887): 295–296. Discusses W. K. Burton; attributes genius to the legacy left by his father.

Waller, Bryan Charles. "To Annette." *Living Age* 186 (August 1890): 322. This Bryan Waller poem, which laments the death of Conan Doyle's older sister, Annette, suggests that Waller was heartbroken by her death in January of 1890. It also implies that Waller was present in the Doyle household prior to 1875 when Annette departed for Portugal, never to return, to work as a governess.

Watts, M. T. "The mysterious case of the doctor with no patients." *Journal of the Royal*

Society of Medicine 84 (March 1991): 165–166. Describes Doyle's failure to establish a successful practice.

"White Swelling of the Knee." *Boston Medical Surgical Journal* 131 (August 2, 1894): 101–104. Affliction of Henry Highland Garnet.

Whittingham, Charles. "Modern Stonyhurst." *Downside Review* 2 (1883): 146–151. Describes inner workings of Stonyhurst College.

"With Our Books." *Michigan Alumnus* 1 (1894): 11. Discussion of how Doyle's *Micah Clarke* earned him a reputation in England.

PERIODICALS

"A. Conan Doyle is Here." *Philadelphia Record* (October 4, 1894). Doyle and his brother are guests at the Aldine Club in Manhattan. States, "Sherlock Holmes is dead, and I imagine the public glad of it. Although I am going to lecture here, my chief object in coming was to seek a climate that would suit my wife, who is an invalid."

"About Sherlock Holmes." *Evening News (San Jose, California)* (June 29, 1901). "The killing of Sherlock Holmes is now considered by Dr. Doyle's friends to be one of the greatest mistakes ever made by the author."

Ad Sense (September 1903). Regarding *The Return of Sherlock Holmes*, Collier's Magazine "paid the largest price for these stories ever given by a single publication to one author."

"An Exacerbation of Spiritualism." *New York State Journal of Medicine* 23 (March 1923): 217. "We are distressed and pained to read of our distinguished colleague, Sir Arthur Conan Doyle, M.D., wandering in the dusky atmosphere in which ectoplasm is alleged to flourish, believing in 'spirit photography,' which all of us produced for fun years ago."

"An Interesting Young Foreigner." *Harper's Round Table* 6 (December 2, 1884): 71–72. Discussion of John Smyth.

"Arthur Conan Doyle." *British Medical Journal* (January 2, 1932): 25. Review of John Lamond's biography of Doyle; notes that Doyle was "a many-sided personality" who struggled with poverty while a doctor in Southsea.

Banks, Frederick C. "The Contagious Diseases Act." *Medical Times and Gazette* (June 23, 1883): 710. Banks responds to a letter by Doyle published a week earlier. Doyle had lobbied for the restoration of the Contagious Diseases Acts; Banks objects to Doyle's arguments as "absolutely untrue" and resulting from "sheer ignorance."

"Book Notices." *Yale Literary Magazine* 60 (December 1894): 151. Somewhat negative review of Doyle's *Round the Red Lamp*.

"British Leaders in Medicine During the Victorian Age." *British Medical Journal* (June 19, 1897): 1579–1582. Homage to the great physicians of the reign of Queen Victoria—Gull, Christison, Simpson, Addison, Stokes, Clay, Snow, and Lister.

Buffalo Medical Journal 50 (1895): 364. A recap of Doyle's American adventures in 1894, which reveals his love for the Adirondack Mountains, Philadelphia, New England, and the Midwest.

Campbell, Maurice. "Sir Arthur Conan Doyle." *British Medical Journal* (May 23, 1959): 1341. Biographical entry on Doyle; discusses his childhood, education, literary career, and time in South Africa.

"Canon Jessop and Sir Conan Doyle on Medicine." *British Medical Journal* (October 15, 1904): 1026. Notes that Doyle's "short and chequered career as a doctor" included time served as a ship's surgeon and army doctor; practiced in both the country and in city slums.

Chiene, John. "Promoter's Address." *Lancet* (August 8, 1896): 361–364. Dr. Chiene, Professor of Surgery at the University of Edinburgh Medical School, alludes to Lamarckian theory during his address to the graduating class of 1896, noting the presence of both a male and a female element in each cell.

"Conan Doyle. *Northern Budget* (Troy, New York) (October 7, 1900). Doyle tells a reporter who paid him a visit in South Africa that Sherlock Holmes "was not good . . . Sherlock Holmes being merely a mechanical creature, easy to create because he was soulless. Why, one story by Edgar Allen Poe would be worth any number of stories on the plane of Sherlock Holmes." Also alludes to "The Adventure of the Speckled Band" as being his favorite Holmes tale.

"Conan Doyle on the Responsibility of the Boer War." *The Public* 210 (April 12, 1902): 3–9. Article summarizes Doyle's charges against the Boers in South Africa.

"Conan Doyle's MD Thesis." *British Medical Journal* (March 27, 1982): 985. Doyle is able to complete his medical dissertation in a remarkably brief period of time. This, despite the death of a patient under his personal care, an interrogation by the police regarding his possible culpability in the patient's demise, and the courting of his future wife (the sister of his dead patient) all during this precise time frame.

"Conan Doyle's Mentor." *Philadelphia Record* (January 20, 1894). Article dedicated to Joseph Bell.

"Current Literature." *Sydney Morning Herald* (May 10, 1902). Doyle caved in to public demand and brought Sherlock Holmes back to solve a "thrilling adventure, rich in tangle and mystery" titled *The Hound of the Baskervilles*.

Douglas, James. "Is Conan Doyle Mad?" *Sunday Express* 14 (September 25, 1921): 6. The author writes that "Doyle asserts that 'the human race is on the very eve of a tremendous revolution of thought, marking a final revulsion from materialism.' He predicts that it will 'give religion a foundation of rock instead of quicksand.'"

Doyle, Arthur Conan. "The 'New' Scientific Subject." *British Journal of Photography* (July 20, 1883): 418. Here, Doyle argues against the credibility of pseudosciences. "He tells us that scientific men have discovered a force in all living things which they have named 'Od'. What scientific men? At the risk of being flippant I should submit that it is very odd that such a force should be mentioned in no text-book of science."

—. "Gelseminum as a Poison." *British Medical Journal* (September 20, 1879): 483. Doyle mentions personal use of gelseminum to treat neuralgia; notes that he frequently exceeded

accepted maximum dosage and experienced no ill effect beyond diarrhea.

—. "My First Book: *Juvenilia*." *The Idler* (1893): 633–640. Autobiographical story about Doyle's first experiences with reading. Influenced by English authors like Walter Scott, Tennyson, and Dickens, as well as American writers such as Bret Harte, Mark Twain, and Nathaniel Hawthorne.

—. "Notes on a Case of Leucocythaemia." *Lancet* (March 25, 1882): 490. Doyle writes of a "large tumour," but he fails to realize his patient had anatomical anomalies.

—. "On the Slave Coast With a Camera." *British Journal of Photography* (March 31, 1882): 185–186. Doyle recounts his use of the ship bathroom as a darkroom.

—. "On the Slave Coast With a Camera." *British Journal of Photography* (April 7, 1882): 202–203. Doyle mentions that he had the opportunity to photograph a war chief named "Wawirra." In what is perhaps *not* a coincidence, Doyle had just written about an Australian river named Wawirra a few weeks earlier.

—. "The Remote Effects of Gout." *Lancet* (November 29, 1884): 978. Doyle examines the effects of gout on three generations of a single family. Indicates an interest in tracking disease within families that may have contributed to his selection of *tabes dorsalis* as a thesis topic.

—. "Up an African River With the Camera." *British Journal of Photography* (July 28, 1882): 431–432. Description of his journey aboard the steamship *Mayumba*.

—. "Where to Go With the Camera: Southsea: Three Days in Search of Effects." *British Journal of Photography* (June 22, 1883): 359–361. Doyle refers to two friends, the "Lunatic" and the "Man of Science," and mentions that a Mr. Barnden of the Gresham Insurance Society joins them on the excursion to Southsea.

—. "Where to Go With the Camera: To the Waterford Coast and Along It." *British Journal of Photography* (August 24, 1883): 497–498. Doyle writes about an 1881 trip to Dublin and the Blackwater Valley on which he was accompanied by his friend Cunningham, who does not appear in his letters from that time.

Eclectic Magazine 14 (September 1891): 427. Doyle's opinion of book piracy.

Edinburgh Museum of Art and Science 38 (1891): 350. Before his untimely death from smallpox, Cosmo Innes Burton began to remodel the Chemical section of the Edinburgh Museum of Science in respect to nomenclature and arrangement.

"English Views on the Effects of the Copyright Law." *Publishers Weekly* 47 (February 16, 1895): 331. Doyle is quoted as having said, "[I]t will be impossible to judge fairly of the effects of the law until it has had a fair trial, of at least ten years."

"From the Lighthouse Window." *Light* 41 (October 23, 1921): 685. "Mr. Douglas, it will be remembered, wrote a striking article last month, entitled, 'Is Conan Doyle Mad?'"

"General Booth in Washington." *Herald and Presbyter* 14 (November 28, 1894): 394. Reports that General William Booth was in Washington at the same time of Doyle's book tour.

Glasgow Herald (July 26, 1894). Joseph Mahoney calls himself "Sherlock Holmes the Second" after helping catch and detain a watch thief.

Innes, Cosmo. "Smoke Testing for Drains." *Illustrated Carpenter and Builder* (January 23, 1885): 67. Details of smoke rockets for determining leaks in sewer drains.

"In Literary England." *Newark Sunday Call* (June 17, 1894). "Upon Poe and Hawthorne he is especially lavish in his praise, and looks upon the former as the greatest writer America ever produced . . . Conan Doyle is an ardent advocate of the gospel of an amalgamation of the literature of the English-speaking nations." **N.B.:** It was Hawthorne that Doyle thought was "the greatest writer America ever produced."

"James Douglas and Conan Doyle." *Public Opinion* 120 (September 30, 1921): 327. James Douglas—after reviewing Doyle's *Wanderings of a Spiritualist*—wrote, "His world-famous character, Sherlock Holmes, is a master of the science of induction and deduction. Doyle could not have created Sherlock Holmes if he had not been deeply versed in the laws of evidence."

Jones, Harold Emery. "The Original of Sherlock Holmes." *Collier's* (January 9, 1904): 14–15. Cites teachers at the University of Edinburgh Medical School.

Kraus, Joseph. "Science Versus Spiritualism." *Science and Invention* 11 (June 1923): 111. "Doyle is absolutely sincere in everything he preaches." He is reported by Kraus to be a true believer in Spiritualism.

Lang, Andrew. "At the Sign of the Ship." *Longman's Magazine* 23 (1894): 431–440. Parody of Sherlock Holmes.

Lansberg, Leon. "Ectoplasm Does It Exist?" *Science and Invention* 11 (July 1923): 214. Doyle is mentioned for his defense of ectoplasm's existence.

"The Late W. K. Burton." *Photography Magazine* 11(Sept. 21, 1899): 626. Tribute to William K. Burton.

Life 774 (October 21, 1897): 338. Doyle, ever the prankster, is quoted as having said, "All is discovered! Fly at once!"

"Literary Notes." *St. Joseph Daily News* (November 22, 1894). Doyle states that "the finest detective service is done in Paris."

Maurice, Arthur Bartlett. "Concerning Mr. Sherlock Holmes." *Collier's* (March 28, 1908): 12–14. Discusses the genesis of Sherlock Holmes.

—. "Sir Arthur Conan Doyle." *Collier's* (March 28, 1908): 11–12. Discusses Doyle's career and personality.

—. "Concerning Conan Doyle." *Collier's* (March 28, 1908): 14. Elaborates on Doyle's dramatic power.

"Medical News." *Medical Times and Gazette* (August 7, 1869): 179. Announcement of the marriage of Reginald Hoare to Amy Jane Tovey.

"Medicine in the Novel." *Medical Press* (February 1, 1905): 119. Criticizes Doyle for medical errors made by Sherlock Holmes and Dr. John Watson in stories; errors undermine

Holmes' genius and offend doctors' "professional pride."

"Message From Book-land." *Lewiston Evening News* (October 13, 1894). "Dr. Conan Doyle, when asked what American authors are now most in England, said: 'Personally I am very fond of Miss Wilkins's work, although I do not think her short stories nearly so good as a performance as "Pembroke." That book struck me as the best novel that has come out of America since Hawthorne's time.'"

—. (November 24, 1894). "Conan Doyle is no snob. It is refreshing to hear his hearty acknowledgment of the debts he owes to Parkman, Irving, Hawthorne, Cooper and Poe."

"The Method of Sherlock Holmes." *British Medical Journal* (December 30, 1893): 1442–1443. Reports that Doyle's medical education, particularly training under Joseph Bell, was critical to the creation of Sherlock Holmes.

"Obituary." *British Architect* (June 22, 1900): 434. William K. Burton's obituary.

"Obituary: Charles Clay." *British Medical Journal* (September 23, 1893): 712–713. Obituary of Dr. Clay, pioneer of abdominal surgery "Father of the Ovariotomy."

"Obituary: John Doyle." *Art Journal London* 7 (March 1, 1868): 47. Biographic obituary about Conan Doyle's grandfather "who, for so long a time, baffled all inquiry as to his identity under the monogram 'HB'."

"Obituary: Professor William Rutherford, M.D." *Medical Press* 118 (March 1, 1899): 232–233. Somewhat akin to Sherlock Holmes, Professor Rutherford "appeared to be conceited and supercilious."

"Obituary: Sir Douglas Maclagan, M.D., L.L.D. Edin." *Scottish Medical and Surgical Journal* 6, (1900) 451–453. Chair of Medical Jurisprudence and Public Health. Part of the defense in the Madeleine Smith case and the Pritchard case.

"Obituary: William Budd." *British Medical Journal* (January 31, 1880): 163–166. Obituary of William Budd, father of Doyle's friend, George T. Budd. The Budds lived in Dartmoor, later to become the setting for Doyle's works *The Hound of the Baskervilles* and "The Adventure of the Cardboard Box."

"Personal and Political." *Lewiston Evening News* (October 8, 1894). Doyle hints at possibly resurrecting Sherlock Holmes.

Publishers Weekly 1184 (October 6, 1894): 547. Reports that "Dr. Doyle is living at the Aldine Club" while touring New York.

"Professor Annandale on Homeopathy, etc." *Michigan Medical News* (October 10, 1881): 296. Reports on Doyle's capping-ceremony on the day he received his M.B. degree from the University of Edinburgh.

"Professor Annandale on Quackery." *London Medical Press and Circular* (August 24, 1881): 179. Transcribes valedictory address given by Annandale to Doyle and the other new graduates of the University of Edinburgh; Annandale warns that quackery is extending into the medical profession.

"Psychical Research." *Medical Times* 50 (June 1922): 172. "That lovable Celt of incorrigible imagination, Sir Arthur Conan Doyle, not being given to conventional religious or ethylic modes of intoxication, has yielded himself to the lure of the spirit world."

Ralph, Julian. "Conan Doyle's Work of Love." *McClure's Magazine* 18 (1902): 429–432. Doyle's position on the war in South Africa.

"Regulating the Rate of Filtration Through Sand." *Minutes of Proceedings of the Institution of Civil Engineers* 112 (1893): 321. Discusses William Burton work on water filtration in Japan.

"Scottish Hospitals and Medical Schools." *Lancet* (September 12, 1868): 370–371. Notes that Joseph Bell owns the most modern ophthalmologic equipment available; Doyle would later specialize in ophthalmology under Bell, using his knowledge to try to free George Edalji.

"Sherlock Holmes Again." *Beaver Times* (*Beaver, Pennsylvania*) (August 3, 1901). "Dr. Doyle not only resurrects 'Sherlock Holmes' in *The Hound of the Baskervilles*, but he does so without one single word of either explanation or apology."

Simpson, Alexander Russell. "Introductory Lecture on the Ninth Medical Congress and American Gynaecology." *British Medical Journal* (November 5, 1887): 977–980. An address delivered in Washington, D.C. by the University of Edinburgh Professor of Midwifery and Diseases of Women and Children, in which he calls for "a scheme for uniformity of obstetric nomenclature."

"Sir Conan Doyle." *Boston Evening Transcript* (August 25, 1902). Dr. Bell is reported to have said that he regarded Doyle as one of his "best students."

"Sir Conan Doyle: Home Life of the Newly Made Baronet." *Boston Evening Transcript* (August 25, 1902). A general history of the Doyle family.

"Social Whirl." *Motor Car Journal* (October 31, 1908): 751. Describes Doyle and Max Pemberton as avid motorists.

"Stephen Joseph Perry, F.R.S." *Nature* (January 23, 1890): 279–280. Discusses Perry, Stonyhurst teacher noted for his contributions toward astronomy.

Stoker, Bram. "Sir Arthur Conan Doyle Tells of His Career and Work, His Sentiments Towards America, and His Approaching Marriage." *New York World* (July 28, 1907): 1. To Stoker, his interviewer and distant relation, Doyle reveals character names considered before settling on "Sherlock Holmes." Also discusses how Doyle "drifted into the study of medicine" and erroneously lists order of medical assistantships.

"The Streets of London." *Lancet* (March 11, 1865): 265–266. Describes the London fog.

"Tee Shots." *Golf Illustrated* (September 29, 1899): 445. Describes Joseph Bell as an enthusiastic golfer.

"Topics of the Day." *Medical Times and Gazette* (June 16, 1883): 671. Reprints part of letter by Doyle condemning the repeal of the Contagious Diseases Act.

"Topics of the Day." *The Post Express (Rochester, New York)* (March 3, 1902). "Dr. Conan Doyle has brought Sherlock Holmes back to the land of the living. A new series of detective stories is contemplated."

"The Trial of Edward William Pritchard." *Medical Times and Gazette* 2 (July 15, 1865): 64–75. Dr. Henry Duncan Littlejohn medico-legal evidence is presented.

"The Trial of Pritchard, the Poisoner." *Lancet*. March 10, 1906: 685–686. Synopsis of Dr. Littlejohn's involvement in the conviction of Dr. Pritchard.

"The Week." *Medical Times and Gazette* (September 3, 1881): 286–288. Joseph Bell takes Queen Victoria on a tour "through wards Nos. 10, 11, and 12" of the Surgical Hospital.

Woodhead, G. Sims. "William Rutherford, M.D., F.R.S.S., Lond. and Edin." *Edinburgh Medical Journal*, 434–436. Obituary of Dr. Rutherford, which names his favorite hobbies as "music and art."

OFFICIAL DOCUMENTS/ PAMPHLETS/SPEECHES

Foreign Relations of the United States; Doc. No. 204; Washington, D.C.: Government Printing Office; 1882; Mr. Smyth to Mr. Blaine.

—. Doc. No. 205; Washington, D.C.: 1882; Mr. Smyth to Mr. Blaine.

—. Doc. No. 206; Washington, D.C.: 1882; Mr. Smyth to Mr. Blaine. [Extract]

—. Doc. No. 207; Washington, D.C.: 1882; Mr. Smyth to Mr. Blaine.

Index to the Executive Documents of the House of Representatives; Vol. 20; Washington, D.C.: Government Printing Office 1881–1882; pg. 11.

—. Doc. No. 289: 1878–1879; Mr. Turner to Mr. Evarts.

—. Doc. No. 323: 1878–1879; Mr. Smyth to Mr Evarts.

—. Doc. No. 326: 1878–1879; Mr. Smyth to Mr. Seward.

Papers Relating to the Foreign Relations of the United States, No. 436, Mr. Smyth to Mr. Blaine, Washington, D.C. Government Printing Office, 1882, pg. 738.

Smyth, John Henry. "The African in Africa and the African in America" (1895). Delivered at the Cotton State Exposition in Atlanta, Georgia.

About the Authors

Daniel Friedman, MD, received his BA in history from Stony Brook University, and his medical degree from St. George's University School of Medicine. He is a practicing pediatrician in Floral Park, New York, and assistant clinical professor at the Northwell-Hofstra University Medical School. He is the co-author of *The Strange Case of Dr. Doyle*, and a frequent contributing writer to Sherlock Holmes magazines and journals worldwide. He has received, along with his father, Eugene, the Sydney Passengers Montpelier Award in 2021 and was jointly named with his father "runner-up" for Best Article of the Year by the *Canadian Holmes*. Daniel is an avid comic book collector and contributing writer to Roy Thomas' *Alter Ego* magazine. He has also been published with famed Egyptologist and television celebrity Robert ("Mr. Mummy") Brier in *KMT Magazine*. In his spare time, he is a singer/songwriter and bass guitarist with the Friedman Brothers Band and lead vocalist for New Jersey-based Ignite the Atmosphere. Dr. Friedman resides in Miller Place on Long Island with his wife, Elena, and their three children, Amanda, David, and Andrew.

Eugene Friedman, MD, received his BA in history from New York University, and his medical degree from New York Medical College. He was Chief Resident in Pediatrics at New York Medical College and twice was the recipient of the Arthritis Foundation of New York's Research Fellowship. During the Vietnam War, he served in the military as a Major in the US Army as Assistant Chief of Pediatrics at Martin Army Hospital at Fort Benning, Georgia. Dr. Friedman has been in private practice for more than forty years. He has held multiple leadership positions in organized medicine, including two terms as president of the Long Island Jewish Medical Center Staff Society; Chief Medical Officer of Allied and has devoted himself to the education of Allied Physicians Group, and as a trustee and overseer at Northwell Health System. He regards his role as an educator and preceptor of future physicians, nurse practitioners, and physician assistants as the most rewarding aspect of his career. He is the co-author of *The Strange Case of Dr. Doyle* and is a published translator of nineteenth-century French poetry. He and his wife, Sheryl, live on Long Island and have five children and fifteen grandchildren.

Index

NOTE: Any *italicized* names listed below are those of characters from various works of fiction cited throughout this book.

THE STRANGE CASE OF DR. DOYLE

A Journey into Madness & Mayhem

Daniel Friedman, MD,
and Eugene Friedman, MD

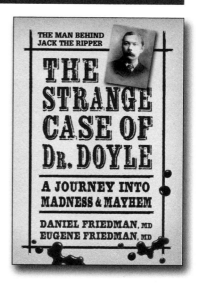

London. 1910. A procession of well-attired gentlemen and ladies are clearly out of place among the stalls and pushcarts of the Whitechapel District. As the group makes its way through the crowded streets, the tour guide stops now and then to point out various places where the mutilated bodies of the women had been found. Although the murders occurred twenty-two years prior, the man leading the group seems to know every detail and aspect of each slaying. Of those things he does not know, he offers freely his own insightful conjecture. This is, however, no average tour of brutal acts. It is a close look at infamous serial killer Jack the Ripper's trail of blood. And the man leading the group is none other than Sir Arthur Conan Doyle—famous creator of fictional character Sherlock Holmes, the world's greatest detective. In *The Strange Case of Dr. Doyle,* we learn what draws one famous Englishman to another in ways that are as fascinating as they are shocking.

Sir Arthur Conan Doyle actually led a tour group to the sites of the Whitechapel Murders in the year 1905. While we do not have an existing description of that tour, authors Daniel Friedman, MD, and Eugene Friedman, MD, have meticulously pieced together Doyle's own words to create a riveting account of his publicly stated beliefs on each of these horrific murders. As Doyle takes the group on his tour, the reader learns about the victims and the way each died. The authors have also included new pieces of evidence to understand better the murderer known to history only as Jack the Ripper.

Interspersed throughout the tour is the Friedmans' unique and well-researched account of the life of the young Conan Doyle, which was shrouded in more mystery than any of his own works of fiction. The authors have uncovered facts about which few, if any, Doyle biographers have ever been aware. Doyle was able to reinvent himself so fully through his own writings that few recognized the more disturbing elements that were cut out of his own life story. What these two authors have uncovered in their investigation of Jack the Ripper and Sir Arthur will no doubt spark passion and debate among Sherlockian fans for years to come. *The Strange Case of Dr. Doyle* proves once again that truth—elementary as it may be—is always stranger than fiction.

$17.95 USD • 320 pages • 6 x 9-inch quality paperback • B&W Photos & Illustrations
True Crime/Biography • ISBN 978-0-7570-0431-5

THE NEW REVELATION

My Personal Investigation of Spiritualism

Sir Arthur Conan Doyle

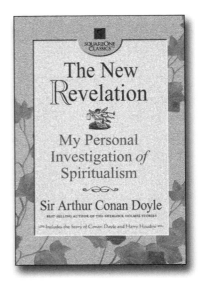

The spiritual movement in the early part of the twentieth century had few, if any, proponents greater than Sir Arthur Conan Doyle—a medical doctor, soldier, intellectual, and world-renowned author. He believed fully in the principles of Spiritualism, which embraced areas that we refer to today as ESP, New Age philosophy, metaphysics, and psychic experiences. It accepted the existence of a soul and an afterlife, and it offered an intriguing view of our existence in relationship to a greater being. Life was a continuum—a progression into ever-greater knowledge and understanding that linked the souls of all people. Doyle was convinced that the principles of Spiritualism were both reasonable and able to be proven.

In 1918, Sir Arthur published *The New Revelation*—a firsthand account of his personal investigation into the world of Spiritualism. This work became the most influential statement of the movement. In it, Sir Arthur presents his case on the merits of Spiritualism in a clear and concise manner. The reader follows along as Sir Arthur, in a voice reminiscent of Dr. Watson, calmly and deliberately examines psychic experiences, life after death, mediums, automatic writing, and more.

Sir Arthur Conan Doyle tirelessly lectured around the world on behalf of Spiritualism. It was a task he carried out until his death in 1930. While some may view this work as a historical footnote, the answers to Sir Arthur's basic questions regarding life and death are as relevant today as they were then.

In addition to this classic work, readers will find an original Introduction, which provides an insightful look at Doyle—the man and his passionate pursuits. It recounts his personal life and explores his experiences with Spiritualism. Also included is an Afterword that brilliantly captures Sir Arthur's friendship with famed magician Harry Houdini as documented through their personal correspondence.

$12.95 USD • 120 pages • 5.5 x 8.5-inch quality paperback • ISBN 978-0-7570-0017-1

Sir Arthur Conan Doyle's

1887

A Study in Scarlet

1890

The Sign of the Four

1891

"A Scandal in Bohemia"

"The Red-Headed League"

"A Case of Identity"

"The Boscombe Valley Mystery"

"The Five Orange Pips"

"The Man With the Twisted Lip"

1892

"The Adventure of the Blue Carbuncle"

"The Adventure of the Speckled Band"

"The Adventure of the Engineer's Thumb"

"The Adventure of the Noble Bachelor"

"The Adventure of the Beryl Coronet"

"The Adventure of the Copper Beeches"

"The Adventure of Silver Blaze"

1893

"The Adventure of the Cardboard Box"

"The Adventure of the Yellow Face"

"The Adventure of the Stockbroker's Clerk"

"The Adventure of the *Gloria Scott*"

"The Adventure of the Musgrave Ritual"

"The Adventure of the Reigate Squire"

"The Adventure of the Crooked Man"

"The Adventure of the Resident Patient"

"The Adventure of the Greek Interpreter"

"The Adventure of the Naval Treaty"

"The Final Problem"

1901

The Hound of the Baskervilles

1903

"The Adventure of the Empty House"

"The Adventure of the Norwood Builder"

"The Adventure of the Dancing Men"

1904

"The Adventure of the Solitary Cyclist"

"The Adventure of the Priory School"

"The Adventure of Black Peter"

"The Adventure of Charles Augustus Milverton"

"The Adventure of the Six Napoleons"